The Critical Reader

The Complete Guide to SAT Reading

2nd Edition

by

Erica L. Meltzer

For Reprints and Permissions, please see p. 350.

Dedication

To Ricky, who pestered me to write this book until I finally acquiesced

Table of Contents

Introduction

Eight years elapsed between my last SAT®, which I took as a senior in high school, and the first time I was asked to tutor reading for the SAT. I distinctly remember sitting in Barnes and Noble, hunched over the Official Guide, staring at the questions in horror and wondering how on earth I had ever gotten an 800 at the age of 17. Mind you, I felt completely flummoxed by the SAT after I had spent four years studying literature in *college*.

Somehow or other, I managed to muddle through my first reading tutoring sessions. I tried to pretend that I knew what I was doing, but to be perfectly honest, I was pretty lost. I had to look up answers in the back of the book. A lot. I lost count of the number of times I had to utter the words, "I think you're right, but give me one second and let me just double-check that answer..." It was mortifying. No tutor wants to come off as clueless in front of a sixteen-year old, but I was looking like I had no idea what I was doing. Grammar I could handle, but when it came to teaching reading, I was in way over my head. I simply had no idea how to put into words what had always come naturally to me. Besides, half the time I wasn't sure of the right answer myself.

Luckily for me, fate intervened in the form of Laura Wilson, the founder of WilsonPrep in Chappaqua, New York, whose company I spent several years writing tests for. Laura taught me about the major passage themes, answer choices patterns, and structures. I learned the importance of identifying the main point, tone and major transitions, as well as the ways in which that information can allow a test-taker to spot correct answers quickly, efficiently, and without second-guessing. I discovered that the skills that the SAT tested were in fact the exact same skills that I had spent four years honing.

As a matter of fact, I came to realize that, paradoxically, my degree in French was probably more of an aid in teaching reading than a degree in English would have been. The basic French literary analysis exercise, known as the *explication de texte linéaire*, consists of close reading of a short excerpt of text, during which the reader explains how the text functions rhetorically from beginning to end – that is, just how structure, diction, and syntax work together to produce meaning and convey a particular idea or point of view. In other words, the same skills as those tested on the SAT – the old test as well as the new version. I had considered *explications de texte* a pointless exercise (Rhetoric? Who studies *rhetoric* anymore? That's so nineteenth century!) and resented being forced to write them in college – especially during the year I spent at the Sorbonne, where I and my (French) classmates did little else – but suddenly I appreciated the skills they had taught me. Once I made the connection between what I had been studying all that time and the skills tested on the SAT, the test suddenly made sense. I suddenly had something to fall back on when I was teaching, and for the first time, I found that I no longer had to constantly look up answers.

I still had a long way to go as a tutor, though: at first I clung a bit too rigidly to some methods (e.g. insisting that students circle all the transitions) and often did not leave my students enough room to find their own strategies. As I worked with more students, however, I began to realize just how little I could take for granted in terms of pre-existing skills: most of them, it turned out, had significant difficulty even identifying the point of an argument, never mind summing it up in five or so words. A lot of them didn't even realize that passages contained arguments at all; they thought that the authors were simply "talking about stuff." As a result, it never even occurred to them to identify which ideas a given author did and did not agree with. When I instructed them to circle transitions like *however* and *therefore* as a way of identifying the key places in an argument, many of them found it overwhelming to do so at the same time they were trying to absorb the literal content of a passage – more than one student told me they could do one or the other, but not both at the same time. In one memorable gaffe, I told a student that while he often did not have to read every word of the more analytical passages, he did need to read all of the literary passages, only to have him respond that he couldn't tell the difference. He thought of all the passages as literary because the blurbs above them all said they came from books, and weren't all books "literary?" It never occurred to me to tell him that he needed to look for the word "novel" in the blurb above the passage in order to identify works of *fiction*. When I pointed out to another student that he had answered a question incorrectly because he hadn't realized that the author of the passage disagreed with a particular idea, he responded without a trace of irony that the author had spent a lot of time talking about that idea – no one had ever introduced him to the idea that writers often spend a good deal of time fleshing out ideas that they *don't* agree with. And this was a student scoring in the mid-600s!

Eventually, I got it: I realized that I would have to spend more time – sometimes a lot more time – explaining basic contextual pieces of information that most adult readers took for granted and, moreover, I would have to do so at the same time I covered actual test-taking strategies. Without the fundamentals, all the strategy in the world might not even raise a score by 10 points. My goal in this book is to supply some of those fundamentals while also covering some of the more advanced skills the exam requires.

I would, however, like to emphasize that this book is intended to help you work through and "decode" College Board material. It is not – and should not be used as – a replacement for the Official Guide. To that end, I have provided a list of the Reading questions from the tests in the College Board Official Guide, 3rd Edition (also available through Khan Academy), corresponding to the relevant question type at the end of each chapter.

The tests can be downloaded from the Khan Academy website as follows:

Test 1:   https://collegereadiness.collegeboard.org/pdf/sat-practice-test-1.pdf
Answers: https://collegereadiness.collegeboard.org/pdf/sat-practice-test-1-answers.pdf

Test 2:   https://collegereadiness.collegeboard.org/pdf/sat-practice-test-2.pdf
Answers: https://collegereadiness.collegeboard.org/pdf/sat-practice-test-2-answers.pdf

Test 3:   https://collegereadiness.collegeboard.org/pdf/sat-practice-test-3.pdf
Answers: https://collegereadiness.collegeboard.org/pdf/sat-practice-test-3-answers.pdf

Test 4:   https://collegereadiness.collegeboard.org/pdf/sat-practice-test-4.pdf
Answers: https://collegereadiness.collegeboard.org/pdf/sat-practice-test-4-answers.pdf

As you work through this book, you will undoubtedly notice that some of the passages are reused in multiple exercises. Although you may find it somewhat tedious to work through the same passages multiple times, that repetition was a deliberate choice on my part. This book is not designed to have you whiz through passage after passage, but rather to have you study the workings of a limited number of passages in depth. As you work through the exercises, you may also notice that different questions accompanying the same passage are targeting the same concepts, merely from different angles. Again, that is a deliberate choice. The goal is to allow you to solidify your understanding of these concepts and the various ways in which they can be tested so that they will leap out at you when you are taking the test for real.

In addition, I have done my best to select passages that reflect the content and themes of the redesigned SAT (based on the Official Guide, 3rd Edition). The new exam focuses much more heavily than the old on science and social science topics, with a notable focus on the recent onslaught of new technologies (the Internet, the rise of social media, "green" energy) and new business models (flexible and individual vs. company-based and traditional) as well as the consequences of those developments. While some passages will address their downsides, you can assume that the overwhelming emphasis will be on their positive – and transformative – aspects.

That said, this book can of course provide no more than an introduction to the sorts of topics you are likely to encounter on the SAT. While the College Board has been very vociferous (to invoke an "irrelevant" term) about proclaiming that the redesigned test will reflect exactly what students are studying in school, the reality is of course a bit more complex. Common Core or no Common Core, American high schools have nothing even remotely resembling a core curriculum, with the result that a student high school A might emerge from AP US History with a solid understanding of how Locke and Rousseau influenced the American revolutionaries, while a student at high school B the next town over might emerge from AP US History not even knowing their names. No short-term SAT prep program, "disruptive" and Internet-based or otherwise can easily compensate for knowledge gaps built up over a dozen years or more. So while some of the passages you encounter on the SAT may indeed seem familiar and accessible, others may seem very foreign. On p. 13, I have provided a list of suggested reading resources, and I strongly encourage you to devote some time to exploring them.

Unfortunately, there is no such thing as a "pure" reading test the way there is such thing as a pure math test. To some extent, your ability to understand what you read is always bound up with your existing knowledge. Research shows that when students whose overall reading skills are weak are asked to read about subjects they are highly familiar with, their comprehension is *better* than that of students whose reading skills are stronger across the board. The more familiar you are with a subject, the less time and energy you will have to spend trying to understand a text about it, and the faster you'll move through the passage as a whole. You'll also be familiar with any vocabulary associated with the topic, which means you won't have to worry as hard about keeping track of unfamiliar terminology.

Moreover, you will probably find it much easier to identify correct and incorrect answer choices. While it is true that answers that are true in the real world will not necessarily be right, it is also true that correct answers will not be false in the real world. If you see an answer that you know is factually true based on your pre-existing knowledge of a topic, you can potentially save yourself a lot of time by checking that answer first.

Finally, encountering a passage about a subject you already know something about can be very calming on a high-pressure test like the SAT because you will no longer be dealing with a frightening unknown. Instead of trying to assimilate a mass of completely new information in the space of a few minutes, you can instead "place" what you are reading in the context of your existing knowledge. No matter how strongly the College Board might insist that the SAT is simply testing skills, and that all of the Reading questions can be answered on the basis of the information in the passages alone, the SAT is also testing your knowledge of the subjects those passages discuss for the simple reason that it would be impossible to design a reading test that did not!

Provided that you have solid comprehension skills and contextual knowledge, success in Reading is also largely a question of approach, or method. Because the test demands a certain degree of flexibility – no single strategy can be guaranteed to work 100% of the time – I have also tried to make this book a toolbox of sorts. My goal is to provide you with a variety of approaches and strategies that you can choose from and apply as necessary, depending on the question at hand. Whenever possible, I have provided multiple explanations for questions, showing how you might arrive at the answer by working in different ways and from different sets of starting assumptions. The ability to adapt is what will ultimately make you unshakeable – even at eight o'clock on a Saturday morning.

Erica Meltzer
New York City
July 2015

Suggested Reading

Gerald Graff, Cathy Birkenstein, and Russell Durst: *They Say/I Say: The Moves that Matter in Academic Writing*, 2nd Edition. New York: W.W. Norton and Company, 2009.

Periodicals:

The New York Times
(particularly the op-ed section, http://www.nytimes.com/pages/opinion/index.html, and the "Room for Debate" feature)

The Wall Street Journal, www.wsj.com

The Economist, www.economist.com

Harvard Business Review, www.hbr.com

The Boston Globe "Ideas" Section, www.bostonglobe.com/ideas (5 free articles/month)

Scientific American, www.scientificamerican.com

National Geographic, www.nationalgeographic.com

Newsweek, www.newsweek.com

Time Magazine, www.time.com

Smithsonian Magazine, www.smithsonianmag.com

The Atlantic Monthly, www.theatlantic.com/magazine

Reason Magazine, www.reason.com

Wired, www.wired.com

The New Atlantis: A Journal of Technology and Society, www.thenewatlantis.com

For links to many additional resources containing SAT-level material and above, please visit Arts & Letters Daily at www.aldaily.com.

Fiction, suggested authors: by Jane Austen, Charlotte/Anne Brontë, Charles Dickens, George Orwell, Toni Morrison, Edith Wharton, Virginia Woolfe

Historical Documents, Sources:
http://www.ushistory.org/documents/
http://www.ourdocuments.gov/content.php?page=milestone
https://thesocialstudiesteacher.wordpress.com/important-historical-documents/

1. Overview of SAT Reading

The redesigned SAT contains one 65-minute reading section that will always be the first section of the exam. The section consists of four long single passages and one set of shorter paired passages, accompanied by a total of 52 questions (9-11 questions per passage or paired passage set).

The breakdown of passage topics is as follows:

- Fiction (1 passage)

- Social science (1-2 passages)

- Natural science (1-2 passages)

- Historical Documents, aka the "Great Global Conversation" (1 passage or 1 set of paired passages)

- Paired passages (1 set, science or social science)

Each passage or set of paired passages will range in length from 500-750 words; science and social science passages will also include 1-2 graphs or charts related in some way to the topics of those passages. In some instances, the graphic (or graphics) will clearly support an idea or phenomenon discussed in the passage; in other cases, the relationship between the graphic and the passage will be less clear-cut.

The majority of the Reading questions will be text-based; however, science and social science passages accompanied by graphs or charts will also contain several questions pertaining to those graphics. Some of these questions will ask you consider information from the graphic alone, while other questions will require you to integrate information from both the passage and the graphic.

What Does SAT Reading Test?

To some extent, the SAT reading test is a reading comprehension test, but it would perhaps be more accurate to call it an *argument* comprehension test. **It does not simply test the ability to find bits of factual information in a passage, but rather the capacity to understand how arguments are constructed and the ways in which specific textual elements (e.g. words, phrases, punctuation marks) work together to convey ideas.** The focus is on moving beyond what a text says to understanding how the text says it. Comprehension, in other words, is necessary but not sufficient.

The skill that the SAT requires is therefore something I like to call **"rhetorical reading."** Rhetoric is the art of persuasion, and reading rhetorically simply means reading to understand an author's argument as well as the rhetorical role or *function* that various pieces of information play in creating that argument.

Reading this way is an acquirable skill, not an innate aptitude. It just takes practice.

While the primary focus of the redesigned SAT is on having students use evidence to justify their responses – that is, requiring them to identify which section of a passage most directly supports their answers – the exam does still test a number of other skills. The most important of these skills include drawing relationships between specific wordings and general/abstract ideas; distinguishing between main ideas and supporting evidence; understanding how specific textual elements such as diction (word choice), syntax, and style convey meaning and tone; keeping track of multiple viewpoints and understanding/inferring relationships between arguments and perspectives; and recognizing that it is possible for an author to agree with some aspects of an idea while rejecting others.

That might sound like an awful lot to manage, but don't worry; we're going to break it down.

These skills are tested in various ways across a variety of different question types.

- **Big picture** questions test your understanding of the passage as a whole. They may ask you summarize, identify main points, or determine the overall purpose of a passage.

- **Literal comprehension** questions test your understanding of what is indicated or stated directly in the passage.

- **Inference** questions test your understanding of what is suggested or stated indirectly in the passage.

- Both literal comprehension and inference questions will frequently be followed by **supporting evidence** questions, which test your ability to identify the specific information in the passage that supports the answer to the previous question.

- **Function** or **purpose** questions test your understanding of the **rhetorical role** (e.g. support, refute, criticize) that various pieces of information play within a passage.

- **Vocabulary in context** questions test your ability to use context clues to identify alternate meanings of common words.

- **Rhetorical strategy** and **passage organization** questions test your understanding of passage structure as well as the effects of particular rhetorical figures.

- **Tone** and **attitude** questions test your understanding of how specific words or phrases contribute to an author's tone.

- **Supporting and undermining claims** questions ask you to identify information, in either a passage or an answer choice, that would either support or contradict an idea presented within the passage.

- **Analogy** questions test your ability to identify parallels between situations.

- **Paired passage** questions test your ability to compare texts with different, often conflicting, points of view, and to infer how each author would likely react to the other's point of view.

- **Information graphic (infographic)** questions test your ability to interpret information presented in graph or table form, and to determine whether and how it supports various pieces of information in a passage.

Each chapter in this book is devoted to a specific type of question and is followed by exercises that allow you to practice that particular skill.

Managing the Reading Section as Whole

The 65 minutes you have to complete the 52 questions in the reading section are both a blessing and a curse. On one hand, you have over an hour to read and answer questions for just five passages; on the other hand, reading passage after passage for a straight hour without interruption can start to feel like a slog. Even though you have a good amount of time, you still want to use it as efficiently and effectively as possible. Regardless of whether you're aiming for a 600 or an 800, your goal is simple: to correctly answer as many questions as possible within the allotted time. You are under no obligation to read the passages and/or answer the questions in the order in which they appear. In fact, you can divvy up those 65 minutes and 52 questions in any way you wish.

If you're a strong reader across the board, or you simply have a very strong aversion to skipping around, you may find it easiest to read the passages and answer the questions in the order they're presented (skipping and possibly coming back to anything that seems excessively confusing). If you have very pronounced strengths and weaknesses or consistently have difficulty managing time on standardized tests, however, keep reading.

One way to ensure that you use your time most effectively is to **do the passages in order of most to least interesting** or **easiest to hardest**. Working this way ensures that you'll pick up easy points – points that you might not get as easily if you saw those questions after struggling through a passage you hated. You won't get tired or frustrated early on, then spend the rest of the section trying to make up for the time you lost struggling through a difficult passage at the start. You might even finish the first couple of passages in less than the allotted time, meaning that you won't have to rush through the more difficult material.

It's true that this strategy requires you to spend about 10-15 seconds upfront skimming the beginning of each passage and seeing which one(s) seem least painful, but it can often be a worthwhile tradeoff.

If you don't want to spend time trying to figure out which passages to start and end with, however, you can come in with a plan of attack based on your strengths and weaknesses. **If there's a particular type of passage that you consistently find easy, do it first.** That way, you automatically start with your strongest passage without having to waste time. Likewise, **if there's a type of passage you consistently have trouble with, leave it for last**. When you're struggling through those last few questions, you can at least console yourself with the knowledge that the section is almost over.

For example, a student who excels in science and graph reading but who dislikes more humanities-based passages might prefer the following order. (Note that this strategy will also necessitate some looking around since passages will not always appear in the same order).

1. Science

2. Social Science

3. Paired Passages

4. Historical Documents

5. Fiction

On the flip side, a student who is strong in the humanities but who finds science passages and graphs challenging might do the passages in this order:

1. Fiction

2. Historical Documents

3. Social Science

4. Paired Passages

5. Science

There are, of course, many possible combinations. In order to figure out which one works most effectively for you, you will most likely have to spend some time experimenting to see what order is most comfortable.

Just as you can read the passages in an order that works to your advantage, you can also answer questions in an order that helps you leverage your skills to maximum effect.

To reiterate: while you should always fill in an answer for every question, you do not need to devote serious time to answering every question. In fact, you may be better off planning from the start to guess on a certain number of questions. If you are not aiming for a perfect score, answering all of the questions may actually make it *more* difficult for you to achieve your goal.

Think of it this way: most time problems come about not because people spend too much time answering every question but rather because they spend an excessive amount of time answering a small number of questions, leaving them too little time to think through other, easier questions carefully. As a result, they feel pressured and rush, incorrectly answering questions they otherwise could have gotten right. If they were to eliminate those three or four time-consuming questions completely, they would have far more time to answer the remaining questions and thus be considerably more likely to get them right. The goal then becomes to ensure that all of the easier questions are answered before any of the more challenging questions are even considered.

One factor that can make implementing this strategy challenging, however, is that there is no way to predict where in the section easy vs. hard questions will fall. A very difficult question might be placed next to one that is very straightforward. You must therefore spend some time learning to recognize which questions you are normally able to answer easily and which ones you frequently struggle with so that you already have a clear sense of where to focus the majority of your attention when you walk into the test.

Although "easy" and "hard" are to some extent subjective, **there are some types of questions – most notably combined passage/graphic, Passage 1/Passage 2 relationship, and support/undermine – that tend to be both challenging and time consuming.** If you are not aiming for a top score, you may want to skip them entirely and spend your time focusing on more straightforward questions instead.

The Answer Isn't Always *In* the Passage

One of the great truisms of SAT prep is that "the answer is always in the passage," but in reality this statement is only half true: **the information necessary to answer the questions is always provided in the passage, but not necessarily the answer itself.** The SAT tests the ability to draw relationships between specific wordings and general ideas – so while the correct answer will always be *supported by* specific wording in the passage (which you will sometimes be explicitly asked to identify), the whole point is that you are responsible for making the connection. That, in essence, is the test.

As a rule, therefore, the correct answers to most questions will not usually be stated word-for-word in the text. In fact, **if the phrasing of an answer choice mimics the phrasing of the passage too closely, you should approach it with a healthy dose of suspicion.** The correct answer will usually refer to an **idea** that has been discussed in the passage and that has simply been **rephrased**. Your job is therefore to identify that idea and look for an answer choice that rewords it using **synonyms**. Same idea, different words.

Understanding Answer Choices

Each SAT Reading question is accompanied by four answer choices, labeled A) through D). Despite the multiple-choice format, the presence of multiple answers does not somehow make incorrect answers any more valid or make correct answers any less so.

Although one or more incorrect answers may sound convincing, there is always a specific reason – supported by the passage – that wrong answers are wrong. Often, they describe a situation that *could* be true but that the passage does not explicitly indicate *is* true. They may also employ relatively abstract language that many test-takers find confusing or difficult to comprehend. That said, incorrect answers typically fall into the following categories:

- Off-topic

- Too broad (e.g. the passage discusses *one* scientist while the answer refers to *scientists*)

- Too extreme (e.g. the passage is neutral or slightly negative/positive but the answer is extremely negative/positive)

- Half-right, half-wrong (e.g. right information, wrong point of view)

- Could be true but not enough information

- True for the passage as a whole, but not for the specific lines in question

- Factually true but not stated in the passage

On most questions, many test-takers find it relatively easy to eliminate a couple of answers but routinely remain stuck between two plausible-sounding options. Typically, the incorrect answer will fall into either the "could be true but not enough information" or the "half-right, half-wrong" category. In such cases, you must be willing to read very carefully in order to determine which answer the passage truly supports.

Understanding Line References

A line reference simply tells you where a particular word or phrase is located – it does **not** tell you that the answer will be in that line or set of lines. A question that reads, "The author uses digital and video offerings (line 35) as examples of…" is telling you the phrase *digital and video offerings* is in line 35. The answer could be in line 25, but it could also be in line 23 or 27 or even 35.

In addition, **the most important places in the passage, the ones that you need to pay the most attention to, are not necessarily the ones indicated by the questions**. Focusing excessively on a particular set of lines can make you lose sight of the bigger picture.

At the other extreme, only a small part of the line reference may sometimes be important. In fact, **the longer a line reference, the lower the chance that all of it will be important**. There's no sense spending time puzzling over eight or ten lines that you've spent time carefully marking off if all you need to focus on is the first sentence or a set of dashes.

Strategies for Reading Passages

One of the major challenges of SAT reading is that questions are arranged in two ways: first, in rough chronological order of the passage (although answers to "supporting evidence" questions may be found *after* the line reference in the following question), and afterward, in non-chronological order for infographic questions. In addition, some "big picture" questions that appear either at the beginning or in the middle of a question set may not provide line references. As a result, some jumping around is unavoidable. If you can understand the gist of the author's argument, though, you will likely be able to identify some correct answers – even those to "detail" questions – without having to hunt through the passage. You will also find it easier to answer "supporting evidence" questions because in many cases, you will already have a good idea of the information the correct lines must include.

There are essentially two major ways to read passages. Regardless of which strategy you choose, you should read the passage as quickly as you can while still absorbing the content. Do your best to focus on the parts you understand and try to avoid spending time puzzling over confusing details or turns of phrase (which may or may not ultimately be relevant), and repeatedly re-reading sections you do not grasp immediately.

The **first option** is to read the entire passage with the goal of understanding the big picture, then answering the questions in one block after you are done reading. This strategy tends to work best for people who have excellent focus and comprehension, and who are strong at identifying and summarizing arguments.

Read the passage slowly until you figure out the **point – usually at the end of the introduction** – and underline it. Then, focus on the first (topic) and last sentence of each paragraph carefully, skimming through the body of each paragraph and circling major transitions/strong language. Finally, read the conclusion carefully, paying particular attention to and **underlining the last sentence or two because the main point will often be restated at the end of the conclusion.**

Working this way will allow you to create a mental "map" of the passage: the introduction and conclusion will most likely give you the main point, and each topic sentence will generally provide you with the point of the paragraph, allowing you to understand how it fits into the argument as a whole. Then when you're asked to think about the details, you'll already understand the ideas that they support and have a sense of their purpose within the passage.

If you consistently spend too much time reading passages, you can try another version of this approach, reading the introduction slowly until you figure out the point, then reading the first and last sentence of each body paragraph carefully and skipping the information in between. Then, read the conclusion slowly and underline the end. That way, you'll get the major points without losing time.

If your comprehension is outstanding, you can simply move on to the next section of the passage (the place where the idea clearly changes) once you've grasped the point of any particular section of the passage you happen to be reading – regardless of how long that section may be. You can worry about the details when you go back.

The **second option** is to read the passage in sections, say a paragraph or two at a time, answering the more straightforward line-reference questions as you read. When you turn to a new passage, start by skimming through the questions. Notice which ones have specific lines references, then go to the passage and mark off those lines in the passage. (Note: bracketing lines is generally faster and more efficient than underlining.) Then, as you read the passage, you can answer those questions as you come to them, **keeping in mind that the answers to some questions will not be located directly in the lines referenced, and that you may need to read before/after in order to locate the necessary information.**

This is often a good approach for people who difficulty recognizing main ideas, or who have difficulty maintaining focus when they are confronted with too much information. Breaking passages down into smaller "chunks" can make them seem more manageable.

This can also be a helpful strategy for people who are concerned about spending too much time reading the passages and not having enough left over to comfortably answer all the questions. Knowing that you've answered even three or four of the questions by the time you get done with the passage can allow you to work more calmly through the remaining questions.

An important note about "supporting evidence" questions: If you choose to answer some of the questions as you work through the passage, you need to be careful with "supporting evidence" questions. They come in two types: ones in which the first question of the pair contains a line reference, and ones in which the first question of the pair does not contain a line reference.

When the first question of the pair does contain a line reference, you can probably answer both questions as you read the passage. Pay close attention to the lines you use to determine your answer to the first question; assuming you understand the passage, those lines will likely be cited in the correct answer to the second question, allowing you to answer both questions simultaneously. (Don't worry, we're going to look at some examples of how to do this a little later on.) For this reason, **you should make sure to mark both questions in this type of pair as you look through the questions**. If you overlook the "supporting evidence" question initially, you'll end up having to backtrack after you're done with the passage and re-locate information you've already found.

On the other hand: **when the first question of a "supporting evidence" pair does not contain a line reference, you should not normally try to answer both questions as you read, and you should <u>not</u> mark the line references in the second question.** If you attempt to pay attention to all those various places and connect them to the first question as you read, you will almost certainly become confused.

Answering the questions as you read the passage can work well if you are a strong reader, but it does have some potential drawbacks. Reading passages in bits can cause you to get lost in the details and lose sight of the argument. So while this method can be effective if you tend to have trouble understanding the big picture, it cannot fully compensate for that weakness. Strategies allow you to leverage the skills you do have, but they cannot substitute for the ones you don't. To be sure, it is possible to get many – or even all – of the questions right working this way. It's just that the process will be much more tedious and open to error.

You might be wondering why we're not going to seriously address the possibility of skipping the passage entirely and just jumping to the questions. If time is a serious problem for you, you might think that this option represents your best shot at finishing on time. After all, those passages are long! While I don't dispute that this strategy can be effective for the right person, I do not normally recommend it.

The main problem is that is does not take into account what the SAT is actually testing, namely relationships between ideas – particularly between main ideas and supporting details. In order to determine relationships between ideas, you need context for them, which is very difficult to determine if you're reading bits and pieces of a passage in isolation. You therefore run the serious risk of misunderstanding certain sections – or even the entire passage.

Moreover, unless you are able to split your attention and glean main ideas at the same time you are hunting for answers to detail-based questions (an extremely sophisticated skill), you will have no way of using the big picture to "shortcut" detail-based questions. You are likely to spend considerable time hunting through the passage, re-reading aimlessly as you try to figure out where to look. What is intended to be a time-saving strategy thus ends up requiring more time than would have been involved in simply reading the passage.

If you have a serious time problem, you are much better off simply reading a few key places – introduction, topic sentences, conclusion – so that you at least have a gist of what the passage is talking about when you look at the questions.

Skimming Effectively Means Knowing What to Focus On

If you ask those rare lucky people who can easily complete a test with half an hour left over how they finish so quickly, they'll probably just shrug and tell you that there's no magic trick involved; they're just reading the passages and answering the questions. What most highly skilled readers often do not recognize, though, is that their "naturally" fast reading is actually the result of a combination of specific skills. But because expert readers generally perform those skills subconsciously, they can't explain how they do what they do or teach someone else to do it. The good news is that those skills can be learned. You probably won't become a champion speed-reader overnight, but you can learn to read more quickly and effectively.

Brute speed, no doubt, is a useful thing to have , but it is not the whole story. In reality, **the key is to read efficiently**. If you understand main ideas, you can often use a general, "bird's eye" view to answer some questions without even looking back, leaving you plenty of time to worry about questions that require more time.

One of the most common mistakes people make is to read as if every sentence were equally important. As a result, when they encounter something they don't understand, they assume it must be crucial and read it again. And if they still don't understand it, they read again. And maybe even a third and fourth time. Before they know it, they've spent almost a minute reading and rereading a single sentence. When they finally move on, they're not only confused and frustrated (which makes it harder to concentrate on the rest of the passage) but they've also lost sight of what the passage is actually about.

What's more, when most people skim through a passage, they simply try to read *everything* faster, with the result that they don't understand the passage as more than a string of vaguely related sentences. When they look at the question, they have only a fuzzy idea of what they just read. Because they haven't focused on the key places indicating main ideas and concepts, they're often perplexed when they encounter "big picture" questions that ask about the passage as a whole. And because they've just been worrying about each individual piece of information, they have difficulty thinking about where information would logically be located when confronted with questions without line references.

Effective skimming, on the other hand, involves reading <u>selectively</u>. Some sections are read very slowly, while others are glanced through or even skipped over entirely. Reading this way requires much more thought and focus, but it is also much faster and, when done properly, actually improves comprehension. In order know what to read slowly and what to skip, however, you must be able to recognize what information is important.

As a general rule, authors tend to be pretty clear about the parts of their writing that they want you to pay attention to: if they're really generous, they'll even come right out and tell you what the point is. Even if they're not quite that blatant, however, they usually make a decent effort to tell you what's important – if not through words, then through punctuation.

So first, **you should circle any words or phrases that indicate the author is making a** point, e.g. *the point is, goal,* or *intention,* along with the word *important* and any of its synonyms (*significant, central, essential, key*) and any italicized words. If you see one of these terms in the middle of a paragraph as you're racing through, you need to slow down, circle it, and read that part carefully. **If the author says it's important, it's important.** There's no trick.

Second, you need to learn to recognize when an argument changes or when new and important information is being introduced: transitions such as *however, therefore, in fact;* "unusual" punctuation such as dashes, italics, and colons; strong language such as *only, never,* and *most;* and "explanation" words such as *answer, explain,* and *reason* are all "clues" that tell you to pay attention. If one of these elements appears either **in or around** the lines you're given to read, **the answer will typically be located right around that spot.** If you are able to do so while still absorbing the meaning of the passage, you should mark these key elements as you read so you'll know what to pay attention to when you go back to answer the questions. To be clear the goal is not to look for transitions just for the sake of doing so. You don't need to circle every last *and* or *but* that appears. In fact, you probably shouldn't. Rather, the goal is to use the "clues" that the passage provides as a means of identifying the *major* points of the argument – the places where you most need to pay close attention.

If, on the other hand, you feel that looking for transitions will interfere with your comprehension, then you should not worry about them when you read through the passage initially. It is far more important that you gain a clear understanding of the passage. When you go back to answer the questions, however, you do need to take them into account because they will typically indicate where the answers are located.

In the passage on the following page, key elements are in bold. **The chart on p. 203 provides a full list of key words, phrases, and punctuation, as well as their functions.**

The following passage is adapted from "Makerspaces, Hackerspaces, and Community Scale Production in Detroit and Beyond," © 2013 by Sean Ansanelli.

During the mid-1980s, spaces began to emerge across Europe where computer hackers could convene for mutual support and camaraderie. In the past few years, the idea of fostering such shared, physical spaces
5 has been rapidly adapted by the diverse and growing community of "makers", who seek to apply the idea of "hacking" to physical objects, processes, or anything else that can be deciphered and improved upon.

A hackerspace is described by hackerspaces.org as
10 a "community-operated physical space where people with common interests, often in computers, technology, science, digital art or electronic art, can meet, socialize, and/or collaborate." Such spaces can vary in size, available technology, and membership structure (some
15 being completely open), but generally share community-oriented characteristics. **Indeed, while** the term "hacker" can sometimes have negative connotations, modern hackerspaces thrive off of community, openness, and assimilating diverse **viewpoints – these** often being the
20 only guiding principles in otherwise informal organizational structures.

In recent years, the city of Detroit has emerged as a hotbed for hackerspaces and other DIY ("Do-It-Yourself") experiments. Several hackerspaces
25 can already be found throughout the city and several more are currently in formation. **Of course,** Detroit's attractiveness for such projects can be partially attributed to cheap real estate, which allows aspiring hackers to acquire ample space for experimentation. Some observers
30 have **also** described this kind of making and tinkering as embedded in the DNA of Detroit's residents, who are able to harness substantial intergenerational knowledge and attract like-minded individuals.

Hackerspaces (or "makerspaces") can be found in
35 more commercial forms, **but** the vast majority of spaces are self-organized and not-for-profit. **For example,** the OmniCorp hackerspace operates off member fees to cover rent and new equipment, from laser cutters to welding tools. OmniCorp also hosts an "open hack night"
40 every Thursday in which the space is open to the general public. Potential members are required to attend at least one open hack night prior to a consensus vote by the existing members for **admittance; no** prospective members have yet been denied.
45 A visit to one of OmniCorp's open hack nights reveals the **vast variety** of activity and energy existing in the space. In the main common room alone, activities range from experimenting with sound installations and learning to program Arduino boards to building speculative "oloid"
50 shapes - all just for the sake of it. With a general atmosphere of mutual support, participants in the space are continually encouraged to help others.

One of the **most active** community-focused initiatives in the city is the Mt. Elliot Makerspace. Jeff Sturges,
55 former MIT Media Lab Fellow and Co-Founder of OmniCorp, started the Mt. Elliot project with the aim of replicating MIT's Fab Lab model on a smaller, cheaper scale in Detroit. "Fab Labs" are production facilities that consist of a small collection of flexible computer
60 controlled tools that cover several different scales and various materials, with the **aim to make "almost anything"** (including other machines). The Mt. Elliot Makerspace now offers youth-based skill development programs in **eight areas: Transportation,** Electronics,
65 Digital Tools, Wearables, Design and Fabrication, Food and Music, and Arts. The range of activities is meant to provide not only something for everyone, **but** a well-rounded base knowledge of making to **all** participants.

While the center receives some foundational support,
70 the space also derives **significant support** from the local community. Makerspaces throughout the city connect the space's youth-based programming directly to school curriculums.

The growing interest in and development of
75 hacker/makerspaces has been **explained**, in part, as a result of the growing maker movement. Through the combination of cultural norms and communication channels from open source production as well as increasingly available technologies for physical
80 production, amateur maker communities have developed in virtual and physical spaces.

Publications such as *Wired* are noticing the **transformative potential** of this emerging movement and have sought to devote significant attention to its
85 development. Chief editor Chris Anderson recently published a book entitled *Makers*, in which he proclaims that the movement will become the next Industrial Revolution. Anderson argues such developments will allow for a new wave of business opportunities by
90 providing mass-customization rather than mass-production.

The **transformative potential** of these trends goes beyond new business opportunities or competitive advantages for economic growth. **Rather, these trends**
95 **demonstrate the potential to actually transform economic development models entirely**.

Using Key Words: Managing Questions Without Line References

Just as you must be able to recognize key words and phrases within passages, so must you be able to recognize key words and phrases within *questions*. This is a crucial skill for questions that are not accompanied by line references – while many of these questions will be accompanied by supporting evidence questions that direct you to look at specific places in the passage, you will also encounter detail-based questions in which line references are **not** provided in either the question or the answer choices. In such cases, you must be able to locate the necessary information efficiently by using the wording of the question for guidance.

For example, consider this from a hypothetical passage about sustainable energy:

1

The author suggests that a reduction in <u>fossil fuel subsidies</u> could lead to

A) greater cooperation among nations.
B) decreased economic stability.
C) higher transportation costs.
D) more sustainable infrastructure.

This question is relatively straightforward, but it gives no indicated of where in the passage the answer might be located. If you happen to remember the answer from the passage, you're in luck. If you don't remember, however, you have to know how to find the information in a way that will not involve staring at the passage and aimlessly (and increasingly nervously) skimming random parts of it.

The first step is to identify and **underline** the key word(s) or phrase in the question. That word or phrase is the specific focus of the question, i.e. the topic, and will virtually always follows the word *indicates/conveys* or *suggests/implies*. In this case, the key phrase is *fossil fuel subsidies*.

Then, you should go back to the passage to skim for that word or phrase, **dragging your index finger down the page as you scan**. This may seem like a minor detail, but in fact it is extremely important: it establishes a physical connection between your eye and the page, focusing you and reducing the chance that you will overlook the necessary information.

As you skim, you should **pay particular attention to the first (topic) and last sentence** of each paragraph because they are most likely to include important points. Even if they don't provide the information necessary to answer the question, they will often provide important clues about where the information *is* located.

Each time the key word or phrase appears, stop and read a sentence or two above and below for context. If that section of the passage does not answer the question, move on and check the next place the key word/phrase shows up. **Your goal is to avoid falling into a loop of reading and re-reading a section, searching for information that isn't there.**

How to Work Through Questions with Line References

While your approach will vary depending on the specific question, in general I recommend the following strategy:

1) Read the question <u>slowly</u>.

Put your finger on each word of the question as you read it; otherwise you may miss key information, and every letter of every word counts.

When you're done, take a second or two to make sure you know exactly what it's asking. If the question is phrased in an even slightly convoluted manner, rephrase it in your own words in a more straightforward way until you're clear on what you're looking for. If necessary, scribble the rephrased version down.

This is not a minor step. If, for example, a question asks you the purpose of a sentence, you must re-read it with the goal of understanding what role the sentence plays within the argument. If you re-read it with a different goal, e.g. understanding what the sentence is literally saying, you can't work toward answering the question that's actually being asked.

2) Go back to the passage and re-read the lines given in the question. If the question seems to call for it, read from a sentence or two above to a sentence or two below.

Purpose/function questions often require more context and, as a result, you should be prepared to read both before and after the line reference. The answers to most other question types are usually found within the lines referenced, but there are exceptions. If the line reference begins or ends halfway through a sentence, however, make sure you back up or keep reading so that you cover the entire sentence in which it appears. If a line reference begins close to the beginning of a paragraph, you should automatically read from the first sentence of the paragraph because it will usually give you the point of the paragraph.

There is unfortunately no surefire way to tell from the wording of a question whether the information necessary to answer that question is included in the line reference. If you read the lines referenced and have an inordinate amount of difficulty identifying the correct answer, or get down to two answers and are unable to identify which is correct, that's often a sign that the answer is actually located somewhere else. Go back to the passage, and read the surrounding sentences.

For long line references: a long line reference is, paradoxically, a signal that you <u>don't</u> need to read all of the lines. Usually the information you need to answer the question will be in either the first sentence or two, the last sentence or two, or in a section with key punctuation (dashes, italics, colon). Start by focusing on those places and forgetting the rest; they'll almost certainly give you enough to go on.

3) Answer the question in your own words, and write that answer down.

This step is not necessary on very straightforward questions, but it can be a big help on questions that require multiple steps of logic, particularly Passage 1/Passage 2 relationship questions. Writing things down keeps you focused, reminds you what you're looking for, and prevents you from getting distracted by plausible-sounding or confusing answer choices.

The goal is not to write a dissertation or come up with the exact answer in the test. You can be very general and should spend no more than a few seconds on this step; a couple of words scribbled down in semi-legible handwriting will suffice. The goal is to identify the general information or idea that the correct answer must include. Again, make sure you're answering the question that's actually being asked, not just summarizing the passage.

If you do this step, you should spend **no more than a few seconds** on it. If you can't come up with anything, skip to step #4.

4) Read the answers carefully, A) through D), in order.

If there's an option that contains the same essential idea you put down, choose it because it's almost certainly right. If it makes you feel better, though, you can read through the rest of the answers just to be sure, but make sure you don't get distracted by things that sound vaguely plausible and start second-guessing yourself.

If you can't identify the correct answer...

5) Cross out the answers that are absolutely wrong.

Try not to spend more than a couple of seconds on each answer choice. If an option clearly makes no sense in context of the question or passage, get rid of it.

When you cross out an answer, put a line through the entire thing; do not just cross out the letter. As far as you're concerned, it no longer exists.

Leave any answer that's even a remote possibility, even if you're not quite sure how it relates to the passage or question. **Remember: your understanding of an answer has no effect on whether that answer is right or wrong. You should never cross out an answer because you're confused or haven't really considered what it's saying.**

If you get down to two answers, go back to the passage again and start checking them out. Whatever you do, do not just sit and stare at them. The information you need to answer the question is in the passage, not in your head.

When you're stuck between two answers, there are several ways to decide between them.

First, go back to the passage and see if there are any major transitions or strong language you missed the first time around; you may have been focusing on the wrong part of the line reference, or you may not have read far enough before/after the line reference. If that is the case, the correct answer may become clear once you focus on the necessary information.

The correct answer will usually contain a synonym for a key word in the passage, so if a remaining choice includes this feature, you should pay very close attention to it.

You can also pick one specific word or phrase in an answer to check out when you go back to the passage. For example, if the lines in question focus on a single scientist and the answer choice mentions *scientists*, then the answer is probably beyond the scope of what can be inferred from the passage. Likewise, if an answer focuses on a specific person, thing, or idea not mentioned in the lines referenced, there's also a reasonable chance that it's off topic.

Remember: that the more information an answer choice contains, the greater the chance that some of that information will be wrong.

Finally, you can reiterate the main point of the passage or paragraph, and think about which answer is most consistent with it. That answer will most likely be correct.

6) If you're still stuck, see whether there's a choice that looks like a right answer.

If you still can't figure out the answer, you need to switch from reading the passage to "reading" the test. Working this way will allow you to make an educated guess, even if you're not totally sure what's going on. Does one of the answers you're left with use extremely strong or limiting language (*no one, always, ever*)? There's a pretty good chance it's wrong. Does one of them use a common word (e.g. *compromised, conviction*) in its second meaning? There's a pretty good chance it's right. You might want to pay particularly close attention to the latter.

In addition, ask yourself whether all of the answers you're left with actually make sense in context of both the test and the real world. For example, an answer stating that no scientific progress has been made in recent years is almost certain to be wrong. Yes, you should be very careful about relying on your outside knowledge of a subject, but it's okay to use common sense too!

7) If you're still stuck, skip it or guess.

You can always come back to it later if you have time. And if you're still stuck later on, you need to pick your favorite letter and fill it in. You should never leave anything blank.

Starting on the next page, we're going to look at some examples.

The sharing economy is a little like online shopping, which started in America 15 years ago. At first, people were worried about security. But having made a successful purchase from, say, Amazon, they
5 felt safe buying elsewhere. Similarly, using Airbnb or a car-hire service for the first time encourages people to try other offerings. Next, consider eBay. Having started out as a peer-to-peer marketplace, it is now dominated by professional "power sellers" (many of whom started
10 out as ordinary eBay users). The same may happen with the sharing economy, which also provides new opportunities for enterprise. Some people have bought cars solely to rent them out, for example. Incumbents are getting involved too. Avis, a car-hire firm, has a share
15 in a sharing rival. So do GM and Daimler, two carmakers. In the future, companies may develop hybrid models, listing excess capacity (whether vehicles, equipment or office space) on peer-to-peer rental sites. In the past, new ways of doing things online have not displaced the
20 old ways entirely. But they have often changed them. Just as internet shopping forced Walmart and Tesco to adapt, so online sharing will shake up transport, tourism, equipment-hire and more.
The main worry is regulatory uncertainty. Will
25 room-4-renters be subject to hotel taxes, for example? In Amsterdam officials are using Airbnb listings to track down unlicensed hotels. In some American cities, peer-to-peer taxi services have been banned after lobbying by traditional taxi firms. The danger is that
30 although some rules need to be updated to protect consumers from harm, incumbents will try to destroy competition. People who rent out rooms should pay tax, of course, but they should not be regulated like a Ritz-Carlton hotel. The lighter rules that typically govern
35 bed-and-breakfasts are more than adequate. The sharing economy is the latest example of the internet's value to consumers. This emerging model is now big and disruptive enough for regulators and companies to have woken up to it. That is a sign of its immense potential.
40 It is time to start caring about sharing.

1 ▆▆▆▆▆▆▆▆▆▆▆▆▆▆▆▆▆▆▆▆▆▆▆▆

The author suggests that the sharing economy (line 11) could eventually

A) grow larger than the traditional economy.
B) be controlled by a particular group of sellers.
C) rely mostly on hybrid models.
D) depend exclusively on former eBay users.

The first thing to remember about a question like this is that the line reference is telling us only that the phrase *sharing economy* – the key phrase – appears in line 11. The information we need to answer the question is not necessarily in line 11. Let's start by reading the entire sentence in which the phase appears:

The same may happen with the sharing economy, which also provides new opportunities for enterprise.

Unfortunately, we don't really get much information from this sentence. It tells us that *the same may happen*, but we don't actually know what that thing is.

In order to figure out what *the same* refers to, we need to back up some more and read the previous couple of sentences as well:

> **Next, consider eBay. Having started out as a peer-to-peer marketplace, it is now dominated by professional "power sellers" (many of whom started out as ordinary eBay users).**

Now we're getting someplace. The passage is telling us that the sharing economy as a whole, like eBay, could eventually become dominated (=controlled) by professional "power sellers" (=a particular group of sellers). So the answer is B).

Notice that the correct answer takes the wording of the passage and **rephrases it in more general terms**. The specific people mentioned in the passage ("power sellers") become the much more general "a particular group of sellers."

Notice also that if we had started reading at line 10 or 11 and kept going from there, we would never have found the answer in the passage. We might have eventually stumbled across it by process of elimination, but the process would have been much less straightforward. There would be considerable room for all sorts of confusion.

If the method described above seems like a reasonable – not to mention simpler – way to work, great. This book will provide you with numerous ways to help you figure things out on your own and reduce your reliance on the answer choices.

You might, however, be thinking something like, "Well *you* make it seem easy enough, but *I* would probably get confused if I tried to figure that out on my own." Or perhaps you're thinking something more along the lines of, "Ew… that seems like way too much *work*. Can't I just look at the answer choices?" So for you, here goes. One by one, we're going to consider the answer choices – very, very carefully.

A) grow larger than the traditional economy

No, this answer is completely off topic. It might sound like a reasonable possibility, but there is no information about how the sharing economy compares to the traditional economy, either now or in the future. In fact, the phrase *traditional economy* never even appears. So A) is out.

B) be controlled by a particular group of sellers

The "vague" answer. As a matter of fact, the **"vague" wording suggests that the answer is correct** – even in the absence of any other information. But again, if you started reading in line 10 or 11 and never backed up, it's likely you would never find the information indicating that it was right. As discussed above, this answer rephrases the idea that a professional group of sellers could eventually come to dominate the entire sharing economy, just as they came to dominate eBay.

C) rely mostly on hybrid models

Half-right, half wrong. This answer takes a random word from the passage and uses it to create an answer that could sound either vaguely plausible or confusing (especially if you don't know what a hybrid is), but it does nothing to answer the question. The passage does indicate that some companies may develop hybrid models to list their inventory; it does not, however, suggest in any way that the sharing economy will come to rely *mostly* on hybrid models.

A hybrid, by the way, is something that is created by combining parts from two sources. For example, a hybrid car is a car that contains both a gasoline engine and an electric engine, either of which can be used to power it.

D) depend exclusively on former eBay users

First off, the extreme word *exclusively* is a big warning sign that this answer is probably wrong, so you should be suspicious of it from the start. It's true that the author does *mention* eBay users right before the key phrase, but there's no direct relationship between the two things – the author is simply pointing out that many of the "power sellers" who eventually came to dominate eBay started out as regular users. We cannot in any way infer that the sharing economy as a whole will depend *only* on former eBay users ("power sellers" or otherwise). That is an interpretation that goes far beyond what the passage supports.

Besides, if you think about it logically, this answer doesn't really make sense. Even if you don't know anything about the sharing economy, the passage indicates that it involves a variety of companies in different fields (Amazon, Airbnb, GM). The idea that the sharing economy could depend only on former eBay users is completely at odds with that fact.

If you do know some basic things about the sharing economy, you can think of it this way: correct answers must always be supported by the passage, but they must also correspond to reality – many of the passages on the SAT are connected to current trends, debates, and controversies, and as a result, correct answers must reflect real-world facts.

To be clear: Factually correct answers are not necessarily right, but factually incorrect answers are virtually guaranteed to be wrong.

And now, before we get started for real, some tidbits of test-prep wisdom:

If you're not in the habit of reading things written for educated adults, start. Now.

If you're unsure where to begin, check out Arts & Letters Daily (http://www.aldaily.com), which has links to dozens of publications written at SAT level and above. You cannot, however, read passively and expect your score to magically rise. Rather, you must **actively** and **consistently** practice the skills introduced in this book. Circle/underline the point, major transitions, and words that reveal tone; pay close attention to the introduction and conclusion for the topic and the author's opinion (see how quickly you can get the gist); look for phrases that reveal "they say" and "I say;" notice when words are used in non-literal ways, and look up unfamiliar words; and practice summarizing arguments briefly. The more you develop these skills independently, the easier it will become to apply them to the test.

The SAT isn't really just about the SAT.

One of the most frequently repeated truisms about the SAT is that you have to forget all of your outside knowledge and just worry about what's in the passage. That's mostly true… but not completely. First, just to be clear, an answer can be both factually correct and wrong if that particular fact is not discussed in the passage. That's what most people mean when they say to forget about outside knowledge. The reality, however, is that reading does not exist in a vacuum. It is always dependent upon ideas and debates that exist outside of the SAT. The more you know about the world, the more easily you'll be able understand what you're reading. And if you see an answer you know is factually correct, it can't hurt to check it first.

Read exactly what's on the page, in order, from left to right.

This piece of advice may seem overwhelmingly obvious, but I cannot stress how important it is. When people feel pressured, they start glomming onto random bits of information without fully considering the context. While it is not necessary to read every word of a passage to get the gist of it, skipping around randomly is unlikely to help you either! Pay attention to what the author is telling you to pay attention to: when you see italics or words like "important" or "the point is," you need to slow down and go word by word. **Put your finger on the page, and bracket or underline as you read; the physical connection between your eye and your hand will force you to focus in a way you wouldn't if you were just looking at the page. You're also far less likely to miss key information.**

Be as literal as you possibly can.

While your English teacher might praise you for your imaginative interpretations, the College Board will not. Before you can understand the function of a piece of information or make a reasonable inference about it, you have to understand exactly what it's saying – otherwise, you'll have a faulty basis for your reasoning. When you sum things up, stick as closely as possible to the language of the passage. People often get themselves into trouble because they think that there's a particular way they're supposed to interpret passages that they just don't "get," when in reality they're not supposed to interpret anything. **In short, worry about what the author is actually saying, not what she or he might be trying to say.**

Answering SAT Reading questions is a process.

If you look at the answers with an assumption about what the correct one will say but don't see a choice that says it, you need to be willing to revise your original assumption and re-work through the question from scratch. Yes, this does take some time, but if you can get through most of the questions quickly, having to slow down occasionally won't make much of an impact. No, this is not easy to do when you're under pressure, but that's the mindset with which you have to approach the test.

Draw a line through the entire answer, not just the letter.

Your goal is to deal with the smallest amount of information possible at any given time, and looking at answers you've already eliminated is an unnecessary distraction. If you get down to one option and it doesn't seem to work, you can always erase the lines, but only if you...

Always work in pencil.

It's a lot harder to re-consider answer choices when you've crossed them out in ink.

Flexibility is key.

To obtain a very high score, you need to be able to adapt your approach to the question at hand. People who insist on approaching every question the same way tend to fall short of their goals, while those who start out scoring in the stratosphere tend to adjust automatically (even if they think they're just reading the passage and answering the question every time). Sometimes you'll be able to answer a question based on your general understanding of the passage and won't need to reread anything. Sometimes you'll be able to go back to the passage, answer the question on your own, and then easily identify the correct answer when you look at the choices. Other times the answer will be far less straightforward and you'll have to go back and forth between the passage and the questions multiple times, eliminating answers as you go. Yet other times it might make more sense for you to begin by looking at the answer choices and eliminating those that are clearly wrong, then go back to the passage and seeing which remaining choice best fits. It's up to you to stay flexible and find the strategy that will get you to the answer most easily. For that reason, I have done my best, whenever possible, to offer multiple ways of approaching a given question.

The path to a perfect score is not linear.

Whereas math and writing scores can often be improved those last 100 or so points if you spend time internalizing just a few more key rules, the same cannot be said for reading. If you want a 750+ score, you *cannot skip steps* and start guessing or skimming through answers – you'll keep making just enough mistakes to hurt yourself. The SAT is a standardized test: if you keep approaching it the same way, you'll keep getting the same score. It's designed to work that way. If you want your score to change radically, you have to approach the test in a radically different way. Raising your score is also not just about how much practice you do: it does not matter how well you know the test if you do not fully understand what you are reading. Getting into the right mindset can take five minutes or five months, but until you've absorbed it, your score will probably stay more or less the same.

Don't rush.

I took the SAT twice in high school: the first time, I raced through the reading section, answering questions mostly on instinct, not thinking anything through, and finishing every section early. I was an incredibly strong reader and even recognized one of the passages from a book I'd read for pleasure, but I got a 710.

The second time I understood what I was up against: I broke down every single question, worked through it step-by-step, wrote out my reasoning process, and worked every question out meticulously as if it were a math problem. It was one of the most exhausting things I'd ever done, and when I stumbled out of the exam room, I had absolutely no idea how I'd scored. I'd literally been focusing so hard I hadn't left myself the mental space to worry about how I was doing. Working that way was *hard*, but it got me an 800.

Summoning that level of focus is not easy. It's also terrifying because you don't have the "well, I maybe didn't try as hard as I could have" excuse. If you bomb, you have nowhere to put the blame. If you have excellent comprehension and can stand to do it, though, working that precisely is almost foolproof. It might take longer than you're used to in the beginning, but the more you go through the process, the more accurate you'll become and the less time you'll take. Skipping steps may save you time, but your score will suffer as a result.

Every passage has two authors – the author of the passage and the author(s) of the test – and you need to be able to read both of them.[*]

The highest scorers are often able to use a combination of close reading skills and knowledge about the test itself (themes, biases, types of answers likely to be correct), and they are able to employ both of those skills as needed in order to quickly identify the answer choices most likely to be correct and then check them out for real.

When I was in high school and uncertain about an answer, I trained myself to always ask, "What would the test writers consider correct?" It didn't matter that I couldn't put the patterns into words then; the point was that I was able to convince myself that what *I* personally thought was irrelevant. To score well, you have to think of the test in terms of what the College Board wants – not what you want. You have to abandon your ego completely and approach the test with the mindset that *the College Board is always right and what you think doesn't matter*. Even if that thought makes you want to throw up, you have to get over it and put yourself at the mercy of the test. Then, once you've gotten the score you want, you can put it out of your mind and never have to worry about it again (or at least until your own children take it).

The ability to do this is really important: occasionally the logic on certain questions will not be airtight. In those instances, you need to be able to consider the choices on their own and ask which one looks most like the sort of answer that is usually correct. It's not fair that the test writers can get away with being sloppy, but if it happens, you need to be prepared.

---

[*]I need to thank Debbie Stier for putting this idea into words so eloquently. They're hers, not mine, and thanks to her, I've spent a lot more time thinking – and talking – about the necessity of reading the test at two levels.

Be willing to consider that the test might break its own "rules."

For example, you can usually assume that answers containing extreme language such as *always, never, awe, incomprehensible, impossible,* etc. are incorrect and cross them off as soon as you see them. But you can't *always* assume that a particular pattern holds without carefully considering what the passage is actually saying. Correct answers, especially to inference questions, will very occasionally contain words such as *always* or *only.* If you're trying to score 800 or close to it, you need to stay open to the possibility that an answer containing one of those words could on occasion be correct.

Remember: provided that doing so won't result in a lawsuit, the College Board is free to ignore its own rules. General patterns are just that: general. That means you will sometimes encounter exceptions.

Fit the answer to the passage, not the passage to the answer.

If an answer could only *sort of kind of maybe possibly be true if you read the passage in a very specific way,* it's not right. Don't try to justify anything that isn't directly supported by specific wording in the passage.

Every word in the answer choice counts.

One incorrect word in an answer choice is enough to make the entire answer wrong. It doesn't matter how well the rest of the answer works; it doesn't matter how much you like the answer or think it should be right. If the author of the passage is clearly happy about a new scientific finding and an answer choice says "express skepticism about a recent finding," the answer choice is wrong. The fact that the words "a recent finding" might have appeared in the passage is irrelevant if the answer does not correctly indicate the author's attitude toward it. On the other hand...

Just because information is in the passage doesn't mean it's important.

One of the things the SAT tests is the ability to recognize important information and ignore irrelevant details. Reading SAT passages is not about absorbing every last detail but rather about understanding what you need to focus on and what you can let go. And that means...

Don't get stuck.

In my experience, students often encounter time problems because either 1) they get hung up on a section of the passage that they find confusing – a part that sometimes turns out to be irrelevant – and waste a lot of time re-reading it; or 2) they get stuck between two answer choices and sit there staring at them. To avoid falling into one of these traps, push yourself to keep moving. Go back to the passage and check out a specific aspect of one of the answers, circle things, write down what you know, or cross things out that clearly don't make sense. Doing something is better than doing nothing. Furthermore...

If something confuses you, ignore it and focus on what you do understand.

You have a limited amount of time to get through each section, and that means you need to be constantly figuring things out. **Skip around.** If you don't know how to work through a problem, you need to leave it and work on something you *can* answer. It doesn't matter if you have to leave a couple of the most time-consuming questions blank if doing so allows you to answer everything else correctly. Sometimes, there's no way to make certain questions (e.g. passage/graphic, support/undermine) go quickly. If they take too much time and you're not fixated on getting a perfect score, you can probably afford to skip a couple.

SAT Reading is not a guessing game.

This is just as true as it was before the wrong-answer penalty was abolished. Yes, you might be able to jack up your score a bit by guessing strategically on a relatively small number of questions, but there is still no substitute for carefully thinking your way through each question. The chance of your reaching your score goal simply by being a lucky guesser on more than a few questions is very small indeed.

If you consistently get down to two choices and always pick the wrong one, that's a sign that you either don't really know how to answer the questions or that you're not reading carefully enough. I've had a lot of students tell me they always got down to two and then guessed wrong when in fact they were missing the entire point of the passage. That's not a test-taking problem; that's a comprehension problem.

If you are just not reading carefully enough, slow down, put your finger on the page, make sure you're getting every single word, and make a concerted effort to think things through before you pick an answer.

On the other hand, if you really aren't sure how to choose between answers, you need to figure out what particular skills you're missing and work on them. If you're misunderstanding the passage and/or answer choices because you don't know vocabulary words, you need to keep a running list of unfamiliar words. The fact that vocabulary is no longer directly tested is irrelevant. You're unlikely to see any truly obscure words on the test, and anything you see once is something you're likely encounter again.

If you're getting thrown by complicated syntax, you need to spend more time reading SAT-level material. If you can't figure out what the author thinks, you need to focus on key phrases and places (e.g. last sentence of the first paragraph, end of the conclusion).

You also need to spend some time getting familiar with the kinds of answers that usually appear as correct and incorrect choices: if you know, for example, that *apathetic* and *ambivalent* are often wrong answers to tone questions, and that *emphatic*, *appreciative*, and *disdainful* often appear as correct answers, you'll be a lot less tempted to pick one of the former – even if you thought you *might* be able to argue for an interpretation that made one of them work. **Remember: just because an answer is there doesn't mean it can be correct.** If you look for reasons to keep answers, you'll never get down to one. But on the other hand…

Don't assume you'll always recognize the right answer when you see it

Incorrect answers are written to sound plausible. You might get away with jumping to the answers on easy and medium questions, but you'll almost certainly fall down on at least some of the hard ones, unless you do some legwork upfront. The test is designed that way. The fact that there are answer choices already there does not excuse you from having to think.

This is especially true for "function" or "purpose" questions. Because correct answers are phrased in a more general manner than the text itself, they do not always initially appear to be correct – or even directly related to the passage. **Confusing does not equal wrong**. If there's any chance an answer could work, you have to leave it until you see something better. Sometimes the right answer just won't say what you're expecting it to say, and in those cases, you need to keep an open-enough mind to consider that you've been thinking in the wrong direction and be willing to go back and revise your original assumption.

In addition, correct answers – especially those to questions about what Passage 1/Passage 2 authors agree on – may occasionally depend on a seemingly minor detail or less important facet of an author's argument; consequently, many test takers eliminate them automatically, without stopping to actually consider whether they do in fact answer the question. This does not make the response any less correct – it just makes it harder to identify at first glance.

There are no trick questions.

Reading questions may require you to apply very careful logic or make fine distinctions between ideas – but they're also set up so that you can figure them out logically. The right answer might be something that you're not expecting, but it can still be reasoned out. Wrong answers are wrong because they are based on various kinds of faulty reasoning. If you think your way carefully through a question and put the answer in your own words, then see an option choice that truly says the same thing, it's almost certainly correct.

Go back to the passage and read.

Even if you think you're certain of what the passage says in the lines cited, you probably need to go back and read it anyway (unless you can reason out the answer based on the main point). Stress makes memory unreliable; don't assume you can trust yours. You could be absolutely certain that you remember the author mentioning a particular idea in line 15 when in fact it doesn't show up until five or ten lines later and refers to something that *someone else* thinks. Don't play games or be cocky. Just take the extra few seconds and check.

Don't ever read just half a sentence.

Context counts. If you only read the first or last half of a sentence, you might miss the fact that the author thinks exactly the *opposite* of what that half of the sentence says. You might also overlook the exact information you need to answer a question.

If the answer isn't in the lines you're given, it must be somewhere else.

If you read the lines you're given in the question and can't figure out the answer, chances are the information you need is located either before or after. Don't just assume you're missing something and read the same set of lines over and over again or, worse, guess. Again: be willing to revise your original assumption and start over. Yes, this will take time (although probably not as much as you think), but you're a lot more likely to get the question right.

When in doubt, reread the end of the conclusion.

The point of the passage is more likely to be located at the end of the conclusion, usually the last sentence or two, than it is just about anywhere else. If you get lost and start to panic, stop and reread it to focus yourself. It won't work all the time, but it will work often enough.

Writing things down is not a sign of weakness.

Most people don't have a huge problem writing down their work for Math problems; the same, alas, cannot be said for Reading. Unfortunately, one of the biggest differences between people scoring pretty well vs. exceptionally well is often their degree of willingness to write down each step of a problem. The very highest scorers tend to view writing each step down as a crucial part of the process necessary to get the right answer, whereas lower scorers often resent having to write things down, viewing it as a drag on their time or a sign of weakness that they should be above. It's not either of those things. Writing things down does not have to take a long time – you should abbreviate as much as possible, and the only person who has to read your handwriting is you. Writing also keeps you focused and takes some pressure off of your memory; everything you write down is one less thing your brain has to manage. If you're really certain what you're looking for, you probably don't need to spend the time. If you have any hesitation, though, it's worth your while. When you're under a lot of pressure, having even one less thing to worry about is a big deal. Besides, you probably wouldn't try to figure the hardest math problems out in your head, so why on earth would you work that way for reading?

The order in which you read the passage and do the questions doesn't really matter.

What truly matters is that you have the necessary close reading and reasoning skills to figure out or recognize the correct answers. **Strategy is not a substitute for skill**; rather, it's a way of leveraging the skills you do have to work efficiently and with the least possible amount of second-guessing.

Don't fight the test.

It doesn't matter how much you want the answer to be C) instead of B). It never will be, and unless you want to file a complaint with the College Board, you're stuck. Instead of arguing about why your answer should have been right, try to understand why it was wrong – chances are you misunderstood something or extrapolated a bit too far along the way. If you're serious about improving, your job is to adapt yourself to the mindset of the test because it certainly won't adapt itself to yours. Who knows, you might even learn something.

2. Vocabulary in Context

We're going to start by looking at vocabulary-in-context questions, which are among the most common types of questions to appear: every passage/set of paired passages will contain at least one. Compared to other types of reading questions, they also tend to be relatively straightforward and less dependent on your understanding of the passage as a whole. It is usually possible to determine the correct answer simply by looking at the sentence in which the word appears.

There are two types of vocabulary-in-context questions: most test alternate meanings of common words, but some also test first meanings of more challenging, less common words. In addition, you may sometimes be asked to identify the meaning of short phrases that contain words used in non-literal ways (e.g. *in its wake* means "as a consequence"). Regardless of which type you are asked about, the principle on which these questions are based can be summed up as follows:

Context determines meaning

On the SAT, words can be used to mean whatever an author happens to want them to mean, regardless of their dictionary definition(s). As a matter of fact, it doesn't even matter if you know the definition of the word being tested, as long as you 1) can use context clues to understand the word in question, and 2) can figure out the definitions of the words in the answer choices. Sometimes the word being tested will in fact be used in a way that's fairly similar to its most common meaning – but then again, sometimes it won't.

The one thing you can be reasonably certain of, however, is that a *common* word will not be used to mean what it most commonly means (e.g. *spill* will not mean "knock over"). If it did, there would be no reason to test that word in the first place! As a general rule, if you see the usual definition of a word among the answer choices, you should start by assuming that it's wrong and only reevaluate that assumption if nothing else seems to work.

It also means that when you see a question that says, "In line 14, *want* most nearly means…," you can think of the question as saying, "In line 14, ------- most nearly means." The fact that the word *want* as opposed to some other word, happens to be used in the original text is essentially irrelevant.

Strategies:

1) Plug in your own word and find the answer choice that matches

The only potential difficulty involved in this approach is that sometimes, even if you supply a perfectly adequate synonym for the word in question, the correct answer will be a less common word, or the second meaning of a common word – one that you may not recognize as having the same meaning as the word you supplied.

2) Plug each answer choice into the sentence

Frequently, you'll be able to hear that a particular choice does not sound correct or have the right meaning within the context of a sentence. The only potential downside is that sometimes, as is true for #1, the correct word is not a word you would think to use. As a result, you might talk yourself out of choosing that answer (or eliminate it immediately) because you think it sounds funny.

3) Play positive/negative, then plug in

If you can determine from context whether the word is positive or negative, you can often eliminate at least two or three of the answer choices. You can then plug the remaining answers back into the sentence and see which one works best.

While some people feel most comfortable using a single approach for all vocabulary-in-context questions, it is also true that certain questions lend themselves better to certain approaches. On some straightforward questions you may find it easiest to plug in your own word, while on other, less clear-cut questions, a combination of positive/negative and process of elimination might be the most effective way of working toward the answer.

Important: sometimes you will not be able to determine the meaning of a word from the sentence in which it appears. In such cases, you need to establish a slightly larger context. Read from the sentence above to the sentence below – one of those sentences will very likely contain a synonym for the word in question and thus for one of the answer choices.

Starting on the next page, we're going to look at some examples.

Every time a car drives through a major intersection, it becomes a data point. Magnetic coils of wire lay just beneath the pavement, registering each passing car. This starts a cascade of information: Computers tally the

5   number and speed of cars, shoot the data through underground cables to a command center and finally translate it into the colors red, yellow and green. On the seventh floor of Boston City Hall, the three colors splash like paint across a wall-sized map.

10   To drivers, the color red means stop, but on the map it tells traffic engineers to leap into action. Traffic control centers like this one—a room cluttered with computer terminals and live video feeds of urban intersections— represent the brain of a traffic system. The city's network

15   of sensors, cables and signals are the nerves connected to the rest of the body. "Most people don't think there are eyes and ears keeping track of all this stuff," says John DeBenedictis, the center's engineering director. But in reality, engineers literally watch our every move,

20   making subtle changes that relieve and redirect traffic.
        The tactics and aims of traffic management are modest but powerful. Most intersections rely on a combination of pre-set timing and computer adaptation. For example, where a busy main road intersects with a quiet residential

25   street, the traffic signal might give 70 percent of "green time" to the main road, and 30 percent to the residential road. (Green lights last between a few seconds and a couple minutes, and tend to shorten at rush hour to help the traffic move continuously.) But when traffic

30   overwhelms the pre-set timing, engineers override the system and make changes.

1

As used in line 21, "modest" most nearly means

A) proper.
B) simple.
C) timid.
D) inexpensive.

Solution:

When you look at the sentence in which the word *modest* appears, you can see that it contains an important clue – the word *but* indicates that *modest* is being used in opposition to *powerful*. The most direct opposite of *powerful* is *weak*, but unfortunately that isn't an option here. Still, we're looking for something in that general area.

A) and D) are simply off-topic; *proper* is in no way the opposite of *powerful*, and there's no mention of money, so *inexpensive* is out. If you don't know what *timid* (shy) means, you'll have to work by process of elimination. When vocabulary is involved, **you should always work from what you do know to what you don't know**. If you're not sure about a word, ignore it and deal with everything you know for sure first.

Simple makes sense in context. Even though the traffic management system isn't particularly complex (the next sentence tells us that it relies on a combination of just two things: pre-set timing and computer adaptations), it can still accomplish a lot. So B) is the answer.

Let's look another example. The language in this passage is a bit more challenging, so we're going to spend more time on it.

The following passage is adapted from Susan B. Anthony's Remarks to the Woman's Auxiliary Congress of the Public Press Congress, May 23, 1893.

Mrs. President and Sisters, I might almost say daughters—I cannot tell you how much joy has filled my heart as I have sat here listening to these papers and noting those characteristics that made each in its
5 own way beautiful and masterful. I would in no ways lessen the importance of these expressions by your various representatives, but I want to say that the words that specially voiced what I may call the up-gush of my soul were to be found in the paper read by Mrs. Swalm
10 on "The Newspaper as a Factor of Civilization." I have never been a pen artist and I have never succeeded with rhetorical flourishes unless it were by accident. But I have always admired supremely that which I could realize the least. The woman who can coin words and
15 ideas to suit me best would not be unlike Mrs. Swalm, and when I heard her I said: "That is worthy of Elizabeth Cady Stanton."
While I have been sitting here I have been thinking that we have made strides in journalism in the last forty
20 years. I recall the first time I ever wrote for a paper. The periodical was called the *Lily*. It was edited—and quite appropriately—by a Mrs. Bloomer. The next paper to which I contributed was the *Una*. These two journals were the only avenues women had through
25 which to face themselves in type to any extent worthy of note before the war. The press was as kind as it knew how to be. It meant well and did all for us it knew how to do. We couldn't ask it to do more than it knew how. But that was little enough and I tried an experiment
30 editing a newspaper myself. I started a paper and ran it for two years at a vast cost to every one concerned in it. I served seven years at lecturing to pay off the debt and interest on that paper and I considered myself fortunate to get off as easily as that.

1

As used in line 8, "voiced" most nearly means

A) recorded.
B) rose.
C) strained.
D) conveyed.

2

As used in line 31 "concerned" most nearly means

A) worried.
B) involved.
C) bothered.
D) altered.

Solution #1:

Let's start by considering the context. Anthony is talking about how impressed she is with the speeches (i.e. papers) that came before hers, and how she's been paying attention to the specific features that made each speech so great. The sentence in which the word *voiced* appears is quite long, but we really need to get the gist of it – basically, Anthony is saying that of all the speeches, she particularly liked Mrs. Swalm's speech because it *voiced the gush-up of [her] soul*. In other words, it "voiced" her deepest feelings. So *voiced* means something along the lines of *expressed*. *Conveyed* is closest to *expressed*, so D) is correct.

If you find it too difficult to wade through all that language and figure out just what Anthony is trying to get across in that sentence, you can work around your confusion. If you know that she's talking about speeches and words, you can make an educated guess. *Rose* simply doesn't make sense, so B) is out. *Strained* is negative, and if you look at the previous sentence, the word *beautiful* and *masterful* are clearly positive. So C) can be eliminated as well.

Next, you can plug in. The sentence is sufficiently long that you can start after the comma – if you go all the way back to the beginning, you might lose track of what it's saying.

A)   **...but I want to say that the words that specially <u>recorded</u> what I may call the up-gush of my soul were to be found in the paper read by Mrs. Swalm on "The Newspaper as a Factor of Civilization."**

That doesn't really make sense. Words can *be* recorded by someone, but they can't actually record anything themselves. Even if you find the antiquated language difficult to decipher, that fact hasn't changed since the nineteenth century. (And no one was recording anything in the nineteenth century anyway.)

B)   **...but I want to say that the words that specially <u>conveyed</u> what I may call the up-gush of my soul were to be found in the paper read by Mrs. Swalm on "The Newspaper as a Factor of Civilization."**

Yes, that makes sense. Words are used to "convey" things – that's their purpose. Even if you understand nothing else in the sentence, you are likely to recognize that. There's no trick.

Solution #2:

This question is a good deal more straightforward than the previous question, as long as you don't fall for the trap in A). "Worried" is the most common definition of *concerned*, which means that you can eliminate it from the get-go. Notice that it's the first answer choice; it's placed where it is because a given percentage of test-takers will reliably choose it without looking back. If an answer seems too obvious and you haven't gone back to the passage or thought about it carefully, there's a good chance it's too good to be true.

Let's go back and look at the sentence in which the word in question appears. In this case, the larger context isn't all that important, but we can back up a sentence or so to be safe.

> **But that was little enough and I tried an experiment editing a newspaper myself. I started a paper and ran it for two years at a vast cost to every one ------- in it.**

If you had to plug in your own word, there's a pretty good chance you'd come up with something like *involved*, which is in fact the answer.

Playing process of elimination, we can eliminate C) because *bothered* is similar to *worried*, and we already know that the former is not correct. In addition, you can probably hear that it sounds wrong in context: the phrase *bothered in it* is not idiomatic. D) doesn't fit either. There's nothing in the passage about changing, and like C), it doesn't work idiomatically.

Now try some additional questions on your own. Answer choices are not included initially because the point of this exercise is to work through the question as far as you can before looking at the answers.

Mrs. President and Sisters, I might almost say daughters—I cannot tell you how much joy has filled my heart as I have sat here listening to these papers and noting those characteristics that made each in its
5 own way beautiful and masterful. I would in no ways lessen the importance of these expressions by your various representatives, but I want to say that the words that specially voiced what I may call the up-gush of my soul were to be found in the paper read by Mrs. Swalm
10 on "The Newspaper as a Factor of Civilization." I have never been a pen artist and I have never succeeded with rhetorical flourishes unless it were by accident. But I have always admired supremely that which I could realize the least. The woman who can coin words and
15 ideas to suit me best would not be unlike Mrs. Swalm, and when I heard her I said: "That is worthy of Elizabeth Cady Stanton."
While I have been sitting here I have been thinking that we have made strides in journalism in the last forty
20 years. I recall the first time I ever wrote for a paper. The periodical was called the *Lily*. It was edited—and quite appropriately—by a Mrs. Bloomer. The next paper to which I contributed was the *Una*. These two journals were the only avenues women had through
25 which to face themselves in type to any extent worthy of note before the war. The press was as kind as it knew how to be. It meant well and did all for us it knew how to do. We couldn't ask it to do more than it knew how. But that was little enough and I tried an experiment
30 editing a newspaper myself. I started a paper and ran it for two years at a vast cost to every one concerned in it. I served seven years at lecturing to pay off the debt and interest on that paper and I considered myself fortunate to get off as easily as that.

3

As used in line 14, "coin" most nearly means

1) Underline context clues

2) Your word OR positive/negative:

_____

A) gain.
B) spend.
C) think up.
D) learn about.

4

As used in line 24, "avenues" most nearly means

1) Underline context clues

2) Your word OR positive/negative:

_____

A) routes.
B) means.
C) escapes.
D) conventions.

Answers and explanations are at the end of this chapter.

"Hard" Words

In announcing the rollout of the new exam, the College Board was quite vocal in publicizing the fact that the SAT would no longer test "obscure" vocabulary, instead focusing on "relevant" words in context. While that made for a nice sound bite as well as a good marketing pitch, it very deliberately ignored one very important fact: virtually none of the words that the pre-2016 SAT tested were truly "obscure" (and those that were more unusual could normally be dealt with either through a knowledge of roots or process of elimination). Rather, the words tested were the sorts of moderately sophisticated words that regularly appear in college/adult-level reading but that the average high school student – that is, one who did not regularly read texts written for college-educated adults – was unlikely to know. And most members of the press simply parroted the College Board's official stance, trotting out a couple of outlier, multisyllabic horrors as proof. Apparently, it never occurred to them that words that would have seemed "weird" when they were in high school would now strike them as utterly unremarkable if encountered among the pages of *The New York Times*.

The problem, of course, is that many of those words tested on the old exam are still important – a pesky little fact of which the College Board is perfectly aware. The result is that some of the types of challenging words tested on the old SAT will continue to be tested – it's just that now they're considered "relevant" simply by virtue of appearing on the new test.

The good news for you, oh lucky post-January 2016 test taker, is that you do not need to be able to spit out the definitions of these words yourself – you simply need to be able to glean their meanings from context. That said, it doesn't hurt to actually know what they mean.

For example, consider this excerpt from an 1850 speech by Daniel Webster:

I wish to speak to-day, not as a Massachusetts
man, nor as a Northern man, but as an American, and
a member of the Senate of the United States. It is
fortunate that there is a Senate of the United States; a
5 body not yet moved from its propriety, not lost to a just
sense of its own dignity and its own high responsibilities,
and a body to which the country looks, with confidence,
for wise, moderate, patriotic, and healing counsels.
It is not to be denied that we live in the midst of strong
10 agitations, and are surrounded by very considerable
dangers to our institutions and government. The
imprisoned winds are let loose. The East, the North,
and the stormy South combine to throw the whole sea
into commotion, to toss its billows to the skies, and
15 disclose its profoundest depths.

1

As used in line 10, "agitations" most nearly means

A) considerations.
B) decisions.
C) disturbances.
D) defenses.

If you look at the sentence in which the word *agitations* appears, the phrase *very considerable dangers* provides an important clue that the correct definition must be negative. Only C) fulfills that criterion, and in fact, "agitations" are disturbances or turmoil.

Second Meanings and Answer Choices

Sometimes vocabulary can also be tested in very indirect ways – even on questions that appear to test something else entirely. Whenever possible, you should always pay close attention to answer choices that contain second meanings. If you have difficulty recognizing when words are being used in alternate meanings, or if having to think about answer choices this way seems too complicated given all the other things you have to worry about, this is probably not a good strategy for you. But if you are an exceptionally strong reader and want to have some fun with the test, this is a "game" you might want to play. **To be clear: you should never choose an answer simply because it contains a second meaning. You should, however, give such answers special consideration and/or look at them first.**

Yogi Berra, the former Major League baseball catcher and coach, once remarked that you can't hit and think at the same time. Of course, since he also reportedly said, "I really didn't say everything I said,"
5   it is not clear we should take his statements at face value. Nonetheless, a widespread view — in both academic journals and the popular press — is that thinking about what you are doing, as you are doing it, interferes with performance. The idea is that once you
10 have developed the ability to play an arpeggio on the piano, putt a golf ball or parallel park, attention to what you are doing leads to inaccuracies, blunders and sometimes even utter paralysis. As the great choreographer George Balanchine would say to his
15 dancers, "Don't think, dear; just do."
    Perhaps you have experienced this destructive force yourself. Start thinking about just how to carry a full glass of water without spilling, and you'll end up drenched. How, exactly, do you initiate a telephone
20 conversation? Begin wondering, and before long, the recipient of your call will notice the heavy breathing and hang up. Our actions, the French philosopher Maurice Merleau-Ponty tells us, exhibit a "magical" efficacy, but when we focus on them, they degenerate
25 into the absurd. A 13-time winner on the Professional Golfers Association Tour, Dave Hill, put it like this: "You can't be thinking about the mechanics of the sport while you are performing."

1

The passage indicates that focusing on one's actions as they are performed

A) is an important component of improving a skill.
B) is more common among experts than it is among other people.
C) can result in a compromised performance.
D) leads to a superior level of performance.

This is a fairly straightforward question, but we're only interested in one word in one answer. Choice C) contains the word *compromised*. Now, *compromised* usually means "came to an agreement," but here it's being used in its second meaning: "put at risk." That single word suggests that C) deserves close attention. And in fact, C) is the answer.

The view discussed in the first paragraph can be summarized as "paying attention to an action while you do it makes you worse at it." But if you interpret *compromise* as meaning "come to an agreement," C) won't make sense. And that's precisely why the answer is written that way.

Common Second Meanings

Affect (v.) – To take on, assume; affected (adj.) – behaving in an artificial/pretentious way

Afford – Grant (e.g. an opportunity)

Appreciate – To take into account, recognize the merits of, OR to increase in value

Appropriate (app-ro-pre-ATE) – To take from, steal

Arrest – To stop (not just put handcuffs on a criminal)

Assume – To take on responsibility for, acquire (e.g. to assume a new position)

Austerity – Extreme financial restraint, eliminating all excess spending

Badger (v.) – To pester/annoy (e.g. reporters badgered the candidate after the scandal broke)

Bent – Liking or preference for

Capacity – Ability

Chance (v.) – To attempt

Check – To control (e.g. *The vaccine checked the spread of the disease*)

Coin (v.) – To invent (e.g. coin a phrase)

Compromise (v.) – To endanger or make vulnerable (e.g. to compromise one's beliefs)

Constitution – Build (e.g. a football player has a solid constitution)

Conviction – Strong belief. Noun form of *convinced.*

Couch (v.) – To hide

Currency – acceptance, approval (of an idea)

Discriminating – Able to make fine distinctions (e.g. a *discriminating* palate)

Dispatch – Speed, efficiency (e.g. *She completed the project promptly and with great dispatch*)

Doctor (v.) – To tamper with, alter

Economy – Thrift (e.g. a writer who has an *economical* style is one who uses few words)

Embroider – To falsify, make up stories about

Execute – To carry out

Exploit – Make use of, take advantage of (does not carry a negative connotation)

Facility – Ability to do something easily (e.g. *a facility for learning languages*

Foil – To put a stop to (e.g. to foil a robbery), OR a secondary character in a play/novel

Grave/Gravity – Serious(ness)

Grill – To question intensely and repeatedly (e.g. *The police officers grilled the suspect thoroughly*)

Hamper – To get in the way of, hinder

Harbor – To possess, hold (e.g. to harbor a belief)

Hobble – Prevent, impede

Mint – To produce money, or as an adjective = perfect, like new

Pedestrian – Unremarkable, uninteresting

Plastic/plasticity – Able to be changed, malleable (e.g. brain plasticity)

Provoke – Elicit (e.g. a reaction)

Qualify – To provide more information or detail about

Realize – To achieve (a goal)

Reconcile – To bring together opposing or contradictory ideas

Relate/Relay - To pass on information, give an account of (a story)

Reservations – Misgivings

Reserve – To hold off on (e.g. to reserve judgment)

Ruffled – Flustered, nonplussed (Unruffled – calm)

Sap (v.) – To drain (e.g. of energy)

Scrap (v.) – To eliminate

Shelve/Table (v.) – To reject or discard (e.g. an idea or proposal)

Sound – Firm, stable, reliable, valid (e.g. a sound argument)

Spare, Severe – Plain, unadorned

Static – Unchanging (i.e. in a state of *stasis*)

Store (n.) – Reserve

Sustain (v.) – To withstand

Temper – To moderate, make less harsh

Train – To fixate on (e.g. one's eyes on something)

Uniform – Constant, unvarying

Unqualified – Absolute

Upset (v.) – To interfere with an expected outcome

Want – Lack

Yield – To reveal (e.g. an experiment yields results)

Additional Words to Know

Acquiesce – Give in, surrender; synonym for *capitulate*

Alleviate/Ameliorate – To make better, reduce pain; synonyms for *mitigate*

Ambivalent – To have mixed feelings, be torn

Anomaly – Abnormality, deviation from the norm

Bolster – Provide support for (e.g. an argument)

Chronicle – To record, tell the story of

Comprehensive – Thorough, complete

Condone – Disregard or pardon an illegal or objectionable act

Dearth – Lack of

Didactic – Intended to teach

Digression – Section of a text that deviates from the main topic

Empirical – Derived from experiment or observation

Idealistic – Cherishing noble or high-minded principles, opposite of pragmatic

Illustrious – Famous, renowned

Ingenious – Clever

Innate – Inborn

Innovation – New invention or discovery

Lofty – High-minded

Myriad - Many

Partisan – Strong adherent to a party or idea

Postulate – Propose an explanation for

Pragmatic, Prudent – Practical

Scrutinize – Examine Closely

Stipulate – Specify a requirement

Substantiate – Prove; unsubstantiated – unproven

Synthesize – Bring together, integrate

Timid – Shy, fearful

Undermine – Attack indirectly

Unequivocal – Absolute, certain (equivocal = uncertain)

Vernacular – Common, everyday speech

Vocabulary in Context Exercises

1. Math poses difficulties. There's little room for eyewitness testimony, seasoned judgment, a skeptical eye or transcendental rhetoric.

1

As used in line 2, "seasoned" "most nearly means

A) determined
B) tasteful
C) experienced
D) objective

2. Around the middle of the 20th century, science dispensed with the fantasy that we could easily colonize the other planets in our solar system. Science fiction writers absorbed the new reality: soon, moon and
5 asteroid settings replaced Mars and Venus.

1

As used in line 4 "dispensed with" most nearly means

A) distributed
B) disposed of
C) identified with
D) renewed

3. Until the past few years, physicists agreed that the entire universe is generated from a few mathematical truths and principles of symmetry, perhaps throwing in a handful of parameters like the mass of an electron.
5 It seemed that we were closing in on a vision of our universe in which everything could be calculated, predicted, and understood. However, two theories, eternal inflation and string theory, now suggest that the same fundamental principles from which the laws of
10 nature derive may lead to many different self-consistent universes, with many different properties.

1

As used in line 4, "parameters" most nearly means

A) restrictions
B) hypotheses
C) calculations
D) theories

2

As used in line 5, "closing in on" most nearly means

A) experimenting
B) approaching
C) hypothesizing
D) shutting down

4.   The world is complex and interconnected, and the evolution of our communications system from a broadcast model to a networked one has added a new dimension to the mix. The Internet has made us all less
5 dependent on professional journalists and editors for information about the wider world, allowing us to seek out information directly via online search or to receive it from friends through social media. But this enhanced convenience comes with a considerable risk: that we
10 will be exposed to what we want to know at the expense of what we need to know. While we can find virtual communities that correspond to our every curiosity, there's little pushing us beyond our comfort zones to or into the unknown, even if the unknown may have
15 serious implications for our lives. There are things we should probably know more about—like political and religious conflicts in Russia or basic geography. But even if we knew more than we do, there's no guarantee that the knowledge gained would prompt us to act in a
20 particularly admirable fashion.

1

As used in line 10 "at the expense of" most nearly means

A) in the event of
B) without consideration of
C) with the understanding that
D) with the sacrifice of

2

As used in line 15 "serious" most nearly means

A) profound
B) focused
C) concentrated
D) sincere

3

As used in line 19 "prompt" most nearly means

A) advocate
B) require
C) motivate
D) instruct

5.   Citrus greening, the plague that could wipe out Florida's $9 billion orange industry, begins with the touch of a jumpy brown bug on a sun-kissed leaf. From there, the bacterial disease incubates in the
5 tree's roots, then moves back up the trunk in full force, causing nutrient flows to seize up. Leaves turn yellow, and the oranges, deprived of sugars from the leaves, remain green, sour, and hard. Many fall before harvest, brown necrotic flesh ringing failed stems.
10   For the past decade, Florida's oranges have been literally starving. Since it first appeared in 2005, citrus greening, also known by its Chinese name, huanglongbing, has swept across Florida's groves like a flood. With no hills to block it, the Asian citrus
15 psyllid—the invasive aphid relative that carries the disease—has infected nearly every orchard in the state. By one estimate, 80 percent of Florida's citrus trees are infected and declining.
20   The disease has spread beyond Florida to nearly every orange-growing region in the United States. Despite many generations of breeding by humanity, no citrus plant resists greening; it afflicts lemons, grapefruits, and other citrus species as well. Once a
25 tree is infected, it will die. Yet in a few select Floridian orchards, there are now trees that, thanks to innovative technology, can fight the greening tide.

1

As it is used in line 9, "ringing" most nearly means

A) nourishing
B) implanting
C) growing
D) surrounding

2

As it is used in line 24, "select" most nearly means

A) exclusive
B) preferred
C) particular
D) conventional

6. Chimps do it, birds do it, even you and I do it.
Once you see someone yawn, you are compelled to
do the same. Now it seems that wolves can be added
to the list of animals known to spread yawns like a
5 contagion.
   Among humans, even thinking about yawning can
trigger the reflex, leading some to suspect that catching
a yawn is linked to our ability to empathize with other
humans. For instance, contagious yawning activates the
10 same parts of the brain that govern empathy and social
know-how. And some studies have shown that humans
with more fine-tuned social skills are more likely to
catch a yawn.

1

As used in line 10, "govern" most nearly means

A) elect
B) control
C) charge
D) rule

7. The following passage is adapted from Daniel Webster's
speech to the Senate in support of the Compromise of
1850, the congressional effort to resolve the issues
propelling the United States toward a civil war.

   I wish to speak to-day, not as a Massachusetts
man, nor as a Northern man, but as an American, and
a member of the Senate of the United States. It is
fortunate that there is a Senate of the United States; a
5 body not yet moved from its propriety, not lost to a just
sense of its own dignity and its own high responsibilities,
and a body to which the country looks, with confidence,
for wise, moderate, patriotic, and healing counsels.
It is not to be denied that we live in the midst of strong
10 agitations, and are surrounded by very considerable
dangers to our institutions and government. The
imprisoned winds are let loose. The East, the North,
and the stormy South combine to throw the whole sea
into commotion, to toss its billows to the skies, and
15 disclose its profoundest depths. I do not affect to regard
myself, Mr. President, as holding, or as fit to hold, the
helm in this combat with the political elements; but I
have a duty to perform, and I mean to perform it with
fidelity, not without a sense of existing dangers, but not
20 without hope. I have a part to act, not for my own
security or safety, for I am looking out for no fragment
upon which to float away from the wreck, if wreck there
must be, but for the good of the whole, and the
preservation of all; and there is that which will keep me
25 to my duty during this struggle, whether the sun and the
stars shall appear, or shall not appear for many days.
I speak to-day for the preservation of the Union.

1

As used in line 15, "affect" most nearly means

A) object
B) claim
C) influence
D) defend

2

As used in line 19, "fidelity" most nearly means

A) rebellion
B) excitement
C) disbelief
D) steadfastness

8. To understand what the new software—that is, analytics—can do that's different from more familiar software like spreadsheets, word processing, and graphics, consider the lowly photograph. Here the
5 relevant facts aren't how many bytes constitute a digital photograph, or a billion of them. That's about as instructive as counting the silver halide molecules used to form a single old-fashioned print photo. The important feature of a digital image's bytes is that, unlike
10 crystalline molecules, they are uniquely easy to store, transport, and manipulate with software. In the first era of digital images, people were fascinated by the convenience and malleability (think PhotoShop) of capturing, storing, and sharing pictures. Now, instead of
15 using software to manage photos, we can mine features of the bytes that make up the digital image. Facebook can, without privacy invasion, track where and when, for example, vacationing is trending, since digital images reveal at least that much. But more importantly, those
20 data can be cross-correlated, even in real time, with seemingly unrelated data such as local weather, interest rates, crime figures, and so on. Such correlations associated with just one photograph aren't revealing. But imagine looking at billions of photos over weeks,
25 months, years, then correlating them with dozens of directly related data sets (vacation bookings, air traffic), tangential information (weather, interest rates, unemployment), or orthogonal information (social or political trends). With essentially free super-computing,
30 we can mine and usefully associate massive, formerly unrelated data sets and unveil all manner of economic, cultural, and social realities.

For science fiction aficionados, Isaac Asimov anticipated the idea of using massive data sets to predict
35 human behavior, coining it "psychohistory" in his 1951 Foundation trilogy. The bigger the data set, Asimov said then, the more predictable the future. With big-data analytics, one can finally see the forest, instead of just the capillaries in the tree leaves. Or to put it in more
40 accurate terms, one can see beyond the apparently random motion of a few thousand molecules of air inside a balloon; one can see the balloon itself, and beyond that, that it is inflating, that it is yellow, and that it is part of a bunch of balloons en route to a birthday party. The
45 data/software world has, until now, been largely about looking at the molecules inside one balloon.

1

As in line 15, "mine" most nearly means

A) exploit
B) contain
C) respond
D) describe

2

As used in line 31, "unveil" most nearly means

A) reveal
B) analyze
C) alter
D) uphold

3

As used in line 34 "anticipated" most nearly means

A) waited for
B) accumulated
C) foresaw
D) explained

9. This passage is adapted from Sharon Tregaskis, "What Bees Tell Us About Global Climate Change," © 2010 by *Johns Hopkins Magazine*.

Standing in the apiary on the grounds of the U.S. Department of Agriculture's Bee Research Laboratory in Beltsville, Maryland, Wayne Esaias digs through the canvas shoulder bag leaning against his leg in search of
5 the cable he uses to download data. It's dusk as he runs the cord from his laptop—precariously perched on the beam of a cast-iron platform scale—to a small, battery-operated data logger attached to the spring inside the scale's steel column. In the 1800s, a scale like this
10 would have weighed sacks of grain or crates of apples, peaches, and melons. Since arriving at the USDA's bee lab in January 2007, this scale has been loaded with a single item: a colony of *Apis mellifera*, the fuzzy, black-and-yellow honey bee. An attached, 12-bit
15 recorder captures the hive's weight to within a 10th of a pound, along with a daily register of relative ambient humidity and temperature.

On this late January afternoon, during a comparatively balmy respite between the blizzards that
20 dumped several feet of snow on the Middle Atlantic states, the bees, their honey, and the wooden boxes in which they live weigh 94.5 pounds. In mid-July, as last year's unusually long nectar flow finally ebbed, the whole contraption topped out at 275 pounds, including
25 nearly 150 pounds of honey. "Right now, the colony is in a cluster about the size of a soccer ball," says Esaias, who's kept bees for nearly two decades and knows without lifting the lid what's going on inside this hive. "The center of the cluster is where the queen is, and
30 they're keeping her at 93 degrees—the rest are just hanging there, tensing their flight muscles to generate heat." Provided that they have enough calories to fuel their winter workout, a healthy colony can survive as far north as Anchorage, Alaska. "They slowly eat their
35 way up through the winter," he says. "It's a race: Will they eat all their honey before the nectar flows, or not?" To make sure their charges win that race, apiarists have long relied on scale hives for vital management clues. By tracking daily weight variations, a beekeeper can
40 discern when the colony needs a nutritional boost to carry it through lean times, whether to add extra combs for honey storage and even detect incursions by marauding robber bees—all without disturbing the colony. A graph of the hive's weight—which can

45 increase by as much as 35 pounds a day in some parts of the United States during peak nectar flow — reveals the date on which the bees' foraging was was most productive and provides a direct record of successful pollination. "Around here, the bees make
50 their living in the month of May," says Esaias, noting that his bees often achieve daily spikes of 25 pounds, the maximum in Maryland. "There's almost no nectar coming in for the rest of the year." A scientist by training and career oceanographer at NASA, Esaias
55 established the Mink Hollow Apiary in his Highland, Maryland, backyard in 1992 with a trio of hand-me-down hives and an antique platform scale much like the one at the Beltsville bee lab. Ever since, he's maintained a meticulous record of the bees' daily
60 weight, as well as weather patterns and such details as his efforts to keep them healthy. In late 2006, honey bees nationwide began disappearing in an ongoing syndrome dubbed colony collapse disorder (CCD). Entire hives went empty as bees inexplicably
65 abandoned their young and their honey. Commercial beekeepers reported losses up to 90 percent, and the large-scale farmers who rely on honey bees to ensure rich harvests of almonds, apples, and sunflowers became very, very nervous. Looking for clues, Esaias
70 turned to his own records. While the resulting graphs threw no light on the cause of CCD, a staggering trend emerged: In the span of just 15 seasons, the date on which his Mink Hollow bees brought home the most nectar had shifted by two weeks—from late May
75 to the middle of the month. "I was shocked when I plotted this up," he says. "It was right under my nose, going on the whole time." The epiphany would lead Esaias to launch a series of research collaborations, featuring honey bees and other pollinators, to investigate
80 the relationships among plants, pollinators, and weather patterns. Already, the work has begun to reveal insights into the often unintended consequences of human interventions in natural and agricultural ecosystems, and exposed significant gaps in how we understand the
85 effect climate change will have on everything from food production to terrestrial ecology.

As used in line 41, "lean" most nearly means

A) tilted
B) scarce
C) compact
D) sunken

As used in line 42, "incursions" most nearly means

A) intentions
B) introductions
C) intrusions
D) initiatives

As used in lines 49-50, "make their living" most nearly means

A) grow heavier
B) accumulate money
C) behave aggressively
D) are most productive

As used in line 68, "rich" most nearly means

A) plentiful
B) costly
C) heavy
D) fragrant

10. The following passage is adapted from the novel
Summer by Edith Wharton, initially published in 1917.

The hours of the Hatchard Memorial librarian were
from three to five; and Charity Royall's sense of duty
usually kept her at her desk until nearly half-past four.
But she had never perceived that any practical
5 advantage thereby accrued either to North Dormer or to
herself; and she had no scruple in decreeing, when it
suited her, that the library should close an hour earlier.
A few minutes after Mr. Harney's departure she formed
this decision, put away her lace, fastened the shutters,
10 and turned the key in the door of the temple of
knowledge. The street upon which she emerged was
still empty: and after glancing up and down it she began
to walk toward her house. But instead of entering she
passed on, turned into a field-path and mounted to a
15 pasture on the hillside.

She let down the bars of the gate, followed a trail
along the crumbling wall of the pasture, and walked on
till she reached a knoll where a clump of larches shook
out their fresh tassels to the wind. There she lay down
20 on the slope, tossed off her hat and hid her face in the
grass. She was blind and insensible to many things, and
dimly knew it; but to all that was light and air, perfume
and color, every drop of blood in her responded. She
loved the roughness of the dry mountain grass under
25 her palms, the smell of the thyme into which she crushed
her face, the fingering of the wind in her hair and
through her cotton blouse, and the creak of the larches
as they swayed to it.

She often climbed up the hill and lay there alone for
30 the mere pleasure of feeling the wind and of rubbing her
cheeks in the grass. Generally at such times she did not
think of anything, but lay immersed in an inarticulate
well-being. Today the sense of well-being was
intensified by her joy at escaping from the library. She
35 liked well enough to have a friend drop in and talk to
her when she was on duty, but she hated to be bothered
about books. How could she remember where they
were, when they were so seldom asked for? Orma Fry
occasionally took out a novel, and her brother Ben was
40 fond of what he called "jography," and of books
relating to trade and bookkeeping; but no one else asked
for anything except, at intervals, "Uncle Tom's Cabin,"
or "Opening of a Chestnut Burr," or Longfellow. She
had these under her hand, and could have found them
45 in the dark; but unexpected demands came so rarely
that they exasperated her like an injustice....

She had liked the young man's looks, and his short-
sighted eyes, and his odd way of speaking, that was abrupt
yet soft, just as his hands were sun-burnt and sinewy, yet

50 with smooth nails like a woman's. His hair was
sunburnt-looking too, or rather the colour of bracken
after frost; eyes grey, with the appealing look of the
shortsighted, his smile shy yet confident, as if he knew
lots of things she had never dreamed of, and yet
55 wouldn't for the world have had her feel his superiority.
But she did feel it, and liked the feeling; for it was new
to her. Poor and ignorant as she was, and knew herself
to be—humblest of the humble even in North Dormer,
where to come from the Mountain was the worst
60 disgrace—yet in her narrow world she had always ruled.
It was partly, of course, owing to the fact that lawyer
Royall was "the biggest man in North Dormer"; so
much too big for it, in fact, that outsiders, who didn't
know, always wondered how it held him. In spite of
65 everything—and in spite even of Miss Hatchard—
lawyer Royall ruled in North Dormer; and Charity ruled
in lawyer Royall's house. She had never put it to herself
in those terms; but she knew her power. Confusedly, the
young man in the library had made her feel for the first
70 time what might be the sweetness of dependence. She
sat up and looked down on the house where she held
sway.

It stood just below her, cheerless and untended.
Behind the house a bit of uneven ground with clothes-
75 lines strung across it stretched up to a dry wall, and
beyond the wall a patch of corn and a few rows of
potatoes strayed vaguely into the adjoining wilderness
of rock and fern.

1

As used in line 21 "blind" most nearly means

A) weak
B) ignorant
C) insensitive
D) careless

2

As used in line 42, the phrase "at intervals" most
nearly means

A) on a whim
B) at a steady pace
C) from time to time
D) in a repetitive manner

11. This passage is from Samuel Gompers, "What Does the Working Man Want?" 1890. Gompers, a Scottish Immigrant, was the founder of the American Federation of Labor and helped workers to organize and fight for fairer working conditions.

My friends, we have met here today to celebrate the idea that has prompted thousands of working-people of Louisville and New Albany to parade the streets; that prompts the toilers of Chicago to turn out by their
5 fifty or hundred thousand of men; that prompts the vast army of wage-workers in New York to demonstrate their enthusiasm and appreciation of the importance of this idea; that prompts the toilers of England, Ireland, Germany, France, Italy, Spain, and Austria to defy the
10 manifestos of the autocrats of the world and say that on May the first, 1890, the wage-workers of the world will lay down their tools in sympathy with the wage-workers of America, to establish a principle of limitations of hours of labor to eight hours for sleep,
15 eight hours for work, and eight hours for what we will.
It has been charged time and again that were we to have more hours of leisure we would merely devote it to the cultivation of vicious habits. They tell us that the eight-hour movement can not be enforced, for the
20 reason that it must check industrial and commercial progress. I say that the history of this shows the reverse. I say that is the plane on which this question ought to be discussed—that is the social question. As long as they make this question economic one, I am willing to
25 discuss it with them. I would retrace every step I have taken to advance this movement did it mean industrial and commercial stagnation. But it does not mean that. It means greater prosperity it means a greater degree of progress for the whole people.
30 They say they can't afford it. Is that true? Let us see for one moment. If a reduction in the hours of labor causes industrial and commercial ruination, it would naturally follow increased hours of labor would increase the prosperity, commercial and industrial. If that were true, England and America ought to be at
35 the tail end, and China at the head of civilization.
Why, when you reduce the hours of labor, just think what it means. Suppose men who work ten hours a day had the time lessened to nine, or men who work nine hours a day have it reduced to eight; what
40 does it mean? It means millions of golden hours and opportunities for thought. Some men might say you will go to sleep. Well, the ordinary man might try to sleep sixteen hours a day, but he would soon find he could not do it long. He would probably become interested in

45 some study and the hours that have been taken from manual labor are devoted to mental labor, and the mental labor of one hour produce for him more wealth than the physical labor of a dozen hours.
I maintain that this is a true proposition—that
50 men under the short-hour system not only have opportunity to improve themselves, but to make a greater degree of prosperity for their employers. Why, my friends, how is it in China, how is it in Spain, how is it in India and Russia, how is it in Italy?
55 Cast your eye throughout the universe and observe the industry that forces nature to yield up its fruits to man's necessities, and you will find that where the hours of labor are the shortest the progress of invention in machinery and the prosperity of the people are the
60 greatest. It has only been under the great influence of our great republic, where our people have exhibited their great senses, that we can move forward, upward and onward, and are watched with interest in our movements of progress and reform.

1

As used in line 16, "charged" most nearly means

A) convicted
B) ridiculed
C) claimed
D) endangered

2

As used in line 18, "vicious" most nearly means

A) idle
B) cruel
C) severe
D) ferocious

3

As used in line 20, "check" most nearly means

A) ensure
B) restrict
C) control
D) observe

4

As used in line 49, "proposition" most nearly means

A) offer
B) reminder
C) plan
D) assertion

5

As used in line 52, "degree" most nearly means

A) amount
B) measurement
C) temperature
D) stage

Official Guide/Khan Academy Vocabulary in Context Questions

Test 1

3
8
12
18
40
45
48

Test 2

14
16
25
37
39
43
47

Test 3

2
6
16
17
22
28
31
35
47

Test 4

3
9
10
13
18
24
33
34

Explanations: Vocabulary in Context Exercises

Additional Susan B. Anthony questions

3. C

If you know that the second meaning of *coin* is "think up," then you can assume C) is the answer from the start. Anthony is talking about the qualities of her ideal speechwriter; in that context, *think up* makes perfect sense.

4. B

If you plugged in your own word, you might say something like *ways*. *Means* is a synonym, so it is correct. If you think it sounds strange, you can work by process of elimination. None of the other answers make sense at all in context. The biggest danger here is that you'll avoid picking B) simply because you think it sounds too strange.

End of Chapter Exercises

1. C

This is essentially a straightforward second meanings question since the passage gives very little context – the second meaning of *seasoned* is in fact "experienced," which fits with the passage's meaning: judgment, even experienced judgment, plays no role in math because an answer is always right or wrong. *Determined* and *tasteful* do not fit logically, and *objective* is exactly the opposite of the correct idea.

2. B

The phrase *absorbed the new reality* indicates that an old reality no longer held true. What was that reality? That other planets in our solar system could easily be colonized. Logically, then, *dispensed* must mean something like "got rid of" or "threw out." *Disposed of* is closest in meaning to those phrases, so it is correct.

3.1 A

The beginning of the sentence states that the entire universe is generated from a *few* mathematical truths and principles, and the phrase *perhaps throwing in* indicates that the word in question must be related to "truths" or "principles." B) and C) clearly do not fit and can be eliminated. The phrase *like the mass of an electron* indicates that the unknown word must be something more specific than "theories" – the mass of an electron is not a theory. That leaves A), which is correct. Parameters are limits, and *restrictions* comes closest to that definition.

3.2 B

The beginning of the passage describes how physicists believed they were beginning to understand how to describe the universe mathematically. *Closing in* must therefore mean something like "coming close to." That is the definition of "approaching," so B) is correct.

4.1 D

Consider the context. The first half of the sentence indicates that convenience comes with risk, and the second half of the sentence (the information after the colon) mimics the structure of the first half: *exposed to what we want to know* = convenience (good), and *at the expense of what we need to know* = risk (bad). A) is neutral, and C) is positive, so both can be eliminated. Given the context, the phrase in question must also have to do with getting rid of something, or giving something up – basically, we're spending so much time searching for information we *want* to know that we ignore information we *need* to know. The word *sacrifice* in D) corresponds exactly to the idea of giving something up.

4.2 A

If you plugged in your own word, you might say something like "big" or "major" – the author's point is that people are spending too much time on minor things while missing the big ones. Only *profound* makes sense in that context.

4.3 C

The passage is essentially saying that having knowledge about important things wouldn't necessarily result in doing good things with that knowledge. In that context, the word in question must mean something like "cause" or "get" – *motivate* best captures that meaning, so C) is the correct answer. *Require* and *instruct* do not make sense, and *advocate* (lobby for) does not even make sense grammatically; a person can *advocate for* something, but they cannot *be advocated* to do something.

5.1 D

The passage indicates that citrus greening is a disease that essentially takes over trees. In that context, *surrounding* is the only word that makes sense. In A), *nourishing* is exactly the opposite of what you're looking for; and B) and C) don't make sense when plugged in. The rotten part of the tree isn't "implanting" or "growing" the stems.

5.2 C

The word in question refers to the orchards chosen to receive the potential cure to citrus greening. Although *chosen* does not appear as an option, the correct answer must have a similar meaning. Careful with A) and B). Both *exclusive* and *preferred* are strongly positive and would imply that the orchards chosen to receive the experimental technology were already special in some way; the passage gives no indication that the orchards were special. *Conventional* does not really make sense either – things are normally described as "conventional" in order to set up a contrast with something new. Here, it's the cure that's innovative rather than the orchards themselves. That leaves

particular, which is neutral and captures the idea that a few specific orchards have been chosen.

6. B

Govern is a word that you might associate with history, so careful not to jump to D). A brain can't really *rule* anything; only a leader (person) can rule. B) is a much better fit in this context – certain parts of the brain *control* particular social skills. *Elect* and *charge* do not fit at all in this context.

7.1 B

Consider the context. Webster is describing the fact that the various regions of the United States are in conflict with one another. In the section in which the word in question appears, he is essentially saying that he does not believe it is his job to lead the country ("hold the helm" – a helm is the wheel that steers a ship) but that he does feel a responsibility to intercede. In that context, the phrase *I do not affect to regard myself as holding…the helm* means *I do not believe* or *I do not <u>claim</u> to regard myself.* The answer is therefore B). *Object* and *defend* are the opposite of the word required – Webster is talking about what he does believe, not what he doesn't believe. *Influence* doesn't make sense either; Webster is only discussing his own beliefs, not about trying to affect someone else's beliefs.

7.2 D

The easiest way to answer this question is to know that *fidelity* means "faithfulness," and that *steadfast* is a synonym for "faithful." Otherwise, the fact that Webster is discussing his determination to fulfill his duty offers a big clue that the word means something like "determined." Careful not to get sidetracked by A). Webster is talking about the conflicts between different regions, not his own desire to rebel.

8.1 A

If you consider only the sentence in which the word appears, you get an important clue. The structure of the phrase *instead of <u>using</u> software to* *manage photos, we can mine features* indicates that *mine* must have a similar mean to *use*. In fact, *exploit* means "to make use of." That meaning is further confirmed when the author discusses all of the information that can be acquired by using features of bytes.

8.2 A

If you plugged in your own word here, you might say something like "show" or "expose." *Reveal* is closest in meaning to those words, so it is correct. Consider also the image suggested by the word *unveil* itself: a veil is a covering, and to pull off a veil is to uncover or reveal what is behind it.

8.3 C

The word *predict* in line 34 is an important clue, indicating that the word in question must have a similar meaning – Asimov predicted that data sets could be used to predict behavior. *Foresaw* (literally, "saw before") is closest in meaning, so it is correct.

9.1 B

The phrase *needs a nutritional boost* provides an important clue. Why would colonies need a nutritional boost? Because they aren't getting a lot of nutrients. In other words, nutrients are *scarce*. Even though C) might sound strange to you when it is plugged in, it is the only answer that captures the correct meaning. *Tilted* and *sunken* can only be used to refer to the physical placement of objects, and *compact* means "small" or "not taking up a lot of space," none of which quite fits the context.

9.2 C

Don't get distracted by the word *marauder* (raiders) – it doesn't matter whether you know what it means. Focus on the phrase *robber bees*, which tells you the correct word must be negative. Only *intrusions* is negative – the other answers are neutral/positive – so C) must be correct.

9.3 D

Consider the context: Esaias is talking about when honey production *spikes*, so the word you want must be clearly positive and consistent with that idea. B) can be eliminated immediately because it makes no sense in context (bees can't accumulate money), and C) is negative and can be eliminated immediately as well. Careful with A): the amount of honey the bees produce is increasing, not the weight of the bees themselves. D) correctly states that the bees are most productive, i.e. they produce the most honey.

9.4 A

The passage is talking about improved harvests, so if you plugged in your own word, you'd probably come up with something like "big" or "large." *Plentiful* is just a fancier synonym for those words, so it is correct. Careful with B): *costly* means that the harvests themselves would cost more, not that they would bring in more money. C) doesn't quite work because the focus is on harvest size, not weight. And D) is incorrect because *fragrant* (having a nice odor) is completely unrelated to harvest size.

10.1 B

The word in question is linked to *insensible* (unknowing) by the word *and*, so it must have a similar meaning. *Ignorant* is a synonym for unknowing, so B) is correct.

If you don't know what *insensible* means, consider the slightly larger context. The word *but* after the semicolon in line 22 indicates a contrast between the information before and after. *Blind* and *insensible* are opposed to the things Charity *does* respond to fully (light and air). You can therefore assume that the correct word must means something similar to "not knowing" or "not responding." Even if you cannot get all the way to the answer, you can at least play process of elimination. A) does not fit because *weak* clearly does not make sense; C) does not fit because Charity is upset, the opposite of insensitive; and D) does not fit because there is nothing to suggest that Charity is careless.

10.2 C

An interval is a period of time, and to say something occurred *at intervals* is to say that it occurred periodically, i.e. "from time to time." Be careful with B) and D). There is nothing to imply that the requests came at regular or "steady" intervals, or that they came over and over again in the same way.

11.1 C

In this sentence, Gompers is simply presenting what "they say" (shorter working hours would make people lazy), so if you were to plug in your own word, you might say something like *argued*. *Claimed* is closest in meaning, so it is correct.

11.2 A

If you're not sure what *vicious* means here, think about the larger context. Be careful not to get distracted by the word's usual meaning ("cruel" or "nasty"), which might lead you to B) or D). Gompers' argument throughout the passage is essentially that shorter working hours would give people the time to pursue all sorts of useful activities – that is, they would not become lazy. In this context, *vicious* must mean something like "lazy," and *idle* is the only word that fits that definition.

11.3 B

Think about the point of view that Gompers is disputing: shorter working hours will reduce prosperity. In that context, *check* must mean something like "reduce." *Restrict* is closest in meaning, so B) is correct.

11.4 D

If you're not sure what *proposition* means on its own, consider the information that comes immediately afterward: it's essentially a summary of Gompers' argument (reducing workers' hours is good for everyone). Logically, then, *proposition* must mean

something like "argument." *Assertion* is closest in meaning, so it is correct.

11.5 A

If you're able to plug in your own word, chances are you'll come up with something close to the answer. *Amount* is the only word that makes sense in context; Gompers is arguing that reducing workers' hours would lead to more (i.e. a greater *amount*) of prosperity. Playing process of elimination, B) and C) do not make sense in context; *degree* is clearly not being used in a literal, scientific way here because the passage has nothing to do with science. Be careful not to "twist" *stage* to try to make it fit. That word can be a synonym for *degree* when it refers to a step in a process; however, that's not quite the same thing as *amount*, which fits the idea being conveyed here much more precisely.

3. Making the Leap:
Moving from Concrete to Abstract

Before we look more closely at the various question types, we're going to examine a key element of comprehension – namely, the ability to move between specific wording and more abstract or general ideas. While you probably won't see many (if any) questions that directly test this skill, it is nevertheless crucial for navigating challenging passages.

One of the most common ways that both the authors of SAT Reading passages and the test-writers themselves move between specific phrasings and more general language is by using **pronouns** (*this*, *that*) and **abstract** or **compression nouns** (*notion, assertion, phenomenon*).

If you've already spent some time preparing for the Writing section, you may be familiar with pronouns and antecedents, or referents, but even if you are, here's a refresher:

Pronoun = word that replaces a noun (e.g *she, he, it, they, this, that*)

Antecedent/Referent = noun to which a pronoun refers

As a matter of fact, the testing of pronouns and antecedents is one of the places where the Reading and Writing sections overlap. In the Writing section, the focus is primarily on spotting disagreement errors between pronouns and their antecedents. For example:

Some albino animals have difficulty thriving in the wild because **1** its skin is insufficiently dark to absorb sunlight during harsh winters.

1

A) NO CHANGE
B) it's
C) their
D) they're

In the above sentence, the answer is C) because the singular pronoun *it* refers to the plural noun *albino animals*, which is clearly stated at the beginning of the sentence.

Unfortunately, pronouns and their antecedents tend to be less straightforward in Reading than they are in Writing. In the above sentence, for example, the noun that *its* refers to is right there – *some albino animals* is really the only thing that *its* could logically refer to.

Why Use Pronouns?

When it comes to Reading, determining which nouns pronouns refers to may sometimes require more effort than you are accustomed to; however, the heavy use of pronouns is necessary in all but the simplest texts for reasons of style and clarity. It is important that you be able to connect pronouns back to their referents because without the ability to "track" an idea through a passage, you can easily lose track of the passage's focus and argument.

Compare the following two versions of this passage. First without pronouns:

> …Crowdsourcing is a wonderful tool, but **crowdsourcing** still fails in a very particular way, which is that any evaluation is swayed by the evaluations that have come before **that evaluation**. A barbershop with a one-star rating on Yelp as **that barbershop's** first review is subsequently more likely to accrue more negative reviews—and that same barbershop, were **that barbershop** to receive a four-star rating on Yelp as **that barbershop's** first review, would be more likely to accrue more subsequent positive reviews.

Notice how incredibly awkward and repetitive this version is. Now look at this version, which replaces the repeated nouns with pronouns:

> …Crowdsourcing is a wonderful tool, but **it** still fails in a very particular way, which is that any evaluation is swayed by the evaluations that have come before **it**. A barbershop with a one-star rating on Yelp as **its** first review is subsequently more likely to accrue more negative reviews—and that same barbershop, were **it** to receive a four-star rating on Yelp as **its** first review, would be more likely to accrue more subsequent positive reviews.

Notice how much smoother this version is. You don't get tangled up in the constant repetition of the same phrase, so it's much easier to read.

Pronouns won't always appear by themselves, though. Typically, a pronoun such as *this, that,* or *these* will appear in front of a noun, e.g. *this notion, these movements, such developments.* Sounds a lot more straightforward, right? Well…maybe yes, maybe no.

Sometime around third grade, you probably learned that a noun was a person, place, or thing. Pretty self-explanatory. When you learned that a noun was a "thing," however, you probably understood "thing" to mean an object like a bicycle or an apple or a house. That's certainly true. But words like *idea* or *assertion* or *concept* – words that don't refer to actual physical objects – are also nouns. These nouns are sometimes referred to as **abstract nouns** or **compression nouns** because they compress lots of information into a single word.

These types of words appear frequently in SAT passages, and understanding what they refer to is often crucial to comprehension. **In fact, the ability to recognize the relationship between abstract nouns and the ideas that they refer to is central to making sense out of many, if not most, passages.** It is especially probable that you will encounter this type of language on historical documents passages, which tend to employ very abstract language.

If you can't draw the relationship between the noun, say, *belief,* and the specific belief that it refers to, you probably can't answer a question that asks you to do exactly that. And you certainly can't answer a question that asks you what can be inferred from that argument or what sort of information would support it.

What's more, these nouns, like pronouns, may appear **either before or after** the particular idea (argument, assertion, description, etc.) has been discussed, sometimes even in a different paragraph. If you encounter a question that requires you to identify what such a noun refers to, you must either continue reading to locate the necessary information, or more frequently, **back up and read from before the place where the noun appeared**.

Very often, when students are confused about this type of phase, they either reread the phrase in isolation and try to figure out what it's talking about (impossible) or start reading at the phrase and continue on for several lines, then become confused as to why they have no clearer understanding of the phrase than they did when they started. As a result, they get caught in a loop of reading and re-reading the wrong spot and, consequently, have no reliable means of determining the correct answer.

Let's look at an example. The phrase that includes the compression noun is in bold, and the information that it refers to is underlined.

The world is complex and interconnected, and the evolution of our communications system from a broadcast model to a networked one has added a new dimension to the mix. The Internet has made us all less
5 dependent on professional journalists and editors for information about the wider world, allowing us to seek out information directly via online search or to receive it from friends through social media. **But this enhanced convenience** comes with a considerable risk: that we
10 will be exposed to what we want to know at the expense of what we need to know. While we can find virtual communities that correspond to our every curiosity, there's little pushing us beyond our comfort zones to or into the unknown, even if the unknown may have
15 serious implications for our lives. There are things we should probably know more about—like political and religious conflicts in Russia or basic geography. But even if we knew more than we do, there's no guarantee that the knowledge gained would prompt us to act in a
20 particularly admirable fashion.

The phrase *this enhanced convenience* in lines 8-9 is a classic example of a compression noun. It refers not to a single thing but rather to an entire idea presented in the sentence before it:

The Internet has made us all less dependent on professional journalists and editors for information about the wider world, allowing us to seek out information directly via online search or to receive it from friends through social media.

To make something convenient means to make it easier, and here, the phrase *enhanced (improved) convenience* refers to the fact that the Internet has made people's lives much easier because it allows them to obtain information on their own, eliminating their dependence on others. In the second sentence, the author avoids repeating all of that information by condensing it into a mere two words. If the author did not "compress" the information, the passage would read like this:

> **The Internet has made us all less dependent on professional journalists and editors for information about the wider world, allowing us to seek out information directly via online search or to receive it from friends through social media. But the fact that the Internet has made us less dependent on professional journalists and editors for information about the wider world, allowing us to seek out information directly via online search or to receive it from friends through social media, comes with a considerable risk...**

In the second version, the second sentence repeats virtually all of the information from the first sentence, making it long, awkward and repetitive. In contrast, the phrase *enhanced convenience* allows the author to present his ideas in a much clearer, more direct manner.

Let's look at another example.

Yogi Berra, the former Major League baseball catcher and coach, once remarked that you can't hit and think at the same time. Of course, since he also reportedly said, "I really didn't say everything I said,"
5 but it is not clear we should take his statements at face value. Nonetheless, a widespread view — in both academic journals and the popular press — is that thinking about what you are doing, as you are doing it, interferes with performance. The idea is that once you
10 have developed the ability to play an arpeggio on the piano, putt a golf ball or parallel park, attention to what you are doing leads to inaccuracies, blunders and sometimes even utter paralysis. As the great choreographer George Balanchine would say to his
15 dancers, "Don't think, dear; just do."
    Perhaps you have experienced **this destructive force** yourself. Start thinking about just how to carry a full glass of water without spilling, and you'll end up drenched. How, exactly, do you initiate a telephone
20 conversation? Begin wondering, and before long, the recipient of your call will notice the heavy breathing and hang up. Our actions, the French philosopher Maurice Merleau-Ponty tells us, exhibit a "magical" efficacy, but when we focus on them, they degenerate
25 into the absurd. A 13-time winner on the Professional Golfers Association Tour, Dave Hill, put it like this: "You can't be thinking about the mechanics of the sport while you are performing."

In this case, there's an additional twist thrown in. Not only does the phrase *this destructive force* refer to information that comes before it, but that information is in a different paragraph If you were to encounter a question that required you to understand what that phrase referred to and only read from line 16 on, you would likely become confused. You might eventually find your way to the answer through a combination of gut feeling and guesswork, but you wouldn't really be sure. If, on the other hand, you simply back up and read from the previous paragraph, things become much more straightforward.

The Former and the Latter

One set of compression nouns that have a tendency to give people difficulty is "the former and the latter." Like other compression nouns, they are used to refer back to words or ideas mentioned earlier in the same sentence or in a previous sentence. *The former* is used to refer back to the noun or phrase mentioned first, and *the latter* is used to refer back to the noun or phrase mentioned second.

Let's start with a straightforward example:

> **In the nineteenth century, both Thomas Edison and Nikola Tesla were well-known scientists, but the former is now considered one of the greatest American inventors, while the latter has fallen into obscurity.**

The beginning of the sentence refers to two individual: Thomas Edison and Nikola Tesla. In the second half of the sentence, *the former* refers to Edison because his name occurs first, while *the latter* refers to Tesla because his name occurs second (*latter* is like "later"). That's easy enough to follow, but some passages may use these words in ways that you may have to work somewhat harder to follow.

For example:

> **All bodies in the solar system are heated by sunlight. They rid themselves of this heat in two ways: (1) by emitting infrared radiation and (2) by shedding matter. In long-lived bodies such as Earth, the former process prevails; for others, such as comets, the latter dominates.**

Let's look closely at what's going on in these sentences. If this is an unfamiliar topic for you, that's all the better. The author states that bodies in the solar system eliminate heat from the sun in two ways. Next, he lists those ways. The first way is by emitting infrared radiation, and the second is by shedding matter. When he refers to those ways in the following sentence, *the former* = emitting infrared radiation, while *the latter* = shedding matter.

The final sentence thus means that old planets like Earth get rid of heat by emitting infrared radiation, but other objects like comets get rid of heat by shedding matter.

Note that occasionally, *the latter* may appear **before** *the former*. For example, the paragraph above could be written the following way:

> **All bodies in the solar system are heated by sunlight. They rid themselves of this heat in two ways: (1) by emitting infrared radiation and (2) by shedding matter. For some objects such as comets, <u>the latter</u> dominates; in long-lived bodies such as Earth, <u>the former process</u> prevails.**

Although the order of *the former* and *the latter* is switched, the last sentence has exactly the same meaning it had in the previous version.

Pronoun and Compression Noun Exercises

Directions: underline the word, phrase, or lines <u>within the passage</u> that the compression noun in each sentence refers to.

1.   What drives traffic on most "news" websites is not journalism but a combination of snark and celebrity clickbait. Much of it is churned out in soul-destroying content factories manned by inexperienced—and
5   therefore inexpensive—young people without the time or incentive to dig deeply into anything. This deficit is particularly acute where it matters most: in the kind of expensive, far-flung reporting that is either dangerous to the lives of those doing the work or harmful to the
10   bottom lines of the publications paying for it. The idea that readers will pay the actual cost of meaningful journalism has never been sustainable in the United States and has brought down nearly every entity that has tried to depend on it.

2.   While humpback dolphins look quite similar to other dolphins, their genetics tells a different story. Researchers collected 235 tissue samples and 180 skulls throughout the animals' distribution, representing
5   the biggest dataset assembled to date for the animals. The team analyzed mitochondrial and nuclear DNA from the tissue, which revealed significant variations.
        Although the line between species, sub-species and populations is a blurry one, in this case, the researchers
10   are confident that the humpback dolphin is distinct enough to warrant the "species" title. The mitochondrial DNA turned up genetic signatures distinct enough to signal a separate species, and likewise, differences in the dolphins' skulls supported this divergence. Although
15   the nuclear DNA provided a slightly more confounding picture, it still clearly showed differences between the four species.

3.   Soon after the Big Bang, there were tiny ripples: quantum fluctuations in the density of the seething ball of hot plasma. Billions of years later, those seeds have grown into galaxy clusters — sprawling groups of
5   hundreds or thousands of galaxies bound together by gravity. But there seems to be a mismatch. Results released last year suggest that as much as 40% of galaxy-cluster mass is missing when compared with the amount of clustering predicted by the ripples.
10   The findings have led theorists to propose physics beyond the standard model of cosmology to make up the difference.

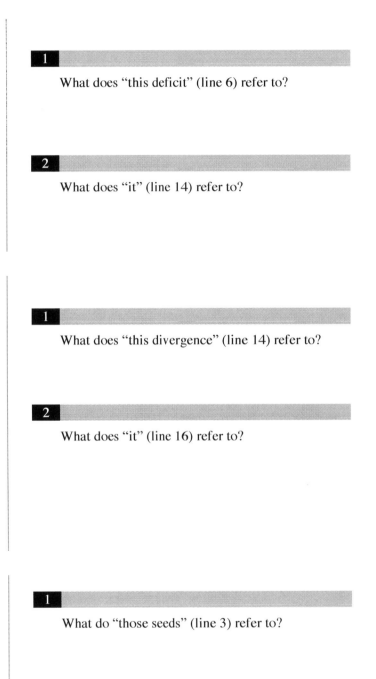

1

What does "this deficit" (line 6) refer to?

2

What does "it" (line 14) refer to?

1

What does "this divergence" (line 14) refer to?

2

What does "it" (line 16) refer to?

1

What do "those seeds" (line 3) refer to?

2

What do "the findings" (line 10) refer to?

4.   The starlings show up over Rome around dusk,
heading for their roosts after a day of feeding in the
countryside. In flocks of several hundred to several
thousand, they form sinuous streams, whirling
5 cylinders, cones or ribbons spread across the sky like
giant flags. Wheeling and dipping together, they
reminded Andrea Cavagna, a physicist at the National
Research Council of Italy, of atoms falling into place
in a superfluid state of matter called a Bose-Einstein
10 condensate. Out of curiosity, Cavagna deployed a
camera to record the flights. As a particle physicist, he
says, "it was refreshing to work with something you
can actually see." But keeping track of a thousand birds
turned out to be much more complicated than a billion
15 billion atoms.
     Cavagna was hardly the first scientist to be intrigued
by these acrobatics—known, in a rare instance of
technical language coinciding with poetry, as
"murmurations." Other animals that travel in groups—
20 schooling fish, most obviously—show the same
uncanny ability to move in apparent unison away from
a predator or toward a food source.

1

What does "they" (line 4) refer to?

2

What do "these acrobatics" (line 17) refer to?

5.   Chimps do it, birds do it, even you and I do it.
Once you see someone yawn, you are compelled to
do the same. Now it seems that wolves can be added
to the list of animals known to spread yawns like a
5 contagion.
     Among humans, even thinking about yawning can
trigger the reflex, leading some to suspect that catching
a yawn is linked to our ability to empathize with other
humans. For instance, contagious yawning activates the
10 same parts of the brain that govern empathy and social
know-how. And some studies have shown that humans
with more fine-tuned social skills are more likely to catch
a yawn.
     Similarly, chimpanzees, baboons and bonobos
15 often yawn when they see other members of their species
yawning. Chimps (Pan troglodytes) can catch yawns
from humans, even virtual ones. At least in primates,
contagious yawning seems to require an emotional
connection and may function as a demonstration of
20 empathy. Beyond primates, though, the trends are less
clear-cut. One study found evidence of contagious
yawning in birds but didn't connect it to empathy.
A 2008 study showed that dogs (Canis lupus familiaris)
could catch yawns from humans, and another showed
25 that dogs were more likely to catch the yawn of a familiar
human rather than a stranger. But efforts to see if dogs
catch yawns from each other and to replicate the results
with humans have so far had no luck.

1

What do "the trends" (line 20) refer to?

2

What does "it" (line 22) refer to?

6.   I wish to speak to-day, not as a Massachusetts
man, nor as a Northern man, but as an American, and
a member of the Senate of the United States. It is
fortunate that there is a Senate of the United States;
5 a body not yet moved from its propriety, not lost to a just
sense of its own dignity and its own high responsibilities,
and a body to which the country looks, with confidence,
for wise, moderate, patriotic, and healing counsels.
It is not to be denied that we live in the midst of strong
10 agitations, and are surrounded by very considerable
dangers to our institutions and government. The
imprisoned winds are let loose. The East, the North,
and the stormy South combine to throw the whole sea
into commotion, to toss its billows to the skies, and
15 disclose its profoundest depths. I do not affect to regard
myself, Mr. President, as holding, or as fit to hold, the
helm in this combat with the political elements; but I
have a duty to perform, and I mean to perform it with
fidelity, not without a sense of existing dangers, but not
20 without hope. I have a part to act, not for my own
security or safety, for I am looking out for no fragment
upon which to float away from the wreck, if wreck there
must be, but for the good of the whole, and the
preservation of all; and there is that which will keep me
25 to my duty during this struggle, whether the sun and the
stars shall appear, or shall not appear for many days.
I speak to-day for the preservation of the Union.

1

What does "a body" (lines 5 and 7) refer to?

2

What does "its" (lines 14 and 15) refer to?

3

What does "it" (line 18) refer to?

7.   For some activists, eating local foods is no
longer just a pleasure—it is a moral obligation. Why?
Because shipping foods over long distances results
in the unnecessary emission of the greenhouse gases
5 that are warming the planet. This concern has
given rise to the concept of "food miles," that is,
the distance food travels from farm to plate. Activists
particularly dislike air freighting foods because it uses
relatively more energy than other forms of trans-
10 portation. Food miles are supposed to be a simple way
to gauge food's impact on climate change.
       But food miles advocates fail to grasp the simple
idea that food should be grown where it is most
economically advantageous to do so. Relevant
15 advantages consist of various combinations of soil,
climate, labor, and other factors. It is possible to grow
bananas in Iceland, but Costa Rica really has the better
climate for that activity. Transporting food is just one
relatively small cost of providing modern consumers
20 with their daily bread, meat, cheese, and veggies.
Concentrating agricultural production in the most
favorable regions is the best way to minimize human
impacts on the environment.

1

What does "This concern" (line 5) refer to?

2

What does "that activity" (line 18) refer to?

8. It was one hundred and forty-four years ago that members of the Democratic Party first met in convention to select a Presidential candidate. A lot of years passed since 1832, and during that time it would
5 have been most unusual for any national political party to ask a Barbara Jordan to deliver a keynote address. But tonight, here I am. And I feel that notwithstanding the past that my presence here is one additional bit of evidence that the American Dream need not forever be
10 deferred.

Now that I have this grand distinction, what in the world am I supposed to say? I could list the problems which cause people to feel cynical, angry, frustrated: problems which include lack of integrity in government;
15 the feeling that the individual no longer counts; feeling that the grand American experiment is failing or has failed. I could recite these problems, and then I could sit down and offer no solutions. But I don't choose to do that either. The citizens of America expect more.

1

What does "this grand distinction" (line 11) refer to?

9. The most ancient of all societies, and the only one that is natural, is the family: and even so the children remain attached to the father only so long as they need him for their preservation. As soon as this
5 need ceases, the natural bond is dissolved. The children, released from the obedience they owed to the father, and the father, released from the care he owed his children, return equally to independence. If they remain united, they continue so no longer naturally, but voluntarily; and
10 the family itself is then maintained only by convention.

This common liberty results from the nature of man. His first law is to provide for his own preservation, his first cares are those which he owes to himself; and, as soon as he reaches years of discretion, he is the sole
15 judge of the proper means of preserving himself, and consequently becomes his own master.

The family then may be called the first model of political societies: the ruler corresponds to the father, and the people to the children; and all, being born free
20 and equal, alienate their liberty only for their own advantage. The whole difference is that, in the family, the love of the father for his children repays him for the care he takes of them, while, in the State, the pleasure of commanding takes the place of the love which the chief
25 cannot have for the peoples under him.

1

What does "they" (line 9) refer to?

2

What does "this common liberty" (line 11) refer to?

10.   The sharing economy is a little like online
shopping, which started in America 15 years ago. At
first, people were worried about security. But having
made a successful purchase from, say, Amazon, they
5 felt safe buying elsewhere. Similarly, using Airbnb or
a car-hire service for the first time encourages people to
try other offerings. Next, consider eBay. Having started
out as a peer-to-peer marketplace, it is now dominated
by professional "power sellers" (many of whom started
10 out as ordinary eBay users). The same may happen with
the sharing economy, which also provides new
opportunities for enterprise. Some people have bought
cars solely to rent them out, for example. Incumbents
are getting involved too. Avis, a car-hire firm, has a share
15 in a sharing rival. So do GM and Daimler, two carmakers.
In the future, companies may develop hybrid models,
listing excess capacity (whether vehicles, equipment or
office space) on peer-to-peer rental sites. In the past,
new ways of doing things online have not displaced the
20 old ways entirely. But they have often changed them.
Just as internet shopping forced Walmart and Tesco to
adapt, so online sharing will shake up transport, tourism,
equipment-hire and more.
     The main worry is regulatory uncertainty. Will
25 room-4-renters be subject to hotel taxes, for example?
In Amsterdam officials are using Airbnb listings to track
down unlicensed hotels. In some American cities,
peer-to-peer taxi services have been banned after
lobbying by traditional taxi firms. The danger is that
30 although some rules need to be updated to protect
consumers from harm, incumbents will try to destroy
competition. People who rent out rooms should pay tax,
of course, but they should not be regulated like a Ritz-
Carlton hotel. The lighter rules that typically govern
35 bed-and-breakfasts are more than adequate. The sharing
economy is the latest example of the internet's value to
consumers. This emerging model is now big and
disruptive enough for regulators and companies to have
woken up to it. That is a sign of its immense potential. It
40 is time to start caring about sharing.

1

What does "it" (line 8) refer to?

2

What do "they" and "them" (line 20) refer to?

3

What does "this emerging model" (line 37)
refer to?

11. The following passage is adapted from "Scientists Discover Salty Aquifer, Previously Unknown Microbial Habitat Under Antarctica," © 2015 by Dartmouth College.

Using an airborne imaging system for the first time in Antarctica, scientists have discovered a vast network of unfrozen salty groundwater that may support previously unknown microbial life deep under the coldest, driest
5 desert on our planet. The findings shed new light on ancient climate change on Earth and provide strong evidence that a similar briny aquifer could support microscopic life on Mars. The scientists used SkyTEM, an airborne electromagnetic sensor, to detect and map
10 otherwise inaccessible subterranean features.

The system uses an antennae suspended beneath a helicopter to create a magnetic field that reveals the subsurface to a depth of about 1,000 feet. Because a helicopter was used, large areas of rugged terrain could
15 be surveyed. The SkyTEM team was funded by the National Science Foundation and led by researchers from the University of Tennessee, Knoxville (UTK), and Dartmouth College, which oversees the NSF's SkyTEM project.

20 "These unfrozen materials appear to be relics of past surface ecosystems and our findings provide compelling evidence that they now provide deep subsurface habitats for microbial life despite extreme environmental conditions," says lead author Jill Mikucki,
25 an assistant professor at UTK. "These new below-ground visualization technologies can also provide insight on glacial dynamics and how Antarctica responds to climate change."

Co-author Dartmouth Professor Ross Virginia is
30 SkyTEM's co-principal investigator and director of Dartmouth's Institute of Arctic Studies. "This project is studying the past and present climate to, in part, understand how climate change in the future will affect biodiversity and ecosystem processes," Virginia says.
35 "This fantastic new view beneath the surface will help us sort out competing ideas about how the McMurdo Dry Valleys have changed with time and how this history influences what we see today."

The researchers found that the unfrozen brines form
40 extensive, interconnected aquifers deep beneath glaciers and lakes and within permanently frozen soils. The brines extend from the coast to at least 7.5 miles inland in the McMurdo Dry Valleys, the largest ice-free region in Antarctica. The brines could be due to freezing and/or 45 deposits. The findings show for the first time that the Dry Valleys' lakes are interconnected rather than isolated; connectivity between lakes and aquifers is important in sustaining ecosystems through drastic climate change, such as lake dry-down events. The findings also challenge

50 the assumption that parts of the ice sheets below the pressure melting point are devoid of liquid water.

In addition to providing answers about the biological adaptations of previously unknown ecosystems that persist in the extreme cold and dark of the Antarctic
55 winter, the new study could help scientists to understand whether similar conditions might exist elsewhere in the solar system, specifically beneath the surface of Mars, which has many similarities to the Dry Valleys. Overall, the Dry Valleys ecosystem – cold,
60 vegetation-free and home only to microscopic animal and plant life – resembles, during the Antarctic summer, conditions on the surface on Mars.

SkyTEM produced images of Taylor Valley along the Ross Sea that suggest briny sediments exist at
65 subsurface temperatures down to perhaps -68°F, which is considered suitable for microbial life. One of the studied areas was lower Taylor Glacier, where the data suggest ancient brine still exists beneath the glacier. That conclusion is supported by the presence of Blood
70 Falls, an iron-rich brine that seeps out of the glacier and hosts an active microbial ecosystem.

Scientists' understanding of Antarctica's underground environment is changing dramatically as research reveals that subglacial lakes are widespread
75 and that at least half of the areas covered by the ice sheet are akin to wetlands on other continents. But groundwater in the ice-free regions and along the coastal margins remains poorly understood.

1

What do "the findings" (line 5) refer to?

2

What does "this history" (line 37) refer to?

3

What does "that conclusion" (line 69) refer to?

This passage is adapted from Sharon Tregaskis, "What Bees Tell Us About Global Climate Change," © 2010 by *Johns Hopkins Magazine*.

Standing in the apiary on the grounds of the U.S. Department of Agriculture's Bee Research Laboratory in Beltsville, Maryland, Wayne Esaias digs through the canvas shoulder bag leaning against his leg in search of
5 the cable he uses to download data. It's dusk as he runs the cord from his laptop—precariously perched on the beam of a cast-iron platform scale—to a small, battery-operated data logger attached to the spring inside the scale's steel column. In the 1800s, a scale like this
10 would have weighed sacks of grain or crates of apples, peaches, and melons. Since arriving at the USDA's bee lab in January 2007, this scale has been loaded with a single item: a colony of *Apis mellifera*, the fuzzy, black-and-yellow honey bee. An attached, 12-bit
15 recorder captures the hive's weight to within a 10th of a pound, along with a daily register of relative ambient humidity and temperature.

On this late January afternoon, during a comparatively balmy respite between the blizzards that
20 dumped several feet of snow on the Middle Atlantic states, the bees, their honey, and the wooden boxes in which they live weigh 94.5 pounds. In mid-July, as last year's unusually long nectar flow finally ebbed, the whole contraption topped out at 275 pounds, including
25 nearly 150 pounds of honey. "Right now, the colony is in a cluster about the size of a soccer ball," says Esaias, who's kept bees for nearly two decades and knows without lifting the lid what's going on inside this hive. "The center of the cluster is where the queen is, and
30 they're keeping her at 93 degrees—the rest are just hanging there, tensing their flight muscles to generate heat." Provided that they have enough calories to fuel their winter workout, a healthy colony can survive as far north as Anchorage, Alaska. "They slowly eat their
35 way up through the winter," he says. "It's a race: Will they eat all their honey before the nectar flows, or not?" To make sure their charges win that race, apiarists have long relied on scale hives for vital management clues. By tracking daily weight variations, a beekeeper can
40 discern when the colony needs a nutritional boost to carry it through lean times, whether to add extra combs for honey storage and even detect incursions by marauding robber bees—all without disturbing the colony. A graph of the hive's weight—which can

45 increase by as much as 35 pounds a day in some parts of the United States during peak nectar flow – reveals the date on which the bees' foraging was was most productive and provides a direct record of successful pollination. "Around here, the bees make
50 their living in the month of May," says Esaias, noting that his bees often achieve daily spikes of 25 pounds, the maximum in Maryland. "There's almost no nectar coming in for the rest of the year." A scientist by training and career oceanographer at NASA, Esaias
55 established the Mink Hollow Apiary in his Highland, Maryland, backyard in 1992 with a trio of hand-me-down hives and an antique platform scale much like the one at the Beltsville bee lab. Ever since, he's maintained a meticulous record of the bees' daily
60 weight, as well as weather patterns and such details as his efforts to keep them healthy. In late 2006, honey bees nationwide began disappearing in an ongoing syndrome dubbed colony collapse disorder (CCD). Entire hives went empty as bees inexplicably
65 abandoned their young and their honey. Commercial beekeepers reported losses up to 90 percent, and the large-scale farmers who rely on honey bees to ensure rich harvests of almonds, apples, and sunflowers became very, very nervous. Looking for clues, Esaias
70 turned to his own records. While the resulting graphs threw no light on the cause of CCD, a staggering trend emerged: In the span of just 15 seasons, the date on which his Mink Hollow bees brought home the most nectar had shifted by two weeks—from late May
75 to the middle of the month. "I was shocked when I plotted this up," he says. "It was right under my nose, going on the whole time." The epiphany would lead Esaias to launch a series of research collaborations, featuring honey bees and other pollinators, to investigate
80 the relationships among plants, pollinators, and weather patterns. Already, the work has begun to reveal insights into the often unintended consequences of human interventions in natural and agricultural ecosystems, and exposed significant gaps in how we understand the
85 effect climate change will have on everything from food production to terrestrial ecology.

1

What does "the epiphany" (line 77) refer to?

2

What does "the work" (line 81) refer to?

Explanations: Pronoun and Compression Noun Exercises

1.1 This deficit = *news websites' combination of snark and celebrity clickbait…churned out…by young people without the time or incentive to dig deeply into anything* (lines 1-6).

1.2 It = *The idea that readers will pay the actual cost of meaningful journalism*

2.1 This divergence = the fact that humpback dolphins are a separate dolphin species, as indicated by the differences in mitochondrial DNA (line 8-13).

2.2 It = the nuclear DNA (line 15)

3.1 Those seeds = *tiny ripples: quantum fluctuations in the density of the seething ball of hot plasma* (lines 1-3).

3.2 The findings = results indicating that *40% of galaxy-cluster mass is missing when compared with the amount of clustering predicted by the ripples* (lines 6-9).

4.1 They = The starlings (line 1)

4.2 These acrobatics = The birds' movements: *sinuous streams, whirling cylinders, cones or ribbons spread across the sky like giant flags* (lines 4-6).

5.1 The trends = *At least in primates, contagious yawning seems to require an emotional connection and may function as a demonstration of empathy* (lines 17-20).

5.2 It = contagious yawning (lines 21-22)

6.1 A body = the Senate

6.2 Its = the whole sea's (line 13)

6.3 It = a duty (line 18)

7.1 This concern = shipping foods over long distances results in the unnecessary emission of the greenhouse gases that are warming the planet (lines 3-5).

7.2 That activity = growing bananas

8. This grand distinction = the selection of Barbara Jordan to deliver the Democratic keynote address (lines 3-7)

9.1 They = The father and the children (lines 6-7)

9.2 This common liberty = the fact that a father and children can *voluntarily* decide whether to maintain ties after the children are no longer dependent on the father for survival (lines 8-10).

10.1 It = eBay (line 7)

10.2 They = the new ways; them = the old ways (lines 18-20)

10.3 This emerging model = the sharing economy (lines 35-36)

11.1 The findings = the discovery of *a vast network of unfrozen salty groundwater that may support previously unknown microbial life deep under the coldest, driest desert on our planet* (lines 2-5).

11.2 This history = *how the McMurdo Dry Valleys have changed with time* (lines 36-37)

11.3 That conclusion = *ancient brine still exists beneath the glacier* (line 68).

12.1 The epiphany = Esaias's realization that *in the span of just 15 seasons, the date on which his Mink Hollow bees brought home the most nectar had shifted by two weeks—from late May to the middle of the month* (lines 72-75).

12.2 The work = *a series of research collaborations, featuring honey bees and other pollinators, to investigate the relationships among plants, pollinators, and weather patterns* (lines 78-81).

4. The Big Picture

Every SAT will have a number of questions that test your understanding of the passage as a whole (or, in some cases, large sections of it). These question may ask you to identify which statement **best summarizes** a passage/section of a passage, or they may ask you to recognize an author's **point** or **central claim**. While these questions are worded in a straightforward manner, they can also be challenging because they require a leap from the concrete, specific details of a passage to an understanding of its broader themes.

Unsurprisingly, then, I've spent a lot of time teaching people to stop looking so hard at the details. It's not that there's anything wrong with details – it's just that they're not always terribly relevant, or even relevant at all. Very often, smart, detail-oriented students have a tendency to worry about every single thing that sounds even remotely odd while missing something major staring them in the face. Frequently, they blame this on the fact that they've been taught in English class to read closely and pay attention to all the details.

Well, I have some news: when you're in college with a 500 page reading assignment that you have two days to get through, you won't have time to annotate every last detail – nor will your professors expect you to do so. Whether or not you're truly interested in what you're reading, your job will be to get the gist of the author's argument and then focus on a few key areas. And if you can't recognize those key areas, college reading will be, shall we say, a struggle; unlike the books you read in English class, most of what you read in college will not have easily-digestible summaries available courtesy of sparknotes.com. But back to the SAT.

It's fairly common for people to simply grind to a halt when they encounter an unfamiliar turn of phrase. When they realize they haven't quite understood a line, they go back and read it again. If they still don't quite get it, they read it yet again. And before they know it, they've wasted two or three minutes just reading the same five lines over and over again. Then they start to run out of time and have to rush through the last few questions.

Almost inevitably, you will encounter some passages with bits that aren't completely clear – that's part of the test. The goal is to see whether you can figure out their meaning from the general context; you're not expected to get every word, especially not the first time around. If you get the gist, you can figure a lot of other things out, whereas if you focus on one little detail, you'll get . . . one little detail.

Identifying Topics

The topic is **the person, thing, or idea that is the primary subject or focus** of the passage. Usually, **the topic is the word or phrase that appears most frequently throughout the passage, either by name or in rephrased form** (pronoun or compression noun). For example, a computer could also be referred to as "the machine," "the invention," or "the technology."

Normally, the topic will first be mentioned in the introduction; if you're not sure about the topic, the first sentence is usually a good place to start. If the topic is not mentioned in the introduction, however, it will almost certainly appear by the start of the second paragraph.

While this discussion might sound very basic, **the ability to identify topics is crucial because correct answer choices will refer to the topic.** In fact, the correct answer will sometimes be the *only* answer choice to include the topic. Furthermore, many incorrect answer are wrong because they are off topic, and you cannot recognize when a statement is off topic unless you know what the topic *is*.

Let's look at an example of how that could play out in a passage.

Citrus greening, the **plague** that could wipe out Florida's $9 billion orange industry, begins with the touch of a jumpy brown bug on a sun-kissed leaf. From there, **the bacterial disease** incubates in the
5 tree's roots, then moves back up the trunk in full force, causing nutrient flows to seize up. Leaves turn yellow, and the oranges, deprived of sugars from the leaves, remain green, sour, and hard. Many fall before harvest, brown necrotic flesh ringing failed stems.
10   For the past decade, Florida's oranges have been literally starving. Since **it** first appeared in 2005, **citrus greening**, also known by its Chinese name, **huanglongbing**, has swept across Florida's groves like a flood. With no hills to block it, the Asian citrus
15 psyllid—the invasive aphid relative that carries **the disease**—has infected nearly every orchard in the state. By one estimate, 80 percent of Florida's citrus trees are infected and declining.
    The disease has spread beyond Florida to nearly
20 every orange-growing region in the United States. Despite many generations of breeding by humanity, no citrus plant resists **greening**; **it** afflicts lemons, grapefruits, and other citrus species as well. Once a tree is infected, it will die. Yet in a few select Floridian
25 orchards, there are now trees that, thanks to innovative technology, can fight **the greening tide**.

In the passage on the previous page, the topic – citrus greening – is introduced in the very first sentence. In the entire remainder of the passage, it is only referred to by name one additional time (line 12). It is, however, referred to in many other ways: *the plague, the disease, the bacterial disease, huanaglongbing, the greening tide* and, of course, *it*.

If you have difficulty drawing the connection between the original term and its many variations, you can end up not quite getting what the passage is about. You may also misunderstand the **scope** of the passage – that is, whether it's **general** or **specific**.

Often, when I ask students for the topic of a passage like this, I'll get a response like "Ummm… I think it talks about oranges and stuff" or "it mentions Florida," or, a bit closer, "diseases." (Incidentally, I see this uncertainty even in high-scoring students – they know the test well enough to spot wrong answers to detail questions, but when asked to state something as straightforward as the topic in their own words, they're suddenly lost.)

As a matter of fact, the topic is not in fact "diseases." It is actually one specific disease, namely citrus greening. That fact can become very important if you see a question like this:

Citrus greening, the plague that could wipe out Florida's $9 billion orange industry, begins with the touch of a jumpy brown bug on a sun-kissed leaf. From there, the bacterial disease incubates in the
5 tree's roots, then moves back up the trunk in full force, causing nutrient flows to seize up. Leaves turn yellow, and the oranges, deprived of sugars from the leaves, remain green, sour, and hard. Many fall before harvest, brown necrotic flesh ringing failed stems.

1

The references to yellow leaves and green, sour, and hard oranges in lines 6-9 primarily serve to

A) describe some effects of citrus greening.
B) point out the consequence of giving plants too many nutrients.
C) suggest that farmers often harvest their crops too early.
D) demonstrate the difficulty of growing crops in a humid climate.

The only answer that directly refers to the passage's topic is A), which is correct. Yes, this is a fairly straightforward question, but using the big picture lets you jump right to the answer.

To reiterate this for yourself, try an exercise: take a page from a book or piece of writing you're familiar with, one whose topic you know for sure. Now, as fast as you can, **count** how many times that topic – either the noun itself or a rephrased version of it – appears on the page. The number should be pretty high. Since you're already familiar with the subject, it should be easier for you to see the relationship between the topic and the various ways that it's referred to throughout the text. If you find it helpful, keep repeating this exercise until you can consistently identity topics quickly and accurately.

Important: when defining a topic, try to use no more than a couple of words (e.g. rise of social media, city ecosystems, importance of Venus) and avoid saying things like, "Well, so I think that basically the passage is like talking about xyz…" The former takes almost no time and gives you exactly the information you need; the latter is time-consuming, vague, and encourages you to view the topic as much more subjective than it actually is.

What's the Point?

The point of a passage is the **primary idea** that the author wants to convey. After the topic, the point should be the first thing you look for when you read a passage. Once you have identified it and underlined it or written it down, you can often skim through the rest of the passage – but before that, finding it needs to be your main goal.

I cannot state this strongly enough: If you keep the main point in mind, you can often eliminate answer choices simply because they do not make sense in context of it or, better yet, identify the correct answer because it is the only option that is consistent with it.

What's more, **focusing on finding the point means you don't have a chance to get distracted.** It reduces the chance that you'll spend five minutes trying to absorb three lines while losing sight of the big idea. And it stops you from wasting energy trying to convince yourself that the passage is interesting when you're actually bored out of your mind.
But let me begin by saying what a main point is **not**:

- It is not a **topic** such as "bears" or "the rise of social media."

- It is not a **theme** such as "oppression" or "overcoming."

A main point is an **argument** that answers the question "so what?" – it tells us *why* the author thinks the topic is important.

You can use this "formula" to determine the point:

Topic + So What? = Main Point

Sometimes the author will directly state the main point in the passage itself, **most often in the introduction or beginning of the second paragraph, and then again for reiteration at the end of the conclusion.** When you find the point, **you should underline it immediately.** If the author does not state the point directly, you should **write it yourself.**

It isn't terribly effective to discuss writing a main point in the abstract, so let's start by taking a look at the following passage:

Sometime near the end of the Pleistocene, a band
of people left northeastern Asia, crossed the Bering
land bridge when the sea level was low, entered
Alaska and became the first Americans. Since the
5 1930s, archaeologists have thought these people were
members of the Clovis culture. First discovered in
New Mexico in the 1930s, the Clovis culture is known
for its distinct stone tools, primarily fluted projectile
points. For decades, Clovis artifacts were the oldest
10 known in the New World, dating to 13,000 years ago.
But in recent years, researchers have found more and
more evidence that people were living in North and
South America before the Clovis.
    The most recently confirmed evidence comes from
15 Washington. During a dig conducted from 1977 to 1979,
researchers uncovered a bone projectile point stuck in
a mastodon rib. Since then, the age of the find has been
debated, but recently anthropologist Michael Waters
and his colleagues announced a new radiocarbon date
20 for the rib: 13,800 years ago, making it 800 years older
than the oldest Clovis artifact. Other pre-Clovis
evidence comes from a variety of locations across the
New World.

When they first start working with me, a lot of my students aren't quite clear on the difference between describing the content of a passage and summarizing its argument. Since the ability to summarize arguments quickly and accurately is among the skills most crucial for success on SAT Reading, this can become a major stumbling block.

Describing content = recounting the information presented in the text, often in sequential "first x, then y, and finally z" form, without necessarily distinguishing between main points and supporting evidence.

Summarizing an argument = identifying the essential point that the author wants to convey and eliminating any unnecessary detail. The goal is not to cover all of the information presented or to relate it in the sequence it appears in the passage, but rather to pinpoint the **overarching idea** that encapsulates the author's point.

Summarizing arguments requires you to make a leap from concrete to abstract because you must move beyond simply recounting the information presented to recognizing which parts are most important and relating them to other, more general ideas. As a result, you must be able to separate the larger, more important ideas (beginning/end of a paragraph) from the details (middle of a paragraph). If you are able to identify main ideas, you will also find it much easier to identify information that supports them.

When I first ask someone to summarize the main point of a passage, however, they generally respond in one of two ways:

1) They state the topic

The Clovis People

2) They describe the content

Uh… so the guy, he basically talks about how these people, I think they were called the Clovis people, right? They were like the first people who came across the Bering Strait to America… Oh no, wait, they weren't actually the first people to come across, it's just that they thought that those people were first. But so anyway those people settled in New Mexico, I think it said like 13,000 years ago? Only now he's saying that there were other people who were actually there before the Clovis, and then he says something about a mastodon rib and then something about radiocarbon dating (I remember 'cuz we learned about it in Chem this year). Oh yeah, and then he mentions the New World.

Notice how long, not to mention how vague, this version is. It doesn't really distinguish between important and unimportant information; everything gets mushed in together, and frankly it doesn't make a lot of sense. This summary gives us exactly zero help in terms of figuring out the main point. It also wastes *colossal* amounts of time.

This is not what you want to do.

Argument Summary:

New evidence shows the first inhabitants of the Americas were NOT Clovis people.

Notice how this version just hits the big idea and omits the details. All the details.

Argument Summary in super-condensed SAT terms:

New: CP $\neq$ 1st / Am.

Now notice how this version cuts out absolutely everything in order to focus on the absolute essentials. It doesn't even attempt to incorporate any sort of detail beyond the subject of the passage (Clovis People) and the "so what?" (they weren't the first people in the Americas). In four words and a number, we've captured the essential information *without wasting any time.*

Point of a Paragraph

As mentioned earlier, the point of a paragraph is most likely to be located in two places: the **first (topic) sentence**, whose purpose is to state the point, or the **last sentence**, whose purpose is to reiterate the point. While secondary points may be introduced in between, the body of a paragraph is primarily intended to provide details or evidence to support the point.

For example, consider the following paragraph, which follows this pattern:

Sometimes it seems surprising that science functions at all. In 2005, medical science was shaken by a paper with the provocative title "Why most published research findings are false." Written by John
5 Ioannidis, a professor of medicine at Stanford University, it didn't actually show that any particular result was wrong. Instead, it showed that the statistics of reported positive findings was not consistent with how often one should *expect* to find them. **As Ioannidis concluded more**
10 **recently, "many published research findings are false or exaggerated, and an estimated 85 percent of research resources are wasted."**

The first sentence serves to introduce the main point, and the last sentence serves to reinforce it. The information in between expands on the original claim, explaining just what the author means by the assertion *Sometimes it seems surprising that science functions at all.*

On the next page, we're going to look at a passage whose length is more typical of what you'll encounter on the SAT.

The following passage is adapted from Verlyn Klinkenborg, "Our Vanishing Night." © 2008 by the National Geographic Society.

If humans were truly at home under the light of the moon and stars, we would go in darkness happily, the midnight world as visible to us as it is to the vast number of nocturnal species on this planet. Instead,
5 we are diurnal creatures, with eyes adapted to living in the sun's light. This is a basic evolutionary fact, even though most of us don't think of ourselves as diurnal beings any more than we think of ourselves as primates or mammals or Earthlings.
10 Yet it's the only way to explain what we've done to the night: We've engineered it to receive us by filling it with light. This kind of engineering is no different than damming a river. Its benefits come with consequences—called light pollution—whose
15 effects scientists are only now beginning to study. Light pollution is largely the result of bad lighting design, which allows artificial light to shine outward and upward into the sky, where it's not wanted, instead of focusing it downward, where
20 it is. **Ill-designed lighting washes out the darkness of night and radically alters the light levels—and rhythms—to which many forms of life, including ourselves, have adapted.** MAIN POINT
For most of human history, the phrase "light
25 pollution" would have made no sense. Imagine walking toward London on a moonlit night around 1800, when it was Earth's most populous city. Nearly a million people lived there, making do, as they always had, with candles and lanterns. Only a few
30 houses were lit by gas, and there would be no public gaslights for another seven years. From a few miles away, you would have been as likely to smell London as to see its dim glow. Now most of humanity lives under intersecting domes of light,
35 of scattering rays from overlit cities and suburbs, from light-flooded highways and factories. In most cities the sky looks as though it has been emptied of stars, leaving behind a vacant haze that mirrors our fear of the dark and resembles the urban
40 glow of dystopian science fiction. We've grown so used to this pervasive orange haze that the original glory of an unlit night—dark enough for the planet Venus to throw shadows on Earth—is wholly beyond our experience, beyond memory almost. We've lit up
45 the night as if it were an unoccupied country, when nothing could be further from the truth. Light is a powerful biological force, and on many species it acts as a magnet. Migrating at night, birds are apt to collide with brightly lit tall buildings; immature birds

50 on their first journey suffer disproportionately. And because a longer day allows for longer feeding, it can also affect migration schedules. The problem, of course, is that migration is a precisely timed biological behavior. Leaving early may mean
55 arriving too soon for nesting conditions to be right.
It was once thought that light pollution only affected astronomers, who need to see the night sky in all its glorious clarity. And, in fact, some of the earliest efforts to control light pollution were made
60 to protect the view from Lowell Observatory. Unlike astronomers, most of us may not need an undiminished view of the night sky for our work, but like most other creatures we do need darkness. Darkness is as essential to our internal clockwork,
65 as light itself. The regular oscillation of waking and sleep in our lives is nothing less than a biological expression of the regular oscillation of light on Earth. So fundamental are these rhythms to our being that altering them is like altering gravity.
70 For the past century or so, we've been performing an open-ended experiment on ourselves, extending the day, shortening the night, and short-circuiting the human body's sensitive response to light. The consequences of our bright new world are more
75 readily perceptible in less adaptable creatures living in the peripheral glow of our prosperity. But for humans, too, light pollution may take a biological toll. **In a very real sense, light pollution causes us to lose sight of our true place in the universe, to**
80 **forget the scale of our being, which is best measured against the dimensions of a deep night with the Milky Way—the edge of our galaxy— arching overhead.**

Repetition of Main Point

Although the author states the main point very clearly, you could simplify it further by writing something like "LP = BAD b/c unnatural" (light pollution is bad because it's unnatural).

That information would come in handy if you encountered the following question:

1

What is the author's main point about the drawbacks of modern light use?

A) It is less efficient than light use in earlier centuries.
B) It distorts authentic relationships between people and the natural world.
C) It distributes light to different locations unequally.
D) It can have a negative impact on the economy.

Even though B) is phrased somewhat differently from the main point, the general idea is the same. Saying that light pollution "distorts (deforms) authentic relationships between people and the natural world" is simply an alternate, wordier way of saying that it's unnatural.

While you may have some difficulty "translating" the specific wording of the passage into the more abstract phrasing of the answer choices, your task will be far more difficult if you're not sure what idea you're looking in the first place.

If, on the other hand, you simply understand the passage as a mass of details, you'll be much more likely to opt for an answer that mentions a word or phrase you remember from the passage but that doesn't actually capture the big picture.

They Say/I Say: A Passage is a Conversation

The "they say/I say" model is one of the most important concepts necessary for making sense out of SAT Reading passages, simply because so many passages make use of it in one way or another. It's also the name of a book written by Gerald Graff and Cathy Birkenstein, professors at the University of Illinois, Chicago, and if you have time (even if you don't have time), you need to run out and buy yourself a copy because it's very possibly the best work ever written to bridge the gap between high school and college learning. Although the book focuses on writing rather than reading, it covers many of the core "formulas" that appear in SAT passages and demystifies academic writing like nothing else.

So what is the "they say/I say" model? Well, let me start by saying this: most of the writing that you do in high school tends to be fairly one-sided. Unless you're explicitly asked to agree or disagree with someone else's opinion, most of your writing for school probably involves coming up with an original thesis and "proving" it by supporting it with various pieces of evidence that you've come up with on your own. Throughout the process, the focus is relentlessly on *your* thoughts, *your* ideas, *your* evidence. Potential objections to your argument? You probably don't spend two or three paragraphs describing them, let alone explaining their weaknesses. If you mention them at all, you probably discuss them pretty superficially. And if you are disagreeing with someone else's idea, you probably don't spend much time talking about the parts of their argument that you *do* agree with.

The writing that professional authors do is different. They're not writing for a grade, or to please their teacher, or to show that they've mastered the five-paragraph essay. They're not writing in a box. **On the contrary, they see themselves as part of a conversation.** They're always writing in response to what other people have said – usually because they don't agree with those other people's ideas, although they may agree with certain aspects of them. (If they agreed completely, they would have no reason to write!) So either directly or indirectly, they will often refer back to the people they are "conversing" with. They examine the history of the idea they are discussing, consider common interpretations and beliefs, and weigh the merits and shortcomings of those beliefs.

As a result, authors will sometimes spend a significant portion of a passage discussing ideas with which they *do not* agree. **In fact, the author's opinion may not emerge until halfway through the passage or later – occasionally not until the conclusion.** Although authors will sometimes state flat-out that a particular idea is wrong, just as often they will be far less direct. They'll "imply skepticism" by putting particular words or phrases in quotation marks or ask rhetorical questions such as, *but is this really the case?* They'll use words like *imply, suggest,* and *support,* not "prove."

Just because they don't frame things in terms of absolute right or wrong does not, however, mean that they lack clear opinions. Regardless of how much time an author spends discussing other people's ideas ("they say"), sooner or later they'll tell you what they think ("I say") – and that's something you need to pay very close attention to because **the "I say" is the point of the passage**. On the flipside, what "they say" is the **counterargument** (we're going to look more closely at those later on.)

While the "they say/I say" model can be found in virtually every type of passage, it is particularly common in science/social science passages, many of which are organized in terms of the "people used to believe x, but now they believe y." In this structure, the author typically begins by discussing an accepted idea or theory, then, at a certain point, explains why that theory is wrong, and why a new theory – the theory the author believes – is correct.

The following list provides some common phrases that indicate when the author is talking about other peoples' ideas versus their own ideas.*

They Say

- Some people (scientists, readers, critics, etc.) believe…
- Many people think that…
- Most people think that…
- is commonly thought that…
- Accepted/conventional wisdom holds that…
- In the past…
- For a long time/decades/hundreds of years…
- Traditionally, people have believed that…

I Say

- However, But in fact, In reality…
- But is it really true/the case that…?
- It seems to me that…
- It now seems (clear) that…
- Recently, it has been found that…
- People now think…
- New research/evidence shows/suggests that
- Another possibility is that…

A single passage will often contain two and occasionally three different points of view, and a Passage 1/Passage 2 pair can contain even more, but it's up to you to keep track of what the author thinks and what other people think. **Don't try to remember: write it down quickly or underline it and draw a huge arrow or a star next to it.** If an author bounces back and forth between different viewpoints, the above phrases become important "signposts" that allow you to keep track of which side the author is discussing.

To reiterate : when you are asked to juggle multiple points of view, relying on your memory is a recipe for disaster. If you're already scoring well, you may be able to do it up to a point, but chances are you're not always defining things precisely. If you don't know which idea(s) the author agrees/disagrees with and cannot summarize those ideas simply and accurately, you risk choosing answers that are the opposite of the ones you should be choosing.

*For an index of rhetorical templates, please see *They Say/I Say: The Moves that Matter in Academic Writing* by Gerald Graff and Cathy Birkenstein.

Using What "They Say" to Predict Main Point and Attitude

One of the reasons that it is so crucial you be able to recognize the types of the phrases that signal "they say/I say" is that those phrases often allow you to identify the point of the passage *before the author even states it.* Think of it this way: if the introduction of a passage includes a sentence with the words "many people think…," that's an absolute giveaway that the idea that follows is what "they say," and that the author's attitude toward that idea will be negative. **The main point of the passage is virtually guaranteed to be the opposite of "their" idea**, and by definition, the author will always have a positive attitude toward the main point. So from a single sentence, it is possible to predict the main point AND the author's likely attitude in various parts of the passage.

You should always keep reading just to make sure, but once you've confirmed that the author does in fact hold the view that the introduction suggests, you can often skim through much of the body of the passage. For example, consider a passage that begins this way.

> **Some scientists conclude** that music's influence may
> be a chance event, arising from its ability to hijack brain
> systems built for other purposes such as language, emotion
> and movement.

The phrase *some scientists conclude* is the equivalent of a flashing red signal that the author disagrees with the idea that music's influence is a "chance event." We can very reasonably assume that the author believes music's influence is **not** a chance event, and the remainder of the passage will explain why.

Some passages will also present what "they say" a bit more subtly. For example:

> The Amazon Kindle—a "new and improved" version
> of which has just been released—comes on like a technology
> for our times: crisp, affordable, hugely capacious, capable of
> connecting to the Internet, and green. How could one argue
> 5 with any of that? Or with the idea that it will make the reading
> of texts once again seductive, using the same technology that
> has drawn people away from the page back to it.

Although it isn't quite as obvious that the author is introducing what "they say" as it is in the previous example, there are a number of clues. First, the quotation marks in the first line suggests **skepticism** (the author does not actually believe that the Kindle is really new and improved). Second, the rhetorical question *How could one argue with any of that?* in lines 4-5 implies that author's answer is *Well actually, I can argue.*

As a general rule, the presence of a contradictor such as *however, but,* or *nevertheless* will signal the transition from the "they say" to the "I say." Whenever one of those words appears, you need to pay special attention to it. Not only will it provide important information about how the passage is structured, but it will also tell you where in the passage to focus because the **author's opinion will virtually always be stated after that transition**.

Look at the passage below: it's a classic example of this kind of structure. We've looked at it before, but now we're going to look at it in a slightly different way.

If you simply scan the passage without really reading it, you should be able to spot the word *but* in line 11. That single word suggests that everything before it will have something to do with the old model (bad), and that everything after it will have something to do with the new model (good). Sure enough, that's exactly how the passage works. Key phrases are underlined.

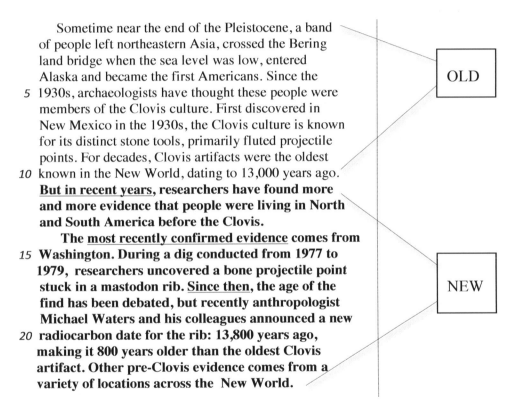

Sometime near the end of the Pleistocene, a band of people left northeastern Asia, crossed the Bering land bridge when the sea level was low, entered Alaska and became the first Americans. Since the
5 1930s, archaeologists have thought these people were members of the Clovis culture. First discovered in New Mexico in the 1930s, the Clovis culture is known for its distinct stone tools, primarily fluted projectile points. For decades, Clovis artifacts were the oldest
10 known in the New World, dating to 13,000 years ago. **But in recent years, researchers have found more and more evidence that people were living in North and South America before the Clovis.**
**The most recently confirmed evidence comes from
15 Washington. During a dig conducted from 1977 to 1979, researchers uncovered a bone projectile point stuck in a mastodon rib. Since then, the age of the find has been debated, but recently anthropologist Michael Waters and his colleagues announced a new
20 radiocarbon date for the rib: 13,800 years ago, making it 800 years older than the oldest Clovis artifact. Other pre-Clovis evidence comes from a variety of locations across the New World.**

OLD

NEW

In order to keep yourself on track and avoid confusion, you should jot down for yourself the old idea and the new idea (what the author believes). And by "jot down," I mean scrawl in shorthand – you don't get points for neatness, and it should take you a few seconds at most.

O = CP 1ˢᵗ NA   (Clovis people first in North America)
N = Ppl in NA pre-CP   (People were in North America before Clovis)

If you are truly concerned that writing these things down will take too much time, simply label them in the passage as is done above.

Important: Whether you write the point yourself or simply underline it, you must remember to look back at your notes! Otherwise, they're useless. I've lost count of the number of times a student of mine has underlined the exact sentence where an answer was located but still gotten a question wrong simply because they forgot to look back at what they'd written.

1

The reference to the bone projectile point (line 16) serves primarily to

A) provide support for the claim that the Americas were inhabited before the Clovis arrived.
B) describe a tool used by prehistoric people in the Americas.
C) suggest that the Clovis people arrived in the Americas earlier than previously thought.
D) emphasize the difficulty of life during the Pleistocene era.

What's the author's point (i.e. claim)? That the Clovis People were NOT the first people to inhabit the Americas (OR: there were people in the Americas BEFORE the Clovis People).

We learn later in the passage the projectile point was dated at 13,800 years old but that the Clovis People only arrived 13,000 years ago. The author is therefore mentioning the projectile point as *evidence* that people inhabited the Americas before 13,000 years ago, i.e. before the Clovis People arrived. So the answer is A).

If you didn't have the main point straight, you could easily pick C), which is just a little bit off. It's not that the Clovis **themselves** arrived earlier than previously thought – it's that **another group** arrived before the Clovis.

Notice that the details of the line in question are borderline irrelevant: it doesn't matter if you know anything about projectile points and mastodons. All that counts is your ability to understand the importance of those details in context of the larger argument. If you understand the argument, you can see how the details fit; if you miss the argument, you'll have to start all over again with each new question.

In longer passages, references to what "they say" and what "I say" may be interspersed throughout the passage. You must read carefully in order to make sure you do not confuse what the author says *other* people think with what the author actually thinks.

In the passage on the following page, references to what "they say" are underlined, and references to what "I say" are in bold. You can see that the author jumps back and forth between discussing his own ideas and other people's ideas. We'll also examine this type of structure more closely in later chapters.

This passage is adapted from Barry Schwartz, "More Isn't Always Better," © 2006 by Harvard Business Review.

Marketers assume that the more choices they offer, the more likely customers will be able to find just the right thing. They assume, for instance, that offering 50 styles of jeans instead of two increases the chances that
5 shoppers will find a pair they really like. **Nevertheless, research now shows that there can be too much choice; when there is, consumers are less likely to buy anything at all, and if they do buy, they are less satisfied with their selection.**

10 It all began with jam. In 2000, psychologists Sheena Iyengar and Mark Lepper published a remarkable study. On one day, shoppers at an upscale food market saw a display table with 24 varieties of gourmet jam. Those who sampled the spreads received a coupon for $1 off
15 any jam. On another day, shoppers saw a similar table, except that only six varieties of the jam were on display. The large display attracted more interest than the small one. **But when the time came to purchase, people who saw the large display were one-tenth as likely to buy as
20 people who saw the small display.**

Other studies have confirmed this result that more choice is not always better. As the variety of snacks, soft drinks, and beers offered at convenience stores increases, for instance, sales volume and customer
25 satisfaction decrease. Moreover, as the number of retirement investment options available to employees increases, the chance that they will choose any decreases. These studies and others have shown not only that excessive choice can produce "choice
30 paralysis," but also that it can reduce people's satisfaction with their decisions, even if they made good ones. My colleagues and I have found that increased choice decreases satisfaction with matters as trivial as ice cream flavors and as significant as jobs.

35 These results challenge what we think we know about human nature and the determinants of well-being. Both psychology and business have operated on the assumption that the relationship between choice and well-being is straightforward: The more choices people
40 have, the better off they are. In psychology, the benefits of choice have been tied to autonomy and control. In business, the benefits of choice have been tied to the benefits of free markets more generally. Added options make no one worse off, and they are bound to make
45 someone better off.

**Choice *is* good for us, but its relationship to satisfaction appears to be more complicated than we had assumed. There is diminishing marginal utility in having alternatives; each new option subtracts a little
50 from the feeling of well-being, until the marginal benefits of added choice level off. What's more, psychologists and business academics alike have largely ignored another outcome of choice: More of it requires increased time and effort and can lead to
55 anxiety, regret, excessively high expectations, and self-blame if the choices don't work out. When the number of available options is small, these costs are negligible, but the costs grow with the number of options. Eventually, each new option makes us feel
60 worse off than we did before.**

Without a doubt, having more options enables us, most of the time, to achieve better objective outcomes. Again, having 50 styles of jeans as opposed to two increases the likelihood that customers will find a pair
65 that fits. **But the subjective outcome may be that shoppers will feel overwhelmed and dissatisfied. This dissociation between objective and subjective results creates a significant challenge for retailers and marketers that look to choice as a way to enhance the
70 perceived value of their goods and services.**

**Choice can no longer be used to justify a marketing strategy in and of itself. More isn't always better, either for the customer or for the retailer. Discovering how much assortment is warranted is a
75 considerable empirical challenge. But companies that get the balance right will be amply rewarded.**

Fiction Passages: What if the Main Point Isn't Obvious?

Because fiction passages are not based on arguments but instead revolve around characters' actions/reactions and relationships, their "main points" can be more challenging. Furthermore, most passages are altered to fit into 85 or so lines, and the edits can sometimes be awkward. Add that to the lack of context, and it's no wonder that figuring out just what is happening can be a challenge.

Regardless of how faithful they are to the original, however, fiction passages typically focus on a specific situation, character trait, or relationship. **You can also think of the point as an extremely condensed (4-6 word) summary of the passage** – it answers the question "what is this passage about?" In fact, most fiction passages will be accompanied by a "summary" question, so if you've already summarized the passage for yourself, you'll have far less work to do and may be able to jump to the answer immediately.

As is true for all other types of passages, you should pay careful attention to major transitions, unusual punctuation, and strong language because they will virtually always appear at key places in the passage. You should also pay particular attention to the places where important information is likely to appear: the introduction will present the character(s) and the general scenario, and the conclusion will reiterate the essential information that the author wants to convey about them.

If you are a very strong reader and capable of getting the gist from a limited number of places, you may be able to skim through larger sections the same way you would in a passage about, say, the Internet. That said, fiction passages are often structured more unpredictably than non-fiction passages, and **you may need to read larger sections of fiction passages more closely**, trying to get a sense of who's involved and what they want (or don't want) but being careful not to waste too much time on unfamiliar words or turns of phrase.

In addition, you should be careful to consider only the information provided by the author and not attempt to speculate about any larger meaning. What counts is your ability to understand the literal events of the passage and how they are conveyed by specific words and phrases. That's it. If you do go looking for some larger symbolism or start to make assumptions not explicitly supported by the passage, you can easily lose sight of the basics. In fact, most people have problems with passages like these not because there's a profound interpretation that can only be perceived through some quasi-mystical process, but rather because they aren't sufficiently *literal*. On the next page, we're going to look at an example.

The passage is divided into two sections – as you read, think about why the division occurs where it does.

The following passage is adapted from the novel *Summer* by Edith Wharton, originally published in 1917.

The hours of the Hatchard Memorial librarian were from three to five; and Charity Royall's sense of duty usually kept her at her desk until nearly half-past four. But she had never perceived that any practical
5 advantage thereby accrued either to North Dormer or to herself; and she had no scruple in decreeing, when it suited her, that the library should close an hour earlier. A few minutes after Mr. Harney's departure she formed this decision, put away her lace, fastened the shutters,
10 and turned the key in the door of the temple of knowledge. The street upon which she emerged was still empty: and after glancing up and down it she began to walk toward her house. But instead of entering she passed on, turned into a field-path and mounted to a
15 pasture on the hillside.

She let down the bars of the gate, followed a trail along the crumbling wall of the pasture, and walked on till she reached a knoll where a clump of larches shook out their fresh tassels to the wind. There she lay down
20 on the slope, tossed off her hat and hid her face in the grass. She was blind and insensible to many things, and dimly knew it; but to all that was light and air, perfume and color, every drop of blood in her responded. She loved the roughness of the dry mountain grass under
25 her palms, the smell of the thyme into which she crushed her face, the fingering of the wind in her hair and through her cotton blouse, and the creak of the larches as they swayed to it.

She often climbed up the hill and lay there alone for
30 the mere pleasure of feeling the wind and of rubbing her cheeks in the grass. Generally at such times she did not think of anything, but lay immersed in an inarticulate well-being. Today the sense of well-being was intensified by her joy at escaping from the library. She
35 liked well enough to have a friend drop in and talk to her when she was on duty, but she hated to be bothered about books. How could she remember where they were, when they were so seldom asked for? Orma Fry occasionally took out a novel, and her brother Ben was
40 fond of what he called "jography," and of books relating to trade and bookkeeping; but no one else asked for anything except, at intervals, "Uncle Tom's Cabin," or "Opening of a Chestnut Burr," or Longfellow. She had these under her hand, and could have found them
45 in the dark; but unexpected demands came so rarely that they exasperated her like an injustice....

She had liked the young man's looks, and his short-sighted eyes, and his odd way of speaking, that was abrupt yet soft, just as his hands were sun-burnt and sinewy, yet

50 with smooth nails like a woman's. His hair was sunburnt-looking too, or rather the colour of bracken after frost; eyes grey, with the appealing look of the shortsighted, his smile shy yet confident, as if he knew lots of things she had never dreamed of, and yet
55 wouldn't for the world have had her feel his superiority. But she did feel it, and liked the feeling; for it was new to her. Poor and ignorant as she was, and knew herself to be—humblest of the humble even in North Dormer, where to come from the Mountain was the worst
60 disgrace—yet in her narrow world she had always ruled. It was partly, of course, owing to the fact that lawyer Royall was "the biggest man in North Dormer"; so much too big for it, in fact, that outsiders, who didn't know, always wondered how it held him. In spite of
65 everything—and in spite even of Miss Hatchard— lawyer Royall ruled in North Dormer; and Charity ruled in lawyer Royall's house. She had never put it to herself in those terms; but she knew her power. Confusedly, the young man in the library had made her feel for
70 the first time what might be the sweetness of dependence. She sat up and looked down on the house where she held sway.

If you're not sure how to determine the "point" of a passage like this, don't worry. We're going to break it down.

Even if fiction passages do not contain arguments, they can often be divided into sections – usually no more than two or three. This passage can be divided into two basic sections:

1) Lines 1-46

In the first section, we are introduced to Charity Royall, the character on whom the passage focuses. We learn that she works as a librarian, that she dislikes her job, and that she's eager to escape from it. If we had to sum it up in a few words, we might say "Charity hates job." (Someone inclined to doodle could also write "Charity ☹ job.") This section contains a lot of description, so if you get the gist after a while, you can just skip down.

2) Lines 47-end

Sections change when new information is introduced or a shift in topic occurs. The introduction of a new character (the man) in line 47 indicates that a new section is beginning. This is where things start to get interesting. We learn that Charity is intrigued by the man and by the prospect of a different life that he represents, but we also learn that she "rules" in her house.

Taking both parts of the passage together, we thus have the central conflict: Charity is torn between her current life, part of which is unpleasant (she hates her job) and part of which is pleasant (she rules at home), and, the passage implies, the possibility of another life as the young man's wife. The first part of the passage thus serves to set up the second part – it explains why Charity would want her life to change.

The really, important part of the passage comes at the end. That's hardly a surprise because most **writing, even fiction, is usually structured so that the most important idea comes last**. What do we learn there? That Charity is *confused*. So a main point, we could put down something like: "Charity torn old/new life."

Note that this statement does not even try to cover all of the events. It simply states the **main conflict** the story is there to convey. It does not "interpret" anything – it simply condenses the information that is directly stated by the author. If we wanted to incorporate both parts of the passage into a main point, however, we could say:

C hates job BUT power at home, meets man → question life

So to sum up, **if you find yourself confused, focus on the conclusion**, particularly the end of the conclusion. Don't waste time trying to figure out the relationship between the various parts of the passage if you're not sure upfront. If you understand the point of the conclusion, chances are that'll be the point of the beginning as well. You can then use that information to answer various "big picture" questions.

1

Which choice best summarizes the first two paragraphs of the passage (lines 1-28)?

A) A woman who dislikes her job seeks solace in nature.
B) A woman works hard at her job but is persuaded to leave by a customer.
C) A woman feels overwhelmed by the demands of her job and desires solitude in a library.
D) A woman spends a day in the wilderness to avoid an unpleasant task.

2

Which choice provides the most accurate summary of this passage?

A) A character is forced to make a momentous decision after an unexpected meeting.
B) A character feels uncertain about her life following a significant encounter.
C) A character holds great power at work but feels powerless in her own home.
D) A character works hard at her job but is persuaded to leave it by a man she meets.

Solution #1:

The easiest way to answer this question is to use the main point. If you've written that Charity hates her job, you can start by making an educated guess that A) is likely to be correct. And in fact, A) describes precisely what happens in the first two paragraphs: Charity dislikes her job and leaves it early one day to go sit on a grassy hill (=nature) and make herself feel better (=seek solace).

If you haven't written the point, focus on the beginning of the first paragraph and the end of the second. The first paragraph begins by describing Charity's decision to leave work, and the second paragraph ends with her lying on a grassy hill. That sequence corresponds to A).

Solution #2:

If you've written the main point, you're already most of the way toward the answer. Basically, Charity is all torn up over the fact that she met this guy (=a significant encounter) and now can't figure out what she wants (=feels uncertain). So the answer is B).

Careful with A). Charity is thrown into confusion by her meeting with the young man, but she isn't actually *forced* to make a "momentous decision." C) reverses the facts: Charity is powerless at *work*. And D) is wrong because no one persuades Charity to leave work.

Order of Events

You may be also encounter questions that ask to determine the sequence in which events discussed in the passage take place. Although having a solid big picture understanding of the passage can help, that knowledge alone will not necessarily get you all the way to the answer. The reason is that these questions are more likely to accompany passages that jump around in time – that is, they discuss events occurring both at the time of the passage as well as before the time of the passage, **but those events may be mentioned in the passage in a order that is different from the order in which they actually occurred**. This is normally accomplished through the use of **flashback**, a technique in which an author describes an event or situation that occurred before the main action of the story.

For example, in the passage we've been looking at, the scene between Charity and the young man is introduced halfway through the passage; however, the event itself took place **before** the action of the passage itself, and Charity is simply remembering it during the passage. Understanding that timeline would become very important if you encountered a question like this:

1

Which choice best describes the sequence of events described in this passage?

A) A woman dislikes her job and seeks solace in nature, where she reflects on a memorable encounter.

B) A woman works hard at her job but is persuaded to leave; she then returns home, where she interacts with another character.

C) A woman feels overwhelmed by the demands of her job and encounters a man with whom she spends the afternoon.

D) A woman has a significant encounter while at work, then leaves because she feels too conflicted to continue.

The most important thing to understand about a question like this is that it is not asking what order the events are discussed in the passage but rather what order the events actually occurred in.

If you're not clear about the fact that Charity's encounter with the man does **not** occur during the action of the passage, you might be tempted to pick C) or D). In contrast, A) is the only answer that indicates the encounter occurred before the time of the passage.

Supporting Examples: Working Backwards

Some questions will test your understanding of main points less directly. In fact, they will not explicitly ask about the main point at all. Rather, they'll test it "backwards," providing an example or list of examples that the author uses at a certain point in the passage and asking you to identify what those items are examples of. Why use examples? To support the point. So the correct answer will restate the point, sometimes the point of a particular section and sometimes the point of the passage as a whole. Since **main points typically come <u>before</u> supporting examples, you should back up and read from at least a sentence before the line reference**. If you start at the line reference and keep going, you risk overlooking the information you need entirely.

Let's look at an example:

Some scientists, unsurprisingly, balk at *Jurassic Park*. After all, the science is so inaccurate! Velociraptor was smaller and had feathers. Dilophosaurus wasn't venomous. Tyrannosaurus rex could not run so fast.
5 That opening scene where the paleontologists just wipe sand off of an intact and perfectly preserved dino skeleton is hogwash. In any case, near-complete DNA molecules cannot survive in fossils for tens of thousands of years, much less tens of millions. Also:
10 did you know that most of the dinosaurs depicted in *Jurassic Park* actually lived in the Cretaceous period? This is the pedant's approach to science fiction, and it does have its uses. Among other things, how would scientists be able to maintain bonding rituals within
15 their tribe if they could not rally around movies that get their specialties wrong? Astronomers have *Armageddon* and *Contact*; volcanologists have *Volcano* and *Dante's Peak*; physicists have the *Stars Trek* and *Wars*; and paleontologists have *Jurassic Park*. (Artificial
20 intelligence researchers are another story — most of them would be out of a job if not for the movies.)
More importantly, *Jurassic Park* isn't simply after the facts. Nor, as many reviewers complained at the time of its initial release, does the movie seek to tell
25 stories about fully three-dimensional human characters. Rather, it offers us a fable about the natural world and man, and the relation between the two: about science, technology, imagination, aspiration, folly, power, corruption, hubris, wild nature in its many forms, and,
30 most importantly, dinosaurs.

1

The author mentions *Volcano*, *Dante's Peak*, *Star War* and *Jurassic Park* (lines 17-19) as examples of

A) the pedant's approach to science fiction.
B) works that contain scientific inaccuracies.
C) films enjoyed by a wide range of scientists.
D) forms of entertainment that popularized scientific inquiry.

We're going to start with the sentence before the list — we know that it's important because it ends with a question mark ("interesting" punctuation). What do we learn from that sentence? That the author is talking about movies that *got science wrong*. So the movies included in the list are ones that got science wrong, i.e. contained scientific inaccuracies. So the answer is B).

Let's look at another example.

The following passage is adapted from Susan B. Anthony's Remarks to the Woman's Auxiliary Congress of the Public Press Congress, May 23, 1893.

Mrs. President and Sisters, I might almost say daughters—I cannot tell you how much joy has filled my heart as I have sat here listening to these papers and noting those characteristics that made each in its
5 own way beautiful and masterful. I would in no ways lessen the importance of these expressions by your various representatives, but I want to say that the words that specially voiced what I may call the up-gush of my soul were to be found in the paper read by Mrs. Swalm
10 on "The Newspaper as a Factor of Civilization." I have never been a pen artist and I have never succeeded with rhetorical flourishes unless it were by accident. But I have always admired supremely that which I could realize the least. The woman who can coin words and
15 ideas to suit me best would not be unlike Mrs. Swalm, and when I heard her I said: "That is worthy of Elizabeth Cady Stanton."
    While I have been sitting here I have been thinking that we have made strides in journalism in the last forty
20 years. I recall the first time I ever wrote for a paper. The periodical was called the *Lily*. It was edited—and quite appropriately—by a Mrs. Bloomer. The next paper to which I contributed was the *Una*. These two journals were the only avenues women had through
20 which to face themselves in type to any extent worthy of note before the war. The press was as kind as it knew how to be. It meant well and did all for us it knew how to do. We couldn't ask it to do more than it knew how. But that was little enough and I tried an experiment
25 editing a newspaper myself. I started a paper and ran it for two years at a vast cost to every one concerned in it. I served seven years at lecturing to pay off the debt and interest on that paper and I considered myself fortunate to get off as easily as that.

1

The author uses the phrase "rhetorical flourishes" (line 12) as an example of

A) an accomplishment admired in women.
B) an outdated form of communication.
C) a skill at which she does not excel.
D) a task that she tried for many years to master.

The question asks what the phrase *rhetorical flourishes* is an **example** of, so it's telling us that the phrase is being used to support a **point**. Our job is to figure out what that point is.

The question refers to line 12, but we're going read the **entire sentence** in which the key phrase appears. The following sentence starts with *but*, so we're going to read it as well.

What do we learn from those sentences? That rhetorical flourishes are something Anthony *never succeeded at unless it were by accident.* They're something she admires in other people, but that she has never been able to "realize" (i.e. achieve – note the second meaning!). In other words, she stinks at them, i.e. she does NOT excel. So the answer is C).

Main Point vs. Primary Purpose

Very often, when students encounter a question asking about the **primary purpose** of a passage, they reiterate the **main point**, then become confused when an answer corresponding to it does not appear among the answer choices. While it is important to determine the main point, that information alone will not necessarily give you the purpose.

The purpose and point of the passage are related, sometimes directly and sometimes in ways that are less obvious, but they are not precisely the same thing.

> **Main Point** – The primary **argument** the author is making. It is usually stated more or less directly in the passage, in the introduction, the conclusion, or all three.

> **Primary Purpose** – The **goal** of the passage as a whole (e.g. *describe, emphasize, refute*). While the primary purpose is based on the overall passage, there is often a key sentence that will point to a particular answer.

For example, consider the following passage:

In an essay in 1984—at the dawn of the personal computer era—the novelist Thomas Pynchon wondered if it was "O.K. to be a Luddite," meaning someone who opposes technological progress. A better question
5 today is whether it's even possible. Technology is everywhere, and a recent headline at an Internet humor site perfectly captured how difficult it is to resist: "Luddite invents machine to destroy technology quicker." Like all good satire, the mock headline comes
10 perilously close to the truth. Modern Luddites do indeed invent "machines"—in the form of computer viruses, cyberworms and other malware—to disrupt the technologies that trouble them.
   But despite their modern reputation, the original
15 Luddites were neither opposed to technology nor inept at using it. Many were highly skilled machine operators in the textile industry. Nor was the technology they attacked particularly new. Moreover, the idea of smashing machines as a form of industrial protest did
20 not begin or end with them. In truth, the secret of their enduring reputation depends less on what they did than on the name under which they did it.

1

The primary purpose of the passage is to

A) point out that the Luddites' modern reputation is based on a misconception.
B) emphasize the destructive nature of the Luddites' actions.
C) describe some of the machines invented by modern Luddites.
D) indicate that perception of the Luddites has changed over time.

Main Point: Luddites NOT anti-tech, mod. rep = WRONG (the Luddites weren't opposed to technology; their modern reputation is wrong). The word *But* in line 14 signals the transition to the "I say," which is by definition the point. That point corresponds exactly to A). We don't even need to check the other answers.

Now let's look back at the Wharton passage. We've already seen a question asking about the main point, but this time we're going to look at it in term of overall purpose.

The following passage is adapted from the novel *Summer* by Edith Wharton, originally published in 1917.

The hours of the Hatchard Memorial librarian were from three to five; and Charity Royall's sense of duty usually kept her at her desk until nearly half-past four. But she had never perceived that any practical
5 advantage thereby accrued either to North Dormer or to herself; and she had no scruple in decreeing, when it suited her, that the library should close an hour earlier. A few minutes after Mr. Harney's departure she formed This decision, put away her lace, fastened the shutters,
10 and turned the key in the door of the temple of knowledge. The street upon which she emerged was still empty: and after glancing up and down it she began to walk toward her house. But instead of entering she passed on, turned into a field-path and mounted to a
15 pasture on the hillside.

She let down the bars of the gate, followed a trail along the crumbling wall of the pasture, and walked on till she reached a knoll where a clump of larches shook out their fresh tassels to the wind. There she lay down
20 on the slope, tossed off her hat and hid her face in the grass. She was blind and insensible to many things, and dimly knew it; but to all that was light and air, perfume and color, every drop of blood in her responded. She loved the roughness of the dry mountain grass under
25 her palms, the smell of the thyme into which she crushed her face, the fingering of the wind in her hair and through her cotton blouse, and the creak of the larches as they swayed to it.

She often climbed up the hill and lay there alone for
30 the mere pleasure of feeling the wind and of rubbing her cheeks in the grass. Generally at such times she did not think of anything, but lay immersed in an inarticulate well-being. Today the sense of well-being was intensified by her joy at escaping from the library. She
35 liked well enough to have a friend drop in and talk to her when she was on duty, but she hated to be bothered about books. How could she remember where they were, when they were so seldom asked for? Orma Fry occasionally took out a novel, and her brother Ben was
40 fond of what he called "jography," and of books relating to trade and bookkeeping; but no one else asked for anything except, at intervals, "Uncle Tom's Cabin," or "Opening of a Chestnut Burr," or Longfellow. She had these under her hand, and could have found them
45 in the dark; but unexpected demands came so rarely that they exasperated her like an injustice…

She had liked the young man's looks, and his short-sighted eyes, and his odd way of speaking, that was abrupt yet soft, just as his hands were sun-burnt and sinewy,
50 with smooth nails like a woman's. His hair was sunburnt-looking too, or rather the colour of bracken after frost; eyes grey, with the appealing look of the shortsighted, his smile shy yet confident, as if he knew lots of things she had never dreamed of, and yet
55 wouldn't for the world have had her feel his superiority. But she did feel it, and liked the feeling; for it was new to her. Poor and ignorant as she was, and knew herself to be—humblest of the humble even in North Dormer, where to come from the Mountain was the worst
60 disgrace—yet in her narrow world she had always ruled. It was partly, of course, owing to the fact that lawyer Royall was "the biggest man in North Dormer"; so much too big for it, in fact, that outsiders, who didn't know, always wondered how it held him. In spite of
65 everything—and in spite even of Miss Hatchard—lawyer Royall ruled in North Dormer; and Charity ruled in lawyer Royall's house. She had never put it to herself in those terms; but she knew her power. **Confusedly, the young man in the library had made her feel for**
70 **the first time what might be the sweetness of dependence. She sat up and looked down on the house where she held sway.**

1

The primary purpose of the passage is to

A) illustrate a family's daily life in a small town.
B) describe how a significant encounter causes a a character to reevaluate her life.
C) call attention to the difference between a character's public and private behavior.
D) explain the influence of books on a main character's life.

If you encounter a "purpose of a passage" question right after you've finished reading the passage, your immediate thought might be, "Oh no, I was so focused on trying to get what was going on in the passage that I wasn't really thinking about the purpose. You mean now I have to go back and reread the whole thing so that I can figure it out?" Either that, or you might be inclined to leave that question for last, working through the detail-based questions first and using them to figure out the big picture.

Leaving a big picture question for the end is certainly a fair strategy if you find it helpful (rereading an entire passage for the sake of a single question, on the other hand, is a very bad idea), but if you get a good sense of the passage the first time you read it, you should be able to handle these questions upfront.

Even though this question asks about the purpose rather than the point, we need to start by reiterating the "point:"

C hates job BUT power at home, meets man → question life (Charity hates her job even though she's powerful at home, but then she meets a guy and starts to question what she really wants.)

Or: **C unhappy but unsure/change**; or **What does C want?**; or even more simply: **C = confused**

As discussed earlier, the most important part of the passage is the end of the conclusion, and it gives us pretty much all the information we need.

The correct answer is basically going to tell us that the purpose of the passage is to describe this girl who meets a guy and realizes that she doesn't know what the heck she wants. That's pretty much what B) says. It just phrases it from a slightly different angle and with more general wording. Charity's meeting with the man is "a significant encounter." We know it's significant because it causes her to start wondering what she really wants.

Otherwise, A) is wrong because the passage focuses on a single character, not a family; C) is wrong because the passage doesn't really tell us much about Charity's behavior at all – the focus is on her thoughts and feelings. Her interactions with other characters are mentioned, and she's certainly alone for a good portion of the passage, but Wharton does not go out of her way to call the reader's attention to any difference in how she *acts* in those two situations. D) is just plain wrong – the passage makes it clear that Charity can't stand her job at the library. There's also nothing to suggest that books themselves have influenced her life (for good or bad), only that she dislikes the job of working with them.

The Big Picture Exercises

1.   To understand what the new software—that is,
analytics—can do that's different from more familiar
software like spreadsheets, word processing, and
graphics, consider the lowly photograph. Here the
5 relevant facts aren't how many bytes constitute a digital
photograph, or a billion of them. That's about as
instructive as counting the silver halide molecules used
to form a single old-fashioned print photo. The important
feature of a digital image's bytes is that, unlike
10 crystalline molecules, they are uniquely easy to store,
transport, and manipulate with software. In the first era
of digital images, people were fascinated by the
convenience and malleability (think PhotoShop) of
capturing, storing, and sharing pictures. Now, instead of
15 using software to manage photos, we can mine features
of the bytes that make up the digital image. Facebook
can, without privacy invasion, track where and when,
for example, vacationing is trending, since digital images
reveal at least that much. But more importantly, those
20 data can be cross-correlated, even in real time, with
seemingly unrelated data such as local weather, interest
rates, crime figures, and so on. Such correlations
associated with just one photograph aren't revealing.
But imagine looking at billions of photos over weeks,
25 months, years, then correlating them with dozens of
directly related data sets (vacation bookings, air traffic),
tangential information (weather, interest rates,
unemployment), or orthogonal information (social or
political trends). With essentially free super-computing,
30 we can mine and usefully associate massive, formerly
unrelated data sets and unveil all manner of economic,
cultural, and social realities.
    For science fiction aficionados, Isaac Asimov
anticipated the idea of using massive data sets to predict
35 human behavior, coining it "psychohistory" in his 1951
Foundation trilogy. The bigger the data set, Asimov said
then, the more predictable the future. With big-data
analytics, one can finally see the forest, instead of just
the capillaries in the tree leaves. Or to put it in more
40 accurate terms, one can see beyond the apparently
random motion of a few thousand molecules of air inside
a balloon; one can see the balloon itself, and beyond that,
that it is inflating, that it is yellow, and that it is part of a
bunch of balloons en route to a birthday party. The
45 data/software world has, until now, been largely about
looking at the molecules inside one balloon.

1

The main idea of the passage is that

A) Bytes have allowed people to capture and
edit images in innovative ways.
B) New forms of technology allow users'
activities to be tracked without violating
privacy.
C) Recent developments in technology have
transformed the way data is acquired and
analyzed.
D) Modern technology was described in science
fiction novels long before it was invented.

2

The author's central claim in the second
paragraph is that

A) The predictions of science fiction writers
tend to be more accurate than those of
scientists.
B) All human behavior can be understood
through the use of massive data sets.
C) Technological innovation is often inspired by
the natural world.
D) Data sets will reveal unforeseen relationships
between large-scale phenomena.

2. This passage is adapted from Jamaica Kincaid, *Annie John*, © 1985 © Farrar Strauss and Giroux. The protagonist is a girl growing up in the Caribbean.

It was the first day of a new term, Miss Nelson said, so we would not be attending to any of our usual subjects; instead, we were to spend the morning in contemplation and reflection and writing something she
5　described as an "autobiographical essay." In the afternoon, we would read aloud to each other our auto-biographical essays. (I knew quite well about "autobiography" and "essay," but reflection and contemplation! A day at school spent in such a way!
10　Of course, in most books all the good people were always contemplating and reflecting before they did anything. Perhaps in her mind's eye she could see our future and, against all prediction, we turned out to be good people.) On hearing this, a huge sigh went up
15　from the girls.

Half the sighs were in happiness at the thought of sitting and gazing off into clear space, the other half in unhappiness at the misdeeds that would have to go unaccomplished. I joined the happy half, because I
20　knew it would please Miss Nelson, and, my own selfish interest aside, I liked so much the way she wore her ironed hair and her long-sleeved blouse and box-pleated skirt that I wanted to please her.

The morning was uneventful enough: a girl
25　spilled ink from her inkwell all over her uniform; a girl broke her pen nib and then made a big to-do about replacing it; girls twisted and turned in their seats and pinched each other's bottoms; girls passed notes to each other. All this Miss Nelson must have seen and
30　heard, but she didn't say anything—only kept reading her book: an elaborately illustrated edition of the *The Tempest*, as later, passing by her desk, I saw. Midway in the morning, we were told to go out and stretch our legs and breathe some fresh air for a few minutes;
35　when we returned, we were given glasses of cold lemonade and a slice of bun to refresh us.

As soon as the sun stood in the middle of the sky, we were sent home for lunch. The earth may have grown an inch or two larger between the time I had
40　walked to school that morning and the time I went home to lunch, for some girls made a small space for me in their little band. But I couldn't pay much attention to them; my mind was on my new surroundings, my new teacher, what I had written in my nice new
45　notebook with its black-all-mixed-up-with-white cover and smooth lined pages (so glad was I to get rid of my old notebooks, which had on their covers a picture of a wrinkled-up woman wearing a crown on her head and a neckful and armfuls of diamonds and pearls—their
50　pages so coarse, as if they were made of cornmeal).

I flew home. I must have eaten my food. By half past one, we were sitting under a flamboyant tree in a secluded part of our schoolyard, our auto-biographical essays in hand. We were about to read aloud what
55　we had written during our morning of contemplation and reflection. In response to Miss Nelson, each girl stood up and read her composition. One girl told of a much revered and loved aunt who now lived in England and of how much she looked forward to
60　one day moving to England to live with her aunt; one girl told of her brother studying medicine in Canada and the life she imagined he lived there (it seemed quite odd to me); one girl told of the fright she had when she dreamed she was dead, and of the matching
65　fright she had when she woke and found that she wasn't (everyone laughed at this, and Miss Nelson had to call us to order over and over); one girl told of how her oldest sister's best friend's cousin's best friend (it was a real rigmarole) had gone on a Girl Guide
70　jamboree held in Trinidad and met someone who millions of years ago had taken tea with Lady Baden-Powell; one girl told of an excursion she and her father had made to Redonda, and of how they had seen some booby birds tending their chicks. Things
75　went on in that way, all so playful, all so imaginative. I began to wonder about what I had written, for it was the opposite of playful and it was the opposite of imaginative. What I had written was heartfelt, and, except for the very end, it was all too true.

1

Which choice best summarizes the passage?

A) A character is apprehensive about attending new school but is quickly reassured by her teacher.

B) A character is excited about attending a new school but struggles to make friends.

C) A character is eager to complete a school assignment but becomes anxious after observing her classmates' work.

D) A character admires her teacher but is disappointed by her teacher's reaction to her work.

The primary purpose of the passage is to

A) describe the interactions between a young girl and her peers.
B) recount a memorable episode in a young girl's life.
C) explain the influence of an important figure on a young girl's life.
D) explore the consequences of a young girl's decision.

3. The following passaged is adapted from Olympe de Gouges, *Declaration of the Rights of Women*. It was initially published in 1791, during the French Revolution, and was written in response to the *Declaration of the Rights of Man* (1789).

Woman, wake up; the toxin of reason is being heard throughout the whole universe; discover your rights. The powerful empire of nature is no longer surrounded by prejudice, fanaticism, superstition, and
5 lies. The flame of truth has dispersed all the clouds of folly and usurpation. Enslaved man has multiplied his strength and needs recourse to yours to break his chains. Having become free, he has become unjust to his companion. Oh, women, women! When will you cease
10 to be blind? What advantage have you received from the Revolution? A more pronounced scorn, a more marked disdain. In the centuries of corruption you ruled only over the weakness of men. The reclamation of your patrimony, based on the wise decrees of nature –
15 what have you to dread from such a fine undertaking? Do you fear that our legislators, correctors of that morality, long ensnared by political practices now out of date, will only say again to you: women, what is there in common between you and us? Everything, you
20 will have to answer. If they persist in their weakness in putting this hypocrisy in contradiction to their principles, courageously oppose the force of reason to the empty pretensions of superiority; unite yourselves beneath the standards of philosophy; deploy all the
25 energy of your character. Regardless of what barriers confront you, it is in your power to free yourselves; you have only to want to. Let us pass not to the shocking tableau of what you have been in society; and since national education is in question at this moment, let us
30 see whether our wise legislators will think judiciously about the education of women.
   Women have done more harm than good. Constraint and dissimulation have been their lot. What force has robbed them of, ruse returned to them; they had recourse
35 to all the resources of their charms, and the most irreproachable persons did not resist them. Poison and the sword were both subject to them; they commanded in crime as in fortune. The French government, especially, depended throughout the centuries on the nocturnal
40 administrations of women; the cabinet could keep no secrets as a result of their indiscretions; all have been subject to the cupidity and ambition of this sex, formerly contemptible and respected, and since the revolution, respectable and scorned.

45   In this sort of contradictory situation, what remarks could I not make! I have but a moment to make them, but this moment will fix the attention of the remotest posterity. Under the Old Regime, all was vicious, all was guilty; but could not the amelioration of
50 conditions be perceived even in the substance of vices? A woman only had to be beautiful or lovable; when she possessed these two advantages, she saw a hundred fortunes at her feet. If she did not profit from them, she had a bizarre character or a rare philosophy
55 which made her scorn wealth; then she was deemed to be like a crazy woman. A young, inexperienced woman, seduced by a man whom she loves, will abandon her parents to follow him; the ingrate will leave her after a few years, and the older she has
60 become with him, the more inhuman is his inconstancy; if she has children, he will likewise abandon them. If he is rich, he will consider himself excused from sharing his fortune with his noble victims. If some involvement binds him to his duties, he will
65 deny them, trusting that the laws will support him. If he is married, any other obligation loses its rights. Then what laws remain to extirpate vice all the way to its root? The law of dividing wealth and public administration between men and women. It can easily
70 be seen that one who is born into a rich family gains very much from such equal sharing. But the one born into a poor family with merit and virtue – what is her lot? Poverty and opprobrium. If she does not precisely excel in music or painting, she cannot be admitted to
75 any public function when she has all the capacity for it.

1

The central problem that the author describes in in the second paragraph (lines 32-44) is that women

A) are encouraged by their husbands to secretly gather information.
B) have played a significant but unacknowledged role in political life.
C) have been responsible for undermining their own cause.
D) must play a more active role in civic life.

The author's main point in the passage is that

A) women and men must work together to improve conditions for women.
B) women must excel in the arts in order to gain societal approval.
C) women must unite to demand the rights that society has denied them.
D) women's lack of rights can be primarily attributed to government policies.

4. The following passage is adapted from Julian Jackson, "New Research Suggests Dinosaurs Were Warm-Blooded and Active" © 2011 by Julian Jackson.

New research from the University of Adelaide has added to the debate about whether dinosaurs were cold-blooded and sluggish or warm-blooded and active. Professor Roger Seymour from the University's School
5 of Earth & Environmental Sciences has applied the latest theories of human and animal anatomy and physiology to provide insight into the lives of dinosaurs.

Human thigh bones have tiny holes – known as the
10 "nutrient foramen" – on the shaft that supply blood to living bone cells inside. New research has shown that the size of those holes is related to the maximum rate that a person can be active during aerobic exercise. Professor Seymour has used this principle to evaluate
15 the activity levels of dinosaurs.

"Far from being lifeless, bone cells have a relatively high metabolic rate and they therefore require a large blood supply to deliver oxygen. On the inside of the bone, the blood supply comes usually from a single
20 artery and vein that pass through a hole on the shaft – the nutrient foramen," he says.

Professor Seymour wondered whether the size of the nutrient foramen might indicate how much blood was necessary to keep the bones in good repair. For
25 example, highly active animals might cause more bone 'microfractures,' requiring more frequent repairs by the bone cells and therefore a greater blood supply. "My aim was to see whether we could use fossil bones of dinosaurs to indicate the level of bone metabolic rate
30 and possibly extend it to the whole body's metabolic rate," he says. "One of the big controversies among paleobiologists is whether dinosaurs were cold-blooded and sluggish or warm-blooded and active. Could the size of the foramen be a possible gauge for dinosaur
35 metabolic rate?"

Comparisons were made with the sizes of the holes in living mammals and reptiles, and their metabolic rates. Measuring mammals ranging from mice to elephants, and reptiles from lizards to crocodiles, one
40 of Professor Seymour's Honors students, Sarah Smith, combed the collections of Australian museums, photographing and measuring hundreds of tiny holes in thigh bones.

"The results were unequivocal. The sizes of the holes
45 were related closely to the maximum metabolic rates during peak movement in mammals and reptiles," Professor Seymour says. "The holes found in mammals were about 10 times larger than those in reptiles."

These holes were compared to those of fossil
50 dinosaurs. Dr. Don Henderson, Curator of Dinosaurs from the Royal Tyrrell Museum in Alberta, Canada, and Daniela Schwarz-Wings from the Museum für Naturkunde Humboldt University Berliny, German measured the holes in 10 species of
55 dinosaurs from five different groups, including bipedal and quadrupedal carnivores and herbivores, weighing 50kg to 20,000kg.

"On a relative comparison to eliminate the differences in body size, all of the dinosaurs had
60 holes in their thigh bones larger than those of mammals," Professor Seymour says.

"The dinosaurs appeared to be even more active than the mammals. We certainly didn't expect to see that. These results provide additional weight to
65 theories that dinosaurs were warm-blooded and highly active creatures, rather than cold-blooded and sluggish."

Professor Seymour says following the results of this study, it's likely that a simple measurement of
70 foramen size could be used to evaluate maximum activity levels in other vertebrate animals.

<hr>

1

The main purpose of the passage is to

A) Describe an experiment to resolve a scientific controversy and discuss its results.
B) Refute a commonly held belief about dinosaur behavior.
C) Compare the development of dinosaur bones to the development of mammal bones.
D) Explain how foramen size has been used to gauge activity levels in mammals.

Which of the following best summarizes the findings of Professor Seymour's study?

A) Foramen size can be used as a measure of growth rate in dinosaurs and other animals.

B) The density of dinosaurs' thigh bones conclusively proves that dinosaurs were warm-blooded.

C) The size of dinosaurs' foramens indicates that dinosaurs may have behaved more like mammals than like reptiles.

D) The size of the holes in the shaft of dinosaurs' thigh bones strongly suggests that dinosaurs were warm-blooded.

5. This passage is adapted from a 1950 speech by Dean Acheson, who served as Secretary of State from 1949 to 1953 and strongly influenced United States foreign policy during the Cold War.

However much we may sympathize with the Soviet citizens who for reasons bedded deep in history are obliged to live under it, we are not attempting to change the governmental or social structure of the Soviet

5 Union. The Soviet regime, however, has devoted a major portion of its energies and resources to the attempt to impose its system on other peoples. In this attempt it has shown itself prepared to resort to any method or stratagem, including subversion, threats, and even

10 military force.

Therefore, if the two systems are to coexist, some acceptable means must be found to free the world from the destructive tensions and anxieties of which it has been the victim in these past years and the continuance

15 of which can hardly be in the interests of any people.

I wish, therefore, to speak to you about those points of greatest difference which must be identified and sooner or later reconciled if the two systems are to live together, if not with mutual respect, at least in

20 reasonable security.

It is now nearly 5 years since the end of hostilities, and the victorious Allies have been unable to define the terms of peace with the defeated countries. This is a grave, a deeply disturbing fact. For our part, we do not

25 intend nor wish, in fact we do not know how, to create satellites. Nor can we accept a settlement which would make Germany, Japan, or liberated Austria satellites of the Soviet Union. The experience in Hungary, Rumania, and Bulgaria has been one of bitter disappointment and

30 shocking betrayal of the solemn pledges by the wartime Allies. The Soviet leaders joined in the pledge at Tehran that they looked forward "with confidence to the day when all peoples of the world may live free lives, untouched by tyranny, and according to their varying

35 desires and their own consciences." We can accept treaties of peace which would give reality to this pledge and to the interests of all in security.

With regard to the whole group of countries which we are accustomed to thinking of as the satellite area, the

40 Soviet leaders could withdraw their military and police force and refrain from using the shadow of that force to keep in power persons or regimes which do not command the confidence of the respective peoples, freely expressed through orderly representative processes.

45 In this connection, we do not insist that these governments have any particular political or social complexion. What concerns us is that they should be truly independent national regimes, with a will of their own and with a decent foundation in popular feeling.

50 The Soviet leaders could cooperate with us to the end that the official representatives of all countries are treated everywhere with decency and respect and that an atmosphere is created in which these representatives could function in a normal and helpful manner,

55 conforming to the accepted codes of diplomacy.

These are some of the things which we feel that Soviet leaders could do which would permit the rational and peaceful development of the coexistence of their system and ours. They are not things that go to

60 the depths of the moral conflict. They have been formulated by us, not as moralists but as servants of government, anxious to get on with the practical problems that lie before us and to get on with them in a manner consistent with mankind's deep longing for a

65 respite from fear and uncertainty.

Nor have they been formulated as a one-sided bargain. A will to achieve binding, peaceful settlements would be required of all participants. All would have to produce unmistakable evidence of their good faith.

70 All would have to accept agreements in the observance of which all nations could have real confidence.

The United States is ready, as it has been and always will be, to cooperate in genuine efforts to find peaceful settlements. Our attitude is not inflexible, our opinions

75 are not frozen, our positions are not and will not be obstacles to peace. But it takes more than one to cooperate. If the Soviet Union could join in doing these things I have outlined, we could all face the future with greater security. We could look forward to more than

80 the eventual reduction of some of the present tensions. We could anticipate a return to a more normal and relaxed diplomatic atmosphere and to progress in the transaction of some of the international business which needs so urgently to be done.

1

What is the main idea of the passage?

A) The Soviet Union's failure to adhere to international agreements poses an immediate threat to American security.

B) Relations between the Soviet Union and the United States will improve if the Soviet Union offers greater liberties to its citizens.

C) The Soviet Union will be unable to conduct normal relations with other countries until communism has been thoroughly destroyed.

D) The conduct of the United States toward the Soviet Union is a moral dilemma that cannot be easily resolved.

2

The primary purpose of the passage is to

A) Criticize the Soviet Union for its harsh treatment of peoples under its rule.

B) Suggest that the Soviet Union should model its diplomatic process on that of the United States.

C) Propose a course of action that would result in a reduction of tension between the Soviet Union and the United States.

D) Decry the use of a force as a tool for maintaining international order.

3

The main idea of the fourth paragraph (lines 21-37) is that

A) Leaders must act according to their conscience as well as their desires.

B) Control of Soviet satellites will be granted to the United States if the Soviet Union continues to behave unreliably.

C) Soviet control of Germany, Japan, and Austria would inevitably end in disaster.

D) The Soviet Union must abide by its promises in order for the United States to accept its treaties.

6. The following passage is adapted from George Orwell, "Keep the Aspidastra Flying," first published in 1936. Gordon, the protagonist, is a poet.

    Gordon walked homeward against the rattling wind, which blew his hair backward and gave him more of a 'good' forehead than ever. His manner conveyed to the passers-by – at least, he hoped it did—that if he wore
5 no overcoat it was from pure caprice.
    Willowbed Road, NW, was dingy and depressing, although it contrived to keep up a kind of mingy decency. There was even a dentist's brass plate on one of the houses. In quite two-thirds of them, amid the
10 lace curtains of the parlor window, there was a green card with 'Apartments' on it in silver lettering, above the peeping foliage of an aspidistra.*
    Mrs. Wisbeach, Gordon's landlady, specialized in 'single gentlemen'. Bed-sitting-rooms, with gaslight laid
15 on and find your own heating, baths extra (there was a geyser), and meals in the tomb-dark dining-room with the phalanx of clotted sauce-bottles in the middle of the table. Gordon, who came home for his midday dinner, paid twenty-seven and six a week.
20   The gaslight shone yellow through the frosted transom above the door of Number 31. Gordon took out his key and fished about in the keyhole – in that kind of house the key never quite fits the lock. The darkish little hallway – in reality it was only a passage – smelt of
25 dishwater and cabbage. Gordon glanced at the japanned tray on the hall-stand. No letters, of course. He had told himself not to hope for a letter, and nevertheless had continued to hope. A stale feeling, not quite a pain, settled upon his breast. Rosemary might have written!
30 It was four days now since she had written. Moreover, he had sent out to magazines and had not yet had returned to him. The one thing that made the evening bearable was to find a letter waiting for him when he got home. But he received very few letters – four or five in a week
35 at the very most.
    On the left of the hall was the never-used parlor, then came the staircase, and beyond that the passage ran down to the kitchen and to the unapproachable lair inhabited by Mrs. Wisbeach herself. As Gordon came in,
40 the door at the end of the passage opened a foot or so. Mrs. Wisbeach's face emerged, inspected him briefly but suspiciously, and disappeared again. It was quite impossible to get in or out of the house, at any time before eleven at night, without being scrutinized in this
45 manner. Just what Mrs. Wisbeach suspected you of it

was hard to say. She was one of those malignant respectable women who keep lodging-houses. Age about forty-five, stout but active, with a pink, fine-featured, horribly observant face, beautifully grey hair,
50 and a permanent grievance.
    In the familiar darkness of his room, Gordon felt for the gas-jet and lighted it. The room was medium-sized, not big enough to be curtained into two, but too big to be sufficiently warmed by one defective oil lamp. It had
55 the sort of furniture you expect in a top floor back. White-quilted single-bed; brown lino floor-covering; wash-hand-stand with jug and basin of that cheap white ware which you can never see without thinking of chamberpots. On the window-sill there was a sickly
60 aspidistra in a green-glazed pot.
    Up against this, under the window, there was a kitchen table with an inkstained green cloth. This was Gordon's 'writing' table. It was only after a bitter struggle that he had induced Mrs. Wisbeach to give him
65 a kitchen table instead of the bamboo 'occasional' table – a mere stand for the aspidistra – which she considered proper for a top floor back. And even now there was endless nagging because Gordon would never allow his table to be 'tidied up'. The table was in a
70 permanent mess. It was almost covered with a muddle of papers, perhaps two hundred sheets, grimy and dog-eared, and all written on and crossed out and written on again – a sort of sordid labyrinth of papers to which only Gordon possessed the key. There was a film of
75 dust over everything. Except for a few books on the mantelpiece, this table, with its mess of papers, was the sole mark Gordon's personality had left on the room.

*a bulbous plant with broad leaves, often used as a houseplant.

Which choice correctly states the order of events in the passage?

A) A character arrives home, is briefly observed by another character, and retires unhappily to his room.
B) A character arrives home, finds a letter that he has been expecting, and races to his room to read it.
C) A character sneaks into his house, then is stopped by another character with whom he has an unpleasant encounter.
D) A character who is waiting for a letter learns that it has not been sent; later, he narrowly avoids being seen by another character.

The primary purpose of the passage is to

A) describe the habits of a somewhat eccentric character.
B) illustrate the difficulties involved in being a writer.
C) foreshadow an ominous development in a character's life.
D) depict an unusual occurrence in a character's routine.

Official Guide/Khan Academy Big Picture Questions

Test 1

1	Summary
32	Purpose of a passage
33	Main point

Test 2

1	Summary
11	Purpose of a passage
29	Purpose of a passage
33	Main point

Test 3

1	Summary
14	Point of a paragraph
48	Purpose of a paragraph

Test 4

11	Summary of a paragraph
22	Purpose of a passage
41	Purpose of a passage
42	Purpose of a passage

Explanations: The Big Picture Exercises

1.1 C

To find the answer to this question, focus on the end of the passage – the place where the author describes the true significance of all the technology he's described. The point is that big data allows people to see the big picture, and to identify relationships between seemingly unrelated phenomena. Although there's no answer that says so in quite so many words, the correct answer must be related to that idea in some way. A) is very specific, referring only to "bytes." Likewise, D) focuses on science fiction, which is discussed in only a small part of the passage. Careful with B) – it's supported by the passage (lines 16-19), but it's not a main idea. C) is much more general and consistent with the overall focus of the passage – new technology has changed the way data is acquired (through bytes) and analyzed (to reveal hidden relationships).

1.2 D

The key to this question is to understand that the author uses the "tree" and "balloon" metaphors. He's essentially saying that until now, people have only been able to examine various events in isolation, but that with massive data sets, we will be able to understand the "big picture" in a way that was impossible before. That corresponds to D), making it the correct answer.

2.1 C

To make this question manageable, focus on the beginning and the end of the passage, using the answer choices to guide you. Each choice contains "attitude" words, so play positive/negative. The character's attitude at the beginning is positive, as indicated by the exclamation points in line 9 and the phrase *I joined the happy half.* A) can be eliminated because it begins with a negative word ("apprehensive"). Now consider the end. In line 76, the narrator states *I began to wonder at what I had written, for it was the opposite of playful,* indicating that

she is questioning herself (negative). Unfortunately, B), C), and D) all end with negative attitude words. (Note: this step is still important because you may be able to use it to identify the correct answer to other questions.) So think about the context: the narrator isn't "struggling to make friends," so eliminate B). Nor is she "disappointed by her teacher's reaction to her work" – in fact, we have no information about how her teacher reacted. That leaves C), which correctly corresponds to the fact that the narrator becomes nervous after listening to her classmates read their work.

2.2. B

If you were to answer this question very quickly in your own words, you might say something along the lines of "describe some stuff that happened to this girl at school." That might not get you to the answer, but it would get you thinking in the right direction. A) doesn't quite fit: the passage never really discusses the narrator's interaction with her peers. You might not be sure about B), so leave it. C) might seem attractive, but think carefully: although the narrator is very clear that she admires her teacher, we don't get any information about Miss Nelson's specific influence on the narrator's life. D) is incorrect because the only decision the narrator makes in the passage is to write her auto-biographical essay about a topic important to her, and the passage does not really describe the consequences of that decision beyond indicating that the narrator was nervous about reading it. So that leaves B), which is the only answer general enough to encompass the entire passage.

3.1 C

Don't be fooled by the long line reference. You only need the first sentence to answer the question. De Gouges' assertion that *Women have done more harm than good* directly corresponds to the idea that women have undermined their own cause. The answer is therefore C).

3.2 C

If you're written the main point ("women must demand rights/stop hurting each other"), you can probably jump right to C). Otherwise, focus on the beginning of the passage, where de Gouges makes her most impassioned pleas. Throughout the whole first section, she begs women to stand up and reclaim their rights. In line 23 (end of the introduction, often a key place), she directly calls upon women to "unite." Otherwise, A) is incorrect because de Gouges asserts that women must take their rights on their own, without waiting for men to help them (in lines 16-23, she implies that men will resist women's attempts at claiming their rights). B) is incorrect because de Gouges does mention that women can only gain a position in society by excelling in music or painting, but that is a secondary point (mentioned in one place) compared to her insistence that women must demand their rights. D) is incorrect because de Gouges implies that society as a whole, including women themselves, is responsible for women's inferior position.

4.1 A

Lines 31-35 ("One…rate") provide the exact information you need to answer this question. The passage describes Professor Seymour's experiment, which was designed to resolve the "big controversy" of whether dinosaurs were warm-blooded or cold-blooded.

4.2 D

Although it might seem tempting to start by looking at the answers, it is worthwhile to take a moment and state the answer in your own words before looking at the choices. If you're not sure, look at the end of the passage – a good part of the answer is right there in lines 64-68. What were Professor Seymour's findings? Basically, that the large size of the holes in the dinosaurs' thigh bones strongly suggests that dinosaurs were warm-blooded and active. That makes D) the answer. A) is incorrect because Professor Seymour used foramen size as an indicator of *metabolic rate*, not

growth rate. The use of foramen size was also a starting point of his experiment, not a finding. B) is incorrect because the focus was on the size of the holes in dinosaurs' thigh bones, not the density. Furthermore, the study "proved" nothing; it simply added weight to the theory that dinosaurs were warm-blooded. C) is incorrect because the passage says nothing about the relationship between foramen size and *behavior*.

5.1 B

Focus on the end of the passage. What does Acheson indicate? That the United States wants to find a way to peacefully coexist with the Soviet Union. So the answer must be relatively positive. A), C), and D) are all negative, leaving B) as the only option.

5.2 C

Note that this is essentially the same question as 5.1, just phrased a slightly different way. What is Acheson's point, as indicated by the conclusion? That the United States wants to find a way to peacefully coexist with the Soviet Union. That's another way of saying that he wants tensions between the United States and the Soviet Union to be reduced, making C) the answer. Careful with A). Although Acheson does criticize the Soviets' treatment of people living under its regime, that is not his primary point. There is no information to support B) in the passage, and D) goes far beyond the bounds of what can be inferred from the passage. The focus is specifically on US-Soviet relations, not international order in general.

5.3 D

The fact that you have a 17-line reference indicates that you do *not* need to read the whole thing. Focus on the beginning and the end. In this case, the beginning doesn't provide much information relevant to the question. The end, however, gives you more to work with. The statement *We can accept treaties of peace that would give reality to this pledge and to the interests of all in security* indicates that the US would be willing to work with the Soviet Union if the latter would keep its promises. That idea corresponds directly to D).

6.1 A

Start by focusing on the beginning of the passage and matching it to the beginning of one of the answer choices. What does the very beginning of the passage indicate? That Gordon is on his way home. That corresponds most directly to A) and B), so eliminate C) and D). If you have a pretty good grasp of the passage, there's a good chance you remember that Gordon did *not* receive a letter, eliminating B). Otherwise, focus on the end of the passage. It's a description of Gordon's room, and there's nothing about a letter, again pointing to A).

6.2 A

The passage basically recounts an episode from Gordon's life – he comes home, he tries unsuccessfully to avoid his nosy landlady, and then he goes to his extremely messy room. There's absolutely nothing to suggest that something bad is going to happen to him, nor is there any information that would suggest that the events of the passage are anything unusual in Gordon's life. That eliminates C) and D). B) might seem tempting to you, but the passage doesn't really focus on the fact that Gordon is a writer, or the difficulties of that career. The descriptions are more intended to illustrate that Gordon is a somewhat odd person (=somewhat eccentric), a purpose that corresponds to A).

5. Introduction to Supporting Evidence Questions

Before we go any further, it would strongly behoove us to take a look at one of the key features of the redesigned SAT: paired "supporting evidence" questions.

If you look through an SAT Reading section, you'll undoubtedly notice a number of questions that look like this:

2

Which choice provides the best evidence for
the answer to the previous question?

A) Lines 5-7 ("This…declaration")
B) Lines 24-25 ("It…answers")
C) Lines 44-46 ("Between…past")
D) Lines 46-48 ("Still…issued")

The first time most people look at this type of question, their reaction is something along the lines of "Whoa, that looks *really* complicated."

While these questions are necessarily easy (although some of them can be surprisingly straightforward), they are generally not nearly as complicated as they appear – provided that you're prepared and willing to work through them very systematically.

But first, the basics. Supporting evidence questions are primarily paired with two other question types: **literal comprehension** (questions that ask what the passage indicates), and **inference** (questions that ask what the passage implies). As we'll see a little later, these two question types are actually very similar; sometimes, they are nearly interchangeable. While not every single literal comprehension and inference question will be followed by a supporting evidence question, the vast majority will follow this pattern.

Next, the **most important** thing to understand is that paired "supporting evidence" questions are **not really two questions at all but rather a single question broken into two parts**. In fact, **the information needed to answer question #1 will always be**

contained among the answer choices to question #2. The answer to #1 is essentially a rephrased (more general) version of the correct lines cited in #2. "True" supporting evidence questions – ones that ask you to identify the lines that support an idea discussed in the passage – are much rarer, occurring no more than a few times per test.

Third, "supporting evidence" pairs come in two types. In the vast majority of cases, question #1 will not contain a line reference. From time to time, however, question #1 will contain a line reference. Unless you are an extraordinarily strong reader who can simply read and answer every question in order, the two types of questions can require different approaches.

As mentioned earlier, regardless of the order in which you read the passage and answer the questions, you should, **at some point before you answer any of the questions, look through all of them and mark the "supporting evidence" pairs. Furthermore, when a literal comprehension or inference question appears at the bottom of a page, you MUST remember to check the following page for a supporting evidence question.**

If you don't know any better, a likely reaction to these types of questions is as follows: you read the first question and, realizing that there's no line reference, go back to the passage and begin to hunt for the answer. You have a general idea of where it might be, but when you check that spot and don't see it, you start to get a little nervous.

You start skimming faster and faster, your eyes racing over the page, until finally you see something that seems to fit. You're not totally sure, but you've already spent a few minutes looking and can't afford to waste any more time, so you bubble the answer in.

When you see that the next question is a supporting evidence question, though, your stomach sinks. You think that the right answer should be somewhere around the spot where you found the answer to the previous question, but none of quotes are located there.

One by one, you plug in each of the answers. You get rid of two that seem pretty wrong, but the remaining answers both seem possible. You sit and stare at them, not sure how to choose. You still have half a section left, though, so you need to move on. Finally, you pick the one that feels a little more right and hope for the best.

This scenario is one you want to avoid at all costs. If it occurs multiple times, you'll already be exhausted halfway through the section – and you'll still have more than half the test to go.

The key to answering paired questions is to plug the answer choices to question #2 into question #1, then use that information to answer both questions simultaneously.

The line references in the answers to question #2 tell you that the answer to question #1 is either in or very close to one of the four sets of lines provided. Instead of randomly scanning the passage for the answer to question #1, wasting untold amount of time and energy in the process, using the answers to question #2 allows you to focus on four specific places – one of which **must** provide the correct answer

That is why marking question pairs is so important: if you don't know a "supporting evidence" question is coming, you can't use the second question to help you.

So, for example, a set of questions that looks like this...

1

The author indicates which of the following
about mixed-use developments

A)   They are a recent development.
B)   They reduce architectural variety.
C)   They create healthier neighborhoods.
D)   They increase dependence on automobiles.

2

Which choice provides the best evidence for
the answer to the previous question?

A)   Lines 5-7 ("This...complicated")
B)   Lines 24-25 ("It...recognized")
C)   Lines 44-46 ("Between...past")
D)   Lines 46-48 ("Still...issued")

...can be rewritten to look like this:

1

The author indicates which of the following
about mixed-use developments

A)   Lines 5-7 ("This...complicated")
B)   Lines 24-25 ("It...recognized")
C)   Lines 44-46 ("Between...past")
D)   Lines 46-48 ("Still...issued")

Then, one by one, read each line reference and determine whether it provides the answer to question #1. When you find the correct set of lines, you have the answers to both questions.

Remember that you do not necessarily need to check the line references in order. If you remember that the topic of question #1 was discussed in a particular part of the passage and see a line reference corresponding to that section, you might want to start with it.

Important: In some instances, it may be necessary to read before and/or after a line reference for context. If you read the lines in question and are unsure whether they answer the question, do not – I repeat, do not – eliminate the answer simply because you are confused. Read a sentence or two before to a sentence or two after to see where the lines fits within the argument.

In the next chapter, we're going to take a closer look at how to work through these questions.

6. Same Idea, Different Words: Literal Comprehension

Literal comprehension questions ask you to identify what a passage **indicates** or **states**. These most straightforward and common Reading questions essentially require you to understand ideas well enough to recognize accurate **summaries** of them. When you read my example of the typical, long-winded response I get when I ask someone to summarize the main point of a passage, you might have laughed, but the truth is that the ability to pick out the most important ideas in a passage and condense them into a concise, direct statement is a crucial skill both for the SAT and school.

Because this is the SAT, however, those summaries will rarely use the exact same wording as that found in the passage. **The test is whether you understand the ideas well enough to recognize when they're stated using different, often more general, language.** Correct answers thus require you to recognize **paraphrased** versions of ideas, ones that contain **synonyms for key words in the passage.** If you understand the idea, you'll probably be fine; if you're too focused on the details, you might miss it completely.

Most literal comprehension questions will be followed by supporting evidence questions and will not contain line references. In most cases, you should use the line references in the supporting evidence questions to narrow down the location of the answer to the literal comprehension questions.

Literal comprehension questions can be phrased in the following ways:

- The author's discussion of antibiotics indicates that…

- The author claims which of the following is a longstanding tradition?

- Which reaction does Watson have to the statement in lines x-y?

While these questions are asked in a very straightforward way, they can also be challenging. In addition to having to check multiple locations in the passage for the answer, you must sometimes navigate very challenging syntax and vocabulary. Furthermore, you must connect the specific words of the correct set of lines to the more abstract language of the answers.

We're going to start by looking at some examples of literal comprehension questions. The first one is a bit shorter than what you're likely to encounter on the SAT, but it's useful to illustrate a point.

Experimental scientists occupy themselves with observing and measuring the cosmos, finding out what stuff exists, no matter how strange that stuff may be. Theoretical physicists, on the other hand, are
5   not satisfied with observing the universe. They want to know why. They want to explain all the properties of the universe in terms of a few fundamental principles and parameters. These fundamental principles, in turn, lead to the "laws of nature," which govern the behavior
10 of all matter and energy.

1

This passage primarily discusses

A)   the influence of theoretical physicists on other kinds of scientists.
B)   the fundamental principles of theoretical physics.
C)   the differences between two groups of scientists.
D)   the conflict between experimental and theoretical physics.

The first thing that you probably notice when you look at the answer choices is that pretty much all of them contain bits and pieces of ideas mentioned in the passage, and therefore it might seem like any one of them could be right.

But the question is asking what the passage **primarily** discusses, i.e. the **topic** – not what words or phrases happen to appear in the passage. It's asking you to make a leap from the **specific words** to the overall **general idea**.

Let's look at how the passage is organized. That might not seem to have anything to do with this question, but in fact it's the simplest way to answer it.

First, the author describes what experimental scientists do.

Second, the author describes what theoretical physicists do. The phrase *on the other hand* (line 4) is key because it tells us that the author is setting up a **contrast** (=difference).

So the author is describing two groups of scientists and the differences between them. Which is exactly what C) says.

It doesn't matter that the word differences does not appear in the passage – the **idea** of difference is indicated through the transition *on the other hand*, and the correct answer conveys that idea. **Same idea, different words**.

Now let's look at a literal comprehension question paired with a supporting evidence question. We're going to start with a set in which question #1 contains a line reference since it's a bit more straightforward.

The following passage is adapted from Verlyn Klinkenborg, "Our Vanishing Night." © 2008 by the National Geographic Society.

If humans were truly at home under the light of the moon and stars, we would go in darkness happily, the midnight world as visible to us as it is to the vast number of nocturnal species on this planet. Instead,
5 we are diurnal creatures, with eyes adapted to living in the sun's light. This is a basic evolutionary fact, even though most of us don't think of ourselves as diurnal beings any more than we think of ourselves as primates or mammals or Earthlings.
10 Yet it's the only way to explain what we've done to the night: We've engineered it to receive us by filling it with light. This kind of engineering is no different than damming a river. Its benefits come with consequences—called light pollution—whose
15 effects scientists are only now beginning to study. Light pollution is largely the result of bad lighting design, which allows artificial light to shine outward and upward into the sky, where it's not wanted, instead of focusing it downward, where it is.
20 Ill-designed lighting washes out the darkness of night and radically alters the light levels—and rhythms – to which many forms of life, including ourselves, have adapted.
For most of human history, the phrase "light
25 pollution" would have made no sense. Imagine walking toward London on a moonlit night around 1800, when it was Earth's most populous city. Nearly a million people lived there, making do, as they always had, with candles and lanterns. Only a few houses
30 were lit by gas, and there would be no public gaslights for another seven years. From a few miles away, you would have been as likely to smell London as to see its dim glow. Now most of humanity lives under intersecting domes of light, of scattering rays from
35 overlit cities and suburbs, from light-flooded highways and factories. In most cities the sky looks as though it has been emptied of stars, leaving behind a vacant haze that mirrors our fear of the dark and resembles the urban glow of dystopian science
40 fiction. We've grown so used to this pervasive orange haze that the original glory of an unlit night—dark enough for the planet Venus to throw shadows on Earth—is wholly beyond our experience, beyond memory almost. We've lit up the night as if it were
45 an unoccupied country, when nothing could be further from the truth. Light is a powerful biological force, and on many species it acts as a magnet. Migrating at night, birds are apt to collide with brightly lit tall buildings; immature birds on their first journey suffer

50 disproportionately. And because a longer day allows for longer feeding, it can also affect migration schedules. The problem, of course, is that migration is a precisely timed biological behavior. Leaving early may mean arriving too soon for nesting
55 conditions to be right.
It was once thought that light pollution only affected astronomers, who need to see the night sky in all its glorious clarity. And, in fact, some of the earliest efforts to control light pollution were made
60 to protect the view from Lowell Observatory. Unlike astronomers, most of us may not need an undiminished view of the night sky for our work, but like most other creatures we do need darkness. Darkness is as essential to our internal clockwork
65 as light itself. The regular oscillation of waking and sleep in our lives is nothing less than a biological expression of the regular oscillation of light on Earth. So fundamental are these rhythms to our being that altering them is like altering gravity.
70 For the past century or so, we've been performing an open-ended experiment on ourselves, extending the day, shortening the night, and short-circuiting the human body's sensitive response to light. The consequences of our bright new world are more
75 readily perceptible in less adaptable creatures living in the peripheral glow of our prosperity. But for humans, too, light pollution may take a biological toll. In a very real sense, light pollution causes us to lose sight of our true place in the universe, to
80 forget the scale of our being, which is best measured against the dimensions of a deep night with the Milky Way—the edge of our galaxy— arching overhead.

1

Based on the passage, the "intersecting domes of light" (line 34) could best be described as

A) a welcome sight.
B) a recent development.
C) a source of entertainment.
D) an inspiring vision.

2

Which choice provides the best evidence for the answer to the previous question?

A) Lines 12-13 ("This...river")
B) Lines 24-25 ("For...sense")
C) Lines 44-46 ("We've...truth")
D) Lines 46-47 ("Light...magnet")

We're going to start by figuring out the significance of the phrase *intersecting domes of light*. Before we even look back, though, we can make some assumptions based on the main point. We know that the passage is about light pollution, and that the author's attitude toward that topic is **negative**. So if "intersecting domes of light" refers to artificial/polluting light, the answer is probably going to be negative as well. If, on the other hand, the "intersecting domes" are associated with natural light, the answer will probably be positive.

In order to figure that out, we need to go back to the passage and read that phrase in context.

> **Now most of humanity lives under intersecting domes of light, of scattering rays from overlit cities and suburbs, from light-flooded highways and factories.**

The very first word of the sentence provides a big clue – the author isn't a very big fan of what's going on with light these days, so right there you can make a very educated assumption that his attitude is negative. The word *overlit* is another clue. It implies something excessive and unnatural. But if you're not sure, keep reading:

> **In most cities the sky looks as though it has been emptied of stars, leaving behind a vacant haze that mirrors our fear of the dark and resembles the urban glow of dystopian science fiction.**

Now there's no ambiguity. *Vacant haze*, *fear of the dark*, and *dystopian science fiction* are all very clearly negative. So we know the answer will probably be negative – and it definitely won't be positive. A), C), and D) are all positive, so they can be eliminated. B) isn't negative, but it's also the only answer that isn't positive. By process of elimination, it must be correct. Remember that the right answer will sometimes be phrased more neutrally than the passage.

The answer to the first question also gives us a **very important clue** to the answer of the second question – the correct answer will have something to do with **time** and will directly support the idea that light pollution is something pretty recent. We can also assume that the correct set of lines will be relatively close to line 34, where the phrase "intersecting domes of light" appears, although we don't know whether the lines will come before or after.

Now that we have a reasonable idea of what we're looking for, we can check each answer.

A) This kind of engineering is no different than damming a river.

> No. This answer has nothing to do with time, and it has nothing to do with the "intersecting domes of light." It's also pretty far from the original reference.

B) For most of human history, the phrase "light pollution" would have made no sense.

> Yes, this makes sense. *History* is related to time. If "light pollution" made no sense for most of human history, then by definition it is a "recent development."

If you work through a question logically this way and find an answer that fits, you can simply pick it and move on; you always run the risk of second-guessing yourself if you keep going. But if you feel the overwhelming need to glance at the other answers, just to be on the safe side, you can always do so.

C) We've lit up the night as if it were an unoccupied country, when nothing could be further from the truth.

This answer has to do with light, but it does nothing to suggest that the intersecting domes are a "recent development."

D) Light is a powerful biological force, and on many species it acts as a magnet.

Same as C). Even though it mentions light, this answer is otherwise off-topic.

So that leaves us with B), which is correct.

Important: If you're a very strong reader able to keep track of things easily, you can start with the answers closest to the original line reference, but otherwise you should work in order. If, however, the lines that you used to determine the answer to the first question appear as an answer to the second, you can simply pick that answer and move on. It is also a good idea to mark the lines you use to answer the first question so that you don't lose track.

Next, we're going to try a question pair without a line reference in the first question.

Let's look at an example. We're going to start with something short.

For some activists, eating local foods is no longer just a pleasure—it is a moral obligation. Why? Because shipping foods over long distances results in the unnecessary emission of the greenhouse gases
5 that are warming the planet. This concern has given rise to the concept of "food miles," that is, the distance food travels from farm to plate. Activists particularly dislike air freighting foods because it uses relatively more energy than other forms of trans-
10 portation. Food miles are supposed to be a simple way to gauge food's impact on climate change.
    But food miles advocates fail to grasp the simple idea that food should be grown where it is most economically advantageous to do so. Relevant
15 advantages consist of various combinations of soil, climate, labor, and other factors. It is possible to grow bananas in Iceland, but Costa Rica really has the better climate for that activity. Transporting food is just one relatively small cost of providing modern consumers
20 with their daily bread, meat, cheese, and veggies. Concentrating agricultural production in the most favorable regions is the best way to minimize human impacts on the environment.

1

The author indicates that food should be grown in regions where

A) crops can be produced in a cost-effective manner.
B) temperatures remain warm throughout the year.
C) many crops varieties can be grown at the same time.
D) agriculture plays a central role in the economy.

2

Which choice provides the best evidence for the answer to the previous question?

A) Lines 3-5 ("Because…planet")
B) Lines 7-10 ("Activists…transportation")
C) Lines 12-14 ("But…so")
D) Lines 18-20 ("Transporting…veggies")

The first thing we're going to do is plug the second set of answer choices into the first question so that we get this:

1

The author indicates that food should be grown in regions where

A) Lines 3-5 ("Because...planet")
B) Lines 7-10 ("Activists...transportation")
C) Lines 12-14 ("But...so")
D) Lines 18-20 ("Transporting...veggies")

Next, we're going to plug in each set of lines and see whether it answers #1:

A) Because shipping foods over long distances results in the unnecessary emission of the greenhouse gases that are warming the planet.

That might seem generally related to the question in #1, but it doesn't directly answer it. It tells us that pollution is the downside of shipping food, but it says nothing about where food *should* be grown, and any inference we make is going to be too much of a stretch.

B) Activists particularly dislike air freighting foods because it uses relatively more energy than other forms of transportation.

This is completely off topic. Again, it only talks about the downside of transporting food; it says nothing about where food should be grown.

C) But food miles advocates fail to grasp the simple idea that food should be grown where it is most economically advantageous to do so.

Bingo! This gives us exactly what we're looking for. The next step is to back up and find which answer in the previous question rephrases this sentence.

Even if you're not 100% sure what *economically advantageous* means, you can probably figure it out. *Economically* means "having to do with the economy," or more generally, with money, and *advantageous* means "providing an advantage." So the phrase must mean something like "good for the economy." That's the **idea** that the correct answer choice must contain.

When you look at the answer choices, you're going to look for words related to money or the economy. Right there, you're down to A), which contains the word *cost-effective*, and D), which contains the word *economy*. A) matches the general idea – saying that something is produced in a "cost-effective manner" is essentially the same as saying it's produced in an "economically advantageous" one. D), however, is too much of a stretch. The passage says nothing about the superiority of growing crops in places where agriculture plays a *central* role in the economy. It could be true, but we don't really have enough information. So it's A).

127

Other Approaches

If you're a very strong reader and/or excel at playing process of elimination, you'll probably find that you don't always need (or want) to look back at the passage for the first question in a supporting evidence pair. You might also find the strategy discussed above too complicated, preferring to look back at the passage and then answer the questions in order.

If you either remember the answer to the first question or are able to figure it out logically by using the main point or process of elimination, you may find yourself caught off guard – and perhaps a bit irritated – by the supporting evidence question. You understand the gist of the passage and just "know" what the right answer is. Why should you have to go and find evidence for something that seems so obvious? Besides, you're not sure whether you can put into words what you understand instinctively.

The good news, however, is that you're not responsible for putting anything into words yourself; the line references do that part for you. In fact, you pretty much have the answer. You already know what the point is – you just have to find the answer that supports it. All you have to do is put two and two together. If you're a strong enough reader to consistently figure out the point on your own in the first place, you're probably a strong enough reader to figure out what sort of information is consistent with that point.

So now, we're going to work through the two questions in order.

For some activists, eating local foods is no
longer just a pleasure—it is a moral obligation. Why?
Because shipping foods over long distances results
in the unnecessary emission of the greenhouse gases
5 that are warming the planet. This concern has
given rise to the concept of "food miles," that is,
the distance food travels from farm to plate. Activists
particularly dislike air freighting foods because it uses
relatively more energy than other forms of trans-
10 portation. Food miles are supposed to be a simple way
to gauge food's impact on climate change.
  But food miles advocates fail to grasp the simple
idea that food should be grown where it is most
economically advantageous to do so. Relevant
15 advantages consist of various combinations of soil,
climate, labor, and other factors. It is possible to grow
bananas in Iceland, but Costa Rica really has the better
climate for that activity. Transporting food is just one
relatively small cost of providing modern consumers
20 with their daily bread, meat, cheese, and veggies.
Concentrating agricultural production in the most
favorable regions is the best way to minimize human
impacts on the environment.

1

The author indicates that food should be grown in regions where

A) crops can be produced in a cost-effective manner.
B) temperatures remain warm throughout the year.
C) many crops varieties can be grown at the same time.
D) agriculture plays a central role in the economy.

2

Which choice provides the best evidence for the answer to the previous question?

A) Lines 3-5 ("Because…planet")
B) Lines 7-10 ("Activists…transportation")
C) Lines 11-14 ("But…so")
D) Lines 18-20 ("Transporting…veggies")

When you work this way, you should start by identifying/underlining the key word or phrase that indicates the specific focus of the question. In this case, the key phrase is *food should be grown*.

Then, you should go back to the passage to skim for *food should be grown* or a similar phrase, **remembering to drag your index finger down the page as you skim and to pay close attention to the first and last sentence of each paragraph**. Even in a shorter passage, important information is most likely to be located in those key areas.

As you'll see, the information you need is located in the topic sentence of the second paragraph. (*But food miles advocates fail to grasp the simple idea that food should be grown where it is most economically advantageous to do so.*) If you identify that sentence on your own and use it to answer the first question, you can also see that those lines appear as an answer to the second question. You can therefore jump to C) for the supporting evidence question.

To reiterate: if you choose to answer paired "supporting evidence" questions this way, you should quickly bracket off the lines you used to determine the answer to question #1 because you may be able to match them to an answer in question #2. If they're there, you don't need to go back to the passage.

The question we just looked at was based on a detail that most people would be unlikely to remember simply from reading the passage. Although the question itself wasn't outrageously complicated, there was essentially no way to answer both questions without going back to the passage and checking each set of lines.

Sometimes, however, you may be able to use a big picture understanding of the passage to identify the answer to the first question quickly. The simplest way to answer the supporting evidence question is then to check each set of lines against the idea you know it must contain.

On the next page, we're going to look at an example.

Citrus greening, the plague that could wipe out Florida's $9 billion orange industry, begins with the touch of a jumpy brown bug on a sun-kissed leaf. From there, the bacterial disease incubates in the
5 tree's roots, then moves back up the trunk in full force, causing nutrient flows to seize up. Leaves turn yellow, and the oranges, deprived of sugars from the leaves, remain green, sour, and hard. Many fall before harvest, brown necrotic flesh ringing failed stems.
10 For the past decade, Florida's oranges have been literally starving. Since it first appeared in 2005, citrus greening, also known by its Chinese name, *huanglongbing*, has swept across Florida's groves like a flood. With no hills to block it, the Asian citrus
15 psyllid—the invasive aphid relative that carries the disease—has infected nearly every orchard in the state. By one estimate, 80 percent of Florida's citrus trees are infected and declining.
The disease has spread beyond Florida to nearly
20 every orange-growing region in the United States. Despite many generations of breeding by humanity, no citrus plant resists greening; it afflicts lemons, grapefruits, and other citrus species as well. Once a tree is infected, it will die. Yet in a few select Floridian
25 orchards, there are now trees that, thanks to innovative technology, can fight the greening tide.
The pressure to find solutions keeps growing. Even without disease, the orange industry is under stress. It's losing land to housing developments; it's losing
30 customers to the spreading notion that orange juice is a sugary, not healthy, drink.
The citrus industry, slow to prevent the greening disease, has partially redirected its advertising budget and invested heavily in research—reportedly $90 million so
35 far. Southern Gardens Citrus, one of the largest growers, supports Mirkov's work. The federal government, too, has contributed, with this year's farm bill directing $125 million toward the fight against citrus greening.

1

According the writer's description, citrus greening could best be described as

A) mysterious.
B) benign.
C) ancient.
D) devastating.

2

Which choice provides the best evidence for the answer to the previous question?

A) Lines 17-18 ("By...declining")
B) Lines 24-26 ("Yet...tide")
C) Lines 29-31 ("It's...drink")
D) Lines 32-35 ("The citrus...far")

Note that the first question could actually be considered a **vocabulary question in reverse**: instead of recognizing what a word in the passage means, you must use the wording of the passage to identify the correct definition from among the answer choices.

Although the question does not provide a line reference, there is no need to go searching through the passage for the answer. If you're gotten the gist of the passage, you can pretty much answer it on your own. What's the point? CG = BAD (citrus greening is really bad). Assuming you know the definition of *devastating*, that gives you D) right there.

Note that it's irrelevant whether you know the definitions of the other words (especially *benign*, which will be unfamiliar to many test-takers) as long as you do know what *devastating* means.

Now all you have to do is find the lines that say as much. Since a good part of the passage is devoted to making that point, you probably shouldn't try to figure out the lines on your own – there are just too many places where they could be. Even so, it shouldn't be too hard to work from the answers provided. You need not spend more than a few seconds on each answer as long as you have a clear idea of what you're looking for.

A) By one estimate, 80 percent of Florida's citrus trees are infected and declining.

Yes, this is consistent with the idea that citrus greening is "devastating." 80 percent is an enormous loss.

Since this answer fits, you can stop reading right there. If you really wanted to make sure, you could check the remaining answers, but especially in this case, it's not necessary to do so.

Why? Think about how the passage is organized. Everything up until line 24 is basically focused on emphasizing how awful the effects of citrus greening are. After line 24, the focus switches to stopping the disease – so logically, the correct set of lines must be located before line 24. A) is the only option with lines that meet that criterion, so it must be correct.

On the next page, we're going to come back to our long passage.

The following passage is adapted from Verlyn Klinkenborg, "Our Vanishing Night." © 2008 by the National Geographic Society.

If humans were truly at home under the light of the moon and stars, we would go in darkness happily, the midnight world as visible to us as it is to the vast number of nocturnal species on this planet. Instead,
5 we are diurnal creatures, with eyes adapted to living in the sun's light. This is a basic evolutionary fact, even though most of us don't think of ourselves as diurnal beings any more than we think of ourselves as primates or mammals or Earthlings.
10 Yet it's the only way to explain what we've done to the night: We've engineered it to receive us by filling it with light. This kind of engineering is no different than damming a river. Its benefits come with consequences—called light pollution—whose
15 effects scientists are only now beginning to study. Light pollution is largely the result of bad lighting design, which allows artificial light to shine outward and upward into the sky, where it's not wanted, instead of focusing it downward, where it is.
20 Ill-designed lighting washes out the darkness of night and radically alters the light levels—and rhythms – to which many forms of life, including ourselves, have adapted.
For most of human history, the phrase "light
25 pollution" would have made no sense. Imagine walking toward London on a moonlit night around 1800, when it was Earth's most populous city. Nearly a million people lived there, making do, as they always had, with candles and lanterns. Only a few houses
30 were lit by gas, and there would be no public gaslights for another seven years. From a few miles away, you would have been as likely to smell London as to see its dim glow. Now most of humanity lives under intersecting domes of light, of scattering rays from
35 overlit cities and suburbs, from light-flooded highways and factories. In most cities the sky looks as though it has been emptied of stars, leaving behind a vacant haze that mirrors our fear of the dark and resembles the urban glow of dystopian science
40 fiction. We've grown so used to this pervasive orange haze that the original glory of an unlit night—dark enough for the planet Venus to throw shadows on Earth—is wholly beyond our experience, beyond memory almost. We've lit up the night as if it were
45 an unoccupied country, when nothing could be further from the truth. Light is a powerful biological force, and on many species it acts as a magnet. Migrating at night, birds are apt to collide with brightly lit tall buildings; immature birds on their first journey suffer

50 disproportionately. And because a longer day allows for longer feeding, it can also affect migration schedules. The problem, of course, is that migration is a precisely timed biological behavior. Leaving early may mean arriving too soon for nesting
55 conditions to be right.
It was once thought that light pollution only affected astronomers, who need to see the night sky in all its glorious clarity. And, in fact, some of the earliest efforts to control light pollution were made
60 to protect the view from Lowell Observatory. Unlike astronomers, most of us may not need an undiminished view of the night sky for our work, but like most other creatures we do need darkness. Darkness is as essential to our internal clockwork
65 as light itself. The regular oscillation of waking and sleep in our lives is nothing less than a biological expression of the regular oscillation of light on Earth. So fundamental are these rhythms to our being that altering them is like altering gravity.
70 For the past century or so, we've been performing an open-ended experiment on ourselves, extending the day, shortening the night, and short-circuiting the human body's sensitive response to light. The consequences of our bright new world are more
75 readily perceptible in less adaptable creatures living in the peripheral glow of our prosperity. But for humans, too, light pollution may take a biological toll. In a very real sense, light pollution causes us to lose sight of our true place in the universe, to
80 forget the scale of our being, which is best measured against the dimensions of a deep night with the Milky Way—the edge of our galaxy— arching overhead.

1

The author indicates that the alternation between periods of sleep and periods of waking

A) is an essential characteristic of life on Earth.
B) has remained unaffected by artificial light.
C) is less regular in people than it is in animals.
D) cannot be changed in any way.

2

Which choice provides the best evidence for the answer to the previous question?

A) Lines 33-36 ("Now…factories")
B) Lines 52-53 ("The problem…behavior")
C) Lines 68-69 ("So…gravity")
D) Lines 78-80 ("In…being")

In this case, we're going to start by combining the two questions into a single question. There's so much information to wade through that this is the most efficient way to work.

1

The author indicates that the alternation of sleeping and waking cycles in people

A) Lines 33-36 ("Now…factories")
B) Lines 52-53 ("The problem…behavior")
C) Lines 68-69 ("So…gravity")
D) Lines 78-80 ("In…being")

Now we have something concrete to work with. Instead of just randomly skimming the passage looking for bits that seem like they might be relevant, we've narrowed our focus to four places where the answer could potentially be located – one of which **must** be correct.

The next step is to check each answer out. We're looking for information related to **sleeping and waking**, so the correct answer will be related to those key words.

If you're working on your own and feel it helps you, you can bracket off each line reference in the text, either before you start working through the answers or as you come to each one. Just remember that you may need to skim the surrounding lines for context.

A) Now most of humanity lives under intersecting domes of light, of scattering rays from overlit cities and suburbs, from light-flooded highways and factories.

No. This has absolutely nothing to do with sleeping and waking cycles. It's off-topic.

B) The problem, of course, is that migration is a precisely timed biological behavior.

Again, off-topic. The word *migration* is also a big clue that this answer isn't correct. Migration is usually associated with animals, and the question asks about people. If you want to read the surrounding lines to make sure, you'll see that this section is about birds. So B) is out.

C) So fundamental are these rhythms to our being that altering them is like altering gravity.

If you read this sentence on its own, it might not make any sense because you don't know what "these rhythms" refers to (note the abstract noun *rhythms*!). You must therefore back up to the previous sentence. Sure enough, "waking" and "sleep" are mentioned in lines 65-66. Even if you're confused by the phrasing, you can at least know that this answer generally fits with what the question is asking about.

D) In a very real sense, light pollution causes us to lose sight of our true place in the universe, to forget the scale of our being

That's a lovely, poetic thought, but it's unrelated to waking and sleeping. So that leaves C), which is correct. It is the only answer that directly relates to the key words in the question.

Now we're going to backtrack and use the answer to this question to answer the previous question.

1

The author indicates that the alternation between periods of sleep and periods of waking

A) is an essential feature of life on Earth.
B) has remained unaffected by artificial light.
C) is less regular in people than it is in most animals.
D) cannot be altered in any way.

What do lines 68-69 state? That waking and sleeping are *fundamental* to our being – that is, they are **essential features** of being alive. Which is pretty much what A) says.

If that's too much of a leap to make on your own, you can also play process of elimination.

A) See above. If you're not sure, leave it.

B) is exactly the opposite of the main point of the passage – the author's primary concern is the effect that normal sleep rhythms have been (negatively) affected by artificial light.

C) is off-topic. Not only does this particular section of the passage not compare people to most animals but it says nothing about animals whatsoever.

D) The extreme language (*in any way*) as well as the repetition of a word from the passage (*altered*) are immediate tip-offs that this answer probably isn't correct. That said, you need to be careful. The author does state that changing sleeping/waking rhythms is "like altering gravity," but the comparison is not meant literally; it's only intended to convey how central and natural the activities of sleeping and waking are to living beings. The author's whole point, however, is that sleep cycles *can* be – and are being – altered.

Now let's consider what would happen if you decided to answer the questions in order. If you went back to the passage and skimmed through until you found the answer to the first question, you'd pretty much be set for the second question as well. The only danger in a passage this long is that the information you need doesn't appear until close to the end of the passage. If you begin to panic halfway through because you haven't found the answer yet, you can easily fall into a loop of skimming randomly and guessing.

Let's say, though, that you arrived at A) for the first question by process of elimination. You haven't bothered to go back to the passage, but you remember it well enough to be confident that A) is correct. Your job now is to figure out why.

Before you do anything, it's a good idea to take a moment and reiterate for yourself what the point is and what sort of information you're looking for. If you've just been playing process of elimination, it's very easy to be a little fuzzy on that part and then miss something staring you right in the face. In this case, you might just say something like "waking/sleeping = really important f/living things." The correct answer must be consistent with that idea.

At this point, you can simply plug in each answer in turn, looking for an answer that has something to do with sleeping and week. If you go this route, you must make sure to not to eliminate any answer before you've thought it through, and to read before/ after the line references that require context to be understood. You also need to keep the key phrase in mind. If it helps, underline it in the question to focus yourself.

Using Line References to Make Educated Guesses

If you want to get really ambitious, you can also sometimes (but by no means always) use a word/words in an answer choice to identify the answers most likely to be correct. This strategy does require close attention to detail as well as some very logical thinking, but it can also get you to the answer much more quickly. For example, let's take another look at our supporting evidence question.

2

Which choice provides the best evidence for the answer to the previous question?

A) Lines 33-36 ("Now…factories")
B) Lines 52-53 ("The problem…behavior")
C) Lines 68-69 ("So…gravity")
D) Lines 78-80 ("In…being")

Remember that the correct answer to the previous question referred to an *essential feature of life on earth*. If you start with that information and very, very carefully consider the words from the beginnings and ends of line references that appear in the answer choices, you can make an educated guess about the correct answer.

Look for an answer that includes a word consistent with the idea of "something essential to life on Earth." Can you spot it?

It's *gravity*, in choice C). What could be more fundamental to life on Earth than gravity? That one word is enough to suggest that C) is worth serious consideration and that you should check it **first** (not that you should just choose it and move on). When you go back and plug it in, you can see that it does in fact answer the question. As discussed earlier, the lines occur in the context of a discussion about the centrality of sleeping and waking to human existence.

To reiterate, though: you should **never** choose an answer this way without going back to the passage and checking that it does actually make sense in context. This strategy is useful insofar as it can get you to the correct answer *faster*; it is not a substitute for doing work. Leaping to conclusions can get you into a lot of trouble. Better not to risk it.

Literal Comprehension Exercises

1. The world is complex and interconnected, and the evolution of our communications system from a broadcast model to a networked one has added a new dimension to the mix. The Internet has made us all less
5 dependent on professional journalists and editors for information about the wider world, allowing us to seek out information directly via online search or to receive it from friends through social media. But this enhanced convenience comes with a considerable risk: that we
10 will be exposed to what we want to know at the expense of what we need to know. While we can find virtual communities that correspond to our every curiosity, there's little pushing us beyond our comfort zones to or into the unknown, even if the unknown may have
15 serious implications for our lives. There are things we should probably know more about—like political and religious conflicts in Russia or basic geography. But even if we knew more than we do, there's no guarantee that the knowledge gained would prompt us to act in a
20 particularly admirable fashion.

1

The passage indicates that internet users tend to seek information in a manner that is

A) impulsive.
B) unadventurous.
C) creative.
D) reckless.

2

Which lines best support the answer to the previous question?

A) Lines 1-4 ("The world…mix")
B) Lines 4-6 ("The Internet…world")
C) Line 13 ("there's…zones")
D) Lines 17-20 ("But…fashion")

2. Chimps do it, birds do it, even you and I do it. Once you see someone yawn, you are compelled to do the same. Now it seems that wolves can be added to the list of animals known to spread yawns like a
5 contagion.
Among humans, even thinking about yawning can trigger the reflex, leading some to suspect that catching a yawn is linked to our ability to empathize with other humans. For instance, contagious yawning activates the
10 same parts of the brain that govern empathy and social know-how. And some studies have shown that humans with more fine-tuned social skills are more likely to catch a yawn.
Similarly, chimpanzees, baboons and bonobos
15 often yawn when they see other members of their species yawning. Chimps (Pan troglodytes) can catch yawns from humans, even virtual ones. At least in primates, contagious yawning seems to require an emotional connection and may function as a demonstration of
20 empathy. Beyond primates, though, the trends are less clear-cut. One study found evidence of contagious yawning in birds but didn't connect it to empathy. A 2008 study showed that dogs (Canis lupus familiaris) could catch yawns from humans, and another showed
25 that dogs were more likely to catch the yawn of a familiar human rather than a stranger. But efforts to see if dogs catch yawns from each other and to replicate the results have so far had no luck.

1

The passage indicates that the people most likely to catch yawns are

A) detail oriented.
B) easily persuaded.
C) attuned to others.
D) chronically fatigued.

2

Which lines best support the answer to the previous question?

A) Lines 3-5 ("Now…contagion")
B) Lines 9-11 ("For…know-how")
C) Lines 21-22 ("One…empathy")
D) Lines 26-28 ("But…luck")

The passage indicates that the connection between empathy and yawning in birds and dogs, in comparison to humans, is

A) more uncertain.
B) less uncertain.
C) impossible to establish.
D) a controversial topic.

Which lines best support the answer to the previous question?

A) Lines 3-4 ("Now…yawns")
B) Lines 14-16 ("Similarly…yawning")
C) Lines 20-21 ("Beyond…clear-cut")
D) Lines 23-26 ("A 2008…stranger")

3. The following passage is adapted from George Orwell, "Keep the Aspidastra Flying," first published in 1936. Gordon, the protagonist, is a poet.

Gordon walked homeward against the rattling wind, which blew his hair backward and gave him more of a 'good' forehead than ever. His manner conveyed to the passers-by – at least, he hoped it did—that if he wore
5 no overcoat it was from pure caprice.

Willowbed Road, NW, was dingy and depressing, although it contrived to keep up a kind of mingy decency. There was even a dentist's brass plate on one of the houses. In quite two-thirds of them, amid the
10 lace curtains of the parlor window, there was a green card with 'Apartments' on it in silver lettering, above the peeping foliage of an aspidistra.*

Mrs. Wisbeach, Gordon's landlady, specialized in 'single gentlemen'. Bed-sitting-rooms, with gaslight laid
15 on and find your own heating, baths extra (there was a geyser), and meals in the tomb-dark dining-room with the phalanx of clotted sauce-bottles in the middle of the table. Gordon, who came home for his midday dinner, paid twenty-seven and six a week.

20 The gaslight shone yellow through the frosted transom above the door of Number 31. Gordon took out his key and fished about in the keyhole – in that kind of house the key never quite fits the lock. The darkish little hallway – in reality it was only a passage – smelt of
25 dishwater and cabbage. Gordon glanced at the japanned tray on the hall-stand. No letters, of course. He had told himself not to hope for a letter, and nevertheless had continued to hope. A stale feeling, not quite a pain, settled upon his breast. Rosemary might have written!
30 It was four days now since she had written. Moreover, he had sent out to magazines and had not yet had returned to him. The one thing that made the evening bearable was to find a letter waiting for him when he got home. But he received very few letters – four or five in a week
35 at the very most.

On the left of the hall was the never-used parlor, then came the staircase, and beyond that the passage ran down to the kitchen and to the unapproachable lair inhabited by Mrs. Wisbeach herself. As Gordon came in,
40 the door at the end of the passage opened a foot or so. Mrs. Wisbeach's face emerged, inspected him briefly but suspiciously, and disappeared again. It was quite impossible to get in or out of the house, at any time before eleven at night, without being scrutinized in this
45 manner. Just what Mrs. Wisbeach suspected you of it

was hard to say. She was one of those malignant respectable women who keep lodging-houses. Age about forty-five, stout but active, with a pink, fine-featured, horribly observant face, beautifully grey hair,
50 and a permanent grievance.

In the familiar darkness of his room, Gordon felt for the gas-jet and lighted it. The room was medium-sized, not big enough to be curtained into two, but too big to be sufficiently warmed by one defective oil lamp. It had
55 the sort of furniture you expect in a top floor back. White-quilted single-bed; brown lino floor-covering; wash-hand-stand with jug and basin of that cheap white ware which you can never see without thinking of chamberpots. On the window-sill there was a sickly
60 aspidistra in a green-glazed pot.

Up against this, under the window, there was a kitchen table with an inkstained green cloth. This was Gordon's 'writing' table. It was only after a bitter struggle that he had induced Mrs. Wisbeach to give him
65 a kitchen table instead of the bamboo 'occasional' table – a mere stand for the aspidistra – which she considered proper for a top floor back. And even now there was endless nagging because Gordon would never allow his table to be 'tidied up'. The table was in a
70 permanent mess. It was almost covered with a muddle of papers, perhaps two hundred sheets, grimy and dog-eared, and all written on and crossed out and written on again – a sort of sordid labyrinth of papers to which only Gordon possessed the key. There was a film of
75 dust over everything. Except for a few books on the mantelpiece, this table, with its mess of papers, was the sole mark Gordon's personality had left on the room.

*a bulbous plant with broad leaves, often used as a houseplant.

1

Based on the passage, "that kind of house" (line 22) is one that is

A) large and rambling.
B) gloomy and rundown.
C) tidy and cheerful.
D) utterly neglected.

2

Which lines best support the answer to the previous question?

A) Lines 6-8 ("Willowbed...decency")
B) Lines 9-12 ("In...apidastra")
C) Lines 18-19 ("Gordon...week")
D) Lines 26-28 ("He...hope")

3

The passage indicates that the encounter between Gordon and Mrs. Wisbeach was

A) inevitable.
B) drawn out.
C) cordial.
D) unexpected.

4

Which lines best support the answer to the previous question?

A) Lines 32-33 ("The one...home")
B) Lines 36-39 ("On...herself")
C) Lines 42-45 ("It was...manner")
D) Lines 46-50 ("She...grievance")

5

The narrator indicates that the papers in Gordon's room were

A) an unrecognized masterpiece.
B) hidden from view.
C) a source of embarrassment.
D) comprehensible to Gordon alone.

6

Which lines best support the answer to the previous question?

A) Lines 52-55 ("The room...back")
B) Lines 63-65 ("It was...table")
C) Lines 73-74 ("a sort...key")
D) Lines 75-77 ("Except...room")

4. The following passage is adapted from Wiebke Brauer, "The Miracle of Space," © 2014 by *Smart Magazine*.

Imagine a world where you share the available space with others: without signs, sidewalks, or bicycle lanes. A vision otherwise known as shared space –
and one that becomes more and more relevant with
5 the crowding of our cities. While this might sound like urban science fiction or, possibly, impending chaos mixed with survival of the fittest, this particular concept is the declared dream of many traffic planners.
Shared space means streets freed of signs and
10 signals; streets solely governed by right of way, leaving road users to their own devices. In order to restructure public space, it removes all superfluous interventions and contradictory guidelines. Many countries are currently in the process of installing – or at least
15 discussing – such 'lawless' areas: Germany and the Netherlands, Denmark and the UK, Switzerland and the USA, but also Australia and New Zealand.
One could argue that shared spaces have been around for a long time, simply under different terms
20 and titles. Back in the 1970s, for example, residents enjoyed mixed traffic areas, traffic calming, and play streets. And yet, these were not quite the same: Shared space involves a new and radical push for equal rights of all road users, pedestrian and otherwise. And
25 while it was British urban designer Ben Hamilton-Baillie who coined the actual term, the concept itself was developed in the mid-1990s under former Dutch traffic manager Hans Monderman. Shortly before his death in 2006, Monderman explained the basic tenets
30 of shared space as such: "The problem with traffic engineers is that when there's a problem with a road, they always try to add something. To my mind, it's much better to remove things."
Indeed, studies have shown that in many places –
35 where signs and traffic lights have been removed and where each and every one is responsible for their own actions in ungoverned space – the rate of accidents goes down. The reason: the traditional strict separation between cars, cyclists, and pedestrians encourages
40 clashes at crossings. And although shared space requires cars to lower their speed, it also cuts down on journey times since it encourages a continuous flow of traffic instead of bringing it to a halt through traffic signals.
45 Monderman was utterly convinced that shared space would work anywhere in the world because, underneath it all, people are basically the same, despite any cultural differences. In an interview, he stated that "emotions and issues are the same everywhere. You should be able

50 to read a street like a book. If you insist on constantly guiding people and treating them like idiots, you shouldn't be surprised if they act like idiots after a while."
At the same time, the threat of looming idiocy
55 is not the most pressing reason for a future traffic management rethink. Recent city planning, for example, has evolved along the same lines around the world: think highways and flyovers dissecting the city's natural fabric, dedicated pedestrian zones, and
60 large shopping malls. Clear-cut boundaries between driving, work, life, and shopping are emphasized by a thicket of signs. The result: ultimate, well-ordered bleakness. At night, you might find yourself in an empty, soulless pedestrian zone. A lot of the time,
65 urbanization simply translates as uniformity.
In recent years, however, city and traffic planners have decided to tackle this issue with "road space attractiveness" measures to breathe new spirit into lifeless satellite towns. Their goal: a new definition
70 of space and mobility against the background that the notion of "might is right" – and only if those in power stick to the rules – is more than outdated. The unregulated and unorthodox approach of shared space makes it obvious to each and every individual
75 that this concept requires cooperation, that sharing is the new having.
Critics of Monderman and Hamilton-Baillie have voiced that no rules implies the inevitable return of "might is right." Yet who says that chaos
80 reigns in the absence of order? That's a questionable statement. Shared space certainly requires a new mindset and we can't expect a swift shift away from traditional traffic planning – bigger, further, faster.
But the vision of no more set traffic cycles, fewer
85 linear and predefined patterns, of freely flowing and intermingling participants in an open and boundless space, is equally unfettered and fascinating. A vision in the spirit of Pericles who wrote around 450 BC that "you need freedom for happiness and courage
90 for freedom."

1

The passage indicates that in areas where traffic signals are removed, traveling becomes

A) safer and less time consuming.
B) safer and more time consuming.
C) more dangerous and less time consuming.
D) more dangerous and more time consuming.

2

According to the author, recent city planning has primarily resulted in

A) isolated neighborhoods.
B) a lack of variety.
C) stylistic incoherence.
D) urban revitalization.

3

Which lines best support the answer to the previous question?

A) Lines 13-15 ("Many...areas")
B) Lines 30-32 ("The problem...things")
C) Lines 48-49 ("emotions ...everywhere")
D) Lines 64-65 ("A...uniformity")

5. This passage is adapted from a 1950 speech by Dean Acheson, who served as Secretary of State from 1949 to 1953 and strongly influenced United States foreign policy during the Cold War.

However much we may sympathize with the Soviet citizens who for reasons bedded deep in history are obliged to live under it, we are not attempting to change the governmental or social structure of the Soviet

5   Union. The Soviet regime, however, has devoted a major portion of its energies and resources to the attempt to impose its system on other peoples. In this attempt it has shown itself prepared to resort to any method or stratagem, including subversion, threats, and even

10 military force.

Therefore, if the two systems are to coexist, some acceptable means must be found to free the world from the destructive tensions and anxieties of which it has been the victim in these past years and the continuance

15 of which can hardly be in the interests of any people.

I wish, therefore, to speak to you about those points of greatest difference which must be identified and sooner or later reconciled if the two systems are to live together, if not with mutual respect, at least in

20 reasonable security.

It is now nearly five years since the end of hostilities, and the victorious Allies have been unable to define the terms of peace with the defeated countries. This is a grave, a deeply disturbing fact. For our part, we do not

25 intend nor wish, in fact we do not know how, to create satellites. Nor can we accept a settlement which would make Germany, Japan, or liberated Austria satellites of the Soviet Union. The experience in Hungary, Rumania, and Bulgaria has been one of bitter disappointment and

30 shocking betrayal of the solemn pledges by the wartime Allies. The Soviet leaders joined in the pledge at Tehran that they looked forward "with confidence to the day when all peoples of the world may live free lives, untouched by tyranny, and according to their varying

35 desires and their own consciences." We can accept treaties of peace which would give reality to this pledge and to the interests of all in security

With regard to the whole group of countries which we are accustomed to thinking of as the satellite area, the

40 Soviet leaders could withdraw their military and police force and refrain from using the shadow of that force to keep in power persons or regimes which do not command the confidence of the respective peoples, freely expressed through orderly representative processes.

45 In this connection, we do not insist that these governments have any particular political or social complexion. What concerns us is that they should be truly independent national regimes, with a will of their own and with a decent foundation in popular feeling.

50 The Soviet leaders could cooperate with us to the end that the official representatives of all countries are treated everywhere with decency and respect and that an atmosphere is created in which these representatives could function in a normal and helpful manner,

55 conforming to the accepted codes of diplomacy.

These are some of the things which we feel that Soviet leaders could do which would permit the rational and peaceful development of the coexistence of their system and ours. They are not things that go to

60 the depths of the moral conflict. They have been formulated by us, not as moralists but as servants of government, anxious to get on with the practical problems that lie before us and to get on with them in a manner consistent with mankind's deep longing for a

65 respite from fear and uncertainty.

Nor have they been formulated as a one-sided bargain. A will to achieve binding, peaceful settlements would be required of all participants. All would have to produce unmistakable evidence of their good faith.

70 All would have to accept agreements in the observance of which all nations could have real confidence.

The United States is ready, as it has been and always will be, to cooperate in genuine efforts to find peaceful settlements. Our attitude is not inflexible, our opinions

75 are not frozen, our positions are not and will not be obstacles to peace. But it takes more than one to cooperate. If the Soviet Union could join in doing these things I have outlined, we could all face the future with greater security. We could look forward to more than

80 the eventual reduction of some of the present tensions. We could anticipate a return to a more normal and relaxed diplomatic atmosphere and to progress in the transaction of some of the international business which needs so urgently to be done.

What is the author's main point about regimes in the satellite area?

A) Their leaders are susceptible to outside influences because they lack confidence.
B) The United States would not dictate their policies as long as they were elected freely.
C) They should model themselves directly on successful democracies.
D) They should refrain from behaving aggressively toward neighboring countries.

Which lines best support the answer to the previous question?

A) Lines 38-41 ("With...force")
B) Lines 45-48 ("In...regimes")
C) Lines 50-52 ("The Soviet...respect")
D) Lines 67-68 ("A will...participants")

## 3

The author uses Hungary, Romania, and Bulgaria (lines 28-29) as examples of

A) Soviet leaders' betrayal of their pledge at Tehran.
B) newly liberated satellites of the Soviet Union.
C) countries that the United States want to transform into satellites.
D) nations that have expressed the desire to accept peace treaties.

The author describes the Soviet Union as a regime characterized by

A) flexibility.
B) corruption.
C) ruthlessness.
D) loyalty.

Which lines best support the answer to the previous question?

A) Lines 7-10 ("In...force")
B) Lines 16-19 ("I...together")
C) Lines 21-23 ("It is...countries")
D) Lines 31-34 ("The Soviet...tyranny")

6. The following passage is adapted from "Scientists Discover Salty Aquifer, Previously Unknown Microbial Habitat Under Antarctica," © 2015 by Dartmouth College.

Using an airborne imaging system for the first time in Antarctica, scientists have discovered a vast network of unfrozen salty groundwater that may support previously unknown microbial life deep under the coldest, driest
5 desert on our planet. The findings shed new light on ancient climate change on Earth and provide strong evidence that a similar briny aquifer could support microscopic life on Mars. The scientists used SkyTEM, an airborne electromagnetic sensor, to detect and map
10 otherwise inaccessible subterranean features.

The system uses an antennae suspended beneath a helicopter to create a magnetic field that reveals the subsurface to a depth of about 1,000 feet. Because a helicopter was used, large areas of rugged terrain could
15 be surveyed. The SkyTEM team was funded by the National Science Foundation and led by researchers from the University of Tennessee, Knoxville (UTK), and Dartmouth College, which oversees the NSF's SkyTEM project.

20 "These unfrozen materials appear to be relics of past surface ecosystems and our findings provide compelling evidence that they now provide deep subsurface habitats for microbial life despite extreme environmental conditions," says lead author Jill Mikucki,
25 an assistant professor at UTK. "These new below-ground visualization technologies can also provide insight on glacial dynamics and how Antarctica responds to climate change."

Co-author Dartmouth Professor Ross Virginia is
30 SkyTEM's co-principal investigator and director of Dartmouth's Institute of Arctic Studies. "This project is studying the past and present climate to, in part, understand how climate change in the future will affect biodiversity and ecosystem processes," Virginia says.
35 "This fantastic new view beneath the surface will help us sort out competing ideas about how the McMurdo Dry Valleys have changed with time and how this history influences what we see today."

The researchers found that the unfrozen brines form
40 extensive, interconnected aquifers deep beneath glaciers and lakes and within permanently frozen soils. The brines extend from the coast to at least 7.5 miles inland in the McMurdo Dry Valleys, the largest ice-free region in Antarctica. The brines could be due to freezing and/or
45 deposits. The findings show for the first time that the Dry Valleys' lakes are interconnected rather than isolated; connectivity between lakes and aquifers is important in sustaining ecosystems through drastic climate change, such as lake dry-down events. The findings also challenge

50 the assumption that parts of the ice sheets below the pressure melting point are devoid of liquid water.

In addition to providing answers about the biological adaptations of previously unknown ecosystems that persist in the extreme cold and dark of the Antarctic
55 winter, the new study could help scientists to understand whether similar conditions might exist elsewhere in the solar system, specifically beneath the surface of Mars, which has many similarities to the Dry Valleys. Overall, the Dry Valleys ecosystem – cold,
60 vegetation-free and home only to microscopic animal and plant life – resembles, during the Antarctic summer, conditions on the surface on Mars.

SkyTEM produced images of Taylor Valley along the Ross Sea that suggest briny sediments exist at
65 subsurface temperatures down to perhaps -68°F, which is considered suitable for microbial life. One of the studied areas was lower Taylor Glacier, where the data suggest ancient brine still exists beneath the glacier. That conclusion is supported by the presence of Blood
70 Falls, an iron-rich brine that seeps out of the glacier and hosts an active microbial ecosystem.

Scientists' understanding of Antarctica's underground environment is changing dramatically as research reveals that subglacial lakes are widespread
75 and that at least half of the areas covered by the ice sheet are akin to wetlands on other continents. But groundwater in the ice-free regions and along the coastal margins remains poorly understood.

1

The passage indicates that the "unfrozen salty groundwater" (line 3) was once

A) contained in isolated lakes.
B) locked in glaciers.
C) devoid of any life.
D) found at the earth's surface.

2

Which lines best support the answer to the previous question?

A) Lines 5-6 ("The findings…Earth")
B) Lines 20-21 ("These…ecosystems")
C) Lines 31-34 ("This…processes")
D) Lines 47-48 ("connectivity…change")

Based on the passage, a novel finding of the
SkyTEM project was that

A) shifting plates below the Antarctic surface can
   create major earthquakes.
B) certain regions of Antarctica bear a similarity
   to the surface of Mars.
C) interconnected lakes and aquifers create hardy
   ecosystems.
D) biodiversity in Antarctica is decreasing rapidly
   as a result of climate change.

Which lines best support the answer to the
previous question?

A) Lines 8-10 ("The scientists…features")
B) Lines 25-28 ("These…change")
C) Lines 45-49 ("The findings…events")
D) Lines 75-76 ("at least…continents")

7. The following passage is adapted from Jane Austen, *Northanger Abbey*, originally published in 1817.

No one who had ever seen Catherine Morland in her infancy would have supposed her born to be an heroine. Her situation in life, the character of her father and mother, her own person and disposition, were all
5 equally against her. Her father was a clergyman, without being neglected, or poor, and a very respectable man, though his name was Richard—and he had never been handsome. He had a considerable independence besides two good livings—and he was not in the least addicted
10 to locking up his daughters. Her mother was a woman of useful plain sense, with a good temper, and, what is more remarkable, with a good constitution. She had three sons before Catherine was born; and instead of dying in bringing the latter into the world, as anybody
15 might expect, she still lived on—lived to have six children more—to see them growing up around her, and to enjoy excellent health herself. A family of ten children will be always called a fine family, where there are heads and arms and legs enough for the number;
20 but the Morlands had little other right to the word, for they were in general very plain, and Catherine, for many years of her life, as plain as any. She had a thin awkward figure, a sallow skin without colour, dark lank hair, and strong features—so much for her person; and
25 not less unpropitious for heroism seemed her mind. She was fond of all boy's plays, and greatly preferred cricket not merely to dolls, but to the more heroic enjoyments of infancy, nursing a dormouse, feeding a canary-bird, or watering a rose-bush. Indeed she had
30 no taste for a garden; and if she gathered flowers at all, it was chiefly for the pleasure of mischief—at least so it was conjectured from her always preferring those which she was forbidden to take. Such were her propensities—her abilities were quite as extraordinary.
35 She never could learn or understand anything before she was taught; and sometimes not even then, for she was often inattentive, and occasionally stupid. Her mother was three months in teaching her only to repeat the "Beggar's Petition"; and after all, her
40 next sister, Sally, could say it better than she did. Not that Catherine was always stupid—by no means; she learnt the fable of "The Hare and Many Friends" as quickly as any girl in England. Her mother wished her to learn music; and Catherine was sure she should like it,
45 for she was very fond of tinkling the keys of the old forlorn spinner; so, at eight years old she began. She learnt a year, and could not bear it; and Mrs. Morland, who did not insist on her daughters being accomplished in spite of incapacity or distaste, allowed her to leave
50 off. The day which dismissed the music-master was one of the happiest of Catherine's life. Her taste for drawing was not superior; though whenever she could obtain the outside of a letter from her mother or seize upon any other odd piece of paper, she did what she
55 could in that way, by drawing houses and trees, hens and chickens, all very much like one another. Writing and accounts she was taught by her father; French by her mother: her proficiency in either was not remarkable, and she shirked her lessons in both
60 whenever she could. What a strange, unaccountable character!—for with all these symptoms of profligacy at ten years old, she had neither a bad heart nor a bad temper, was seldom stubborn, scarcely ever quarrelsome, and very kind to the little ones, with
65 few interruptions of tyranny; she was moreover noisy and wild, hated confinement and cleanliness, and loved nothing so well in the world as rolling down the green slope at the back of the house.

1

The narrator indicates that on the whole, the Morlands' appearance was

A) unremarkable.
B) intimidating.
C) uncommonly attractive.
D) somewhat peculiar.

2

Which lines best support the answer to the previous question?

A) Lines 5-8 ("Her…handsome")
B) Line 10-12 ("Her…constitution")
C) Lines 17-18 ("A family…family")
D) Lines 20-21 ("but…plain")

3

As presented in the passage, Catherine could best be described as

A) charming
B) heroic
C) rambunctious
D) gifted

4

Which lines best support the answer to the previous question?

A) Lines 30-31 ("and...mischief")
B) Lines 33-34 ("Such...extraordinary")
C) Line 41 ("Not...means")
D) Line 65-66 ("she...cleanliness")

5

The narrator indicates that Mrs. Morland was

A) weak and sickly.
B) sturdy and practical.
C) short-tempered and irritable.
D) creative and enthusiastic.

6

The passage indicates that Catherine responded to her parents' lessons by

A) participating eagerly.
B) turning them into games.
C) avoiding them if possible.
D) refusing to listen.

Test 1

4	**No line reference**
5	**Evidence**
9	No line reference
13	**No line reference**
14	**Evidence**
16	**Line reference**
17	**Evidence**
24	Line reference
36	**No line reference**
37	**Evidence**
38	**Line reference**
39	**Evidence**
43	**No line reference**
44	**Evidence**
50	**P1/P2 relationship, line reference**
51	**Evidence**

Test 2

5	No line reference
6	**No line reference**
7	**Evidence**
9	**No line reference**
10	**Evidence**
22	**No line reference**
23	**Evidence**
35	**No line reference**
36	**Evidence**

40	No line reference
41	Line reference
45	**No line reference**
46	**Evidence**

Test 3

7	No line reference
9	**No line reference**
10	**Evidence**
26	Line reference
37	No line reference
34	No line reference
36	**No line reference**
37	**Evidence**

Test 4

5	No line reference
7	No line reference
12	No line reference
14	**No line reference**
15	**Evidence**
27	**No line reference**
28	**Evidence**
32	No line reference
46	**No line reference**
47	**Evidence**

Explanations: Literal Comprehension Exercises

1.1-2 B, C

Using the point of the passage (people stick to familiar w/Internet) allows you to identify B) as the correct answer to 1.1 right away. When you go to plug in line references, you already know that the correct set of lines must be related to the idea that the Internet does not encourage people to learn about unfamiliar topics. C) contains the only set of lines that explicitly address that idea (*there's little pushing us beyond our comfort zones*), so it is the answer to 1.2

If you don't remember the answer from the passage, the easiest way to approach the question is to plug in line references. The lines cited in A) and B) provide no information about how Internet users behave online, and D) does not talk about how Internet users actually behave – it only speculates about what *might* happen if they found new information. Again, only C) explicitly describes how users behave: they stick to their comfort zones, i.e. they are "unadventurous."

2.1-2 C, B

The easiest way to answer this question is to use the main point and answer the questions in order. Main point: yawns = empathy in primates, BUT animals? (Yawns are associated with empathy in primates, but the association isn't clear in other animals.) Empathy = attuned to others, making C) the answer to 2.1. The correct answer to 2.2 must support the association between empathy and yawning. That answer is B) because lines 9-11 state that yawning is governed by the same parts of the brain as empathy.

2.3-4 A, C

Again, the easiest way to approach this question is to use the main point: yawns = empathy in primates, BUT animals? (Yawns are associated with empathy in primates, but the association isn't clear in other animals.) Not clear = more *un*certain. For

2.4, you're simply looking for a set of lines that indicate it isn't clear whether empathy has anything to do with yawning in animals other than primates. Now think about the organization of the passage: the author first discusses primates, including humans, then switches to non-primates relatively close to the end. You can therefore assume that the correct answer involves one of the later line references, narrowing your choices to C) and D). C) is correct because lines 20-21 state that the relationship between yawning and empathy in non-primates is *less clear-cut* (=more uncertain).

3.1-2 B, A

Since the first question provides a line reference, start by using it. What information do we get about "that kind of house" in and around line 22? That it's "darkish" and smells of "dishwater and cabbage" (lines 23-25). In other words, it's not a very pleasant place. C) can be eliminated because it's clearly positive, and D) is a bit too extreme, so you can assume it's wrong as well. B) might seem to fit better, but if you're not sure, check the line references in 3.2, and see whether they provide any additional direction. A) provides that direction. Lines 6-8 indicate that the neighborhood is "dingy and depressing." That is consistent with B) in 3.1, and A) is the answer to 3.2.

3.3-4 A, C

Because there's no line reference in 3.3, plug in the line references from 3.4 in order. You can eliminate A) quickly because lines 32-33 are about Rosemary's letters, not Mrs. Wisbeach. Lines 36-39 mention Mrs. Wisbeach but provide no information about Gordon's actual encounter with her, so B) can be eliminated as well. C) is correct because lines 42-45 state that *It was quite impossible to get in or out of the house…without being scrutinized*. That means Mrs. Wisbeach caught him every single time, i.e. their encounter was "inevitable." That makes A) the answer to 3.3 and C) the answer to 3.4.

3.5-6 D, C

Because there's no line reference in 3.5, plug in the line references from 3.6 in order. You can eliminate A) quickly because lines 52-55 have nothing to do with Gordon's papers. Lines 63-65 are about the table, not the papers, so B) can be eliminated as well. C) is correct because lines 73-74 indicate that only Gordon possessed the "key" to his "labyrinth of papers." In other words, he was the only person to whom they were comprehensible. That makes D) the answer to 3.5 and C the answer to 3.6.

4.1 A

If you know the main point (eliminating traffic signals improves traffic), you can make an educated guess that either A) or B) is the answer to 4.1 because those are the most positive answers. Then, when you go back to the passage, you only have to determine whether driving without traffic signals takes more or less time. When you go back to the passage, you only need to look for the key word "time." If you scan from the beginning, you'll find the answer in lines 41-42, where the author states that *[removing traffic signals] also* <u>cuts down</u> *on journey times*, i.e. trips become less time-consuming.

4.2-3 B, D

Because there's no line reference, plug in the line references in 4.3 in order. Lines 13-15 only indicate that many countries are creating areas without traffic signals; they do not discuss urban planning. A) can therefore be eliminated. Lines 30-32 provide no information whatsoever about city planning – they only indicate Monderman's problem with traffic engineering. B) can thus be eliminated as well. C) is incorrect because the quote only indicates Monderman's belief that removing traffic signals can work anywhere; it reveals nothing about urban planning. D) is correct because in line 65, the phrase *urbanization simply translates as uniformity* is used to support the idea that *Recent city planning… has evolved along the same lines around the world.* In other words, it's the same everywhere, i.e. "uniform." That makes B) the answer to 4.2 and D) the answer to 4.3.

5.1-2 B, B

Although this is a main point question, it's one that focuses on only a small part of the passage. Unless you remember the answer from your initial reading of the passage, you should plug in the line references from 5.2 and work through them in order. Remember, though, that main points are most likely to be found in topic sentences, so you want to pay particular attention to line references involving them. Be very careful with A). Lines 38-41 do discuss satellite areas, and if you're not working carefully, the reference to "withdrawing force" might seem to support D) in 5.1. The problem, however, is that lines 38-41 focus on the *Soviets'* behavior toward satellite regimes, not on the satellite regimes' behavior toward other countries. So A) doesn't work. For B), the fact that lines 45-48 include a topic sentence should immediately alert you to their potential importance. What do we learn from those lines? That the United States is **not** primarily concerned that *these [satellite] governments have any particular social or political complexion.* In other words, the US doesn't care what the people living under Soviet control choose, as long as they are given the opportunity to choose freely. That idea corresponds to B) in 5.1 and makes B) the correct answer to 5.2 as well.

5.3 A

The question asks what Hungary, Romania, and Bulgaria are examples of, so your job is to figure out what point they're used to support. Remember that the reference to lines 28-29 does not indicate that the answer will be in those lines; it simply gives you a starting point. Since the reference is right in the middle of the paragraph, you need to read from a few lines above to a few lines below for context. The sentence in which the key words from the passage appear indicates that the Soviets have broken their promises ("pledges"), and the next sentence indicates that they pledged their belief in freedom at Tehran. Logically, then, Hungary, Romania, and Bulgaria are examples of the Soviets' broken Tehran pledge, making A) the answer. B) is incorrect because those countries have not been liberated – the passage implies just the opposite. C) is incorrect because Acheson clearly states that United States does not want satellites. D) is incorrect because the passage provides no information about these countries' desire to accept peace treaties.

5.4-5 C, A

If you happen to know something about the Soviet regime, you can probably narrow the answers down to B) and C) right away. Even if you don't know anything about the Soviet Union, however, this is a fairly straightforward question. If you simply plug in line references, you'll hit the answer almost immediately. Lines 7-10 indicate that the Soviet Union *has shown itself prepared to resort to any method or stratagem, including subversion, threats, and even military force.* That is the definition of "ruthless," making C) the answer to 5.4 and A) the answer to 5.5.

6.1-2 D, B

Although you're given a line reference, it provides little information other than the fact that the unfrozen groundwater *may support previously unknown microbial life.* The question asks what this water "once" was, so plug in the line references and see which one provides information about frozen groundwater in the *past.* Lines 5-6 only indicate a possible use for the findings about groundwater; they say nothing about the groundwater in the past, so A) can be eliminated. The key to recognizing B) as the correct answer to 6.2 is to recognize that "these unfrozen materials" refers to unfrozen *groundwater* – if you overlook the fact the author is referring to the same thing two different ways, you'll miss the answer. Lines 20-21 state that the groundwater was part of past *surface* ecosystems, indicating that D) is the correct answer to 6.1 Otherwise, C) and D) can be eliminated in 6.2 because lines 31-34 focus on the future, not the past, and lines 47-48 simply discuss an advantage of interconnected lakes.

6.3-4 C, C

If you remember reading about how the SkyTEM project's findings could help scientists better understand life on Mars, you might be tempted to pick B), then look for a set of lines in 6.4 that support that answer. Unfortunately, there isn't one. So plug in the answers in order, looking for information about the findings from the project. A) in 6.4 is incorrect because 8-10 only describe SkyTEM itself; they say nothing about its finding, novel or otherwise. B) in 6.4 is incorrect because lines 25-28 only indicate what the project *could* find, not what it has actually found. C) in 6.4 is correct because the phrase *findings show for the first time* indicates a "novel" (new) finding, namely that connectivity between bodies of water can help ecosystems handle difficult periods (=create hardier ecosystems). That makes C) the answer to 6.3 as well. D) in 6.4 is incorrect because lines 75-76 do not describe a novel finding specific to the SkyTEM project.

7.1-2 A, D

Unless you happen to remember the discussion of the Morlands' appearance (unlikely, since it comprises a very small section of the passage), the easiest way to work through this question is to plug in the line references in order. A) is incorrect because line 5-8 only provides information about Mr. Morland, not the family as a whole. B) is incorrect because lines 10-12 focus on Mrs. Morland's personality, not her appearance; they also say nothing about the rest of the family. C) is incorrect because lines 17-18 refer to the size of the Morland family, not their appearance. D) is correct because lines 20-21 indicate that the Morlands' appearance was "plain." That is a synonym for "unremarkable," making A) the correct answer to 7.1.

7.3-4 C, D

If you've gotten the gist of the passage, you should be able to eliminate B) and D). The narrator's whole point is that Catherine isn't particularly heroic or gifted. If you're stuck between A) and C), check the answers in 7.4 in order. Lines 30-31 indicate nothing to suggest Catherine was either charming or rambunctious, so eliminate A). Likewise, neither lines 33-34 nor line 41 provide any information about those qualities. D) is correct because the description of Catherine as *noisy and wild* directly supports the idea of rambunctiousness.

7.5 B

Since the question itself does not provide a line reference and there is no supporting evidence question to provide direction regarding the location of the answer, the fastest way to answer this question is to start from the beginning of the passage and skim for references to Mrs. Morland, pulling your finger down the page as you read. Working this way, you'll find the answer very quickly. Lines 10-12 state that Catherine's mother *was a woman of useful plain sense* (=practical), *with a good temper, and, what is more remarkable, with a good constitution* (=sturdy). That makes B) correct.

7.6 C

If you have the gist of the passage, you should be able to eliminate both A) and B) right away. The narrator is pretty clear that Catherine isn't a particularly enthusiastic student. To decide between the remaining answers, however, you'll most likely need to locate the correct section of the passage; unfortunately, there's no supporting evidence question to guide you. The key phrase is "parents' lessons," so starting from the beginning, skim the passage for those words or related phrases. The answer appears in lines 56-60, which indicates that Catherine's mother taught her French and her father accounting, and that *she shirked her lessons in both whenever she could.* In other words, she avoided them if possible, making C) the answer.

7. Reasonable Inferences

Inference questions test what a particular section of a passage **suggests** or **implies**. Like literal comprehension questions, they are often accompanied by supporting evidence questions. They are usually phrased in the following ways:

- In lines x-y, the author suggests that…

- The author most strongly implies which of the following…

- It can be most reasonably inferred that the author considers "those scientists" (lines x-y)…

The most important thing to understand about inference questions is that they are essentially literal comprehension questions with a twist. Correct answers simply make explicit what the passage is implying. All of the information you need is there; you just have to put it together.

It is also essential to understand that inferences on the SAT are much narrower than the kinds of inferences you may be accustomed to making in English class. For example, if you read a novel in which a character becomes angry, you might think that the author is suggesting that the character is a bad person or warning the reader not to behave in the same way. On the SAT, the only thing that you can infer is that the character is not happy and, if it is suggested in the passage, the reason for the character's anger.

It is true that some inference questions will require you to make slightly larger leaps than others, but only *slightly* larger. Although answers to inference questions **will not be stated word-for-word in the passage**, the passage will always contain specific wording that clearly indicates a particular idea, event, or relationship. In fact, **inference questions will frequently be paired with "supporting evidence" questions**. In fact, this structure can actually make these questions easier. Instead of having to consider the entire passage AND make the correct inference, the "supporting evidence" question will at least provide specific locations for the information you need to make a valid inference.

Because inference questions ask you to go a step beyond what the author is literally saying, (although often a smaller step than what you are expecting), you should be prepared to work very carefully and avoid leaping to conclusions. That is true everywhere, but it is especially true here. If you don't feel ready to handle one of these questions when you first encounter it, skip it and come back to it after you have answered the more straightforward questions.

Fallacies and Incorrect Answers

Statements that go outside the bounds of what can be determined logically from a given assertion are known as **fallacies**; incorrect answer choices to inference questions are fallacies, and they involve various types of faulty reasoning. On the SAT fallacies can be difficult to identify because you are required to sift through so much information, some of which is relevant and some of which is not.

The key to dealing with inference questions is to make sure that you are absolutely clear about the literal meaning of the lines in question. Ideally, you should take a couple of seconds, make sure you understand them, **jot down a quick (3-4 word) summary**, then look for the answer closest in *overall meaning* to that statement. That answer should be correct.

Because the right answer might be phrased in a way you're not expecting, though, it is crucial that you not eliminate any answer without making sure you really understand what it says and how it relates to the lines in question. Knowing how to recognize a couple of common fallacies can also help you identify incorrect answers more easily.

One very common type of fallacy involves **speculation**: that is, it *could* be true based on the information in the passage, but usually there simply isn't enough information to judge whether it is *actually* true. Some of these answers are quite obviously wrong because they are so far outside the bounds of what is discussed in the passage that they are patently absurd, while others sound so plausible that it seems that they should be true. In fact, **some of them may be true – they just won't be supported by the passage**.

Another common type of fallacy involves the reasoning, "if x is true in one case, then x is true in all cases/has always been true," or "if x is true for one member of a group, then it is true for all members of that group." In reality, the only thing that x being true in one case suggests is that x is true in that particular case. It does not automatically mean that x will be true in any other case or for any other person.

Such fallacies are characterized by **extreme words** such as *always, never, all,* and *only*. You should be suspicious of any answer choice that contains this type of wording. To be sure, there are cases in which a given statement will imply that a particular fact applies to all situations/people, but they are comparatively rare.

Important: Make sure that you pay close attention to answer choices that are phrased negatively (ones that contain the word *not*) or that contain double negatives (e.g. not impossible = possible). Unless you carefully work out what this type of wording actually means, it is very easy to become confused by it.

This is very important because one of the easiest ways to create a valid inference is to rewrite the original statement from a different angle. For example, if a passage states that a particular star is much older than the Earth, a valid inference is that the star is **not** younger than the Earth.

Let's look at some examples of reasonable and unreasonable inferences. Consider the following sentences:

Every time a car drives through a major intersection, it becomes a data point. Magnetic coils of wire lay just beneath the pavement, registering each passing car.

Because the author refers to "magnetic coils of wire" immediately after he states that a car becomes a data point every time it drives through a major intersection, we can infer that the magnetic coils of wire play a role in turning cars into data points. Although the author does not directly state that one is a result of the other, he strongly implies it by placing those two pieces of information next to one another. Based on how texts normally work, there is simply no other reason to mention the magnetic coils there.

Because the author states that the magnetic coils of wire record the cars from below the pavement, we can infer that coils of wire do not need to be above ground to do their job.

We cannot, however, infer that magnetic coils are the **best** way of tracking cars' movement; these sentences give us nothing to compare the cars to.

Likewise, we cannot infer that magnetic coils are only – or even mostly – used below the pavement, or that their only/primary use is to track cars. Those things may very well be true, but we do not have enough information to determine whether they are actually true.

Let's look at another example. It's excerpted from a passage we've seen before, but we're just going to look at a small part of it.

10 For the past decade, Florida's oranges have been
literally starving. Since it first appeared in 2005,
citrus greening, also known by its Chinese name,
huanglongbing, has swept across Florida's groves
like a flood. With no hills to block it, the Asian citrus
15 psyllid—the invasive aphid relative that carries the
disease—has infected nearly every orchard in the
state. By one estimate, 80 percent of Florida's citrus
trees are infected and declining.

We're going to focus on lines 11-17 – the second and third sentences, particularly the third sentence. We can make several inferences from those lines. First, from the statement *With no hills to block it, the Asian citrus psyllid…has infected nearly every orchard in the state*, we can reasonably infer that the Asian citrus psyllid **can** be stopped by hills. We can also infer that not every orchard in the state has been infected, i.e. **some** orchards in the state have **not** been infected.

If we back up to the second sentence, we can also infer that Florida's citrus groves do not have hills – if they did, the Asian citrus psyllid would not have been able to spread so widely.

Let's look at some more examples.

This passage is from Barbara Jordan's keynote address at the 1976 Democratic National Convention. A Texas native, Jordan was the first African-American woman to represent the Deep South in Congress.

It was one hundred and forty-four years ago that members of the Democratic Party first met in convention to select a Presidential candidate. A lot of years passed since 1832, and during that time it would
5 have been most unusual for any national political party to ask a Barbara Jordan to deliver a keynote address. But tonight, here I am. And I feel that notwithstanding the past that my presence here is one additional bit of evidence that the American Dream need not forever be
10 deferred.

Now that I have this grand distinction, what in the world am I supposed to say? I could list the problems which cause people to feel cynical, angry, frustrated: problems which include lack of integrity in government;
15 the feeling that the individual no longer counts; feeling that the grand American experiment is failing or has failed. I could recite these problems, and then I could sit down and offer no solutions. But I don't choose to do that either. The citizens of America expect more.
20 We are a people in search of a national community. We are a people trying not only to solve the problems of the present, unemployment, inflation, but we are attempting on a larger scale to fulfill the promise of America. We are attempting to fulfill our national purpose,
25 to create and sustain a society in which all of us are equal.

And now we must look to the future. Let us heed the voice of the people and recognize their common sense. If we do not, we not only blaspheme our political heritage, we ignore the common ties that bind all
30 Americans. Many fear the future. Many are distrustful of their leaders, and believe that their voices are never heard. Many seek only to satisfy their private interests. But this is the great danger America faces – that we will cease to be one nation and become instead a collection
35 of interest groups: city against suburb, region against region, individual against individual; each seeking to satisfy private wants. If that happens, who then will speak for America? Who then will speak for the common good?

This is the question which must be answered in 1976:
40 Are we to be one people bound together by common spirit, sharing in a common endeavor; or will we become a divided nation? For all of its uncertainty, we cannot flee the future. We must address and master the future together. It can be done if we restore the belief that we
45 share a sense of national community, that we share a common national endeavor.

There is no executive order; there is no law that can require the American people to form a national community. This we must do as individuals, and if we
50 do it as individuals, there is no President of the United States who can veto that decision.

As a first step, we must restore our belief in ourselves. We are a generous people, so why can't we be generous with each other?
55 And now, what are those of us who are elected public officials supposed to do? We call ourselves "public servants" but I'll tell you this: We as public servants must set an example for the rest of the nation. It is hypocritical for the public official to admonish and
60 exhort the people to uphold the common good if we are derelict in upholding the common good. More is required of public officials than slogans and handshakes and press releases.

If we promise as public officials, we must deliver.
65 If we as public officials propose, we must produce. If we say to the American people, "It is time for you to be sacrificial" – sacrifice. And again, if we make mistakes, we must be willing to admit them. What we have to do is strike a balance between the idea that
70 government should do everything and the idea that government ought to do nothing.

Let there be no illusions about the difficulty of forming this kind of a national community. It's tough, difficult, not easy. But a spirit of harmony will survive
75 in America only if each of us remembers, when self-interest and bitterness seem to prevail, that we share a common destiny.

We cannot improve on the system of government handed down to us by the founders of the Republic.
80 There is no way to improve upon that. But what we can do is to find new ways to implement that system and realize our destiny.

1

The author most strongly suggests which of the following about the "common endeavor" (line 41)

A) It represents an impossible ideal.
B) It has the potential to be destroyed by uncertainty.
C) It cannot be realized through legislation.
D) It represents a merger of individual and corporate interests.

Which choice provides the best evidence for
the answer to the previous question?

A) Lines 33-35 ("But...groups")
B) Lines 42-43 ("For...future")
C) Lines 47-49 ("There is...community")
D) Lines 56-58 ("We...nation")

There are a few ways to go about answering this question.

Option 1: The Short Shortcut

Remember that little "trick" we talked about way back in the "vocabulary in context"
chapter, the one about second meanings?

Well, there's an answer choice here that includes a common word used in its second
meaning: *realized*, in choice C). *Realize* normally means "become aware of," but here it's used
to mean "achieve." That usage signals that C) is likely correct, but you still need to check.

The lines references in the second question tell you that the answer is located somewhere
between lines 33 and 58. If you're a strong reader and skim through that section with a clear
idea of what you're looking for, you'll find the answer in lines 47-51.

No executive order; no law = cannot be realized (accomplished) through legislation.

Option 2: Answer the Question Yourself

The fact that you're given a line reference means that you have a pretty good chance of
being able to answer the question on your own without having to plug in every line
reference.

The only potential downside is that the lines you come up with to support your answer
might not be the same lines provided in the second question, so you might have to do a bit
more reading around than you'd like.

The first thing to do is to define the key phrase *common endeavor*.

Let's consider context of the passage. Jordan's main concern is that the United States is
becoming fragmented into *a collection of interest groups: city against suburb, region against
region, individual against individual; each seeking to satisfy private wants*. In fact, if we were to write a
main point, we might say something like "America must UNITE f/future."

Coming back to the key phrase, Jordan essentially answers the question a couple of lines
down when she states that *We (all Americans) must address and master the future together*. So the
correct answer must be consistent with that idea.

The author most strongly suggests which of the following about the "common endeavor" (line 41)

A) It represents an impossible ideal.
B) It has the potential to be destroyed by uncertainty.
C) It cannot be realized through legislation.
D) It represents a merger of individual and corporate interests.

When you look at the answer choices, though, there's no option that *directly* rephrases the idea that Americans must come together. You can, however, play process of elimination pretty effectively.

A) can be eliminated because Jordan states in line 44 that *it can be done*. The extreme word *impossible* also suggests that the answer is wrong.

B) simply takes a word (*uncertainty*) from the passage and presents it in another context. The passage only states that the future is unavoidable despite the fact that it is uncertain (The phrase *for all* means "despite"). This answer is otherwise off topic.

C) is an answer you might overlook initially, and here you need to be careful not to eliminate it simply because you don't remember anything about it. If you have a very strong sense of logic, you may be able to figure out that if the "endeavor" depends on the American people's uniting, then by definition, it cannot be accomplished by legislation. But if you're not sure, just leave this answer.

D) is completely off topic. The passage says nothing whatsoever about corporate interests.

So that leaves you with C). It's the only one that seems like it could work, but maybe you're not sure why. So now you have to look at each line reference and check to see whether it supports C). While it may be a tedious process, the good news is that you have a very good idea of what the correct set of lines must say.

If you're comfortable doing so, you may simply want to skim through the lines on your own, looking for information consistent with C). Again, you can use the information in the second question to tell you that the answer is located somewhere between 33 and 58. If you're a strong enough reader, you'll probably be able to figure out that *no executive order* and *no law* in line 47 both support C) in the first question and give you C) as the answer to the second question as well.

Alternately, if you'd prefer to simply work through each of the line references provided in the second question, you can answer the question that way. Again, you can play process of elimination. A), B), and D) can all be eliminated because they have nothing to with legislation. That leaves C), which fits perfectly.

Option 3: Plug in Line References

When you're given a line reference in the first question, this method usually isn't ideal – it can end up being unnecessarily confusing and time consuming. But that said, we're going to try it anyway, just so you can see how it works.

Even though we're going to rely more heavily on the passage from the start than we did for the other methods, we still need to do some work upfront.

Again, we're going to define the key phrase "common endeavor" in context of the main point ("Americans must UNITE f/future") so that we know what we're looking for when we go back to the passage.

Now that we have an idea of what we're looking for, we can go and check each set of lines to see whether it matches. Remember, though, that because this is an inference question, the correct answer may be stated from a somewhat different angle.

A) **But this is the great danger America faces – that we will cease to be one nation and become instead a collection of interest groups**

These lines are related to the same general idea as the key phrase, but they only tell us about the *danger*. The endeavor itself is to unite, and these lines talk about the opposite.

B) **For all of its uncertainty, we cannot flee the future.**

No, this has nothing to do with people uniting. It's off topic.

C) **There is no executive order; there is no law that can require the American people to form a national community.**

Even if you're not sure about this one, the phrase *national community* should make you pay closer attention because it's directly related to the idea of people uniting.

D) **We call ourselves "public servants" but I'll tell you this: We as public servants must set an example for the rest of the nation.**

This has nothing to do with the America people uniting.

So the only answer that seems generally consistent with the question is C). Now you can work backwards, looking at the answers to the first question. Lines 47-49 clearly support the idea that the "endeavor" cannot be accomplished through legislation, giving you C) as the answer to the first question.

Now we're going to look at some inference questions without line references. Although these questions may seem more difficult than ones with line references, it is sometimes possible to use the big picture, as well as an understanding of how texts are structured, to identify correct answers without too much fuss.

Every time a car drives through a major intersection, it becomes a data point. Magnetic coils of wire lay just beneath the pavement, registering each passing car. This starts a cascade of information: Computers tally the
5 number and speed of cars, shoot the data through underground cables to a command center and finally translate it into the colors red, yellow and green. On the seventh floor of Boston City Hall, the three colors splash like paint across a wall-sized map.
10 To drivers, the color red means stop, but on the map it tells traffic engineers to leap into action. Traffic control centers like this one—a room cluttered with computer terminals and live video feeds of urban intersections—represent the brain of a traffic system. The city's network
15 of sensors, cables and signals are the nerves connected to the rest of the body. "Most people don't think there are eyes and ears keeping track of all this stuff," says John DeBenedictis, the center's engineering director. But in reality, engineers literally watch our every move,
20 making subtle changes that relieve and redirect traffic.
The tactics and aims of traffic management are modest but powerful. Most intersections rely on a combination of pre-set timing and computer adaptation. For example, where a busy main road intersects with a quiet residential
25 street, the traffic signal might give 70 percent of "green time" to the main road, and 30 percent to the residential road. (Green lights last between a few seconds and a couple minutes, and tend to shorten at rush hour to help the traffic move continuously.) But when traffic
30 overwhelms the pre-set timing, engineers override the system and make changes.

1

It is reasonable to infer that improvements in traffic flow

A) are more difficult to achieve at certain hours of the day.
B) occur near traffic control centers.
C) can be attributed to pre-set systems.
D) are the result of intervention by traffic engineers.

2

Which choice provides the best evidence for the answer to the previous question?

A) Lines 4-7 ("computers…green")
B) Lines 11-14 ("Traffic…system")
C) Lines 18-20 ("But…traffic")
D) Lines 22-23 ("Most…adaptation")

Because this passage isn't too long, it's not out of the question to try answering the first question without using any of the line references.

If you work from the main point (which ideally you should have underlined), you can actually answer this question very, very quickly. What's the point? That traffic engineers see everything. Where is it located? In lines 18-20 ("But…traffic). In the first question, D) essentially rephrases the main point, and C) in the second question cites those exact lines.

If you're not sure you can reliably use this type of shortcut, you can of course plug in.

1

It is reasonable to infer that improvements in traffic flow

A) Lines 4-7 ("computers…green")
B) Lines 11-14 ("Traffic…system")
C) Lines 18-20 ("But…traffic")
D) Lines 22-23 ("Most…adaptation")

A) Computers tally the number and speed of cars, shoot the data through underground cables to a command center and finally translate it into the colors red, yellow and green.

No. This tells us nothing about traffic flow, only about how individual cars' movements are recorded.

B) Traffic control centers like this one—a room cluttered with computer terminals and live video feeds of urban intersections— represent the brain of a traffic system.

This line extends the metaphor between a traffic control center and the human body. It doesn't actually talk about traffic itself.

C) But in reality, engineers literally watch our every move, making subtle changes that relieve and redirect traffic.

Here we finally do have some information about traffic. What do engineers do? They make changes that *relieve* (that is, make it less jammed) *and redirect it*. In other words, they improve its flow. So this answer works. Note also the second meaning of *relieve*.

D) Most intersections rely on a combination of pre-set timing and computer adaptation.

This choice only talks about intersections (specific), not traffic (general).

So the answer is C). Now we can work backwards. If engineers are constantly watching people, making change to *relieve and redirect traffic*, then improved traffic flow must be the result of their intervention. So the answer to the first question is D).

Let's try a longer passage.

The following passage is adapted from Willer Cather, *My Antonia*, originally published in 1918. The narrator recounts his life on the Nebraska plains as a boy.

On the afternoon of that Sunday I took my first long ride on my pony, under Otto's direction. After that Dude and I went twice a week to the post-office, six miles east of us, and I saved the men a good
5 deal of time by riding on errands to our neighbors. When we had to borrow anything, I was always the messenger.

All the years that have passed have not dimmed my memory of that first glorious autumn. The new country
10 lay open before me: there were no fences in those days, and I could choose my own way over the grass uplands, trusting the pony to get me home again. Sometimes I followed the sunflower-bordered roads.

I used to love to drift along the pale-yellow cornfields,
15 looking for the damp spots one sometimes found at their edges, where the smartweed soon turned a rich copper color and the narrow brown leaves hung curled like cocoons about the swollen joints of the stem. Sometimes I went south to visit our German neighbors and to
20 admire their catalpa grove, or to see the big elm tree that grew up out of a deep crack in the earth and had a hawk's nest in its branches. Trees were so rare in that country, and they had to make such a hard fight to grow, that we used to feel anxious about them, and visit them
25 as if they were persons. It must have been the scarcity of detail in that tawny landscape that made detail so precious.

Sometimes I rode north to the big prairie-dog town to watch the brown earth-owls fly home in the late afternoon
30 and go down to their nests underground with the dogs. Antonia Shimerda liked to go with me, and we used to wonder a great deal about these birds of subterranean habit. We had to be on our guard there, for rattlesnakes were always lurking about. They came to pick up an easy
35 living among the dogs and owls, which were quite defenseless against them; took possession of their comfortable houses and ate the eggs and puppies. We felt sorry for the owls. It was always mournful to see them come flying home at sunset and disappear under
40 the earth.

But, after all, we felt, winged things who would live like that must be rather degraded creatures. The dog-town was a long way from any pond or creek. Otto Fuchs said he had seen populous dog-towns in the desert where
45 there was no surface water for fifty miles; he insisted that some of the holes must go down to water—nearly two hundred feet, hereabouts. Antonia said she didn't believe it; that the dogs probably lapped up the dew in the early morning, like the rabbits.

50 Antonia had opinions about everything, and she was soon able to make them known. Almost every day she came running across the prairie to have her reading lesson with me. Mrs. Shimerda grumbled, but realized it was important that one member of the family should
55 learn English. When the lesson was over, we used to go up to the watermelon patch behind the garden. I split the melons with an old corn-knife, and we lifted out the hearts and ate them with the juice trickling through our fingers. The white melons we did not touch, but we
60 watched them with curiosity. They were to be picked later, when the hard frosts had set in, and put away for winter use. After weeks on the ocean, the Shimerdas were famished for fruit. The two girls would wander for miles along the edge of the cornfields, hunting for
65 ground-cherries.

Antonia loved to help grandmother in the kitchen and to learn about cooking and housekeeping. She would stand beside her, watching her every movement. We were willing to believe that Mrs. Shimerda was a
70 good housewife in her own country, but she managed poorly under new conditions. I remember how horrified we were at the sour, ashy-grey bread she gave her family to eat. She mixed her dough, we discovered, in an old tin peck-measure that had been used about the
75 barn. When she took the paste out to bake it, she left smears of dough sticking to the sides of the measure, put the measure on the shelf behind the stove, and let this residue ferment. The next time she made bread, she scraped this sour stuff down into the fresh dough to
80 serve as yeast.

1

It is most reasonable to infer that access to the the land during the narrator's boyhood was

A) reserved for a small group of settlers.
B) less restricted than it became later on.
C) sometimes prohibited by the narrator's neighbors.
D) controlled by Antonia Shimerda's family.

2

Which lines best support the answer to the previous question?

A) Lines 9-12 ("The new…again")
B) Lines 18-22 ("Sometimes…branches")
C) Lines 33-34 ("We…about")
D) Lines 62-65 ("After…cherries")

This question might look complicated, but it's actually a lot simpler than it appears. Although it appears to ask you to wade through a huge amount of information, it can actually be solved relatively quickly – if, that is, you think carefully about what the correct lines are saying.

This time, we're going to start by combining the two questions into one:

1

It is most reasonable to infer that access to the the land during the narrator's boyhood was

A) Lines 9-12 ("The new…again")
B) Lines 18-22 ("Sometimes…branches")
C) Lines 33-34 ("We…about")
D) Lines 62-65 ("After…cherries")

If we start by checking out the line references in order, we'll hit on the answer immediately:

A) The new country lay open before me: there were no fences in those days, and I could choose my own way over the grass uplands, trusting the pony to get me home again. Sometimes I followed the sunflower-bordered roads.

The first thing to notice is that these lines contain a colon, and colons are important because they signal explanations. You always want to pay close attention to the information after a colon, and this is no exception.

What do we learn after the colon? That *there were no fences in those days, and I could choose my own way over the grass uplands*. In other words, the narrator had pretty much unrestricted access to the land. The phrase *in those days* suggests that this is no longer the case – in other words, access to the land was **less restricted** than it became later on.

So not only is A) correct, but it also tells us that B) is the answer to the previous question.

That was a lot easier than it looked, right?

You could, of course, try to work through the two questions in order, but in this case that approach could end up being confusing, not to mention extremely time-consuming. Not only does the passage not provide a line reference, but the aspect of the passage that it asks about is so general that it is hard to pinpoint even a general area where the necessary information would most likely appear. And because the information is hidden in the middle of a paragraph close to the beginning, you are unlikely to remember specific details from that paragraph, mentally categorizing them as "background information." Even if you circled the colon as you read through the passage, the chances of your remembering to look back at that spot to answer the question are exceedingly slim.

Let's look at one more passage.

This passage is adapted from Sharon Tregaskis, "What Bees Tell Us About Global Climate Change," © 2010 by *Johns Hopkins Magazine*.

Standing in the apiary on the grounds of the U.S. Department of Agriculture's Bee Research Laboratory in Beltsville, Maryland, Wayne Esaias digs through the canvas shoulder bag leaning against his leg in search of
5 the cable he uses to download data. It's dusk as he runs the cord from his laptop—precariously perched on the beam of a cast-iron platform scale—to a small, battery-operated data logger attached to the spring inside the scale's steel column. In the 1800s, a scale like this
10 would have weighed sacks of grain or crates of apples, peaches, and melons. Since arriving at the USDA's bee lab in January 2007, this scale has been loaded with a single item: a colony of *Apis mellifera*, the fuzzy, black-and-yellow honey bee. An attached, 12-bit
15 recorder captures the hive's weight to within a 10th of a pound, along with a daily register of relative ambient humidity and temperature.

On this late January afternoon, during a comparatively balmy respite between the blizzards that
20 dumped several feet of snow on the Middle Atlantic states, the bees, their honey, and the wooden boxes in which they live weigh 94.5 pounds. In mid-July, as last year's unusually long nectar flow finally ebbed, the whole contraption topped out at 275 pounds, including
25 nearly 150 pounds of honey. "Right now, the colony is in a cluster about the size of a soccer ball," says Esaias, who's kept bees for nearly two decades and knows without lifting the lid what's going on inside this hive. "The center of the cluster is where the queen is, and
30 they're keeping her at 93 degrees—the rest are just hanging there, tensing their flight muscles to generate heat." Provided that they have enough calories to fuel their winter workout, a healthy colony can survive as far north as Anchorage, Alaska. "They slowly eat their
35 way up through the winter," he says. "It's a race: Will they eat all their honey before the nectar flows, or not?" To make sure their charges win that race, apiarists have long relied on scale hives for vital management clues. By tracking daily weight variations, a beekeeper can
40 discern when the colony needs a nutritional boost to carry it through lean times, whether to add extra combs for honey storage and even detect incursions by marauding robber bees—all without disturbing the colony. A graph of the hive's weight—which can

45 increase by as much as 35 pounds a day in some parts of the United States during peak nectar flow – reveals the date on which the bees' foraging was was most productive and provides a direct record of successful pollination. "Around here, the bees make
50 their living in the month of May," says Esaias, noting that his bees often achieve daily spikes of 25 pounds, the maximum in Maryland. "There's almost no nectar coming in for the rest of the year." A scientist by training and career oceanographer at NASA, Esaias
55 established the Mink Hollow Apiary in his Highland, Maryland, backyard in 1992 with a trio of hand-me-down hives and an antique platform scale much like the one at the Beltsville bee lab. Ever since, he's maintained a meticulous record of the bees' daily
60 weight, as well as weather patterns and such details as his efforts to keep them healthy. In late 2006, honey bees nationwide began disappearing in an ongoing syndrome dubbed colony collapse disorder (CCD). Entire hives went empty as bees inexplicably
65 abandoned their young and their honey. Commercial beekeepers reported losses up to 90 percent, and the large-scale farmers who rely on honey bees to ensure rich harvests of almonds, apples, and sunflowers became very, very nervous. Looking for clues, Esaias
70 turned to his own records. While the resulting graphs threw no light on the cause of CCD, a staggering trend emerged: In the span of just 15 seasons, the date on which his Mink Hollow bees brought home the most nectar had shifted by two weeks—from late May
75 to the middle of the month. "I was shocked when I plotted this up," he says. "It was right under my nose, going on the whole time." The epiphany would lead Esaias to launch a series of research collaborations, featuring honey bees and other pollinators, to investigate
80 the relationships among plants, pollinators, and weather patterns. Already, the work has begun to reveal insights into the often unintended consequences of human interventions in natural and agricultural ecosystems, and exposed significant gaps in how we understand the
85 effect climate change will have on everything from food production to terrestrial ecology.

1

It is most reasonable to conclude that research into the bees' disappearance could result in

A) additional varieties of apples, almonds, and sunflowers.
B) earlier harvests of popular crops.
C) more sophisticated equipment for studying bees' behavior.
D) a better understanding of the consequences of climate change.

2

Which lines best support the answer to the previous question?

A) Lines 58-61 ("Ever...healthy")
B) Lines 65-69 ("Commercial...nervous")
C) Lines 72-74 ("In...weeks")
D) Lines 81-86 ("Already...ecology")

If you stop and think logically about how passages are typically arranged, this question also has the potential to be much easier than it initially appears. We're going to use our understanding of how arguments are organized to quickly identify the section of the passage where the information is most likely to be located.

The question is asking about the possible *results* of research into the bees' disappearance. Discussions of what research *could* lead to in the future tend to come **after** discussions of the research itself. The question is also asking about a pretty broad idea, and **main ideas tend to be located in two places: the introduction and the conclusion.**

When we look at the line-reference options, we can notice that they start at about halfway through the passage and range to the very end of the passage. There's nothing from the beginning of the passage, eliminating the possibility that the information we're looking for is in the introduction. That means the lines we want are most likely to appear at the end, meaning that we're going to start with D).

What do we learn in in lines 81-86? That the research on bees *has exposed significant gaps in how we understand the effect climate change will have on everything from food production to terrestrial ecology.* We can therefore reasonably infer that the research may eventually close some of those gaps, i.e. improve our understanding. That's the whole point of scientific research.

So the answer is D). We never even had to look at any of the other answers. If you did want to check them out, you'd see pretty quickly that while some of them mention the research, none of them discusses the *results* of the research. They're all off topic.

At this point you might be thinking, "But isn't it confusing to skip around like that?" Or "But how do you remember a strategy like that when you're in the middle of a test and have so many other things to think about?"

The important thing to understand is that a strategy like this is based on logic, not memory. Main ideas are most frequently located in introductions and conclusions – that's a fact of how arguments are most often put together, not just something to be memorized. If you can recognize when questions are asking about the big picture, you can make a reasonable assumption about where in the passage to look. In this case, the most logical place for the answer to appear did in fact provide the answer. If it hadn't worked, the next step would have been to check the answers one by one.

Working through Reading questions is sometimes a process of trial-and-error. You make an assumption based on how texts are usually put together and how the test is typically constructed, and much of the time it'll turn out to be right (it is a *standardized* test, after all). If it's not, then your job is to reexamine your original assumption and try to work through the question from a different angle. The SAT is a reasoning test – if you're a strong reader willing to approach the exam with the attitude that you can reason your way systematically through each question, you'll eventually hit on the answer.

Underlying Assumptions

Another type of inference question asks you to recognize an underlying assumption that can be inferred from a particular section of a passage.

Assumption questions do not appear very frequently, but when they do, they are usually phrased in the following ways:

- An important assumption in the passage is that...

- The author's assumption in lines x-y is that...

- An unstated assumption made by the authors about x is that...

Unlike other inference questions, assumption questions will most likely **not** be paired with supporting evidence questions. Unfortunately, **they are also unlikely to be accompanied by line references**. As a result, you must locate the appropriate section of the passage entirely on your own, then determine the correct answer based on that section.

As is true for correct answers to inference questions, correct answers to assumption questions typically rephrase the lines provided in the question from a slightly different standpoint or in a somewhat more general manner. They may also "fill in the blanks" – that is, explicitly spell out information that is only implied in the passage.

Incorrect answers, on the other hand, will go beyond the bounds of what can reasonably be inferred from the passage. They may include information that is factually true but irrelevant to the lines in question. They may also use some of the same wording that is found in the passage and alter it just enough so that it means something different from what it means in the passage.

On the next page, we're going to look at an example.

After the one-way front door, the first supermarket feature you inevitably encounter is the produce department. There's a good reason for this: the sensory impact of all those scents, textures, and colors (think
5 fat tomatoes, glossy eggplants, luscious strawberries) makes us feel both upbeat and hungry. Similarly the store bakery is usually near the entrance, with its scrumptious and pervasive smell of fresh-baked bread; as is the flower shop, with its buckets of tulips, bouquets
10 of roses, and banks of greenery. The message we get right off the bat is that the store is a welcoming place, fresh, natural, fragrant, and healthy, with comforting shades of grandma's kitchen.

The cruel truth is that the produce department is less
15 garden and kitchen than stage set. Lighting is chosen to make fruits and veggies appear at their brightest and best; and – according to Martin Lindstrom, author of *Brandwashed: Tricks Companies Use to Manipulate Our Minds and Persuade Us to Buy*—the periodic sprays of
20 fresh water that douse the produce bins are all for show. Though used to give fresh foods a deceptive dewy and fresh-picked look, the water actually has no practical purpose. In fact, it makes vegetables spoil faster than they otherwise would.

1

An unstated assumption made by the author about vegetables is that their

A) appearance is not a reliable indicator of their freshness.
B) nutritive qualities are frequently overstated.
C) fragrance is off-putting to some customers.
D) location within a supermarket depends on their popularity.

Since you aren't given a line reference, the first thing you need to do is **identify the key word and find it in the passage.** To reiterate: the key word tells us the specific focus (topic) of the question. Here, the key word is *vegetables*, so that's what we're going to look for.

This is where you need to be careful. The beginning of the passage provides some specific examples of vegetables (tomatoes, eggplant), but the key word itself does not appear. To find it, you need to go to the second paragraph. We get *veggies* in line 16, and *vegetables* in line 23.

While your first instinct might be to check these references in order, you're actually better off checking the second one first. Why? Because it's in the last sentence, and the last sentence is always important. That sentence also begins with the transition *In fact*, whose purpose is to emphasize the preceding idea. So it's doubly important.

What doe we learn from that section? That vegetables get sprayed with water so that they'll look fresh, *even though* spraying them makes them spoil faster. In other words, they might look nice, but they might not be all that fresh. That makes the answer A).

Notice that if you'd gotten stuck on the first paragraph, you could have easily fallen into a loop of reading and re-reading, and never figured how to get to the answer. B), C), and D) are never addressed in the passage, but all of them sound plausible enough to seem like reasonable guesses if you don't really know what you're doing.

Let's look at another example.

The following passage is adapted from "The Origin of the Ocean Floor" by Peter Keleman, © 2009 by The National Geographic Society.

At the dark bottom of our cool oceans, 85 percent of the earth's volcanic eruptions proceed virtually unnoticed. Though unseen, they are hardly insignificant. Submarine volcanoes generate the solid underpinnings
5 of all the world's oceans massive slabs of rock seven kilometers thick.

Geophysicists first began to appreciate the smoldering origins of the land under the sea, known formally as ocean crust, in the early 1960s. Sonar
10 surveys revealed that volcanoes form nearly continuous ridges that wind around the globe like seams on a baseball. Later, the same scientists strove to explain what fuels these erupting mountain ranges, called mid-ocean ridges. Basic theories suggest that because ocean
15 crust pulls apart along the ridges, hot material deep within the earth's rocky interior must rise to fill the gap. But details of exactly where the lava originates and how it travels to the surface long remained a mystery.

In recent years mathematical models of the
20 interaction between molten and solid rock have provided some answers, as have examinations of blocks of old seafloor now exposed on the continents. These insights made it possible to develop a detailed theory describing the birth of ocean crust. The process
25 turns out to be quite different from the typical layperson's idea, in which fiery magma fills an enormous chamber underneath a volcano, then rages upward along a jagged crack. Instead the process begins dozens of kilometers under the seafloor, where
30 tiny droplets of melted rock ooze through microscopic pores at a rate of about 10 centimeters a year, about as fast as fingernails grow.

Closer to the surface, the process speeds up, culminating with massive streams of lava pouring
35 over the seafloor with the velocity of a speeding truck. Deciphering how liquid moves through solid rock deep underground not only explains how ocean crust emerges but also may elucidate the behavior of other fluid-transport networks, including the river systems
40 that dissect the planet's surface.

Far below the mid-ocean ridge volcanoes and their countless layers of crust-forming lava is the mantle, a 3,200-kilometer-thick layer of scorching hot rock that forms the earth's midsection and surrounds its
45 metallic core. At the planet's cool surface, upthrusted mantle rocks are dark green, but if you could see them in their rightful home, they would be glowing red- or even white-hot. The top of the mantle is about 1,300 degrees Celsius, and it gets about one degree
50 hotter with each kilometer of depth. The weight of overlying rock means the pressure also increases with depth about 1,000 atmospheres for every three kilometers.

Knowledge of the intense heat and pressure in
55 the mantle led researchers to hypothesize in the late 1960s that ocean crust originates as tiny amounts of liquid rock known as melt almost as though the solid rocks were "sweating." Even a minuscule release of pressure (because of material rising from
60 its original position) causes melt to form in microscopic pores deep within the mantle rock.

Explaining how the rock sweat gets to the surface was more difficult. Melt is less dense than the mantle rocks in which it forms, so it will
65 constantly try to migrate upward, toward regions of lower pressure. But what laboratory experiments revealed about the chemical composition of melt did not seem to match up with the composition of rock samples collected from the mid-ocean ridges,
70 where erupted melt hardens.

Using specialized equipment to heat and squeeze crystals from mantle rocks in the laboratory, investigators learned that the chemical composition of melt in the mantle varies depending on the depth
75 at which it forms; the composition is controlled by an exchange of atoms between the melt and the minerals that make up the solid rock it passes through. The experiments revealed that as melt rises, it dissolves one kind of mineral, orthopyroxene, and
80 precipitates, or leaves behind, another mineral, olivine. Researchers could thus infer that the higher in the mantle melt formed, the more orthopyroxene it would dissolve, and the more olivine it would leave behind. Comparing these experimental findings
85 with lava samples from the mid-ocean ridges revealed that almost all of them have the composition of melts that formed at depths greater than 45 kilometers.

1

An unstated assumption in the author's discussion of mid-ocean ridges is that these ridges

A) are composed of orthopyrexene and olivine.
B) are maintained by the exchange of atoms.
C) are subject to less pressure than mantle rock is.
D) produce a wide range of minerals.

Start by identifying the key phrase (*mid-ocean ridges*) and locating it in the passage. It is very important that you look for the entire phrase because it appears in only a few places in the passage. If you look for something more general, e.g. *ocean*, you won't know where to focus.

The key phrase appears for the first time in line 41, but be careful. Although the phrase *mid-ocean ridge* is there, it's just mentioned in passing; the real focus of the sentence is the mantle. If you overlook that fact and attempt to determine the answer based on that paragraph, you're likely to get caught in a loop of reading and re-reading, trying to figure out why none of the answers seem to fit.

If that does happen to you, remember: **if the answer isn't in the place you're looking, it has to be somewhere else.** (Provided, of course, that you understand the passage.)

So move on. If you keep scanning, focusing on the first and last sentence of each paragraph, you'll hit the second appearance of the key phrase in line 69. At this point, you must remember to **back up** and read for context (as opposed to starting at line 69 and reading from there). The purpose of a final sentence is to reiterate a point or draw a conclusion from the preceding information. In addition, this sentence starts with *but*, and you can't know what it's contradicting until you back up.

What do we learn from that paragraph? Basically, that melt migrates from the mantle upward to areas of lower pressure, ultimately hardening at the mid-ocean ridge. We can therefore assume that the mid-ocean ridge must be under less pressure than the mantle – which is exactly what C) says.

If that seems like an awfully large jump to make on your own, let's play process of elimination.

A) doesn't work because the passage only states that orthopyrexene and olivine are present in *melt*. It says nothing about those minerals in relationship to mid-ocean ridges.

B) is an answer you need to be careful with. The phrase *exchange of atoms* does appear, but only in regard to the chemical composition of melt in the mantle. Again, there is nothing about mid-ocean ridges.

C) See above. If you're not sure, leave it.

D) is vague and therefore seems eminently plausible, but unfortunately there's nothing in the passage to support it. Don't waste too much time looking; if it's not there, it's not there.

Now let's try another one, based on the same passage.

In line 66, the author refers to "laboratory experiments. Which of the following was an assumption researchers made during those experiments?

OR:

In line 66, the author refers to "laboratory experiments. Based on the passage, which of the following is a hypothesis the author suggests was tested in those experiments?

A) Melted rock contains lower levels of orthopyrexene than of olivine.
B) Melt is composed exclusively of olivine and orthopyrexene.
C) Orthopyrexene only dissolves at depths greater than 45 kilometers.
D) Rock sweat and hardened erupted melt have similar chemical compositions.

Although the word *assumption* only appears in the first version, both questions are in fact testing the same thing. In the second version, the word *suggests* indicates that this is an inference question, meaning that the correct answer will not be stated word-for-word in the passage.

While this question is phrased in a more complicated way than the previous questions, it's actually more straightforward. Since you are given a line reference, you at least have a clear starting point.

The key to answering questions like this is to remember that the correct answer only requires you to make a very **small** leap from the passage. If you try to juggle too many pieces of information at once, you'll get confused and end up staring at the answers without any idea of how to decide between them.

We're going to start by reading the sentence that includes the line reference:

> But what laboratory experiments revealed about the chemical composition of melt did not seem to match up with the composition of rock samples collected from the mid-ocean ridges, where erupted melt hardens.

The phrase *did not seem to match up* tell us that researchers found something different from what they were expecting. What did they find? That the chemical composition of the melt from the mantle (i.e. "rock sweat") didn't match the melt from the mid-ocean ridge.

Logically, then, what was their starting assumption? That the chemical composition of the two types of melt would match. That makes D) the correct answer.

Inference Exercises

1.   Sometimes it seems surprising that science functions at all. In 2005, medical science was shaken by a paper with the provocative title "Why most published research findings are false." Written by John
5 Ioannidis, a professor of medicine at Stanford University, it didn't actually show that any particular result was wrong. Instead, it showed that the statistics of reported positive findings was not consistent with how often one should *expect* to find them. As Ioannidis concluded more
10 recently, "many published research findings are false or exaggerated, and an estimated 85 percent of research resources are wasted."

     It's likely that some researchers are consciously cherry-picking data to get their work published.
15 And some of the problems surely lie with journal publication policies. But the problems of false findings often begin with researchers unwittingly fooling themselves: they fall prey to cognitive biases, common modes of thinking that lure us toward wrong but
20 convenient or attractive conclusions. "Seeing the reproducibility rates in psychology and other empirical science, we can safely say that something is not working out the way it should," says Susann Fiedler, a behavioral economist at the Max Planck Institute for Research on
25 Collective Goods in Bonn, Germany. "Cognitive biases might be one reason for that."

     Psychologist Brian Nosek of the University of Virginia says that the most common and problematic bias in science is "motivated reasoning": We interpret
30 observations to fit a particular idea. Psychologists have shown that "most of our reasoning is in fact rationalization," he says. In other words, we have already made the decision about what to do or to think, and our "explanation" of our reasoning is really a justification for
35 doing what we wanted to do—or to believe—anyway. Science is of course meant to be more objective and skeptical than everyday thought—but how much is it, really?

1

The passage suggests that researchers are likely to exaggerate their findings primarily because

A) they are driven by intense competition for funding.
B) they do not take the time to check their data.
C) they want to gain approval from their superiors.
D) they unconsciously persuade themselves that their results are accurate.

2

Which lines best support the answer to the previous question?

A) Lines 7-9 ("Instead...them")
B) Lines 13-14 ("It's...data)
C) Lines 15-16 ("And...policies")
D) Lines 29-30 ("We...idea")

3

An unstated assumption of the passage is that

A) most data falsification occurs unintentionally.
B) scientific findings today are less trustworthy than those made in the past.
C) science is a fundamentally irrational pursuit.
D) in comparison to other people, scientists are more likely to have cognitive biases.

2. The following passage is adapted from Jane Austen, *Northanger Abbey*, originally published in 1817.

No one who had ever seen Catherine Morland in her infancy would have supposed her born to be an heroine. Her situation in life, the character of her father and mother, her own person and disposition, were all
5 equally against her. Her father was a clergyman, without being neglected, or poor, and a very respectable man, though his name was Richard—and he had never been handsome. He had a considerable independence besides two good livings—and he was not in the least addicted
10 to locking up his daughters. Her mother was a woman of useful plain sense, with a good temper, and, what is more remarkable, with a good constitution. She had three sons before Catherine was born; and instead of dying in bringing the latter into the world, as anybody
15 might expect, she still lived on—lived to have six children more—to see them growing up around her, and to enjoy excellent health herself. A family of ten children will be always called a fine family, where there are heads and arms and legs enough for the number;
20 but the Morlands had little other right to the word, for they were in general very plain, and Catherine, for many years of her life, as plain as any. She had a thin awkward figure, a sallow skin without colour, dark lank hair, and strong features—so much for her person; and
25 not less unpropitious for heroism seemed her mind. She was fond of all boy's plays, and greatly preferred cricket not merely to dolls, but to the more heroic enjoyments of infancy, nursing a dormouse, feeding a canary-bird, or watering a rose-bush. Indeed she had
30 no taste for a garden; and if she gathered flowers at all, it was chiefly for the pleasure of mischief—at least so it was conjectured from her always preferring those which she was forbidden to take. Such were her propensities—her abilities were quite as extraordinary
35 She never could learn or understand anything before she was taught; and sometimes not even then, for she was often inattentive, and occasionally stupid. Her mother was three months in teaching her only to repeat the "Beggar's Petition"; and after all, her
40 next sister, Sally, could say it better than she did. Not that Catherine was always stupid—by no means; she learnt the fable of "The Hare and Many Friends" as quickly as any girl in England. Her mother wished her to learn music; and Catherine was sure she should like it,
45 for she was very fond of tinkling the keys of the old forlorn spinner; so, at eight years old she began. She learnt a year, and could not bear it; and Mrs. Morland, who did not insist on her daughters being accomplished in spite of incapacity or distaste, allowed her to leave
50 off. The day which dismissed the music-master was one of the happiest of Catherine's life. Her taste for drawing was not superior; though whenever she could obtain the outside of a letter from her mother or seize upon any other odd piece of paper, she did what she
55 could in that way, by drawing houses and trees, hens and chickens, all very much like one another. Writing and accounts she was taught by her father; French by her mother: her proficiency in either was not remarkable, and she shirked her lessons in both
60 whenever she could. What a strange, unaccountable character!—for with all these symptoms of profligacy at ten years old, she had neither a bad heart nor a bad temper, was seldom stubborn, scarcely ever quarrelsome, and very kind to the little ones, with
65 few interruptions of tyranny; she was moreover noisy and wild, hated confinement and cleanliness, and loved nothing so well in the world as rolling down the green slope at the back of the house.

1

An unstated assumption in the narrator's description of Catherine is that a heroine is typically

A) bold and daring.
B) brilliant and beautiful.
C) wild and rebellious.
D) independent and carefree.

2

The narrator suggests that Catherine's mother responded to her daughter's imperfections with

A) frequent irritation.
B) general indifference.
C) easy indulgence.
D) utter perplexity.

3

Which lines best support the answer to the previous question?

A) Lines 13-15 ("and…on")
B) Lines 20-21 ("for…plain")
C) Lines 38-40 ("Her…did")
D) Line 47-50 ("and…off")

4

The narrator suggests implies that Catherine was strongly motivated to do things that

A) were unusually difficult.
B) were taught by her parents.
C) were not permitted.
D) her siblings could not do.

5

Which lines best support the answer to the previous question?

A) Lines 26-27 ("She…dolls")
B) Lines 30-33 ("and…take")
D) Lines 43-44 ("Her…music")
C) Line 54-56 ("she…another")

6

The narrator's references to a dormouse, canary-bird, and rose bush (lines 28-29) most strongly suggest that Catherine

A) could behave in a cruel manner.
B) preferred to play alone than with other children.
C) rejected a range of conventionally feminine activities.
D) recognized her exceptional behavior.

3. The following passage is adapted from Wiebke Brauer, "The Miracle of Space," © 2014 by *Smart Magazine.*

Imagine a world where you share the available space with others: without signs, sidewalks, or bicycle lanes. A vision otherwise known as shared space – and one that becomes more and more relevant with
5   the crowding of our cities. While this might sound like urban science fiction or, possibly, impending chaos mixed with survival of the fittest, this particular concept is the declared dream of many traffic planners.

Shared space means streets freed of signs and
10 signals; streets solely governed by right of way, leaving road users to their own devices. In order to restructure public space, it removes all superfluous interventions and contradictory guidelines. Many countries are currently in the process of installing – or at least
15 discussing – such 'lawless' areas: Germany and the Netherlands, Denmark and the UK, Switzerland and the USA, but also Australia and New Zealand.

One could argue that shared spaces have been around for a long time, simply under different terms
20 and titles. Back in the 1970s, for example, residents enjoyed mixed traffic areas, traffic calming, and play streets. And yet, these were not quite the same: Shared space involves a new and radical push for equal rights of all road users, pedestrian and otherwise. And
25 while it was British urban designer Ben Hamilton-Baillie who coined the actual term, the concept itself was developed in the mid-1990s under former Dutch traffic manager Hans Monderman. Shortly before his death in 2006, Monderman explained the basic tenets
30 of shared space as such: "The problem with traffic engineers is that when there's a problem with a road, they always try to add something. To my mind, it's much better to remove things."

Indeed, studies have shown that in many places –
35 where signs and traffic lights have been removed and where each and every one is responsible for their own actions in ungoverned space – the rate of accidents goes down. The reason: the traditional strict separation between cars, cyclists, and pedestrians encourages
40 clashes at crossings. And although shared space requires cars to lower their speed, it also cuts down on journey times since it encourages a continuous flow of traffic instead of bringing it to a halt through traffic signals.

45 Monderman was utterly convinced that shared space would work anywhere in the world because, underneath it all, people are basically the same, despite any cultural differences. In an interview, he stated that "emotions and issues are the same everywhere. You should be able
50 to read a street like a book. If you insist on constantly guiding people and treating them like idiots, you shouldn't be surprised if they act like idiots after a while."

At the same time, the threat of looming idiocy
55 is not the most pressing reason for a future traffic management rethink. Recent city planning, for example, has evolved along the same lines around the world: think highways and flyovers dissecting the city's natural fabric, dedicated pedestrian zones, and
60 large shopping malls. Clear-cut boundaries between driving, work, life, and shopping are emphasized by a thicket of signs. The result: ultimate, well-ordered bleakness. At night, you might find yourself in an empty, soulless pedestrian zone. A lot of the time,
65 urbanization simply translates as uniformity.

In recent years, however, city and traffic planners have decided to tackle this issue with "road space attractiveness" measures to breathe new spirit into lifeless satellite towns. Their goal: a new definition
70 of space and mobility against the background that the notion of "might is right" – and only if those in power stick to the rules – is more than outdated. The unregulated and unorthodox approach of shared space makes it obvious to each and every individual
75 that this concept requires cooperation, that sharing is the new having.

Critics of Monderman and Hamilton-Baillie have voiced that no rules implies the inevitable return of "might is right." Yet who says that chaos
80 reigns in the absence of order? That's a questionable statement. Shared space certainly requires a new mindset and we can't expect a swift shift away from traditional traffic planning – bigger, further, faster.

But the vision of no more set traffic cycles, fewer
85 linear and predefined patterns, of freely flowing and intermingling participants in an open and boundless space, is equally unfettered and fascinating. A vision in the spirit of Pericles who wrote around 450 BC that "you need freedom for happiness and courage
90 for freedom."

1

The passage suggests that the most pressing reason for overhauling the way traffic is managed is that

A) the removal of traffic signal results in more varied and vibrant urban spaces.
B) drivers are unlikely to take responsibility for their actions when they are left alone.
C) overreliance on traffic signals makes drivers weak and passive.
D) accidents are more likely to occur when traffic signals are present.

2

Based on the passage, it is reasonable to infer that those in charge of planning traffic

A) are horrified by Hans Monderman's proposal.
B) believe that drivers' behavior does not vary across cultures.
C) believe that abolishing traffic signals would create chaos.
D) are frequently opposed to the use of traffic signals.

3

Which lines best support the answer to the previous question?

A) Lines 7-8 ("this…planners")
B) Lines 20-22 ("Back…streets")
C) Lines 50-53 ("If…while")
D) Lines 56-58 ("Recent…world")

4. This passage is from Samuel Gompers, "What Does the Working Man Want?" 1890. Gompers, a Scottish Immigrant, was the founder of the American Federation of Labor and helped workers to organize and fight for fairer working conditions.

My friends, we have met here today to celebrate
the idea that has prompted thousands of working-people
of Louisville and New Albany to parade the streets;
that prompts the toilers of Chicago to turn out by their
5 fifty or hundred thousand of men; that prompts the vast
army of wage-workers in New York to demonstrate
their enthusiasm and appreciation of the importance of
this idea; that prompts the toilers of England, Ireland,
Germany, France, Italy, Spain, and Austria to defy the
10 manifestos of the autocrats of the world and say that
on May the first, 1890, the wage-workers of the world
will lay down their tools in sympathy with the wage-
workers of America, to establish a principle of
limitations of hours of labor to eight hours for sleep,
15 eight hours for work, and eight hours for what we will.
    It has been charged time and again that were we
to have more hours of leisure we would merely devote
it to the cultivation of vicious habits. They tell us that
the eight-hour movement can not be enforced, for the
20 reason that it must check industrial and commercial
progress. I say that the history of this shows the reverse.
I say that is the plane on which this question ought
to be discussed—that is the social question. As long as
they make this question economic one, I am willing to
25 discuss it with them. I would retrace every step I have
taken to advance this movement did it mean industrial
and commercial stagnation. But it does not mean that.
It means greater prosperity it means a greater degree of
progress for the whole people.
30   They say they can't afford it. Is that true? Let us
see for one moment. If a reduction in the hours of labor
causes industrial and commercial ruination, it would
naturally follow increased hours of labor would
increase the prosperity, commercial and industrial.
35 If that were true, England and America ought to be at
the tail end, and China at the head of civilization.
    Why, when you reduce the hours of labor, just
think what it means. Suppose men who work ten
hours a day had the time lessened to nine, or men who
40 work nine hours a day have it reduced to eight; what
does it mean? It means millions of golden hours and
opportunities for thought. Some men might say you will
go to sleep. Well, the ordinary man might try to sleep
sixteen hours a day, but he would soon find he could
45 not do it long. He would probably become interested in
some study and the hours that have been taken from
manual labor are devoted to mental labor, and the

mental labor of one hour produce for him more wealth
than the physical labor of a dozen hours.
50   I maintain that this is a true proposition—that
men under the short-hour system not only have
opportunity to improve themselves, but to make a
greater degree of prosperity for their employers.
Why, my friends, how is it in China, how is it in
55 Spain, how is it in India and Russia, how is it in Italy?
Cast your eye throughout the universe and observe the
industry that forces nature to yield up its fruits to man's
necessities, and you will find that where the hours of
labor are the shortest the progress of invention in
60 machinery and the prosperity of the people are the
greatest. It has only been under the great influence of
our great republic, were our people have exhibited
their great senses, that we can move forward, upward
and onward, and are watched with interest in our
65 movements of progress and reform.

1

Based on the passage, Gompers implies that in comparison to workers in the United States, workers in China (line 36)

A) enjoy greater prosperity.
B) are more industrious.
C) spend more hours at work.
D) are less fairly compensated.

2

Gompers suggests that one of the main consequences of long working hours in the United States is that

A) civic participation is reduced.
B) important discoveries go unmade.
C) workers are too exhausted to perform their jobs.
D) the quality of work declines.

3

Which lines best support the answer to the previous question?

A) Lines 16-18 ("It...habits")
B) Lines 22-23 ("I...question")
C) Lines 31-34 ("If...industrial")
D) Lines 46-49 ("the hours...hours")

5. The following passage is adapted from Michael Anft, "Solving the Mystery of Death Valley's Walking Rocks," © 2011 by Johns Hopkins Magazine.

For six decades, observers have been confounded by the movement of large rocks across a dry lake bed in California's Death Valley National Park. Leaving flat trails behind them, rocks that weigh up to 100
5 pounds seemingly do Michael Jackson's moonwalk across the valley's sere, cracked surface, sometimes traveling more than 100 yards. Without a body of water to pick them up and move them, the rocks at Racetrack Playa, a flat space between the valley's high cliffs,
10 have been the subject of much speculation, including whether they have been relocated by human pranksters or space aliens. The rocks have become the desert equivalent of Midwestern crop circles. "They really are a curiosity," says Ralph Lorenz, a planetary scientist at
15 the Applied Physics Laboratory. "Some [people] have mentioned UFOs. But I've always believed that this is something science could solve."

It has tried. One theory holds that the rocks are blown along by powerful winds. Another posits that
20 the wind pushes thin sheets of ice, created when the desert's temperatures dip low enough to freeze water from a rare rainstorm, and the rocks go along for the ride. But neither theory is rock solid. Winds at the playa aren't strong enough—some scientists believe that
25 they'd have to be 100 miles per hour or more—to blow the rocks across the valley. And rocks subject to the "ice sailing theory" wouldn't create trails as they moved.

Lorenz and a team of investigators believe that a
30 combination of forces may work to rearrange Racetrack Playa's rocks. "We saw that it would take a lot of wind to move these rocks, which are larger than you'd expect wind to move," Lorenz explains. "That led us to this idea that ice might be picking up the
35 rocks and floating them." As they explained in the January issue of *The American Journal of Physics*, instead of moving along with wind-driven sheets of ice, the rocks may instead be lifted by the ice, making them more subject to the wind's force. The key, Lorenz
40 says, is that the lifting by an "ice collar" reduces friction with the ground, to the point that the wind now has enough force to move the rock. The rock moves, the ice doesn't, and because part of the rock juts through the ice, it marks the territory it has covered.
45 Lorenz's team came to its conclusion through a combination of intuition, lab work, and observation— not that the last part was easy. Watching the rocks travel is a bit like witnessing the rusting of a hubcap. Instances of movement are rare and last for only a few

50 seconds. Lorenz's team placed low-resolution cameras on the cliffs (which are about 30 miles from the nearest paved road) to take pictures once per hour. For the past three winters, the researchers have weathered extreme temperatures and several flat tires to measure how
55 often the thermometer dips below freezing, how often the playa gets rain and floods, and the strength of the winds. "The measurements seem to back up our hypothesis," he says. "Any of the theories may be true at any one time, but ice rafting may be the best explan-
60 ation for the trails we've been seeing. We've seen trails like this documented in Arctic coastal areas, and the mechanism is somewhat similar. A belt of ice sur- rounds a boulder during high tide, picks it up, and then drops it elsewhere." His "ice raft theory" was also
65 borne out by an experiment that used the ingenuity of a high school science fair. Lorenz placed a basalt pebble in a Tupperware container with water so that the pebble projected just above the surface. He then turned the container upside down in a baking tray filled with a
70 layer of coarse sand at its base, and put the whole thing in his home freezer. The rock's "keel" (its protruding part) projected downward into the sand, which simu- lated the cracked surface of the playa (which scientists call "Special K" because of its resemblance to cereal
75 flakes). A gentle push or slight puff of air caused the Tupperware container to move, just as an ice raft would under the right conditions. The pebble made a trail in the soft sand. "It was primitive but effective," Lorenz says of the experiment. Lorenz has spent the
80 last 20 years studying Titan, a moon of Saturn. He says that Racetrack Playa's surface mirrors that of a dried lakebed on Titan. Observations and experiments on Earth may yield clues to that moon's geology. "We also may get some idea of how climate affects
85 geology—particularly as the climate changes here on Earth," Lorenz says. "When we study other planets and their moons, we're forced to use Occam's razor – sometimes the simplest answer is best, which means you look to Earth for some answers. Once you get out
90 there on Earth, you realize how strange so much of its surface is. So, you have to figure there's weird stuff to be found on Titan as well." Whether that's true or not will take much more investigation. He adds: "One day, we'll figure all this out. For the moment, the moving
95 rock present a wonderful problem to study in a beautiful place."

179

1

It is reasonable to conclude that one of the scientists' goals in studying Racetrack Valleys was to

A) investigate how life could be supported on Titan.
B) understand the effects of climate change.
C) understand the geology of a range of planets.
D) discover the limitations of wind power.

2

Which lines best support the answer to the previous question?

A) Lines 23-26 ("Winds…valley")
B) Lines 52-57 ("For…winds")
C) Lines 75-77 ("A gentle…conditions")
D) Lines 83-86 ("We…Earth")

3

The passage implies that scientists rejected the theory that the rocks were carried on sheets of ice pushed by the wind because

A) the winds were too weak to move the rocks.
B) the rocks left a trace of their movement.
C) rock is too dense to be moved by wind.
D) the rocks had too much friction with the ground.

4

Which lines best support the answer to the previous question?

A) Lines 26-28 ("And…moved")
B) Lines 37-39 ("Instead…force")
C) Lines 49-50 ("Instances…seconds")
D) Lines 62-64 ("A belt…elsewhere")

6. The following passage is adapted from "Makerspaces, Hackerspaces, and Community Scale Production in Detroit and Beyond," © 2013 by Sean Ansanelli.

During the mid-1980s, spaces began to emerge across Europe where computer hackers could convene for mutual support and camaraderie. In the past few years, the idea of fostering such shared, physical spaces
5 has been rapidly adapted by the diverse and growing community of "makers", who seek to apply the idea of "hacking" to physical objects, processes, or anything else that can be deciphered and improved upon.

A hackerspace is described by hackerspaces.org as
10 a "community-operated physical space where people with common interests, often in computers, technology, science, digital art or electronic art, can meet, socialize, and/or collaborate." Such spaces can vary in size, available technology, and membership structure (some
15 being completely open), but generally share community-oriented characteristics. Indeed, while the term "hacker" can sometimes have negative connotations, modern hackerspaces thrive off of community, openness, and assimilating diverse viewpoints – these often being the
20 only guiding principles in otherwise informal organizational structures.

In recent years, the city of Detroit has emerged as a hotbed for hackerspaces and other DIY ("Do-It-Yourself") experiments. Several hackerspaces
25 can already be found throughout the city and several more are currently in formation. Of course, Detroit's attractiveness for such projects can be partially attributed to cheap real estate, which allows aspiring hackers to acquire ample space for experimentation. Some observers
30 have also described this kind of making and tinkering as embedded in the DNA of Detroit's residents, who are able to harness substantial intergenerational knowledge and attract like-minded individuals.

Hackerspaces (or "makerspaces") can be found in
35 more commercial forms, but the vast majority of spaces are self-organized and not-for-profit. For example, the OmniCorp hackerspace operates off member fees to cover rent and new equipment, from laser cutters to welding tools. OmniCorp also hosts an "open hack night"
40 every Thursday in which the space is open to the general public. Potential members are required to attend at least one open hack night prior to a consensus vote by the existing members for admittance; no prospective members have yet been denied.
45 A visit to one of OmniCorp's open hack nights reveals the vast variety of activity and energy existing in the space. In the main common room alone, activities range from experimenting with sound installations and learning to program Arduino boards to building speculative "oloid"

50 shapes – all just for the sake of it. With a general atmosphere of mutual support, participants in the space are continually encouraged to help others.

One of the most active community-focused initiatives in the city is the Mt. Elliot Makerspace. Jeff Sturges,
55 former MIT Media Lab Fellow and Co-Founder of OmniCorp, started the Mt. Elliot project with the aim of replicating MIT's Fab Lab model on a smaller, cheaper scale in Detroit. "Fab Labs" are production facilities that consist of a small collection of flexible computer
60 controlled tools that cover several different scales and various materials, with the aim to make "almost anything" (including other machines). The Mt. Elliot Makerspace now offers youth-based skill development programs in eight areas: Transportation, Electronics,
65 Digital Tools, Wearables, Design and Fabrication, Food, Music, and Arts. The range of activities is meant to provide not only something for everyone, but a well-rounded base knowledge of making to all participants.

While the center receives some foundational support,
70 the space also derives significant support from the local community. Makerspaces throughout the city connect the space's youth-based programming directly to school curriculums.

The growing interest in and development of
75 hacker/makerspaces has been explained, in part, as a result of the growing maker movement. Through the combination of cultural norms and communication channels from open source production as well as increasingly available technologies for physical
80 production, amateur maker communities have developed in virtual and physical spaces.

Publications such as *Wired* are noticing the transformative potential of this emerging movement and have sought to devote significant attention to its
85 development. Chief editor Chris Anderson recently published a book entitled *Makers*, in which he proclaims that the movement will become the next Industrial Revolution. Anderson argues such developments will allow for a new wave of business opportunities by
90 providing mass-customization rather than mass-production.

The transformative potential of these trends goes beyond new business opportunities or competitive advantages for economic growth. Rather, these trends
95 demonstrate the potential to actually transform economic development models entirely.

Based on the passage, it can be reasonably inferred that hackerspaces are set up in a manner that is

A) tightly regulated.
B) disorganized and chaotic.
C) casual and accommodating.
D) determined by an elected body.

Which lines best support the answer to the previous question?

A) Lines 3-6 ("In…makers")
B) Lines 17-21 ("modern…structures")
C) Lines 34-36 ("Hackerspaces…profit")
D) Lines 45-47 ("A visit…space")

The author implies that one potential challenge for new hackerspaces involves

A) zoning restrictions.
B) lack of publicity.
C) local protests.
D) property costs.

Which lines best support the answer to the previous question?

A) Lines 16-17 ("Indeed…connotations")
B) Lines 26-29 ("Of…experimentation")
C) Lines 36-39 ("For…tools")
D) Lines 69-71 ("While…community")

7. The following passage is adapted from Julian Jackson, "New Research Suggests Dinosaurs Were Warm-Blooded and Active" © 2011 by Julian Jackson.

New research from the University of Adelaide has added to the debate about whether dinosaurs were cold-blooded and sluggish or warm-blooded and active. Professor Roger Seymour from the University's School
5 of Earth & Environmental Sciences has applied the latest theories of human and animal anatomy and physiology to provide insight into the lives of dinosaurs.

Human thigh bones have tiny holes – known as the
10 "nutrient foramen" – on the shaft that supply blood to living bone cells inside. New research has shown that the size of those holes is related to the maximum rate that a person can be active during aerobic exercise. Professor Seymour has used this principle to evaluate
15 the activity levels of dinosaurs.

"Far from being lifeless, bone cells have a relatively high metabolic rate and they therefore require a large blood supply to deliver oxygen. On the inside of the bone, the blood supply comes usually from a single
20 artery and vein that pass through a hole on the shaft – the nutrient foramen," he says.

Professor Seymour wondered whether the size of the nutrient foramen might indicate how much blood was necessary to keep the bones in good repair. For
25 example, highly active animals might cause more bone 'microfractures,' requiring more frequent repairs by the bone cells and therefore a greater blood supply. "My aim was to see whether we could use fossil bones of dinosaurs to indicate the level of bone metabolic rate
30 and possibly extend it to the whole body's metabolic rate," he says. "One of the big controversies among paleobiologists is whether dinosaurs were cold-blooded and sluggish or warm-blooded and active. Could the size of the foramen be a possible gauge for dinosaur
35 metabolic rate?"

Comparisons were made with the sizes of the holes in living mammals and reptiles, and their metabolic rates. Measuring mammals ranging from mice to elephants, and reptiles from lizards to crocodiles, one
40 of Professor Seymour's Honors students, Sarah Smith, combed the collections of Australian museums, photographing and measuring hundreds of tiny holes in thigh bones.

"The results were unequivocal. The sizes of the holes
45 were related closely to the maximum metabolic rates during peak movement in mammals and reptiles," Professor Seymour says. "The holes found in mammals were about 10 times larger than those in reptiles."

These holes were compared to those of fossil
50 dinosaurs. Dr. Don Henderson, Curator of Dinosaurs from the Royal Tyrrell Museum in Alberta, Canada, and Daniela Schwarz-Wings from the Museum für Naturkunde Humboldt University Berliny, German measured the holes in 10 species of
55 dinosaurs from five different groups, including bipedal and quadrupedal carnivores and herbivores, weighing 50kg to 20,000kg.

"On a relative comparison to eliminate the differences in body size, all of the dinosaurs had
60 holes in their thigh bones larger than those of mammals," Professor Seymour says.

"The dinosaurs appeared to be even more active than the mammals. We certainly didn't expect to see that. These results provide additional weight to
65 theories that dinosaurs were warm-blooded and highly active creatures, rather than cold-blooded and sluggish."

Professor Seymour says following the results of this study, it's likely that a simple measurement of
70 foramen size could be used to evaluate maximum activity levels in other vertebrate animals.

1

Based on the passage, it can be reasonably inferred that a creature with a small foramen would most likely be

A) cold-blooded.
B) warm-blooded.
C) smaller than average.
D) larger than average.

2

An unstated assumption in the passage is that

A) warm- or cold-bloodedness cannot be determined by an animal's activity level.
B) some prehistoric creatures were physiologically similar to modern ones.
C) foramen size can be an unreliable indicator of activity level.
D) mammal bones are significantly larger than reptile bones.

Official Guide/Khan Academy Inference Questions

Test 1

15   Attitude
21   Main point
26

Test 2

26
38

48   No line reference
49   Evidence

Test 3

3   No line reference
4   Evidence
8
23   Assumption

29   No line reference
30   Evidence

32   No line reference
33   Evidence

43   Line reference
44   Evidence

45   No line reference
46   Evidence

49   Assumption

Test 4

8

16   No line reference
17   Evidence

25   No line reference
26   Evidence

31
35
48

Explanations: Inference Exercises

1.1-2 D, D

The easiest way to answer this question is to use the main point (science = wrong b/c cognitive biases), which should allow you to identify D) as the correct answer to 1.1 When you look at the line references in 1.2, you know that the correct answer must be related to cognitive biases. Only D) fits that criterion.

Otherwise, you can work by plugging in the line references from 1.2. You must pay very close attention to the wording of the question however. All of the line references involve possible explanations for exaggerated data, but the question asks about the *primary* reason scientists exaggerate data. That corresponds to the phrase *most common and problematic bias* in D).

1.3 A

The easiest way to answer this question is again to use the main point: science = wrong b/c cognitive biases. What does the author say about cognitive biases? That they involve researchers *unwittingly fooling themselves* (note that this information appears right next to a colon, in lines 17-18). In other words, scientists don't realize they're exaggerating their findings, a fact that corresponds to A).

2.1 B

Virtually the entire passage involves the narrator describing the various ways in which Catherine is unsuited to being a heroine, so it can be inferred that a heroine should be all of the things that Catherine is *not*. One of the major points of the passage is that Catherine is a less-than-brilliant student who prefers to blow off her lessons. It can therefore be inferred that a heroine should be exceptionally intelligent. Likewise, lines 22-24 indicate that Catherine is "plain" – logically, a heroine should be the opposite (beautiful). The other answers refer to attributes that could be associated with Catherine.

2.2-3 C, D

If you happen to recall from your initial reading of the passage that Mrs. Morland is generally good-natured, you might be able to identify C) as the correct answer to 2.2 because it is the only positive option. Otherwise, start by plugging in the line references, looking for information that *suggests* (remember this is an inference question) how Catherine's mother responded to her antics. Lines 13-15 only indicate that Catherine's mother managed to survive giving birth to so many children, so A) can be eliminated. Lines 20-21 focus on the Morlands' physical appearance, and lines 38-40 only indicate that it took Catherine's mother more than three months to teach Catherine the "Beggar's Petition" – they say nothing about how Mrs. Morland reacted. B) and C) can thus be eliminated as well. D) is correct because lines 47-50 indicate that Mrs. Morland allowed her daughter to stop music lessons, indicating that she responded to Catherine's lack of brilliance or perseverance without any fuss. That corresponds most directly to C) in 2.2.

2.4-5 C, B

If you have enough of a sense of the passage to understand that Catherine is somewhat naughty, you can make a reasonable assumption that the answer to 2.4 is C), then plug in the line references to 2.5 looking for lines that support that idea. Otherwise, the question is broad enough that you are best off plugging in the line references, looking for information about what most motivates Catherine. Lines 26-27 indicate she preferred boys' games, but no answer in 2.4 corresponds to that idea. Lines 30-33 correctly suggest Catherine's propensity for doing things that were forbidden, i.e. not allowed, making C) the answer to 2.4. Neither lines 43-44 nor 54-56 provide information about Catherine's preferences that supports an answer in 2.4.

2.6 C

Start by considering the full sentence in which the references appear (lines 26-29). The point of the sentence is that Catherine preferred boys' games, which is simply another way of saying that she "rejected conventionally feminine activities."

3.1 A

If you have a good understanding of the passage as a whole, you may be able to eliminate B) in 3.1 immediately; the passage indicates that drivers are *more* likely to take responsibility for their behavior in the absence of traffic signals. The other answers in 3.1 are all ideas included in the passage – the question is which one the author considers *most* pressing. That is your key phrase, and you should scan the passage for it. It appears in line 54. A) is correct because lines 54-56 state that *At the same time, the threat of looming idiocy is not the most pressing reason for a future traffic management rethink.* The implication is that the information that follows *is* the most pressing reason for a traffic management rethink. What information follows? A description of bland, soulless urban spaces that could be revitalized by the elimination of traffic divisions. That corresponds to A).

3.2-3 D, A

The question in 3.2 provides very little direction, so start by plugging in line references – you'll hit the answer almost immediately. Lines 7-8 state that *this concept is the declared dream of many traffic planners.* What does "this concept" refer to? A world *without signs, sidewalks, or bicycle lanes.* In other words, most traffic planners agree with Monderman that traffic signals should be abolished. The answer to 3.2 is therefore D), and the answer to 3.3 is A).

4.1 C

The question provides a line reference, so start there. The sentence in which "China" appears states that *If that were true, England and America ought to be at the tail end, and China at the head of civilization.*

In order to figure out what "that" refers to, however, you must back up and read the beginning of the paragraph. What does it tell us? That if fewer working hours caused a decline in national prosperity, then more hours would increase prosperity. The statement that *China [would be] at the head of civilization* if that statement were true, implies that Chinese workers put in very long hours. The answer is therefore C).

4.2-3 B, D

This is a general enough question that you are best off plugging in the line references in 4.3, unless you happen to remember the answer to 4.2. In lines 16-18, the phrase *It has been charged* indicates that Gompers is citing the conventional wisdom – what he does not believe. Eliminate A). B) and C) are incorrect because lines 22-23 and 31-34 provide no information about the *consequences* of long working hours. D) is correct because lines 46-49 suggest that workers could make important discoveries if they were given more free time (*the mental labor of one hour produce for him more wealth than the physical labor of a dozen hours*). The answer to 4.2 is therefore B), and the answer to 4.3 is D).

5.1-2 B, D

If you remember the discussion of Titan from the passage, you might be tempted to pick A) – but careful! None of the lines provided in 5.2 supports the idea that the scientists were attempting to understand how Titan could support life. In fact, the passage only directly indicates that scientists wanted to understand Titan's *geology* (lines 82-83). So plug in the line references from 5.2. The only set of lines to directly support an answer in 5.1 is D); in lines 83-86, Lorenz states that *We may also may get some idea of how climate affects geology— particularly as the climate changes here on Earth.* It can thus be inferred that one of his goals in conducting research on Racetrack Playa is to understand the potential effects of climate change.

5.3-4 B, A

5.3 is phrased in a somewhat complicated manner, so start by rephrasing the question to make sure you're clear on what it's asking. You might say something like, "Why did scientists reject the theory that the rocks were carried on ice?" It's unlikely you'll remember that information, so start by plugging in. Lines 26-28 give you the answer immediately – the only challenge is recognizing that they give you the answer. The problem is that these lines refer to the "ice-sailing" theory; you must back up and read the full paragraph in order to recognize that the "ice-sailing" theory posits that the rocks were carried on ice (lines 19-23, "Another…ride"). What does the passage indicate about the weakness in that theory? The passage states that rocks moved by ice *wouldn't create trails as they moved*. Logically, then, scientists rejected the ice-sailing theory because the Racetrack Playa rocks *did* leave trails. That is what B) in 5.3 says, so it is the answer.

6.1-2 C, B

One of the major points that the author makes about makerspaces/hackerspaces is that they're flexible and open/non-exclusive. If you have that big picture understanding, you can immediately identify C) as the most likely answer to 6.1, then check the line references in 6.2 to confirm. Otherwise, start by plugging in the line references. A) is incorrect because lines 3-6 only describe the community of "makers" themselves (diverse and growing); they do not describe the actual organization of makerspaces themselves. B) is correct because lines 17-21 indicate that *community, openness, and assimilating diverse viewpoints* are often hackerspaces' *only* guiding principles. In other words, they're not terribly structured. In 6.1, B) is too extreme because hackerspaces do have *some* guiding principles, just loose ones. C) is a much better fit for the description in the passage.

6.3-4 D, B

This is a real detail-based question, so it's unlikely you'll remember the answer to 6.3. Work by plugging in from 6.4. A) is incorrect because lines 16-17 only state that "hacking" can have negative connotations; they don't indicate any particular challenge to hackerspaces consistent with an answer in 6.3. B) is subtle but correct. Lines 26-29 indicate that Detroit is particularly well-suited to fostering hackerspaces because of "cheap real estate," implying that (higher) real estate costs could pose an obstacle to hackerspace growth elsewhere. The answer to 6.3 is therefore D). No information is either lines 36-39 or 69-71 directly supports any of the answers in 6.3.

7.1 A

Think about the passage and Seymour's experiment as a whole: the primary hypothesis was that since warm-bloodedness is associated with large holes in the bone (high metabolic rate), the presence of large bone holes in dinosaurs would indicate warm-bloodedness. Logically, the opposite would hold true as well: small holes in the bone would indicate cold-bloodedness. That is what A) says, so it is correct.

7.2 B

Again, consider the passage as a whole. The premise of Seymour's study was that foramen size could be studied as an indicator of metabolic level in dinosaurs (prehistoric creatures) because foramen size could be studied as an indicator of metabolic level in reptiles and mammals (present-day creatures). In order for the findings to be meaningful, the bodies of prehistoric creatures must have functioned in a similar way to those of modern-day creatures. That is essentially what B) says, so it is correct.

8. Supporting and Undermining Claims

We've already spent a fair amount of time looking at one type of supporting evidence question, but now we're going to look at another type. While these questions and answers may look similar to the examples we've worked through, there are some important differences. First, the questions are not part of paired sets but rather single questions. Second, their answers consist solely of lines references; you must identify the lines that support an idea discussed within the passage. As mentioned earlier, these questions are rare, appearing no more than a couple of times per test.

Questions that ask you to **support** a claim test your ability to recognize what sort of information would be **consistent** with an argument or idea discussed in the passage.

Questions that ask you to **contradict** a claim are testing your ability to recognize what sort of information would be **inconsistent** with an argument or idea discussed in the passage.

If you approach these questions methodically, they can become quite straightforward. *But you can't get impatient, and you can't skip steps, no matter how much you want to just get the answer.* If you're not really certain what a support/undermine question is asking, OR you don't feel that you can focus properly, you are better off simply skipping it and returning to it if you have time.

The process for answering support/undermine questions can be broken into three steps:

1) Identify the claim and restate it if necessary

If the claim is stated simply in the question, underline it. If it's worded more complexly, rephrase it more simply and write it down. You can't evaluate whether a set of lines would support an idea unless you know what that idea is.

2) Determine what sort of information would support/contradict the claim

You should at least attempt to do this on your own and not assume you'll be able to recognize the information from the answer choices.

3) Check the answers

Remember that in some cases, you may need to read above/below the lines referenced for context. Remember also not to eliminate any answers just because you find them confusing.

Let's look at some examples:

This passage is adapted from Barry Schwartz, "More Isn't Always Better," © 2006 by Harvard Business Review.

Marketers assume that the more choices they offer, the more likely customers will be able to find just the right thing. They assume, for instance, that offering 50 styles of jeans instead of two increases the chances that
5 shoppers will find a pair they really like. Nevertheless, research now shows that there can be too much choice; when there is, consumers are less likely to buy anything at all, and if they do buy, they are less satisfied with their selection.
10   It all began with jam. In 2000, psychologists Sheena Iyengar and Mark Lepper published a remarkable study. On one day, shoppers at an upscale food market saw a display table with 24 varieties of gourmet jam. Those who sampled the spreads received a coupon for $1 off
15 any jam. On another day, shoppers saw a similar table, except that only six varieties of the jam were on display. The large display attracted more interest than the small one. But when the time came to purchase, people who saw the large display were one-tenth as likely to buy as
20 people who saw the small display.
       Other studies have confirmed this result that more choice is not always better. As the variety of snacks, soft drinks, and beers offered at convenience stores increases, for instance, sales volume and customer
25 satisfaction decrease. Moreover, as the number of retirement investment options available to employees increases, the chance that they will choose any decreases. These studies and others have shown not only that excessive choice can produce "choice
30 paralysis," but also that it can reduce people's satisfaction with their decisions, even if they made good ones. My colleagues and I have found that increased choice decreases satisfaction with matters as trivial as ice cream flavors and as significant as jobs.
35   These results challenge what we think we know about human nature and the determinants of well-being. Both psychology and business have operated on the assumption that the relationship between choice and well-being is straightforward: The more choices people
40 have, the better off they are. In psychology, the benefits of choice have been tied to autonomy and control. In business, the benefits of choice have been tied to the benefits of free markets more generally. Added options make no one worse off, and they are bound to make
45 someone better off.
       Choice *is* good for us, but its relationship to satisfaction appears to be more complicated than we

had assumed. There is diminishing marginal utility in having alternatives; each new option subtracts a little
50 from the feeling of well-being, until the marginal benefits of added choice level off. What's more, psychologists and business academics alike have largely ignored another outcome of choice: More of it requires increased time and effort and can lead to
55 anxiety, regret, excessively high expectations, and self-blame if the choices don't work out. When the number of available options is small, these costs are negligible, but the costs grow with the number of options. Eventually, each new option makes us feel
60 worse off than we did before.
       Without a doubt, having more options enables us, most of the time, to achieve better objective outcomes. Again, having 50 styles of jeans as opposed to two increases the likelihood that customers will find a pair
65 that fits. But the subjective outcome may be that shoppers will feel overwhelmed and dissatisfied. This dissociation between objective and subjective results creates a significant challenge for retailers and marketers that look to choice as a way to enhance the
70 perceived value of their goods and services.
       Choice can no longer be used to justify a marketing strategy in and of itself. More isn't always better, either for the customer or for the retailer. Discovering how much assortment is warranted is a
75 considerable empirical challenge. But companies that get the balance right will be amply rewarded.

1

Which choice best supports the author's claim that an excess of choice can lead consumers to become overwhelmed?

A) Lines 3-5 ("They…like")
B) Lines 18-20 ("people…display")
C) Lines 46-48 ("Choice…assumed")
D) Lines 73-75 ("Discovering…challenge")

Although this question asks about the relationship between ideas in the passage, it is unnecessary to find the original claim in the passage – even if you hadn't read a word of it, the question would still tell you exactly what you needed to find evidence supporting, namely that an excess of consumer choice can lead consumers to become overwhelmed.

That's a fairly straightforward argument, but if you wanted to restate it more simply to keep yourself focused, you could write something like, "Too much choice = BAD." Now all you have to do is find the lines that most directly support that idea. That's essentially the main point of the passage, so the answer could be pretty much anywhere. We therefore need to check the answers in order.

A) **They assume, for instance, that offering 50 styles of jeans instead of two increases the chances that shoppers will find a pair they really like.**

No. We're looking for an option that discusses choice leading to *dissatisfaction*. These lines discuss exactly the opposite idea.

B) **People who saw the large display were one-tenth as likely to buy as people who saw the small display.**

Yes, this fits. Consider the context: the author is describing the outcome of Iyengar and Lepper's study, which found that people who are given too many options are often unable to decide at all. If you're clear about that, you can stop right here. If you're not sure, however, keep going.

C) **Choice is good for us, but its relationship to satisfaction appears to be more complicated than we had assumed.**

Careful here. The lines indicate that the relationship between choice and satisfaction is problematic, but they don't **directly** support the idea that people are overwhelmed by too many choices.

D) **Discovering how much assortment is warranted is a considerable empirical challenge.**

The "confusing" answer, filled with unusual phrasing and abstract, challenging phrasing (*warranted, considerable empirical challenge*). In context, these lines simply indicate that it isn't yet clear when choice stops being a good thing and starts being bad. So no, this answer is off topic.

So the answer is B).

This question could also be asked the other way around, as an "undermine" question.

1

A marketer claims that more choices are always beneficial. Which of the following statements in the passage contradicts the student's claim?

A) Lines 3-5 ("They...like")
B) Lines 18-20 ("people...display")
C) Lines 46-48 ("Choice...assumed")
D) Lines 73-75 ("Discovering...challenge")

First of all, note that although this question is phrased from the opposite perspective, it is actually the exact same question we just worked through.

Because the phrasing of the question is more complicated and thus potentially more confusing, you should definitely take a moment and simplify/rewrite the question before looking at the answer choices.

The question is asking us to identify what idea in the passage contradicts the student's claim, so the correct answer must state the **opposite** of the marketer's claim. To find the idea you're looking for, simply stick the word NOT into the original claim.

Original claim: more choice = beneficial

Correct answer: more choice = NOT beneficial

Therefore, the correct answer must support the idea that more choice is not beneficial.

Then work through the answer choices as in the previous version, checking each against that idea. Again, B) is the only option that fits that criterion.

Important: Even if you are a very strong reader with an excellent memory, it is very important that you write down each step of questions like this. Although you may not have any difficult answering them, it is all too easy to forget and accidentally look for exactly the opposite idea you should be looking for. Sooner or later, there's a good chance you'll slip up and lose what should have been relatively easy points. **This is not about your ability to get the question right but rather to ensure that you <u>don't</u> get the question wrong.** Memories do strange things under pressure, and you're better off not taking the risk.

Supporting and Undermining Claims Exercises

1. The sharing economy is a little like online
shopping, which started in America 15 years ago. At
first, people were worried about security. But having
made a successful purchase from, say, Amazon, they
5 felt safe buying elsewhere. Similarly, using Airbnb or
a car-hire service for the first time encourages people to
try other offerings. Next, consider eBay. Having started
out as a peer-to-peer marketplace, it is now dominated
by professional "power sellers" (many of whom started
10 out as ordinary eBay users). The same may happen with
the sharing economy, which also provides new
opportunities for enterprise. Some people have bought
cars solely to rent them out, for example. Incumbents
are getting involved too. Avis, a car-hire firm, has a share
15 in a sharing rival. So do GM and Daimler, two carmakers.
In the future, companies may develop hybrid models,
listing excess capacity (whether vehicles, equipment or
office space) on peer-to-peer rental sites. In the past,
new ways of doing things online have not displaced the
20 old ways entirely. But they have often changed them.
Just as internet shopping forced Walmart and Tesco to
adapt, so online sharing will shake up transport, tourism,
equipment-hire and more.
  The main worry is regulatory uncertainty. Will
25 room-4-renters be subject to hotel taxes, for example?
In Amsterdam officials are using Airbnb listings to track
down unlicensed hotels. In some American cities,
peer-to-peer taxi services have been banned after
lobbying by traditional taxi firms. The danger is that
30 although some rules need to be updated to protect
consumers from harm, incumbents will try to destroy
competition. People who rent out rooms should pay tax,
of course, but they should not be regulated like a Ritz-
Carlton hotel. The lighter rules that typically govern
35 bed-and-breakfasts are more than adequate. The sharing
economy is the latest example of the internet's value to
consumers. This emerging model is now big and
disruptive enough for regulators and companies to have
woken up to it. That is a sign of its immense potential. It
40 is time to start caring about sharing.

1

Which choice provides the best evidence for
the author's claim that sharing-based companies
may face serious challenges from established
companies?

A) Lines 5-7 ("Similarly...offerings")
B) Lines 14-15 ("Avis...rival")
C) Lines 27-29 ("In...firms")
D) Lines 32-34 ("People...hotel")

2. The following passage is adapted from Verlyn Klinkenborg, "Our Vanishing Night." © 2008 by the National Geographic Society.

If humans were truly at home under the light of the moon and stars, we would go in darkness happily, the midnight world as visible to us as it is to the vast number of nocturnal species on this planet. Instead,
5 we are diurnal creatures, with eyes adapted to living in the sun's light. This is a basic evolutionary fact, even though most of us don't think of ourselves as diurnal beings any more than we think of ourselves as primates or mammals or Earthlings.
10 Yet it's the only way to explain what we've done to the night: We've engineered it to receive us by filling it with light. This kind of engineering is no different than damming a river. Its benefits come with consequences—called light pollution—whose
15 effects scientists are only now beginning to study. Light pollution is largely the result of bad lighting design, which allows artificial light to shine outward and upward into the sky, where it's not wanted, instead of focusing it downward, where it is.
20 Ill-designed lighting washes out the darkness of night and radically alters the light levels—and rhythms – to which many forms of life, including ourselves, have adapted.

For most of human history, the phrase "light
25 pollution" would have made no sense. Imagine walking toward London on a moonlit night around 1800, when it was Earth's most populous city. Nearly a million people lived there, making do, as they always had, with candles and lanterns. Only a few houses
30 were lit by gas, and there would be no public gaslights for another seven years. From a few miles away, you would have been as likely to smell London as to see its dim glow. Now most of humanity lives under intersecting domes of light, of scattering rays from
35 overlit cities and suburbs, from light-flooded highways and factories. In most cities the sky looks as though it has been emptied of stars, leaving behind a vacant haze that mirrors our fear of the dark and resembles the urban glow of dystopian science
40 fiction. We've grown so used to this pervasive orange haze that the original glory of an unlit night—dark enough for the planet Venus to throw shadows on Earth—is wholly beyond our experience, beyond memory almost. We've lit up the night as if it were
45 an unoccupied country, when nothing could be further from the truth. Light is a powerful biological force, and on many species it acts as a magnet. Migrating at night, birds are apt to collide with brightly lit tall buildings; immature birds on their first journey suffer

50 disproportionately. And because a longer day allows for longer feeding, it can also affect migration schedules. The problem, of course, is that migration is a precisely timed biological behavior. Leaving early may mean arriving too soon for nesting
55 conditions to be right.

It was once thought that light pollution only affected astronomers, who need to see the night sky in all its glorious clarity. And, in fact, some of the earliest efforts to control light pollution were made
60 to protect the view from Lowell Observatory. Unlike astronomers, most of us may not need an undiminished view of the night sky for our work, but like most other creatures we do need darkness. Darkness is as essential to our internal clockwork
65 as light itself. The regular oscillation of waking and sleep in our lives is nothing less than a biological expression of the regular oscillation of light on Earth. So fundamental are these rhythms to our being that altering them is like altering gravity.
70 For the past century or so, we've been performing an open-ended experiment on ourselves, extending the day, shortening the night, and short-circuiting the human body's sensitive response to light. The consequences of our bright new world are more
75 readily perceptible in less adaptable creatures living in the peripheral glow of our prosperity. But for humans, too, light pollution may take a biological toll. In a very real sense, light pollution causes us to lose sight of our true place in the universe, to
80 forget the scale of our being, which is best measured against the dimensions of a deep night with the Milky Way—the edge of our galaxy— arching overhead.

1

Which choice provides the best evidence for the author's claim that the effects of light pollution are particularly evident in "less adaptable creatures" (line 75)?

A) Lines 4-6 ("Instead...light")
B) Lines 33-34 ("Now...light)
C) Lines 47-49 ("Migrating...buildings")
D) Lines 76-78 ("But...toll")

3. The following passaged is adapted from Olympe de Gouges, *Declaration of the Rights of Women*. It was initially published in 1791, during the French Revolution, and was written in response to the *Declaration of the Rights of Man* (1789).

Woman, wake up; the toxin of reason is being heard throughout the whole universe; discover your rights. The powerful empire of nature is no longer surrounded by prejudice, fanaticism, superstition, and
5 lies. The flame of truth has dispersed all the clouds of folly and usurpation. Enslaved man has multiplied his strength and needs recourse to yours to break his chains. Having become free, he has become unjust to his companion. Oh, women, women! When will you cease
10 to be blind? What advantage have you received from the Revolution? A more pronounced scorn, a more marked disdain. In the centuries of corruption you ruled only over the weakness of men. The reclamation of your patrimony, based on the wise decrees of nature –
15 what have you to dread from such a fine undertaking? Do you fear that our legislators, correctors of that morality, long ensnared by political practices now out of date, will only say again to you: women, what is there in common between you and us? Everything, you
20 will have to answer. If they persist in their weakness in putting this hypocrisy in contradiction to their principles, courageously oppose the force of reason to the empty pretensions of superiority; unite yourselves beneath the standards of philosophy; deploy all the
25 energy of your character. Regardless of what barriers confront you, it is in your power to free yourselves; you have only to want to. Let us pass not to the shocking tableau of what you have been in society; and since national education is in question at this moment, let us
30 see whether our wise legislators will think judiciously about the education of women.
  Women have done more harm than good. Constraint and dissimulation have been their lot. What force has robbed them of, ruse returned to them; they had recourse
35 to all the resources of their charms, and the most irreproachable persons did not resist them. Poison and the sword were both subject to them; they commanded in crime as in fortune. The French government, especially, depended throughout the centuries on the nocturnal
40 administrations of women; the cabinet could keep no secrets as a result of their indiscretions; all have been subject to the cupidity and ambition of this sex, formerly contemptible and respected, and since the revolution, respectable and scorned.

45   In this sort of contradictory situation, what remarks could I not make! I have but a moment to make them, but this moment will fix the attention of the remotest posterity. Under the Old Regime, all was vicious, all was guilty; but could not the amelioration of
50 conditions be perceived even in the substance of vices? A woman only had to be beautiful or amiable; when she possessed these two advantages, she saw a hundred fortunes at her feet. If she did not profit from them, she had a bizarre character or a rare philosophy
55 which made her scorn wealth; then she was deemed to be like a crazy woman. A young, inexperienced woman, seduced by a man whom she loves, will abandon her parents to follow him; the ingrate will leave her after a few years, and the older she has
60 become with him, the more inhuman is his inconstancy; if she has children, he will likewise abandon them. If he is rich, he will consider himself excused from sharing his fortune with his noble victims. If some involvement binds him to his duties, he will
65 deny them, trusting that the laws will support him. If he is married, any other obligation loses its rights. Then what laws remain to extirpate vice all the way to its root? The law of dividing wealth and public administration between men and women. It can easily
70 be seen that one who is born into a rich family gains very much from such equal sharing. But the one born into a poor family with merit and virtue – what is her lot? Poverty and opprobrium. If she does not precisely excel in music or painting, she cannot be admitted to
75 any public function when she has all the capacity for it.

1

Which choice most effectively supports the author's claim that women have undermined their own cause?

A) Lines 40-41 ("the cabinet…indiscretions")
B) Lines 53-55 ("If…wealth")
C) Lines 59-61 ("the older…inconstancy")
D) Lines 73-75 ("If…for it")

4. The following passage is adapted from "Makerspaces, Hackerspaces, and Community Scale Production in Detroit and Beyond," © 2013 by Sean Ansanelli.

During the mid-1980s, spaces began to emerge across Europe where computer hackers could convene for mutual support and camaraderie. In the past few years, the idea of fostering such shared, physical spaces
5 has been rapidly adapted by the diverse and growing community of "makers", who seek to apply the idea of "hacking" to physical objects, processes, or anything else that can be deciphered and improved upon.

A hackerspace is described by hackerspaces.org as
10 a "community-operated physical space where people with common interests, often in computers, technology, science, digital art or electronic art, can meet, socialize, and/or collaborate." Such spaces can vary in size, available technology, and membership structure (some
15 being completely open), but generally share community-oriented characteristics. Indeed, while the term "hacker" can sometimes have negative connotations, modern hackerspaces thrive off of community, openness, and assimilating diverse viewpoints – these often being the
20 only guiding principles in otherwise informal organizational structures.

In recent years, the city of Detroit has emerged as a hotbed for hackerspaces and other DIY ("Do-It-Yourself") experiments. Several hackerspaces
25 can already be found throughout the city and several more are currently in formation. Of course, Detroit's attractiveness for such projects can be partially attributed to cheap real estate, which allows aspiring hackers to acquire ample space for experimentation. Some observers
30 have also described this kind of making and tinkering as embedded in the DNA of Detroit's residents, who are able to harness substantial intergenerational knowledge and attract like-minded individuals.

Hackerspaces (or "makerspaces") can be found in
35 more commercial forms, but the vast majority of spaces are self-organized and not-for-profit. For example, the OmniCorp hackerspace operates off member fees to cover rent and new equipment, from laser cutters to welding tools. OmniCorp also hosts an "open hack night"
40 every Thursday in which the space is open to the general public. Potential members are required to attend at least one open hack night prior to a consensus vote by the existing members for admittance; no prospective members have yet been denied.

45 A visit to one of OmniCorp's open hack nights reveals the vast variety of activity and energy existing in the space. In the main common room alone, activities range from experimenting with sound installations and learning to program Arduino boards to building speculative "oloid"

50 shapes – all just for the sake of it. With a general atmosphere of mutual support, participants in the space are continually encouraged to help others.

One of the most active community-focused initiatives in the city is the Mt. Elliot Makerspace. Jeff Sturges,
55 former MIT Media Lab Fellow and Co-Founder of OmniCorp, started the Mt. Elliot project with the aim of replicating MIT's Fab Lab model on a smaller, cheaper scale in Detroit. "Fab Labs" are production facilities that consist of a small collection of flexible computer
60 controlled tools that cover several different scales and various materials, with the aim to make "almost anything" (including other machines). The Mt. Elliot Makerspace now offers youth-based skill development programs in eight areas: Transportation, Electronics,
65 Digital Tools, Wearables, Design and Fabrication, Food and Music, and Arts. The range of activities is meant to provide not only something for everyone, but a well-rounded base knowledge of making to all participants.

While the center receives some foundational support,
70 the space also derives significant support from the local community. Makerspaces throughout the city connect the space's youth-based programming directly to school curriculums.

The growing interest in and development of
75 hacker/makerspaces has been explained, in part, as a result of the growing maker movement. Through the combination of cultural norms and communication channels from open source production as well as increasingly available technologies for physical
80 production, amateur maker communities have developed in virtual and physical spaces.

Publications such as *Wired* are noticing the transformative potential of this emerging movement and have sought to devote significant attention to its
85 development. Chief editor Chris Anderson recently published a book entitled *Makers*, in which he proclaims that the movement will become the next Industrial Revolution. Anderson argues such developments will allow for a new wave of business opportunities by
90 providing mass-customization rather than mass-production.

The transformative potential of these trends goes beyond new business opportunities or competitive advantages for economic growth. Rather, these trends
95 demonstrate the potential to actually transform economic development models entirely.

Which choice best supports the author's claim that hackerspaces are generally welcoming and tolerant organizations?

A)   Lines 24-26 ("Several...formation")
B)   Lines 43-44 ("no...denied)
C)   Lines 47-50 ("In...shapes")
D)   Lines 69-71 ("While...community")

5. The following passage is adapted from "The Origin of the Ocean Floor" by Peter Keleman, © 2009 by The National Geographic Society.

At the dark bottom of our cool oceans, 85 percent of the earth's volcanic eruptions proceed virtually unnoticed. Though unseen, they are hardly insignificant. Submarine volcanoes generate the solid
5 underpinnings of all the world's oceans massive slabs of rock seven kilometers thick.

Geophysicists first began to appreciate the smoldering origins of the land under the sea, known formally as ocean crust, in the early 1960s. Sonar
10 surveys revealed that volcanoes form nearly continuous ridges that wind around the globe like seams on a baseball. Later, the same scientists strove to explain what fuels these erupting mountain ranges, called mid-ocean ridges. Basic theories suggest that because ocean
15 crust pulls apart along the ridges, hot material deep within the earth's rocky interior must rise to fill the gap. But details of exactly where the lava originates and how it travels to the surface long remained a mystery.

In recent years mathematical models of the
20 interaction between molten and solid rock have provided some answers, as have examinations of blocks of old seafloor now exposed on the continents. These insights made it possible to develop a detailed theory describing the birth of ocean crust. The process
25 turns out to be quite different from the typical layperson's idea, in which fiery magma fills an enormous chamber underneath a volcano, then rages upward along a jagged crack. Instead the process begins dozens of kilometers under the seafloor, where
30 tiny droplets of melted rock ooze through microscopic pores at a rate of about 10 centimeters a year, about as fast as fingernails grow.

Closer to the surface, the process speeds up, culminating with massive streams of lava pouring
35 over the seafloor with the velocity of a speeding truck. Deciphering how liquid moves through solid rock deep underground not only explains how ocean crust emerges but also may elucidate the behavior of other fluid-transport networks, including the river systems
40 that dissect the planet's surface.

Far below the mid-ocean ridge volcanoes and their countless layers of crust-forming lava is the mantle, a 3,200-kilometer-thick layer of scorching hot rock that forms the earth's midsection and surrounds its
45 metallic core. At the planet's cool surface, upthrusted mantle rocks are dark green, but if you could see them in their rightful home, they would be glowing red- or even white-hot. The top of the mantle is about 1,300 degrees Celsius, and it gets about one degree
50 hotter with each kilometer of depth. The weight of overlying rock means the pressure also increases with depth about 1,000 atmospheres for every three kilometers.

Knowledge of the intense heat and pressure in
55 the mantle led researchers to hypothesize in the late 1960s that ocean crust originates as tiny amounts of liquid rock known as melt almost as though the solid rocks were "sweating." Even a minuscule release of pressure (because of material rising from
60 its original position) causes melt to form in microscopic pores deep within the mantle rock.

Explaining how the rock sweat gets to the surface was more difficult. Melt is less dense than the mantle rocks in which it forms, so it will
65 constantly try to migrate upward, toward regions of lower pressure. But what laboratory experiments revealed about the chemical composition of melt did not seem to match up with the composition of rock samples collected from the mid-ocean ridges,
70 where erupted melt hardens.

Using specialized equipment to heat and squeeze crystals from mantle rocks in the laboratory, investigators learned that the chemical composition of melt in the mantle varies depending on the depth
75 at which it forms; the composition is controlled by an exchange of atoms between the melt and the minerals that make up the solid rock it passes through. The experiments revealed that as melt rises, it dissolves one kind of mineral, orthopyroxene, and
80 precipitates, or leaves behind, another mineral, olivine. Researchers could thus infer that the higher in the mantle melt formed, the more orthopyroxene it would dissolve, and the more olivine it would leave behind. Comparing these experimental findings
85 with lava samples from the mid-ocean ridges revealed that almost all of them have the composition of melts that formed at depths greater than 45 kilometers.

1

A student states that the ocean crust is formed by explosive volcanic eruptions. Is the student correct or incorrect, and which lines provide the best support?

A) Correct, lines 14-16 ("Basic...gap")
B) Correct, lines 26-28 ("fiery...crack")
C) Incorrect, lines 30-33 ("Tiny...grow")
D) Incorrect, lines 45-48 ("At...white-hot")

Official Guide Supporting/Khan Academy Supporting and Undermining Claims Questions

Test 1   23   Undermine

Test 2   17   Support

Test 3   18   Support

Test 4   49   Support

Explanations: Supporting and Undermining Claims Exercises

1. C

Since the question does not provide a line reference and is sufficiently detail-based that you are unlikely to remember the answer, start by plugging in the line reference. You're looking for a section that discusses challenges to "sharing-based" companies. A) is incorrect because although lines 5-7 discuss examples of sharing-based companies, they focus on the likelihood that people will continue to use them after a single experience; challenges from traditional companies are not mentioned. Be careful with B). The word *rival* might suggest competition to you, but in fact this section is discussing the opposite – Avis is an example of a traditional company that is getting involved in the sharing economy, not opposing it. C) is correct because lines 27-29 provide a clear example of an instance in which existing taxi companies successfully opposed "peer-to-peer" ride-share companies. D) is incorrect because lines 32-34 have nothing to do with challenges by traditional companies; the author simply voices his opinion regarding regulation.

2. C

Don't worry about the line reference provided – the question tells you everything you need to know about the relevant claim. The correct answer must provide an example of a creature that has not adapted to light pollution. The question is broad enough that you can't assume the correct answer will be located anywhere near line 75, so plug each answer in. A) is incorrect because lines 4-6 state that humans *have* adapted to living in sunlight. That's the opposite of what you're looking for. (If you do consider the line reference in the question, you'll see that the author contrasts humans to "less adaptable creatures," indicating that the correct section of the passage will not refer to humans.) B) is incorrect for the same reason as A). Lines 33-34 provide an example of adaptation to light. C) is correct because the description of birds in lines 47-49 clearly indicates these creatures have *not* adapted

to constant light (they *collide with brightly lit tall buildings*). D) is incorrect because lines 76-78 simply state that light pollution *may take a biological toll* – they do not provide a specific example of a negative effect that has already occurred.

3. A

If you don't happen to remember where de Gouges discusses how women have undermined their own cause, the easiest way to find the answer is to skim topic sentences. The information is presented so clearly that this is actually a more efficient means of finding the answer than plugging in each choice. In line 32, de Gouges clearly states that *Women have done more harm than good*, suggesting that the correct set of lines is most likely located nearby. A) contains the only line reference in that paragraph, so check it first because it will almost certainly be used to support that idea. Indeed, lines 39-41 provide a clear example of how women have hurt themselves, indicating that *the cabinet (French government) could keep no secrets as a result of their indiscretions.*

4. B

The question indicates that the correct answer must support the idea that hackerspaces *are generally welcoming and tolerant organizations*, so plug in each set of lines and see whether it fits. A) is incorrect because lines 24-26 only indicate that hackerspaces can be found throughout Detroit; there's no information about whether they're welcoming or not, and you can't infer that information from those lines. B) is correct because the fact that *no prospective members have yet been denied* most directly suggest that makerspaces are pretty relaxed about whom they let join. C) is incorrect because lines 47-50 provide no information about makerspaces' atmosphere; they only indicate what people actually do there. D) is incorrect because lines 69-71 only indicate that makerspaces are supported by the community. Again, there is no information about whether makerspaces are welcoming.

5. C

If you've paid attention to important information in the passage and use your notes, you may be able to answer this question rather quickly. The key is to be aware of the "old model/new model" structure, because that is exactly what this question targets. The third paragraph indicates that *the typical layperson's idea* of how ocean crust forms revolves around a massive underwater explosion. That's the *wrong* idea. In line 28, the word *Instead* signals the transition to the correct explanation: tiny droplets of melted rock ooze up at an incredibly slow rate. That information indicates that the student alluded to in the question is incorrect, and that the answer is C). If you haven't clued into that information while reading the passage and plug in the answers in order, you run a serious risk of falling into the trap in B). That answer cites the lines describing what people typically believe, but the phrase *the typical layperson's idea* isn't included in the line reference. If you miss that information, you could easily think that the description in B) is what actually occurs and choose that answer. A) is incorrect because lines 14-16 only state that hot material within the earth rises to the surface, but they do not explain *how* that occurs; and D) is incorrect because lines 45-48 only describe the rocks before they rise to the surface, saying nothing about how that change takes place.

9. Reading for Function

If you've already spent some time studying for the SAT, you've most likely had the following experience: you see a question that asks you the primary purpose of a few lines or a paragraph. You go back, read the lines, and feel pretty confident that you understand what they're saying. When you look at the answers, however, they don't seem to have anything to do with what you've just read. You go back to the passage, frantically re-reading, trying to figure out what you've missed, then look back at the answers. Clear as mud. You get rid of a couple that are obviously wrong but find yourself stuck between B) and C), which both seem equally plausible. You remember hearing that C) is the most common answer, so you decide to just pick it and hope for the best.

This scenario typically stems from the fact that most people don't truly understand that "function" questions are not asking *what* the lines say but rather *why* they say it. In short, you cannot understand function without understanding content, but understanding content alone is not enough to understand function.

One of the things that people often find very foreign is the fact that the SAT not only tests the ability to comprehend *what* is written in a passage but also *how* it's written. Unlike literal comprehension questions, which require you to identify a paraphrased version of an idea contained in the passage, **function questions ask you to move beyond understanding the literal meaning of specific content in the passage to understanding the more abstract role of that content within the larger context of the passage or paragraph**. In other words, these questions ask you to identify **the point that the information in question supports**. In this sense, "function" questions are very similar to "example" questions – both ask you to work backwards from the supporting evidence to the larger idea.

While answers to "function" questions are based on the specific wording in the passage, you should keep in mind that **the answers themselves are not stated word-for-word in the passage.** In fact, the answer choices will sometimes be phrased in much more general or abstract language than what appears in the passage; you are responsible for drawing the connection between the two.

That said, you should **always keep in mind the topic of the passage because the correct answer may refer to it**, either directly or in rephrased form.

Types of Function Questions

Function questions can ask about either a small section of a passage (punctuation, word, set of lines, paragraph) or the passage as a whole. (Note: questions that ask about the purpose of a passage are discussed in the chapter entitled "The Big Picture" for the sake of consistency.)

They are typically phrased in the following ways:

- The main purpose of the second paragraph (line x-y) is to…

- The quotation/phrase, etc. in lines x-y primarily serves to…

- The author makes the comparison in lines x-y in order to…

And their answers fall into two categories:

1. Those that can **only** be answered by looking at the specific wording in the lines provided in the question. In such cases, the lines will typically contain punctuation, phrasing, or an important transition that points to a particular answer.

2. Those that **cannot** be obtained by looking at the lines provided in the question but that instead depend on contextual information.

For the second type of question especially, line references simply tell you where the information in question is located – they do *not* tell you its relationship to anything else in the passage. **The information necessary to obtain the answer will often be either before the line(s) referred to in the question, or, less frequently, after.**

Unfortunately, there is no way to tell upfront which category a particular question will fall into. As a result, **you should generally be prepared to read a sentence or two before and after the lines provided, then focus on the appropriate section as necessary.**

Important: if the lines given in the question are relatively close to the beginning of a paragraph, you should begin reading from there – topic sentences will nearly always give you the point of a paragraph, making it much easier for you to understand the role of a particular word or sentence within it. If the lines are in the middle of a paragraph, especially a long paragraph, you probably do not need to go all the way back to the beginning of it but can instead back up a sentence or couple of sentences as necessary.

Since one of the main focuses of the SAT is the relationships between ideas, it follows that the majority of the questions tend to be based on the places in a passage where ideas come into contact into with one another – that is, where new information is introduced, or where there is a change in focus, point of view, or tone.

The relationships between these ideas are sometimes indicated through the use of specific words/phrases and punctuation, which correlate with particular function words. The chart on the next page lists some of the more common key words, phrases, and types of punctuation, along with the functions that they typically indicate.

Functions of Key Words and Punctuation

Continuers		Contradictors
Continue/Support And Also In addition Furthermore Moreover As well as First/In the first place Next Then Finally For example For instance One reason/another reason **Explain** Because The reason is The answer is Explanation That is Colon Dash **Draw a conclusion** So Consequently Therefore Thus Thereby As a result **Compare** Similarly Like/likewise As Just as Much as/like	**Define** That is/That is to say Properly speaking Colon Dash Parentheses **Speculate** If May Maybe Might Could Perhaps It is possible **Emphasize** Indeed In fact Let me be clear Italics Capital letters Exclamation point Repetition (of a word, phrase) **Indicate Importance** Important Significant Essential Fundamental Central Key The point/goal is	**Contrast** But However Yet Still (Al)though On the contrary On the other hand In contrast Whereas While Despite In spite of Nevertheless Instead Rather than Misguided False **Question, Imply skepticism** But is it really true…? Question mark Quotation marks **Qualify** Dashes Parentheses

Let's look at some examples.

Every time a car drives through a major intersection, it becomes a data point. Magnetic coils of wire lay just beneath the pavement, registering each passing car. This starts a cascade of information: Computers tally the
5 number and speed of cars, shoot the data through underground cables to a command center and finally translate it into the colors red, yellow and green. On the seventh floor of Boston City Hall, the three colors splash like paint across a wall-sized map.
10 To drivers, the color red means stop, but on the map it tells traffic engineers to leap into action. Traffic control centers like this one—a room cluttered with computer terminals and live video feeds of urban intersections— represent the brain of a traffic system. The city's network
15 of sensors, cables and signals are the nerves connected to the rest of the body. "Most people don't think there are eyes and ears keeping track of all this stuff," says John DeBenedictis, the center's engineering director. But in reality, engineers literally watch our every move,
20 making subtle changes that relieve and redirect traffic.
The tactics and aims of traffic management are modest but powerful. Most intersections rely on a combination of pre-set timing and computer adaptation. For example, where a busy main road intersects with a quiet residential
25 street, the traffic signal might give 70 percent of "green time" to the main road, and 30 percent to the residential road. (Green lights last between a few seconds and a couple minutes, and tend to shorten at rush hour to help the traffic move continuously.) But when traffic
30 overwhelms the pre-set timing, engineers override the system and make changes.

1

The reference to "the color red" (line 10) serves mainly to

A) emphasize the importance of obeying traffic signals.
B) indicate that drivers and traffic engineers can react to information in different ways.
C) explain why traffic engineers are more active than other workers.
D) point out a striking feature of the map in Boston City Hall.

Solution: If we're going to try to answer the question on our own, the first thing we need to do is make sure we understand what it's asking. The phrase *serves mainly to* indicates that it's a "purpose" or "function" question. We could therefore rephrase the question as, "Why does the author use the phrase *the color red* in that spot?" or "What point does the author use the phrase *the color red* to support?"

Although you might be rolling your eyes and saying, "Duh, yeah, that's *obviously* what it's asking," rephrasing the question is crucial because it forces you to clarify just what sort of information you're looking for. If you skipped this step, you might simply start by summarizing what the lines say – which is not what you're being asked to do.

The fact that this is a function question tells us that we need to establish **context**. In this case, the line in question is part of the first sentence of the paragraph, i.e. the topic sentence. Because the purpose of a topic sentence is to introduce a topic, we probably don't need to back up. We do, however, need to make sure to read the **entire** sentence in which *the color red* – the key phrase – appears (lines 10-11).

Notice that the sentence is divided into two parts separated by a comma, and that the key phrase appears in the first part. Very often, when people encounter a sentence that contains multiple parts like this, they read only until the comma (or from the comma) and miss the information they need to answer the question.

That is exactly what could happen here. The second half of the sentence begins with the transition *but*, signaling the introduction of new, contradictory information. When *but* (or its synonyms *however* and *yet*) appears, you should always pay close attention to the word itself and the information that follows. If you stop before the *but*, you'll miss key information.

Let's examine the full sentence:

To drivers, the color red means stop, <u>but</u> on the map it tells traffic engineers to leap into action.

What do we learn from reading the entire sentence, especially considering the presence of the word *but* ? That the color red means **different things** to drivers (stop) vs. traffic engineers (leap into action). Which is what B) says. **Same idea, different words.**

If you'd rather play process of elimination, though, we can do that too:

A) emphasize the importance of obeying traffic signals

This might seem like a fairly reasonable answer, especially if you don't take the time to look back at the passage. After all, everyone knows that a red light means "stop." The passage is also about traffic, which is mentioned in the answer choice too. The problem is that if you consider the context, this answer is way **off topic**. The remainder of the paragraph focuses on the ways in which traffic engineers are able to keep track of what goes on in the streets of a city. Traffic safety never even enters into the discussion.

B) indicate that drivers and traffic engineers can react to information in different ways

If you go back to the passage and read lines 10-11 carefully, this probably won't be excessively difficult to identify as the right answer. (If, on the other hand, you try to rely on your memory, you could get into trouble.) Again, the word *but* provides a shortcut: by definition, a sentence with that word in it is discussing two contradictory, or **different**, ideas.

C) explain why traffic engineers are more active than other workers

In general, you need to be careful with comparisons. In this case, the comparison is between traffic engineers and drivers; other workers are not mentioned. Don't get distracted by the word *active*. If you don't read the passage carefully but instead just glance at the sentence, you might see the phrase *leap up* and assume that since someone who leaps up is active, then C) is right. **If any part of the answer is wrong, the whole answer is wrong.**

D) point out a striking feature of the map in Boston City Hall

Again, this answer seems vaguely plausible. If you did happen to back up and read from the previous sentence, you would see that the map in Boston City Hall is indeed mentioned. Since red is a striking color, you might then assume that the reference to it is included for that reason. Sure, there's nothing in the passage that explicitly *says* that, but hey, there's nothing to really suggest that interpretation is wrong either.

The problem with this reasoning is that it is based on **associative thinking** – connecting things that are only loosely related because you have personal associations with them – and it can get you into a lot of trouble on the SAT. Many wrong answers mention things/people that would seem to be logically grouped together but that are not described in that way in the passage. The fact that two ideas are discussed close to one another does not necessarily mean that there is a relationship between them.

Let's look at another question.

Every time a car drives through a major intersection, it becomes a data point. Magnetic coils of wire lay just beneath the pavement, registering each passing car. This starts a cascade of information: Computers tally the
5 number and speed of cars, shoot the data through underground cables to a command center and finally translate it into the colors red, yellow and green. On the seventh floor of Boston City Hall, the three colors splash like paint across a wall-sized map.
10 To drivers, the color red means stop, but on the map it tells traffic engineers to leap into action. Traffic control centers like this one—a room cluttered with computer terminals and live video feeds of urban intersections— represent the brain of a traffic system. The city's network
15 of sensors, cables and signals are the nerves connected to the rest of the body. "Most people don't think there are eyes and ears keeping track of all this stuff," says John DeBenedictis, the center's engineering director. But in reality, engineers literally watch our every move,
20 making subtle changes that relieve and redirect traffic.
The tactics and aims of traffic management are modest but powerful. Most intersections rely on a combination of pre-set timing and computer adaptation. For example, where a busy main road intersects with a quiet residential
25 street, the traffic signal might give 70 percent of "green time" to the main road, and 30 percent to the residential road. (Green lights last between a few seconds and a couple minutes, and tend to shorten at rush hour to help the traffic move continuously.) But when traffic
30 overwhelms the pre-set timing, engineers override the system and make changes.

1

The author mentions "sensors, cables, and signals" (line 15) in order to

A) describe a problem commonly faced by traffic engineers.
B) point out some important differences between traffic control centers and the brain.
C) list some items typically found in traffic control centers.
D) provide examples of ways drivers' actions can be monitored remotely.

Solution: Once again here, we're dealing with a "function" questions, so the question we're really answering is, "why does the passage mention 'sensors, cables, and signals?'" Or, "what point are 'sensors, cables, and signals' included to support?"

This time, the line reference is smack in the middle of the paragraph, where supporting evidence usually appears. Main ideas, in contrast, tend to appear at beginnings and ends of paragraphs. That means that the information we need to answer the question is most likely not in the lines referenced. In order to figure out what point the equipment in line 15 is included to support, we need to pay particular attention to the beginning and the end of the paragraph.

The beginning of the paragraph introduces the comparison between a traffic control center and the brain so, logically, the sentence in which the key phrase appears (*The city's network of sensors, cables and signals are the nerves connected to the rest of the body.*) serves to further develop that comparison. The problem is that no answer contains that idea. That means we need to read the rest of the paragraph, paying particular attention to the last sentence. The fact that it begins with the word *but* suggests that it will indeed be very important.

What idea is presented in the last sentence? Traffic engineers are able to watch people's every move. Why? Because of the sensors, cables, and signals that relay information from the streets back to them. So the phrase in question is there to explain how traffic engineers can monitor drivers' behavior from a distance, i.e. remotely. That makes the correct answer D).

Granted, this question is much less straightforward than the previous one; figuring it out without consulting the answer is a challenge. At the same time, however, you cannot assume that you will automatically recognize the correct answer when you see it. Sometimes you will have to do a bit more work upfront than you'd prefer to avoid getting confused.

A) describe a problem commonly faced by traffic engineers

This answer is probably the easiest to eliminate. The paragraph doesn't discuss a problem at all. It's completely off topic.

B) point out some important differences between traffic control centers and the brain

Remember that every word in an answer choice counts – it only takes one wrong word to make the whole thing incorrect. That's the case here. The author draws a *comparison* between traffic control centers and the brain, but this answer only mentions *differences*, which aren't discussed at all. This answer is exactly the opposite of what's going on in the passage.

C) list some items typically found in traffic control centers

This is the answer you really need to be careful with because the passage does mention traffic control centers and sensors, cables, and signals in very close proximity to one another. If you don't read very carefully, you can easily assume that this answer is correct.

The problem, however, is that passage states only that computer terminals and live video feeds are items found in traffic control centers (lines 12-13). In the next sentence, the author indicates that sensors, cables, and signals are the "nerves" present throughout the city – not in traffic control centers. So C) is out.

**D) provide examples of ways drivers' actions
    can be monitored remotely**

If you work by process of elimination and conclusively eliminate the other answers for the reasons discussed above, you can safely choose this answer. If, however, you simply read the answers without checking each one, you can easily eliminate this type of answer – either because you don't remember the information, or because you don't think it "sounds" right.

If you're stuck between D) and another answer, you can follow the same steps described above to check this answer out. When you get to the end of the paragraph, you can see that it directly supports this answer.

On the next page, we're going to look at a full-length passage.

The following passage is adapted from Verlyn Klinkenborg, "Our Vanishing Night." © 2008 by the National Geographic Society.

If humans were truly at home under the light of the moon and stars, we would go in darkness happily, the midnight world as visible to us as it is to the vast number of nocturnal species on this planet. Instead,
5 we are diurnal creatures, with eyes adapted to living in the sun's light. This is a basic evolutionary fact, even though most of us don't think of ourselves as diurnal beings any more than we think of ourselves as primates or mammals or Earthlings.
10 Yet it's the only way to explain what we've done to the night: We've engineered it to receive us by filling it with light. This kind of engineering is no different than damming a river. Its benefits come with consequences—called light pollution—whose
15 effects scientists are only now beginning to study. Light pollution is largely the result of bad lighting design, which allows artificial light to shine outward and upward into the sky, where it's not wanted, instead of focusing it downward, where it is.
20 Ill-designed lighting washes out the darkness of night and radically alters the light levels—and rhythms – to which many forms of life, including ourselves, have adapted.

For most of human history, the phrase "light
25 pollution" would have made no sense. Imagine walking toward London on a moonlit night around 1800, when it was Earth's most populous city. Nearly a million people lived there, making do, as they always had, with candles and lanterns. Only a few houses
30 were lit by gas, and there would be no public gaslights for another seven years. From a few miles away, you would have been as likely to smell London as to see its dim glow. Now most of humanity lives under intersecting domes of light, of scattering rays from
35 overlit cities and suburbs, from light-flooded highways and factories. In most cities the sky looks as though it has been emptied of stars, leaving behind a vacant haze that mirrors our fear of the dark and resembles the urban glow of dystopian science
40 fiction. We've grown so used to this pervasive orange haze that the original glory of an unlit night—dark enough for the planet Venus to throw shadows on Earth—is wholly beyond our experience, beyond memory almost. We've lit up the night as if it were
45 an unoccupied country, when nothing could be further from the truth. Light is a powerful biological force, and on many species it acts as a magnet. Migrating at night, birds are apt to collide with brightly lit tall buildings; immature birds on their first journey suffer

50 disproportionately. And because a longer day allows for longer feeding, it can also affect migration schedules. The problem, of course, is that migration is a precisely timed biological behavior. Leaving early may mean arriving too soon for nesting
55 conditions to be right.

It was once thought that light pollution only affected astronomers, who need to see the night sky in all its glorious clarity. And, in fact, some of the earliest efforts to control light pollution were made
60 to protect the view from Lowell Observatory. Unlike astronomers, most of us may not need an undiminished view of the night sky for our work, but like most other creatures we do need darkness. Darkness is as essential to our internal clockwork
65 as light itself. The regular oscillation of waking and sleep in our lives is nothing less than a biological expression of the regular oscillation of light on Earth. So fundamental are these rhythms to our being that altering them is like altering gravity.
70 For the past century or so, we've been performing an open-ended experiment on ourselves, extending the day, shortening the night, and short-circuiting the human body's sensitive response to light. The consequences of our bright new world are more
75 readily perceptible in less adaptable creatures living in the peripheral glow of our prosperity. But for humans, too, light pollution may take a biological toll. In a very real sense, light pollution causes us to lose sight of our true place in the universe, to
80 forget the scale of our being, which is best measured against the dimensions of a deep night with the Milky Way—the edge of our galaxy— arching overhead.

1

The passage's discussion of diurnal creatures primarily serves to

A) provide an explanation for the rise of light pollution.
B) point out that animals respond to light in different ways.
C) suggest that human understanding of the natural world is incomplete.
D) demonstrate the necessity of conserving natural resources.

Although it may appear that this question is asking you to wade through an enormous amount of information, it's actually not nearly as complicated as it seems.

The most effective **shortcut** would be to use our knowledge of the topic: light pollution. The only answer that mentions the topic directly is A), suggesting that we should pay special attention to it. But we still need to prove it.

The first thing to do is to locate the key phrase, *diurnal creatures*. In this case, it happens to be right in line 5. If you start from the beginning of the passage and put your index finger on the page as you skim, you'll find it almost immediately.

Once we've found the key phrase, the next step is to figure out what it refers to and why it's important. While your first instinct may be to panic because you don't know what *diurnal* means, the author is kind enough to define it for us, first implicitly (opposing it to *nocturnal*, a term that more people are likely to know) and then explicitly with the phrase *with eyes adapted to living in the sun's light*. So basically, it means that people like to be awake and active during the day.

This is where a lot of people stop and look at the answers, expecting to see an option that rephrases that idea and then getting confused (and then panicking, and then ultimately guessing) when they don't. But remember: there's one more step. The passage is asking us *why* that information is there. So far, we only understand its literal meaning.

Even if people remember to read around the lines, they're still likely to fall into one more trap – they confine themselves to the paragraph in which the key phrase appears. There are, however, several features of the first sentence in the *following* paragraph that suggest it's well worth looking at. First, it begins with *Yet*, a contradictor that almost always signals a key piece of the author's argument will follow; second, it contains the very strong word *only*; and third, it contains both the word *explain* AND a colon, which signals an explanation. It is very rare to encounter a sentence that contains so many key elements at once.

What do we learn when we read the entire sentence? That *it* – the fact that people like light – explains why they've decided to keep the lights on all the time, i.e. why they've created light pollution. So the answer is in fact A).

Playing process of elimination, B) is wrong because the passage is talking about people, not animals (*primates* and *mammals* are used to refer to human beings). C) is wrong because its scope is way too broad – the passage is specifically about light pollution, not the natural world in general. Although D) may sound like a nice, reasonable answer, the phrase *natural resources* makes this answer too broad as well. Furthermore, the passage doesn't focus on conserving natural resources but rather on light pollution. Besides, the issue isn't waste – it's that constant exposure to light has interfered with normal sleeping/waking cycles.

"Vague" Answers

So far, we've looked at questions whose answer choices were relatively self-explanatory – that is, they all spelled out ideas that the information in question could potentially support. Not all answer choices to "function" questions will be this specific, however. Sometimes, you'll see something like this:

A) justify an approach
B) qualify a statement
C) promote a theory
D) refute a claim

When confronted with a set of answers this abstract, a lot of people's initial reaction is confusion. What on earth, they wonder, does *that* have to do with the passage?

The key is to understand that these types of answers move from concrete to abstract in two different ways: first, through a function word such as *explain* or *refute*; and second, by rephrasing the **content** of the passage in a more general way.

Although the phrasing of these questions can take some getting used to, the process for answering them is the same: read from a sentence or two before the line reference to a sentence or two after to get the full context, and pay attention to strong language and "unusual" punctuation. These key places – sometimes consisting of no more than a word or two – will often provide sufficient information to answer the question.

Important: Remember that a long line reference does not necessarily mean that all of the lines are important. Generally speaking, the longer the line reference, the smaller the amount of it that is directly relevant to the question.

Let's look at some examples:

Most people have so-called flashbulb memories of where they were and what they were doing when something momentous happened. (Unfortunately, staggeringly terrible news seems to come out of the
5 blue more often than staggeringly good news.) But as clear and detailed as these memories feel, psychologists have discovered they are surprisingly inaccurate.

1

The function of the last sentence (lines 5-7) is to

A) acknowledge a point.
B) indicate a misconception.
C) criticize a tradition.
D) propose an alternative.

Solution: What information does the last sentence convey? That flashbulb memories are *inaccurate*, i.e. a "misconception." That makes the answer B). Easy, right?

The answer also could be phrased this way:

Most people have so-called flashbulb memories of where they were and what they were doing when something momentous happened. (Unfortunately, staggeringly terrible news seems to come out of the
5 blue more often than staggeringly good news.) But as clear and detailed as these memories feel, psychologists have discovered they are surprisingly inaccurate.

1

The function of the last sentence (lines 5-7) is to

A) acknowledge a point
B) highlight an unexpected discovery
C) criticize a tradition
D) propose an alternative

Solution: In this case, the key word is *surprising*. Surprising = unexpected, so the answer is again B).

Now let's try something a little more challenging:

Eating should be seen as pleasure and not penance; something that brings happiness and joy rather than anxiety. By viewing the acquisition and consumption of food as an ethical and moral act, we diminish the
5 fundamental pleasure that eating food provides us. By attaching social worth and political meaning to what we eat, and hoping that consumption can make the world a better place, we will not only fail to improve the world, but in the process lose the essential fact that eating
10 should be about enjoyment.

1

The statement in lines 5-10 ("By attaching...us") primarily serves to

A) criticize an attitude
B) support a claim
C) emphasize a paradox
D) analyze an attitude

Let's start by considering what the statement itself is saying. It's an awfully long sentence, so our first goal is to simplify it.

Basically, the sentence is saying that people who don't eat meat to make the world better (e.g. reduce waste, protect animals) end up doing exactly the opposite of what they set out to do.

That is essentially the definition of a **paradox** – doing something for a particular reason and achieving the opposite result. So the answer is C).

One more:

In an essay in 1984—at the dawn of the personal computer era—the novelist Thomas Pynchon wondered if it was "O.K. to be a Luddite," meaning someone who opposes technological progress. A better question
5 today is whether it's even possible. Technology is everywhere, and a recent headline at an Internet humor site perfectly captured how difficult it is to resist: "Luddite invents machine to destroy technology quicker." Like all good satire, the mock headline comes
10 perilously close to the truth. Modern Luddites do indeed invent "machines"—in the form of computer viruses, cyberworms and other malware—to disrupt the technologies that trouble them.

But despite their modern reputation, the original
15 Luddites were neither opposed to technology nor inept at using it. Many were highly skilled machine operators in the textile industry. Nor was the technology they attacked particularly new. Moreover, the idea of smashing machines as a form of industrial protest did
20 not begin or end with them. In truth, the secret of their enduring reputation depends less on what they did than on the name under which they did it.

1

In context of the passage as a whole, the primary purpose of the second paragraph (lines 14-22) is to

A) concede a point.
B) refute a misconception.
C) criticize a tradition.
D) praise an invention.

Solution:

Before we look at how to solve the question for real, let's look at a common mistake: considering the paragraph only from the standpoint of its content.

Content Summary (what NOT to do)

If you summarized the **content** of the second paragraph, you might say that it describes how the Luddites were skilled machine operators, that they didn't attack new technology, and that they weren't the only people to protest by destroying machines.

When looking at the answer choices, you might seize on the statement ...*the original Luddites were neither opposed to technology nor inept at using it. Many were highly skilled machine operators in the textile industry* and conclude that since the author seems to like the Luddites in those lines, then D) would make sense. You might not be sure about the invention part, but hey, the passage talks about machines, and machines are inventions, so it must be the answer, right? (It's not.)

As discussed earlier, the problem with this approach is that it relies on a fundamental misconception of what the question is asking. The question is not asking what the second paragraph says. Rather, it is asking about second paragraph's function within the passage and its relationship to the first paragraph.

Function

To figure out the second paragraph's function, you must back up and figure out its relationship to the first paragraph. There are only two paragraphs in the passage, so it is unnecessary to take anything else into consideration.

1) Use transitions to narrow it down

Since the question is asking about the function of the second paragraph, you can also look at the first (topic) sentence of that paragraph for clues.

Sure enough, it starts with "But despite..." which tells us immediately that its function is to contradict. B) and C) both generally go along with that idea, but A) and D) do not, so they can be eliminated.

This is where things get tricky – you might be able to get rid of C) based on the fact that the passage isn't really talking about a tradition, but if you don't know how to figure it out for real, you're reduced to guessing.

2) Identify the idea that the second paragraph contradicts

The topic sentence of the second paragraph states, *But despite their modern reputation, the original Luddites were neither opposed to technology nor inept at using it.*

So the question now becomes, "what is the Luddites' modern reputation?"

The first paragraph states that in 1984, Thomas Pynchon used the term *Luddite* to mean "someone who opposes technological progress" – so that's the modern definition.

The second paragraph, however, states that the *original* Luddites were pretty good with machines and not all that opposed to them.

What's the relationship? Well, the second paragraph indicates that the first paragraph's definition of a Luddite as someone opposed to new technology is actually wrong – in other words, the accepted notion of a Luddite is wrong, i.e. *a misconception* to which the author is opposed, i.e. *refuting*. Which gives us B).

Playing Positive and Negative with Function Questions

One of the simplest ways to approach function questions and eliminate answer choices quickly is to play positive/negative with them. Positive passages or portions of passages tend to have positive answers, while negative passages and portions of passages tend to have negative answers.

While answer choices will often contain function verbs more neutral than the language of the passage itself, the information in the rest of the answer may be distinctly positive or negative. Even if this strategy alone does not get you all the way to the correct answer, it can allow you to quickly eliminate one or two choices upfront, giving you more time to focus on the smaller distinctions between the remaining answers.

The chart on p. 217 provides some examples of common positive, negative, and neutral function words that are likely to appear in answer choices.

Let's look at an example:

These are stimulating times for anyone interested in questions of animal consciousness. On what seems like a monthly basis, scientific teams announce the results of new experiments, adding to a preponderance
5   of evidence that we've been underestimating animal minds, even those of us who have rated them fairly highly. New animal behaviors and capacities are observed in the wild, often involving tool use—or at least object manipulation—the very kinds of activity
10 that led the distinguished zoologist Donald R. Griffin to found the field of cognitive ethology (animal thinking) in 1978: octopuses piling stones in front of their hideyholes, to name one recent example; or dolphins fitting marine sponges to their beaks in order to dig for
15 food on the seabed; or wasps using small stones to smooth the sand around their egg chambers, concealing them from predators. At the same time neurobiologists have been finding that the physical structures in our own brains most commonly held responsible for
20 consciousness are not as rare in the animal kingdom as had been assumed. Indeed they are common. All of this work and discovery appeared to reach a kind of crescendo last summer, when an international group of prominent neuroscientists meeting at the University of
25 Cambridge issued "The Cambridge Declaration on Consciousness in Non-Human Animals," a document stating that "humans are not unique in possessing the neurological substrates that generate consciousness." It goes further to conclude that numerous documented
30 animal behaviors must be considered "consistent with experienced feeling states."

1

The reference to hideyholes, marine sponges, and small stones (lines 13-15) serves mainly to

A) describe ways that animals hide themselves from predators.
B) point out that tools produced by animals are less complex than human tools.
C) provide instances of novel animal behavior in the wild.
D) indicate the limits of animal consciousness.

This is a science passage, so its tone is relatively neutral, as is the case for most science passages. If we dig a little deeper, however, we can see that the author's attitude is actually pretty positive. Again, this is hardly a surprise. Many, if not most, science passages will discuss new theories or discoveries, and authors almost always regard new discoveries as good things – that why they're writing about them in the first place.

In this case, the first sentence of the passage, *These are <u>stimulating</u> times for anyone interested in questions of animal consciousness*, tells us that the author has a positive attitude toward his subject. Even if you find the phrasing otherwise somewhat confusing, the presence of the word *new* is also a big clue. We can therefore assume that the correct answer will be either positive or neutral; anything negative can be eliminated.

When we look at the answer choices, we can notice that B) and D) contain negative phrases (*less complex* and *limits*). Both answers can therefore be eliminated immediately.

That leaves us with only two possibilities, but we still have to be careful. Remember that answers to function questions are often found **before** the line reference. A) refers to something that is mentioned *after*; the answer is constructed that way precisely because so many people will start reading at line 13 and not consider any information before it. The problem here is that small stones are only discussed in relation to wasps; they have nothing to do with the other animals/examples mentioned.

The point is actually found all the way back in lines 7-8: *New animal behaviors and capacities are observed in the wild, often involving tool use.* In addition to the word *new*, the dashes in that sentence indicate that it is important. C) rephrases that sentence, so it is correct.

Shortcut: C) uses the word *novel* in its second meaning ("new"). Even in the absence of any other information, that usage suggests that C) is correct.

Very important: as is true for Reading answers in general, function answers that contain extreme language, either positive or negative (e.g. "condemn," "attack," "prove"), are usually incorrect.

A note about "proving" and "disproving:" One common point of confusion concerns the terms "prove" and "disprove." Most high school students are accustomed to hearing teachers tell them to "prove their thesis," and so it seems logical that SAT authors would do the same. This, alas, is one of the major differences between high school and college: while high school assignments tend to be framed in terms of black-and-white, the reality is that authors who write for adult readers are far more **nuanced** – that is, that they discuss *theories* that can be supported, illustrated, challenged, etc., but that cannot be definitively proved or disproved. "Proving and "disproving" are therefore far outside the bounds of what any author could accomplish in 85 lines or so.

* signals an answer that is likely to be incorrect

Positive

Support
Illustrate
Provide/offer an example
Provide/offer evidence
Exemplify
Bolster
Substantiate
Advance (a claim)
Affirm
Defend
Claim
Prove*

Praise

Acknowledge
Concede

Propose
Offer
Suggest

Emphasize
Highlight
Call attention to
Stress
Focus on
Underscore
Reinforce
Reiterate

Explain
Account for
Qualify
Clarify
Articulate
Specify
Define
Justify*

Promote*
Encourage*
Advocate*
Persuade

Negative

Refute
Criticize
Question
Challenge
Dismiss
Disparage
Decry
Contradict
Deny
Imply skepticism
Debate
Dispel
Undermine*
Discredit*
Attack*
Condemn*
Disprove*

Warn
Raise concern

Make fun of
Satirize
Mock
Scoff at*
Jeer at*

Exaggerate

Downplay
Minimize*
Trivialize*

Lament
Bemoan*

Neutral

Describe
Discuss
Present
Characterize
Portray
Depict
Represent
Evoke
Trace
Dramatize
Show

Indicate
Point out
Identify

Introduce

Shift
Change
Digress*

Restate
Summarize
Paraphrase

Hypothesize
Speculate

Analyze
Examine
Explore
Develop
Explicate
Consider
Reflect on

Attribute
Cite
Allude

Simulate*

For a glossary of selected terms, please see p. 232.

Reading for Function Exercises

1.   To understand what the new software—that is, analytics—can do that's different from more familiar software like spreadsheets, word processing, and graphics, consider the lowly photograph. Here the
5 relevant facts aren't how many bytes constitute a digital photograph, or a billion of them. That's about as instructive as counting the silver halide molecules used to form a single old-fashioned print photo. The important feature of a digital image's bytes is that, unlike
10 crystalline molecules, they are uniquely easy to store, transport, and manipulate with software. In the first era of digital images, people were fascinated by the convenience and malleability (think PhotoShop) of capturing, storing, and sharing pictures. Now, instead of
15 using software to manage photos, we can mine features of the bytes that make up the digital image. Facebook can, without privacy invasion, track where and when, for example, vacationing is trending, since digital images reveal at least that much. But more importantly, those
20 data can be cross-correlated, even in real time, with seemingly unrelated data such as local weather, interest rates, crime figures, and so on. Such correlations associated with just one photograph aren't revealing. But imagine looking at billions of photos over weeks,
25 months, years, then correlating them with dozens of directly related data sets (vacation bookings, air traffic), tangential information (weather, interest rates, unemployment), or orthogonal information (social or political trends). With essentially free super-computing,
30 we can mine and usefully associate massive, formerly unrelated data sets and unveil all manner of economic, cultural, and social realities.
    For science fiction aficionados, Isaac Asimov anticipated the idea of using massive data sets to predict
35 human behavior, coining it "psychohistory" in his 1951 Foundation trilogy. The bigger the data set, Asimov said then, the more predictable the future. With big-data analytics, one can finally see the forest, instead of just the capillaries in the tree leaves. Or to put it in more
40 accurate terms, one can see beyond the apparently random motion of a few thousand molecules of air inside a balloon; one can see the balloon itself, and beyond that, that it is inflating, that it is yellow, and that it is part of a bunch of balloons en route to a birthday party. The
45 data/software world has, until now, been largely about looking at the molecules inside one balloon.

1

The reference to "capturing, storing, and sharing pictures" (line 14) primarily serves to

A) underscore a key difference between old and new technologies.
B) point out technological features that were once considered novel.
C) describe how digital images are preserved.
D) emphasize the rapid nature of technological change.

2

The references to local weather, interest rates, and crime figures (lines 21-22) primarily serve to

A) provide examples of disparate subjects that may have hidden connections.
B) emphasize the range of topics covered on news websites.
C) point out local issues that may be of broader interest.
D) call attention to the limits of data analysis.

3

The passage's discussion of Isaac Asimov primarily serves to

A) introduce the concept of science fiction.
B) call attention to an individual who foresaw recent developments.
C) describe the influence of science fiction fans on technological discoveries.
D) emphasize the differences between science fiction and science.

2. The following passage is adapted from a novel by Willa Cather, originally published in 1918. The protagonist has been sent to live with his grandparents in Nebraska.

All the years that have passed have not dimmed my memory of that first glorious autumn. The new country lay open before me: there were no fences in those days, and I could choose my own way over the grass uplands,
5 trusting the pony to get me home again. Sometimes I followed the sunflower-bordered roads.

I used to love to drift along the pale-yellow cornfields, looking for the damp spots one sometimes found at their edges, where the smartweed soon turned a rich copper
10 color and the narrow brown leaves hung curled like cocoons about the swollen joints of the stem. Sometimes I went south to visit our German neighbors and to admire their catalpa grove, or to see the big elm tree that grew up out of a deep crack in the earth and had a
15 hawk's nest in its branches. Trees were so rare in that country, and they had to make such a hard fight to grow, that we used to feel anxious about them, and visit them as if they were persons. It must have been the scarcity of detail in that tawny landscape that made detail so
20 precious.

Sometimes I rode north to the big prairie-dog town to watch the brown earth-owls fly home in the late afternoon and go down to their nests underground with the dogs. Antonia Shimerda liked to go with me, and we used to
25 wonder a great deal about these birds of subterranean habit. We had to be on our guard there, for rattlesnakes were always lurking about. They came to pick up an easy living among the dogs and owls, which were quite defenseless against them; took possession of their
30 comfortable houses and ate the eggs and puppies. We felt sorry for the owls. It was always mournful to see them come flying home at sunset and disappear under the earth.

But, after all, we felt, winged things who would live
35 like that must be rather degraded creatures. The dog-town was a long way from any pond or creek. Otto Fuchs said he had seen populous dog-towns in the desert where there was no surface water for fifty miles; he insisted that some of the holes must go down to water—nearly two
40 hundred feet, hereabouts. Antonia said she didn't believe it; that the dogs probably lapped up the dew in the early morning, like the rabbits.

Antonia had opinions about everything, and she was soon able to make them known. Almost every day she
45 came running across the prairie to have her reading lesson with me. Mrs. Shimerda grumbled, but realized it was important that one member of the family should learn English. When the lesson was over, we used to go up to the watermelon patch behind the garden. I split the
50 melons with an old corn-knife, and we lifted out the hearts and ate them with the juice trickling through our fingers. The white melons we did not touch, but we watched them with curiosity. They were to be picked later, when the hard frosts had set in, and put away for
55 winter use. After weeks on the ocean, the Shimerdas were famished for fruit. The two girls would wander for miles along the edge of the cornfields, hunting for ground-cherries.

Antonia loved to help grandmother in the kitchen
60 and to learn about cooking and housekeeping. She would stand beside her, watching her every movement. We were willing to believe that Mrs. Shimerda was a good housewife in her own country, but she managed poorly under new conditions. I remember how horrified
65 we were at the sour, ashy-grey bread she gave her family to eat. She mixed her dough, we discovered, in an old tin peck-measure that had been used about the barn. When she took the paste out to bake it, she left smears of dough sticking to the sides of the measure, put
70 the measure on the shelf behind the stove, and let this residue ferment. The next time she made bread, she scraped this sour stuff down into the fresh dough to serve as yeast.

1

The reference to the catalpa grove and the elm tree (line 13) primarily serves to

A) illustrate the narrator's love of nature.
B) call attention to the diversity of the natural world.
C) emphasize the barrenness of the landscape.
D) explain why the narrator felt anxious about his new life.

The narrator's reference to ground-cherries (line 58) primarily serves to

A) emphasize the wholesome quality of the Shimerda's new life.
B) demonstrate the difficulty of finding food in the narrator's new home.
C) describe a food that the narrator was desperate to eat.
D) indicate that the Shimerda's diet during their voyage was limited.

## 3

The narrator's statement that Mrs. Shimerda "was a good housewife in her own country" (lines 62-63) primarily serves to

A) highlight a contrast
B) criticize an injustice
C) defend a decision
D) explain a reaction

3. The following passage is adapted from "Makerspaces, Hackerspaces, and Community Scale Production in Detroit and Beyond," © 2013 by Sean Ansanelli.

During the mid-1980s, spaces began to emerge across Europe where computer hackers could convene for mutual support and camaraderie. In the past few years, the idea of fostering such shared, physical spaces
5 has been rapidly adapted by the diverse and growing community of "makers", who seek to apply the idea of "hacking" to physical objects, processes, or anything else that can be deciphered and improved upon.

A hackerspace is described by hackerspaces.org as
10 a "community-operated physical space where people with common interests, often in computers, technology, science, digital art or electronic art, can meet, socialize, and/or collaborate." Such spaces can vary in size, available technology, and membership structure (some
15 being completely open), but generally share community-oriented characteristics. Indeed, while the term "hacker" can sometimes have negative connotations, modern hackerspaces thrive off of community, openness, and assimilating diverse viewpoints – these often being the
20 only guiding principles in otherwise informal organizational structures.

In recent years, the city of Detroit has emerged as a hotbed for hackerspaces and other DIY ("Do-It-Yourself") experiments. Several hackerspaces
25 can already be found throughout the city and several more are currently in formation. Of course, Detroit's attractiveness for such projects can be partially attributed to cheap real estate, which allows aspiring hackers to acquire ample space for experimentation. Some observers
30 have also described this kind of making and tinkering as embedded in the DNA of Detroit's residents, who are able to harness substantial intergenerational knowledge and attract like-minded individuals.

Hackerspaces (or "makerspaces") can be found in
35 more commercial forms, but the vast majority of spaces are self-organized and not-for-profit. For example, the OmniCorp hackerspace operates off member fees to cover rent and new equipment, from laser cutters to welding tools. OmniCorp also hosts an "open hack night"
40 every Thursday in which the space is open to the general public. Potential members are required to attend at least one open hack night prior to a consensus vote by the existing members for admittance; no prospective members have yet been denied.

45 A visit to one of OmniCorp's open hack nights reveals the vast variety of activity and energy existing in the space. In the main common room alone, activities range from experimenting with sound installations and learning to program Arduino boards to building speculative "oloid"

50 shapes – all just for the sake of it. With a general atmosphere of mutual support, participants in the space are continually encouraged to help others.

One of the most active community-focused initiatives in the city is the Mt. Elliot Makerspace. Jeff Sturges,
55 former MIT Media Lab Fellow and Co-Founder of OmniCorp, started the Mt. Elliot project with the aim of replicating MIT's Fab Lab model on a smaller, cheaper scale in Detroit. "Fab Labs" are production facilities that consist of a small collection of flexible computer
60 controlled tools that cover several different scales and various materials, with the aim to make "almost anything" (including other machines). The Mt. Elliot Makerspace now offers youth-based skill development programs in eight areas: Transportation, Electronics,
65 Digital Tools, Wearables, Design and Fabrication, Food, Music, and Arts. The range of activities is meant to provide not only something for everyone, but a well-rounded base knowledge of making to all participants.

While the center receives some foundational support,
70 the space also derives significant support from the local community. Makerspaces throughout the city connect the space's youth-based programming directly to school curriculums.

The growing interest in and development of
75 hacker/makerspaces has been explained, in part, as a result of the growing maker movement. Through the combination of cultural norms and communication channels from open source production as well as increasingly available technologies for physical
80 production, amateur maker communities have developed in virtual and physical spaces.

Publications such as *Wired* are noticing the transformative potential of this emerging movement and have sought to devote significant attention to its
85 development. Chief editor Chris Anderson recently published a book entitled *Makers*, in which he proclaims that the movement will become the next Industrial Revolution. Anderson argues such developments will allow for a new wave of business opportunities by
90 providing mass-customization rather than mass-production.

The transformative potential of these trends goes beyond new business opportunities or competitive advantages for economic growth. Rather, these trends
95 demonstrate the potential to actually transform economic development models entirely.

## 1

The passage's discussion of Europe in the 1980s primarily serves to

A) introduce the concept of hackerspaces.
B) emphasize the unique role of the United States in the hackerspace movement.
C) compare hackerspaces in the United States to foreign hackerspaces.
D) provide a description of a place where hackerspaces have been particularly popular.

The author's statement that "the term 'hacker' can sometimes have negative connotations" (lines 16-17) serves to

A) criticize a movement.
B) anticipate a potential criticism.
C) contrast past and present forms of technology.
D) emphasize the exclusive nature of an organization.

The primary function of the third paragraph (lines 22-33) is to

A) point out that the decline of certain industries can have unexpected benefits.
B) explain why hackerspaces have succeeded in some cities and failed in others.
C) indicate some of the reasons that hackerspaces have flourished in a particular city.
D) demonstrate the effects of geography on the economy.

## 4

The passage's discussion of OmniCorp (line 37) primarily serves to

A) call attention to hackerspaces' urgent need for funds.
B) suggest that money should not play a role in creative enterprises.
C) point out that non-profit hackerspaces are typically more successful than for-profit ones.
D) emphasize that hackerspaces are open and flexible organizations.

The references to *Wired* magazine and Chris Anderson primarily serve to

A) describe a key figure in the maker movement.
B) underscore the economic power of the maker movement.
C) trace the influence of the Industrial Revolution on the maker movement.
D) suggest that mass-production is incompatible with the modern economy.

4. This passage is from Barbara Jordan's keynote address at the 1976 Democratic National Convention. A Texas native, Jordan was the first African-American woman to represent the Deep South in Congress.

It was one hundred and forty-four years ago that members of the Democratic Party first met in convention to select a Presidential candidate. A lot of years passed since 1832, and during that time it would
5 have been most unusual for any national political party to ask a Barbara Jordan to deliver a keynote address. But tonight, here I am. And I feel that notwithstanding the past that my presence here is one additional bit of evidence that the American Dream need not forever be
10 deferred.

Now that I have this grand distinction, what in the world am I supposed to say? I could list the problems which cause people to feel cynical, angry, frustrated: problems which include lack of integrity in government;
15 the feeling that the individual no longer counts; feeling that the grand American experiment is failing or has failed. I could recite these problems, and then I could sit down and offer no solutions. But I don't choose to do that either. The citizens of America expect more.
20 We are a people in search of a national community. We are a people trying not only to solve the problems of the present, unemployment, inflation, but we are attempting on a larger scale to fulfill the promise of America. We are attempting to fulfill our national purpose,
25 to create and sustain a society in which all of us are equal.

And now we must look to the future. Let us heed the voice of the people and recognize their common sense. If we do not, we not only blaspheme our political heritage, we ignore the common ties that bind all
30 Americans. Many fear the future. Many are distrustful of their leaders, and believe that their voices are never heard. Many seek only to satisfy their private interests. But this is the great danger America faces – that we will cease to be one nation and become instead a collection
35 of interest groups: city against suburb, region against region, individual against individual; each seeking to satisfy private wants. If that happens, who then will speak for America? Who then will speak for the common good?

This is the question which must be answered in 1976:
40 Are we to be one people bound together by common spirit, sharing in a common endeavor; or will we become a divided nation? For all of its uncertainty, we cannot flee the future. We must address and master the future together. It can be done if we restore the belief that we
45 share a sense of national community, that we share a common national endeavor.

There is no executive order; there is no law that can require the American people to form a national community. This we must do as individuals, and if we
50 do it as individuals, there is no President of the United States who can veto that decision.

As a first step, we must restore our belief in ourselves. We are a generous people, so why can't we be generous with each other?
55 And now, what are those of us who are elected public officials supposed to do? We call ourselves "public servants" but I'll tell you this: We as public servants must set an example for the rest of the nation. It is hypocritical for the public official to admonish and
60 exhort the people to uphold the common good if we are derelict in upholding the common good. More is required of public officials than slogans and handshakes and press releases.

If we promise as public officials, we must deliver.
65 If we as public officials propose, we must produce. If we say to the American people, "It is time for you to be sacrificial" – sacrifice. And again, if we make mistakes, we must be willing to admit them. What we have to do is strike a balance between the idea that
70 government should do everything and the idea that government ought to do nothing.

Let there be no illusions about the difficulty of forming this kind of a national community. It's tough, difficult, not easy. But a spirit of harmony will survive
75 in America only if each of us remembers, when self-interest and bitterness seem to prevail, that we share a common destiny.

We cannot improve on the system of government handed down to us by the founders of the Republic.
80 There is no way to improve upon that. But what we can do is to find new ways to implement that system and realize our destiny.

1

The passage's discussion of problems facing the American people (lines 12-17) primarily serves to

A) demonstrate the importance of a national community.
B) indicate some attitudes that the author rejects.
C) explain that Americans are justified in fearing the future.
D) emphasize the importance of local communities.

## 2

The author's discussion of fear and distrust in lines 30-32 primarily serves to

A) call attention to the central role of confidence in effective leadership.
B) emphasize the importance of strong regional identities.
C) indicate some factors that pose a threat to national cohesion.
D) demonstrate the necessity of electing powerful representatives.

The reference to interest groups in line 35 primarily serves to

A) defend an action.
B) call attention to a risk.
C) describe an unlikely scenario.
D) propose a course of action.

Jordan's reference to the future in line 43 serves to

A) refute a widely accepted claim.
B) justify a controversial belief.
C) propose a novel alternative.
D) point out an inevitable occurrence.

The function of the quotation marks in lines 55-57 is to

A) indicate some unexpected tasks associated with public office.
B) suggest that certain politicians are not living up to their responsibilities.
C) praise politicians for their commitment to to civic life.
D) implore the American people to consider the common good.

## 6

The reference to "slogans and handshakes and press releases" (lines 62-63) primarily serves to

A) point out superficial actions that fail to address underlying problems.
B) call attention to the public aspect of political office.
C) suggest that politicians should increase their interactions with constituents.
D) emphasize the importance of collaboration between politicians and citizens.

5. The following passage is adapted from Julian Jackson, "New Research Suggests Dinosaurs Were Warm-Blooded and Active" © 2011 by Julian Jackson.

New research from the University of Adelaide has added to the debate about whether dinosaurs were cold-blooded and sluggish or warm-blooded and active. Professor Roger Seymour from the University's School
5 of Earth & Environmental Sciences has applied the latest theories of human and animal anatomy and physiology to provide insight into the lives of dinosaurs.

Human thigh bones have tiny holes – known as the
10 "nutrient foramen" – on the shaft that supply blood to living bone cells inside. New research has shown that the size of those holes is related to the maximum rate that a person can be active during aerobic exercise. Professor Seymour has used this principle to evaluate
15 the activity levels of dinosaurs.

"Far from being lifeless, bone cells have a relatively high metabolic rate and they therefore require a large blood supply to deliver oxygen. On the inside of the bone, the blood supply comes usually from a single
20 artery and vein that pass through a hole on the shaft – the nutrient foramen," he says.

Professor Seymour wondered whether the size of the nutrient foramen might indicate how much blood was necessary to keep the bones in good repair. For
25 example, highly active animals might cause more bone 'microfractures,' requiring more frequent repairs by the bone cells and therefore a greater blood supply. "My aim was to see whether we could use fossil bones of dinosaurs to indicate the level of bone metabolic rate
30 and possibly extend it to the whole body's metabolic rate," he says. "One of the big controversies among paleobiologists is whether dinosaurs were cold-blooded and sluggish or warm-blooded and active. Could the size of the foramen be a possible gauge for dinosaur
35 metabolic rate?"

Comparisons were made with the sizes of the holes in living mammals and reptiles, and their metabolic rates. Measuring mammals ranging from mice to elephants, and reptiles from lizards to crocodiles, one
40 of Professor Seymour's Honors students, Sarah Smith, combed the collections of Australian museums, photographing and measuring hundreds of tiny holes in thigh bones.

"The results were unequivocal. The sizes of the holes
45 were related closely to the maximum metabolic rates during peak movement in mammals and reptiles," Professor Seymour says. "The holes found in mammals were about 10 times larger than those in reptiles."

These holes were compared to those of fossil
50 dinosaurs. Dr. Don Henderson, Curator of Dinosaurs from the Royal Tyrrell Museum in Alberta, Canada, and Daniela Schwarz-Wings from the Museum für Naturkunde Humboldt University Berliny, German measured the holes in 10 species of
55 dinosaurs from five different groups, including bipedal and quadrupedal carnivores and herbivores, weighing 50kg to 20,000kg.

"On a relative comparison to eliminate the differences in body size, all of the dinosaurs had
60 holes in their thigh bones larger than those of mammals," Professor Seymour says.

"The dinosaurs appeared to be even more active than the mammals. We certainly didn't expect to see that. These results provide additional weight to
65 theories that dinosaurs were warm-blooded and highly active creatures, rather than cold-blooded and sluggish."

Professor Seymour says following the results of this study, it's likely that a simple measurement of
70 foramen size could be used to evaluate maximum activity levels in other vertebrate animals.

1

The reference to the size of the foramen (line 34) primarily serves to

A) compare the metabolic rates of different dinosaur species.
B) point out that dinosaurs were able to survive in a range of climates.
C) indicate a means of resolving a scientific dispute.
D) suggest that mammals and reptiles were once closer in size than they are today.

2

The statement that the dinosaurs "appeared to be even more active than mammals" (lines 62-63) serves to

A) emphasize a conventional belief.
B) defend a finding.
C) propose a controversial claim.
D) call attention to a surprising discovery.

225

6. The following passage is adapted from "Scientists Discover Salty Aquifer, Previously Unknown Microbial Habitat Under Antarctica," © 2015 by Dartmouth College.

Using an airborne imaging system for the first time in Antarctica, scientists have discovered a vast network of unfrozen salty groundwater that may support previously unknown microbial life deep under the coldest, driest
5 desert on our planet. The findings shed new light on ancient climate change on Earth and provide strong evidence that a similar briny aquifer could support microscopic life on Mars. The scientists used SkyTEM, an airborne electromagnetic sensor, to detect and map
10 otherwise inaccessible subterranean features.

The system uses an antennae suspended beneath a helicopter to create a magnetic field that reveals the subsurface to a depth of about 1,000 feet. Because a helicopter was used, large areas of rugged terrain could
15 be surveyed. The SkyTEM team was funded by the National Science Foundation and led by researchers from the University of Tennessee, Knoxville (UTK), and Dartmouth College, which oversees the NSF's SkyTEM project.

20 "These unfrozen materials appear to be relics of past surface ecosystems and our findings provide compelling evidence that they now provide deep subsurface habitats for microbial life despite extreme environmental conditions," says lead author Jill Mikucki,
25 an assistant professor at UTK. "These new below-ground visualization technologies can also provide insight on glacial dynamics and how Antarctica responds to climate change."

Co-author Dartmouth Professor Ross Virginia is
30 SkyTEM's co-principal investigator and director of Dartmouth's Institute of Arctic Studies. "This project is studying the past and present climate to, in part, understand how climate change in the future will affect biodiversity and ecosystem processes," Virginia says.
35 "This fantastic new view beneath the surface will help us sort out competing ideas about how the McMurdo Dry Valleys have changed with time and how this history influences what we see today."

The researchers found that the unfrozen brines form
40 extensive, interconnected aquifers deep beneath glaciers and lakes and within permanently frozen soils. The brines extend from the coast to at least 7.5 miles inland in the McMurdo Dry Valleys, the largest ice-free region in Antarctica. The brines could be due to freezing and/or
45 deposits. The findings show for the first time that the Dry Valleys' lakes are interconnected rather than isolated; connectivity between lakes and aquifers is important in sustaining ecosystems through drastic climate change, such as lake dry-down events. The findings also challenge

50 the assumption that parts of the ice sheets below the pressure melting point are devoid of liquid water.

In addition to providing answers about the biological adaptations of previously unknown ecosystems that persist in the extreme cold and dark of the Antarctic
55 winter, the new study could help scientists to understand whether similar conditions might exist elsewhere in the solar system, specifically beneath the surface of Mars, which has many similarities to the Dry Valleys. Overall, the Dry Valleys ecosystem – cold,
60 vegetation-free and home only to microscopic animal and plant life – resembles, during the Antarctic summer, conditions on the surface on Mars.

SkyTEM produced images of Taylor Valley along the Ross Sea that suggest briny sediments exist at
65 subsurface temperatures down to perhaps -68°F, which is considered suitable for microbial life. One of the studied areas was lower Taylor Glacier, where the data suggest ancient brine still exists beneath the glacier. That conclusion is supported by the presence of Blood
70 Falls, an iron-rich brine that seeps out of the glacier and hosts an active microbial ecosystem.

Scientists' understanding of Antarctica's underground environment is changing dramatically as research reveals that subglacial lakes are widespread
75 and that at least half of the areas covered by the ice sheet are akin to wetlands on other continents. But groundwater in the ice-free regions and along the coastal margins remains poorly understood.

1

The reference to brines in line 44 primarily serves to

A) offer an explanation.
B) point out a misconception.
C) refute a hypothesis.
D) define a term.

In context of the passage, the function of the sixth paragraph (lines 52-62) is to

A) describe some characteristics of Antarctic ecosystems not found elsewhere on earth.

B) compare the development of ecosystems in Antarctica to the development of ecosystems on Mars.

C) indicate a possible outcome of the SkyTEM research in Antarctica.

D) explain how microscopic plants and animals survive in extreme conditions.

The reference to microscopic animal and plant life (lines 60-61) primarily serves to

A) emphasize the harshness of the Antarctic climate.

B) describe the effects of iron on microbial life.

C) indicate the importance of research on glaciers.

D) compare an environment on Earth to an environment on another planet.

Official Guide/Khan Academy Function Questions

Test 1

19
22
25
27
34
42
46

Test 2

2
4
8
15
28
34

Test 3

5
11
25

Test 4

4
30
45

Explanations: Reading for Function Exercises

1.1 B

What is the context for "capturing, storing, and sharing pictures?" They are things that people found "fascinating" when they were first introduced. In the next sentence, the transition *Now* indicates that these capabilities are no longer considered so impressive. In other words, they are something that used to be considered novel (new and interesting), making the answer B).

1.2 A

This question can be answered using the main point: big data reveals hidden connections. That is essentially what A) says, so it is the answer. B) and C) are incorrect because the author's focus is on the uses of data, not news. D) is incorrect because the passage focuses on the *possibilities* of data analysis, not its limits.

1.3 B

Why mention Asimov? Because he predicted the current use of mass data sets all the way back in the 1950s. In other word, Asimov "foresaw recent developments." That makes B) the answer.

2.1 C

Why does the narrator refer to the catalpa grove and elm tree? The answer is in the following sentences. The statements that *Trees were so rare in that country...* and *It must have been the scarcity of detail in that tawny landscape* emphasize that landscape was extremely bare, i.e. barren. C) is therefore the answer.

2.2 D

This is a very straightforward question if you remember to back up a sentence – the one thing you *don't* want to do when answering a function question is start at the line reference and keep reading from there. The previous sentence indicates that *the Shimerdas were famished for fruit after weeks on the ocean*, the implication being that they did not have access to fresh produce during their journey. That statement is most consistent with the idea of a "limited diet" in D).

2.3 A

The key to this question is to notice the contradictor *but* in line 63 – it indicates a difference (=contrast) between Mrs. Shimerda's housewifely abilities in her old life, and her lack of those abilities in her new life.

3.1 A

Don't make this question out to be any more complicated than it actually is. If you don't remember where "Europe in the 1980s" is mentioned, start from the beginning of the passage – you'll find the reference immediately, in lines 1-2. Why mention that time and place? Simply to introduce the topic of the passage. There is no mention of the United States in that paragraph, eliminating B) and C). D) can be eliminated as well because the author says nothing to indicate that hackerspaces were "particularly popular" there; he simply states that they originated there.

3.2 B

To answer this question, you need to really consider how the author is presenting his argument in this section of the passage. The sentence that includes lines 16-17 is presented in "while x...in fact y" form. That is, while the idea of hacking might have an iffy reputation, hackerspaces are actually pretty great places. The first half of the sentence effectively functions as a counterargument, i.e. what "they say." Why would the author mention that idea? In order to show that he is aware that other people hold negative views of his topic, but that those negatives views are not true. In other words, he's "anticipating a potential criticism," making the answer B).

3.3. C

The line reference in the question in quite long, indicating that only a small part of it is likely to be relevant. Start by focusing on the first (topic) sentence of paragraph, since that's the place most likely to give you the answer: *In recent years, the city of Detroit has emerged as a hotbed for hackerspaces and other DIY ("Do-It-Yourself") experiments.* That sentence tells you that the paragraph will focus on Detroit. The only answer that corresponds to that fact is C), which rephrases Detroit as "a particular city." Indeed, if you continue to read the paragraph, you will find that it provides a number of reasons for hackerspaces' success in Detroit.

3.4 D

Consider the context of the OmniCorp discussion. The topic sentence of the paragraph indicates that *the vast majority of [hacker]spaces are self-organized and not-for-profit.* The transition *For example* at the beginning of the next sentence indicates that OmniCorp is mentioned to support that idea. Which answer corresponds most closely to the topic sentence? D). Self-organized = open and flexible. In addition, the author mentions that OmniCorp hosts an "open hack night" open to the general public, which also supports D).

3.5 B

Shortcut: use the main point (makerspaces could transform economy), which corresponds directly to B).

If you don't remember where the reference to *Wired* magazine appears, scan the passage (focusing on topic sentence) for that title – as a shortcut look for the italicized word. It appears in the topic sentence beginning in line 82. What do we learn from that sentence? That the makerspace movement has "transformative potential." If you continue reading, the last sentence (main point of the passage) corresponds directly to B). A) is incorrect because Chris Anderson is not a participant in the maker movement; C) is incorrect because the author only draws a parallel between

the change wrought by the Industrial Revolution and those that could result from the maker movement; and D) is incorrect because there is no information to support the idea that mass-production cannot exist in the modern economy – the author only states that mass-customization will *allow for a new wave of business opportunities.*

4.1 B

The key to this question is the sentence begun by the transition *But* in line 18. There, Jordan indicates that she does *not* intend to focus on people's dissatisfaction with the government and with the state of the country in general. In other words, Jordan lists those problems specifically to indicate that she *rejects* the idea that she should focus on them. That makes B) the correct answer.

4.2 C

Like the answer to the previous question, the answer to this question hinges on the transition *but* – in this case, the one that appears in line 33, immediately after the line reference. In that sentence, Jordan indicates that the "great danger" (=pose a threat) is that America will be torn apart by special interests, losing sight of collective goals (=national cohesion). That corresponds to C).

4.3 B

This is essentially the same question as 4.2, just phrased a slightly different way. Again, the key phrase is "great danger" (=a risk). Jordan uses this phrase to emphasize or "call attention to" the threat that Americans will be split apart by an excessive focus on special interests.

4.4 D

This question requires you to be as literal as possible; it also requires you to focus on the wording of the sentence in which the key word ("future") appears. What does that sentence tell us? That *we cannot flee the future.* In other words, it's inevitable. That makes the answer D).

4.5 B

Before you even look at the passage or the answers, consider that the question asks about the function of quotation marks. Why do authors typically use this form of punctuation? To imply skepticism or imply that something isn't really what it seems. The connotation is almost always negative. C) and D) are both positive, so they can be eliminated. Now consider the context: Jordan is describing politicians' *hypocrisy* – that is, they behave in such a way that contradicts their official titles. That corresponds directly to B).

4.6 A

Like the previous question, this question involves a section of the passage in which Jordan contrasts politicians' positive public face with their actual incompetence in upholding the public good. In that context, "slogans and handshakes and press releases" serve as examples of good-looking but fundamentally meaningless gestures that politicians substitute for working to uphold the public good. The answer that corresponds directly to that idea is A).

5.1 C

The key to answering this question is to consider the previous sentence, which states that the debate over whether dinosaurs were warm-blooded or cold-blooded is a *big controversy* (=scientific dispute). In that context, the foramen is a factor (=a means) that scientists can focus on in order to resolve that dispute. That corresponds directly to C).

5.2 D

This is a very straightforward question if you focus on the most relevant information – in this case, it's the sentence immediately following the line reference. The statement *We certainly didn't expect to see that* indicates that the findings came as a surprise, making the answer D).

6.1 A

This question is much simpler than it might initially seem. The key is the word *could*, which indicates that the author is speculating about a possible cause for the brines. In other words, the author is proposing a possible explanation for how they were created, making A) the answer.

6.2 C

As is true for the answer to the previous question, the answer to this question also depends on the word *could*, this time in line 55. That word indicates that the author is again speculating about the consequences of the SkyTEM research (=indicate a possible outcome). That corresponds directly to C).

6.3 D

Make sure you read the entire sentence in which the line reference appears; in that context, the references to plant and animal life serve as examples of ways in which the Antarctic surface resembles the surface of Mars. That corresponds directly to D).

Glossary of Function Words

Account for – Explain

Acknowledge (a point) – Recognize the merit or validity of an idea

Advocate – Synonym for *promote* and *encourage*

Bolster – Support, provide additional evidence for an idea

Concede (a point) – Recognize the merit or validity of an opposing idea

Discredit – Disprove (literally, demonstrate a lack of credibility)

SAT passages are typically concerned with weighing evidence, considering prevailing theories, and proposing new explanations – while authors may have strong opinions about what is and is not true, passages do not, as a rule, contain sufficient information or evidence to definitively prove or disprove anything. *Discredit* is thus unlikely to appear as a correct answer choice.

Dismiss – Deny the importance or validity of an idea

Downplay – Deliberately understate, imply that something is unimportant

Evoke – To summon, call up (a memory, impression, etc.), recreate through description

Explicate – Explain in great detail

Highlight – Emphasize, call attention to

Jeer at – Make fun of in a cruel or harsh manner. More extreme synonym of *mock* and *scoff*. Typically signals a wrong answer.

Minimize – Deliberately understate the importance of an idea. Synonym for *downplay* and *trivialize*.

Mock – Make fun of

Qualify – Provide more information about a statement in order to make it seem less strong or blunt, or to indicate the conditions under which it would be true.

For example, a statement like, "The SAT is the worst test EVER" is extremely strong (not to mention a good example of a **hyperbole**).

To **qualify** it, however, you could say something like, "At least that's what it feels like when you're a junior in high school." That sentence reduces the impact of the first sentence, clarifies when and for whom it would be true, and makes it seem less extreme.

It can be helpful to know that qualifying phrases are sometimes **parenthetical** – that is, they are found within parentheses or dashes – and are almost like asides to the reader. If you look back at the passage and see this kind of construction, "qualify" is almost certain to be correct. For example, consider the following passage:

> In his discovery of the law of the gravity, which would transform the course of scientific thought, Newton was struck by – **if the story can be believed** – an apple that fell from a tree above the spot where he was reclining.

The phrase between the dashes is intended to suggest that this story may not in fact be true. In other words, it is intended to provide information about the truth of – to qualify – the idea that Newton was struck by an apple.

As discussed earlier, answer choices that contain familiar words used in unfamiliar ways are generally correct since the second meaning itself is being tested. Since *qualify* is not being used in its most common sense of "fulfill requirements for," it has a higher than average chance of being correct.

So here's a shortcut: If you have difficulty coming up with an answer on your own and see "qualify a statement" as an option, you should probably begin by taking a very close look at it. This is NOT to say that you should choose it without thinking – **sometimes it will in fact be wrong** – simply that you should consider it first, making sure to look back to the passage and see if it does in fact describe the function of statement or phrase in question.

Satirize – Make fun of by using irony, sarcasm, or parody

Scoff at – Make fun of, suggest that something is unworthy of serious consideration

Simulate – Recreate an experience

Since SAT passages are primarily analytical and argumentative and are not intended to recreate a particular experience for the reader, this answer choice makes no sense in virtually every instance that it appears.

Substantiate – Give evidence or support for, back up

Trivialize – Treat as trivial or unimportant. Synonym for *downplay* and *minimize* but more extreme.

Undermine – Weaken or attack the foundation of; subvert secretly.

Undermine is also unlikely to appear as a correct answer because SAT passages are not long enough to allow for the kind of in-depth evidence necessary to actually weaken a theory at its base.

Underscore – Call attention to. Synonym for *emphasize* and *highlight*.

10. Tone and Attitude

Tone and attitude questions appear relatively rarely, but you can plan to encounter a few of them on every test. (Note: attitude question involving paired passages are discussed in chapter 13.) These questions essentially ask whether the author's language and attitude toward a subject are positive, negative, or neutral; they may also ask you to identify the relationship between specific wording and the tone. These questions are typically phrased in the following ways:

- What main effect does the quotation by Kim (lines x-y) have on the tone of the passage?

- The author would most likely view the events described in lines x-y as...

- The information in lines x-y suggests that the author would view advocates of Anderson's theory with...

As a general rule, "extreme" answers to tone/attitude questions are incorrect, while correct answers are moderate. Thus, if an author's attitude is positive, the answer is more likely to be **approving** or **appreciative** than **awed**; if the author's attitude is negative, the answer is more likely to be **skeptical** or **dubious** (doubtful) than **angry**; and if an author uses strong language, the answer is likely to be a more neutral word such as **emphatic** or **decisive**.

There are several reasons for this pattern: first is that the tone of most SAT passages tends to be relatively neutral. Most positive passages are slightly positive, and most negative passages are slightly negative. There are exceptions, however, so you must ultimately consider each question on its own merits. The second reason is that many of the passages concern arguments that can never be definitively proven – there's always another side. As a result, authors are unlikely to say that a given piece of evidence *conclusively* proves a new theory. Instead, they use **qualifying statements** and say that evidence *suggests* a theory has some merit. The second statement is much more **cautious** or **tentative** than the first, and SAT answers tend to reflect that fact.

Note: Because hearing how a passage *sounds* is a key element in identifying tone, it can help to read the lines in question aloud, albeit very quietly; however, this strategy will only work if you are able to "translate" the words on the page into normal speech.

Neutral Tone, Definite Opinion

While the terms "tone" and "attitude" are sometimes used interchangeably, they are not precisely the same thing, and it is important to understand the distinction between them.

An author can present information about a topic in a tone that is relatively neutral (or "objective" or "impartial") but still have a distinct opinion about which ideas are correct and which ones incorrect. **A lack of strong language does not imply a neutral <u>attitude</u>**. The information necessary to figure out what the author thinks will always be provided, even though you may have to read closely to identify it.

You should be particularly careful with science passages. There, especially, it is important not to confuse a dry or objective tone with an absence of opinion or point of view. SAT passages are, for all intents and purpose, not just recitations of factual information but rather chosen because they contain some sort of argument. More precisely, they frequently contain the "old idea vs. new idea" structure in which the author first discusses a prevailing theory (negative attitude), then at a certain point turns around and describes a new theory (positive attitude). While there will certainly be indications that the author rejects the former and embraces the latter, the overall *tone* may remain fairly neutral when discussing both.

Let's start with a more straightforward example, though:

> The so-called machine-learning approach…links
> several powerful software techniques that make it
> possible for the robot to learn new tasks rapidly with a
> relatively small amount of training. The new approach
> 5 includes a powerful artificial intelligence technique
> known as "deep learning," which has previously been
> used to achieve major advances in both computer
> vision and speech recognition. Now the researchers have
> found that it can also be used to improve the actions of
> 10 robots working in the physical world on tasks that require
> both machine vision and touch.

In this passage, the author's **positive tone** is revealed in a number of words and phrases:

- *make it possible*
- *powerful artificial intelligence technique*
- *major advances*
- *improve the actions*

Taken together, all of these elements indicate that the author considers this technology important and holds it in very high regard. His *tone*, however, is relatively restrained. He does not say that that this technology is "extraordinary," nor does he say that it is the "most important" invention ever. Instead, he understates his enthusiasm by using **qualifying words** such as *relatively small* and *major advance*. His tone, therefore, could be characterized as **appreciative** or **approving**.

Inferring Attitude

Being able to distinguish between tone and attitude can become very important when you are asked about attitude alone. These questions require the opposite of the approach required by tone questions: you must focus on *what* the author is saying rather than *how* the author is saying it.

While answers to many "attitude" questions are indicated fairly directly in the passage, some questions may ask you to move a step beyond what is literally stated and infer what the author of the passage or a person/group discussed in the passage would be likely to think about a particular idea or group of people.

While these kinds of questions are always present in Passage 1/Passage 2 sets, it is also possible for them to accompany single passages that discuss multiple points of view.

Although answers to these questions cannot be directly found in the passage, they are always directly suggested and remain very close in meaning to the information that *is* explicitly stated. You should, however, work through them very methodically, breaking them into steps to avoid missing key information.

Let's look at an example.

Sometime near the end of the Pleistocene, a band of people left northeastern Asia, crossed the Bering land bridge when the sea level was low, entered Alaska and became the first Americans. Since the
5 1930s, archaeologists have thought these people were members of the Clovis culture. First discovered in New Mexico in the 1930s, the Clovis culture is known for its distinct stone tools, primarily fluted projectile points. For decades, Clovis artifacts were the oldest
10 known in the New World, dating to 13,000 years ago. But in recent years, researchers have found more and more evidence that people were living in North and South America before the Clovis.
    The most recently confirmed evidence comes from
15 Washington. During a dig conducted from 1977 to 1979, researchers uncovered a bone projectile point stuck in a mastodon rib. Since then, the age of the find has been debated, but recently anthropologist Michael Waters and his colleagues announced a new radiocarbon date
20 for the rib: 13,800 years ago, making it 800 years older than the oldest Clovis artifact. Other pre-Clovis evidence comes from a variety of locations across the New World.

1

The "researchers" (line 11) would most likely view advocates of the theory described in lines 4-6 with

A) admiration because they offer a novel perspective.
B) skepticism because they do not acknowledge important new evidence.
C) hostility because they threaten to overturn decades of research.
D) suspicion because their methods are unreliable.

2

Which lines best support the answer to the previous question

A) Lines 1-4 ("Sometime...Americans)
B) Lines 6-9 ("First...points")
C) Lines 9-10 ("For...ago")
D) Lines 17-21 ("Since...artifact")

As discussed earlier, the passage follows a predictable pattern: it discusses an old theory (the Clovis people were the first people to inhabit North America) and a new theory (a group of people inhabited North America before the Clovis arrived).

When discussing these two theories, the author's *tone* remains relatively neutral. Instead of saying, for example, that the theory that the Clovis were the first inhabitants of North America is *absolutely* wrong, he simply states that "more evidence" suggests that is not the case. In contrast, his **attitude** toward the old idea is negative, while the attitude toward the new idea is positive. We're going to use that information to answer both questions. Because we have line references for the first question, we're going to answer them in order.

1) What's the theory in lines 4-6?

The Clovis were the first people in North America.

2) What do the researchers believe?

People were living in North and South America before the Clovis. (The Clovis were NOT the first people in North America.)

3) What's the relationship?

The information in steps 1 and 2 indicates opposing ideas, so they're going to disagree. That means we're going to look for something negative.

Now, we're going to consider just the first word of each option.

A) Admiration: positive. Cross out.

B) Skepticism: negative, relatively neutral. Keep it.

C) Hostility: negative, too strong. Assume it's wrong.

D) Suspicion: negative, relatively neutral. Keep it.

Working this way, we're left with B) and D). B) makes sense because someone who believed that the Clovis were the first people in the North America would be overlooking the evidence described in the second paragraph. D) makes no sense in context; there's no information in the passage to suggest the advocates' methods are unreliable.

So the correct answer is B).

Now for the second question. You could go through and check each option individually, but there's a much faster way to find the answer. We're looking for lines that support the idea that the Clovis were the first people in the Americas, which is part of the "I say."

Because the passage is arranged so that the "they say" comprises most of the first paragraph and the "I say" comprises the second paragraph, the correct lines must be in the second paragraph. D) is the only option that contains lines in the second paragraph, so it must be the answer. And indeed, those lines discuss evidence that the Clovis were not the first people in the Americas.

The Author Always Cares

While the tone of many passages will be objective or neutral, as in the example above, it will also **virtually never be indifferent**, **apathetic**, or **resigned** (or any synonym for those words). If you see one of these answers appear among the answer choices, you should generally begin by assuming it is incorrect.

The reason for this is simple: authors generally care about their subject. If they were indifferent, then pretty much by definition, they wouldn't bother to write about that subject. In addition, the texts for paired passages are chosen specifically because they have distinct points of view – often sharply differing points of view. It is generally possible to infer that the authors of these passages would either agree or disagree with one another's opinions. If there were no relationship, the passages wouldn't have been chosen in the first place.

The only potential **exception** to this rule would be a question about a character in a fiction passage. In that scenario, a character could exhibit a lack of interest. But the chances of that happening are relatively slim. Passages tend to focus on characters who have some level of engagement with the world around them – otherwise, there wouldn't be much to test.

Simplifying Answers and Playing Positive/Negative

Instead of just asking to identify the author's tone from among the various answers, tone questions will generally ask you to identify *how* the use of specific words/phrases contributes to the tone. While these questions may appear to be very complicated, their answers can often be simplified considerably.

Let's look at an example. Just read the passage – don't try to answer the question yet.

The sharing economy is a little like online
shopping, which started in America 15 years ago. At
first, people were worried about security. But having
made a successful purchase from, say, Amazon, they
5 felt safe buying elsewhere. Similarly, using Airbnb or
a car-hire service for the first time encourages people to
try other offerings. Next, consider eBay. Having started
out as a peer-to-peer marketplace, it is now dominated
by professional "power sellers" (many of whom started
10 out as ordinary eBay users). The same may happen with
the sharing economy, which also provides new
opportunities for enterprise. Some people have bought
cars solely to rent them out, for example. Incumbents
are getting involved too. Avis, a car-hire firm, has a share
15 in a sharing rival. So do GM and Daimler, two carmakers.
In the future, companies may develop hybrid models,
listing excess capacity (whether vehicles, equipment or
office space) on peer-to-peer rental sites. In the past,
new ways of doing things online have not displaced the
20 old ways entirely. But they have often changed them.
Just as internet shopping forced Walmart and Tesco to
adapt, so online sharing will shake up transport, tourism,
equipment-hire and more.
   The main worry is regulatory uncertainty. Will
25 room-4-renters be subject to hotel taxes, for example?
In Amsterdam officials are using Airbnb listings to track
down unlicensed hotels. In some American cities,
peer-to-peer taxi services have been banned after
lobbying by traditional taxi firms. The danger is that
30 although some rules need to be updated to protect
consumers from harm, incumbents will try to destroy
competition. People who rent out rooms should pay tax,
of course, but they should not be regulated like a Ritz-
Carlton hotel. The lighter rules that typically govern
35 bed-and-breakfasts are more than adequate. The sharing
economy is the latest example of the internet's value to
consumers. This emerging model is now big and
disruptive enough for regulators and companies to have
woken up to it. That is a sign of its immense potential. It
40 is time to start caring about sharing.

What main effect do the author's statements about the sharing economy in lines 35-40 have on the tone of the passage?

A) They create an emphatic tone, conveying the strength of the author's convictions.
B) They create a resigned tone, focusing on the inevitability of economic change.
C) They create a celebratory tone, praising regulators for adapting.
D) They create a mournful tone, focusing on the destruction of traditional lifestyles.

When you look at a set of answer choices like the ones in the question above, your first reaction might be to feel a bit overwhelmed. After all, they're throwing an awful lot of information at you, and it seems easy to get lost in the details.

One strategy for simplifying things is to just focus on the tone word in each answer and ignore the rest of the information. You can think of the question as asking this:

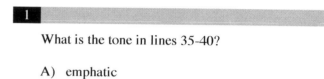

1

What is the tone in lines 35-40?

A) emphatic
B) resigned
C) celebratory
D) mournful

Treating questions this way has both benefits and drawbacks. On one hand, you have less information to deal with, and thus less potential for confusion. On the other hand, you can't rely on the information in the rest of the answer choice to figure out the tone but must instead figure it out on your own. If you can play positive/negative without too much difficulty, though, there's a very good chance you can find your way to the answer.

Some questions may also require a **combination of strategies**: play positive/negative with the "tone" word to eliminate a couple of options, then consider the full answers to decide between the remaining options.

That said, let's keep working through the simplified version:

35   ... The sharing
economy is the latest example of the internet's value to
consumers. This emerging model is now big and
disruptive enough for regulators and companies to have
woken up to it. That is a sign of its immense potential. It
40   is time to start caring about sharing.

The next thing we're going to do is ignore the options provided and answer the question in our own words.

When we look at the section in question, we can notice that it's positive – phrases such as *the internet's value to consumers*, *immense potential*, and *It is time to start caring* indicate that the author thinks that the sharing economy is a pretty great thing. Both *resigned* (accepted of a bad situation) and *mournful* are negative, so we can eliminate B) and D) right away.

That leaves A) and C). The fact that *celebratory* is pretty strong while *emphatic* is more neutral suggests that A) is probably right. In fact, the lines in question – especially the last sentence – do consist mostly of short, strong statements, which support A). Even so, we don't have quite enough information to decide, so we're going to check out the full answers.

35 ... The sharing economy is the latest example of the internet's value to consumers. This emerging model is now big and disruptive enough for regulators and companies to have woken up to it. That is a sign of its immense potential. It 40 is time to start caring about sharing.

What main effect do the author's statements about the sharing economy in lines 35-40 have on the tone of the passage?

A) They create an emphatic tone, conveying the strength of the author's convictions.
B) They create a resigned tone, focusing on the inevitability of economic change.
C) They create a celebratory tone, praising regulators for adapting.
D) They creates mournful tone, focusing on the destruction of traditional lifestyles.

Shortcut: A) contains the word *convictions*, which is used in its second meaning. When most students hear the word *conviction*, they picture a courtroom with a judge announcing "Guilty!" But *conviction* is also the noun form of *convinced* – in this meaning, convictions are simply strong beliefs, and that's the only use that makes sense. That alone is enough to suggest that A) is almost certainly the answer. And when you go back to the passage, it's pretty clear that the author strongly believes the sharing economy is a big deal. So A) works.

The slightly longer way: Remember that when you're stuck between two answers, you want to pick the most specific part of one answer to check out. If the passage supports it, that answer is right; if the passage doesn't support it, the other answer must be right by default.

In this case, C) provides more specific information; it indicates that the passage *[praises] regulators for adapting*. When we go back to the passage, though, the only information we find about regulators is that the author thinks they should have "woken up to" the sharing economy by now. It does not actually say that they have adapted. So C) doesn't work, again leaving A).

Register: Formal vs. Informal

One of the concepts that the SAT tests indirectly is **register** – that is, whether writing is formal or informal. You might assume because the SAT is a Very Serious Test, all the passages must therefore be written in a Very Serious Manner. That is, however, not entirely the case. While it is true that many historical texts will be written in a formal manner, some more contemporary passages – or sections of passages – may be less serious.

For example, compare the following two passage excerpts. Passage 1 is taken from Daniel Webster's 1850 speech *The Union and the Constitution*. Passage 2 is taken from a 2013 editorial that appeared in a major newspaper.

Passage 1

I wish to speak to-day, not as a Massachusetts man, nor as a Northern man, but as an American, and a member of the Senate of the United States. It is fortunate that there is a Senate of the United States; a
5　body not yet moved from its propriety, not lost to a just sense of its own dignity and its own high responsibilities, and a body to which the country looks, with confidence, for wise, moderate, patriotic, and healing counsels. It is not to be denied that we live in the midst of strong
10　agitations, and are surrounded by very considerable dangers to our institutions and government. The imprisoned winds are let loose. The East, the North, and the stormy South combine to throw the whole sea into commotion, to toss its billows to the skies, and
15　disclose its profoundest depths. I do not affect to regard myself, Mr. President, as holding, or as fit to hold, the helm in this combat with the political elements; but I have a duty to perform, and I mean to perform it with fidelity, not without a sense of existing dangers, but not
20　without hope. I have a part to act, not for my own security or safety, for I am looking out for no fragment upon which to float away from the wreck, if wreck there must be, but for the good of the whole, and the preservation of all; and there is that which will keep me
25　to my duty during this struggle, whether the sun and the stars shall appear, or shall not appear for many days. I speak to-day for the preservation of the Union.

Passage 2

Yogi Berra, the former Major League baseball catcher and coach, once remarked that you can't hit and think at the same time. Of course, since he also reportedly said, "I really didn't say everything I said,"
5　it is not clear we should take his statements at face value. Nonetheless, a widespread view — in both academic journals and the popular press — is that thinking about what you are doing, as you are doing it, interferes with performance. The idea is that once you
10　have developed the ability to play an arpeggio on the piano, putt a golf ball or parallel park, attention to what you are doing leads to inaccuracies, blunders and sometimes even utter paralysis. As the great choreographer George Balanchine would say to his
15　dancers, "Don't think, dear; just do."
　　Perhaps you have experienced this destructive force yourself. Start thinking about just how to carry a full glass of water without spilling, and you'll end up drenched. How, exactly, do you initiate a telephone
20　conversation? Begin wondering, and before long, the recipient of your call will notice the heavy breathing and hang up. Our actions, the French philosopher Maurice Merleau-Ponty tells us, exhibit a "magical" efficacy, but when we focus on them, they degenerate
25　into the absurd. A 13-time winner on the Professional Golfers Association Tour, Dave Hill, put it like this: "You can't be thinking about the mechanics of the sport while you are performing."

The first passage is undoubtedly a very **formal** piece of writing. It contains extremely long sentences (up to nine lines) with multiple clauses, sophisticated, abstract vocabulary and phrasing (*propriety, agitations, fidelity, political elements*), and is filled with metaphorical language (*imprisoned winds, toss its billows to the skies, no fragment upon which to float away from the wreck*). The tone could thus be described as **elevated** or **lofty**. Because Webster uses the **first person** (*I*) throughout the passage, the tone could also be characterized as **personal**.

In terms of tone and style, the second passage is the complete opposite of the first. The sentences are far shorter and employ a much more **casual** or **colloquial** level of vocabulary (*blunders, drenched, put it like this*). It contains allusions (references) to popular culture, e.g. Yogi Berra and baseball, and the author frequently addresses the reader directly. In addition, it includes several humorous quotations, including one at the beginning that is patently absurd (*I really didn't say everything I said*), and a rhetorical question (*How, exactly do you begin a phone conversation?*) that is placed to give the impression that the author is thinking things over as she writes. Taken together, these elements create a tone that is **informal** and **conversational.**

Now consider this excerpt from a passage we looked at earlier:

The sharing economy is a little like online shopping, which started in America 15 years ago. At first, people were worried about security. But having made a successful purchase from, say, Amazon, they
5 felt safe buying elsewhere. Similarly, using Airbnb or a car-hire service for the first time encourages people to try other offerings. Next, consider eBay. Having started out as a peer-to-peer marketplace, it is now dominated by professional "power sellers" (many of whom started
10 out as ordinary eBay users). The same may happen with the sharing economy, which also provides new opportunities for enterprise. Some people have bought cars solely to rent them out, for example. Incumbents are getting involved too. Avis, a car-hire firm, has a share
15 in a sharing rival. So do GM and Daimler, two carmakers. In the future, companies may develop hybrid models, listing excess capacity (whether vehicles, equipment or office space) on peer-to-peer rental sites.

In comparison to the examples we just looked at, this one falls somewhere in the middle. It doesn't contain the sophisticated vocabulary and complex syntax (word order) of the first passage, but neither does it include the casual, humorous aspects of the second passage. It simply presents an argument – people are initially nervous about the sharing economy, but their concerns disappear when they participate in it – and supports it with various pieces of evidence. The tone is straightforward and moderately serious. Even though the author clearly has a positive attitude toward the sharing economy, the tone could also be described as **neutral, analytical**, or **objective**. These tone are associated with a **third person point of view** (*he/she/it*).

Certainty and Uncertainty

While SAT authors are rarely over-the-top extreme, they do sometimes voice some very strong opinions. Writing that is **emphatic**, **decisive**, **vehement**, **resolute** or full of **conviction** tends to have some pronounced characteristics:

- It contains short, blunt declarations (e.g. *There is no compelling proof that it's true*).

- It contains strong words and phrases such as *there is no doubt*, *certainly*, *only*, and *most*.

- It lacks qualifying words or phrases such as *sometimes*, *frequently*, or *might* that would soften its meaning.

For example, compare the following two statements:

1) Technology changes everything.

2) In some circumstances, technology has the potential to change people's lives.

The two sentences deal with the same subject, but they do so in very different ways.

The first sentence is striking because it is so short and to-the-point – it simply says what it has to say, and that's that. Its tone could thus be described as **emphatic** or **decisive**.

The second sentence, on the other hand, is filled with **qualifying phrases** (*some*, *has the potential to be*) that tell us that the author wants to avoid making an overly strong statement. Its tone could be described as **tentative**, **hesitant**, or **cautious.**

You are likely to encounter many instances of **speculative** tones. In such cases, the author will discusses hypothetical situations – ones that have not actually occurred but that could occur – and will use words such as *could*, *might*, *probably*, and *perhaps*.

For example:

> A better understanding of archaea's lifestyle and role in nitrogen cycles not only would rewrite ecology textbooks. It **could also have practical applications**, such as devising natural ways to boost a soil's nitrogen
> 5 content without needing to use chemical fertilizers, or designing sewage treatment plants that employ microbes to remove nitrogenous waste more efficiently, or understanding which microbes produce global-warming gases such as nitrous oxide.

In this passage, the word *could* indicates that the author is **speculating** about the potential applications of knowledge regarding archaea's lifestyle and role in nitrogen cycles – that is, knowledge and applications that do not currently exist but that might exist in the future.

Rhetorical questions can also indicate a lack of certainty:

> In our time, reality stars can become "fame-ish" overnight; but the people of the nineteenth century bestowed fame on individuals—mostly male—who they felt had made significant contributions to history. **Why**
> 5 **did the residents of Washington City, the members of government and their families, and, indeed, all of America declare Dolley the nation's "Queen"? What did they understand about Dolley Madison that we don't?**

The questions in the last three lines are key in identifying the author's tone: the fact that the author must ask *why* Dolley Madison was held in such high regard in the nineteenth century, and *what* people today *do not understand* about her indicates that confusion. Thus, we can say that the author is **puzzled, perplexed, uncertain,** or that the tone is **searching**.

Examining Both Sides of an Argument ≠ Ambivalence

One very common point of confusion stems from the fact that SAT authors often acknowledge the merits of arguments that they do not ultimately agree with. That does not, however, mean that those authors are uncertain about *their own* opinions. Even if they discuss other viewpoints extensively, they usually come down firmly on one side (albeit in ways that may strike you as unnecessarily subtle or confusing). As a result, you should be careful with the word **ambivalent** if it appears as an answer choice.

Some of this confusion also stems from difficulty distinguishing between what "they say" vs. "I say." If you don't realize that an author is switching between points of view and miss the signals indicating that they are discussing other people's arguments, you can easily get lost in all the back-and-forth and end up assuming that the author doesn't really have an opinion – and that will almost never be the case.

If you find yourself confused about what the author thinks, you should refer back to the **end of the conclusion** because that is the place where the author is most likely to reaffirm the main point. You can also scan the passage for reversers such as *but, however,* and *rather* since the "I say" will usually be presented after those transitions. While the main point may be introduced at the end of the introduction as well, you should be careful when looking early in the passage since authors can sometimes spend a considerable amount of time repeating what "they" say.

For example, we're going to look back at this passage:

Some scientists, unsurprisingly, balk at *Jurassic Park*. After all, the science is so inaccurate! *Velociraptor* was smaller and had feathers. *Dilophosaurus* wasn't venomous. *Tyrannosaurus rex* could not run so fast.
5   That opening scene where the paleontologists just wipe sand off of an intact and perfectly preserved dino skeleton is hogwash. In any case, near-complete DNA molecules cannot survive in fossils for tens of thousands of years, much less tens of millions. Also:
10 did you know that most of the dinosaurs depicted in *Jurassic Park* actually lived in the Cretaceous period?

They Say

This is the pedant's approach to science fiction, and it does have its uses. Among other things, how would scientists be able to maintain bonding rituals within
15 their tribe if they could not rally around movies that get their specialties wrong? Astronomers have *Armageddon* and *Contact*; volcanologists have *Volcano* and *Dante's Peak*; physicists have the *Stars Trek* and *Wars*; and paleontologists have *Jurassic Park*. (Artificial
20 intelligence researchers are another story — most of them would be out of a job if not for the movies.)
      More importantly, *Jurassic Park* isn't simply after the facts. Nor, as many reviewers complained at the time of its initial release, does the movie seek to tell
25 stories about fully three-dimensional human characters. <u>Rather, it offers us a fable about the natural world and man, and the relation between the two: about science, technology, imagination, aspiration, folly, power, corruption, hubris, wild nature in its many forms, and,</u>
30 <u>most importantly, dinosaurs.</u>

I Say

This is a stellar example of the type of writing that provokes confusion about attitude. If you overlook the significance of the phrase *Some scientists* right at the beginning of the first sentence, you could easily end up thinking that everything that follows represents what the *author* believes. In fact, the author is merely summarizing the reason that *other* scientists balk at (refuse to have anything to do with) *Jurassic Park*. In this case, he goes on for a full 11 lines. The fact that he spends so much time discussing what "they" think does not in any way indicate that he agrees with it. In fact, **there is no relationship between how much time an author spends discussing an idea and whether the author agrees with that idea**.

While the author's attitude toward the "pedant's" view of science in movies is clearly negative, he also acknowledges that *it does have its uses*. It is, however, important to understand that the author's recognition of that fact does not indicate that he has mixed feelings, i.e. is ambivalent. In fact, he states his opinion very clearly at the end of the passage: *Jurassic Park* is important because it raises crucial questions about the morality of science.

Humor, Sarcasm, and Irony

If you encounter humor in an SAT passage, it will probably not be the obvious, over-the-top, laugh-out-loud type of humor that you probably associate with that word. Rather, it will be based on **wordplay** that either involves **punning** on alternate meanings of words, or using words to mean exactly the **opposite** of what they normally mean (the literary equivalent of a kid who rolls his eyes and says "great" when he's asked to stop playing video games and take out the trash). It is up to the reader to recognize that meanings are being flip-flopped *based on the context of the passage* and to connect those meanings to the tone.

One thing to be aware of is that authors often use humor to express **negative attitudes**. It typically appears as part of the "I say," when the author wants to criticize or mock what "they" say without being overly direct or heavy-handed. This stands in direct contrast to the usual positive associations that most people have with humor.

Unfortunately, humor and sarcasm can be more difficult to recognize than other tones because there are no specific types of words that reliably signal their presence (although punctuation such as quotation marks can indicate that an author does not intend for a word to be understood literally). While there is no guarantee that you will encounter questions testing these types of tones, it is to your advantage to be able to recognize them.

For example:

The ethics of eating red meat have been **grilled** recently by critics who question its consequences for environmental health and animal welfare. But if you want to minimize animal suffering and promote more
5 sustainable agriculture, adopting a vegetarian diet might be the worst possible thing you could do.

In the first line, the author puns on the word *grilled* by using it in its second meaning ("question intensely") while simultaneously associating it with its first meaning ("cooking food on a grill"). The play on words creates a **humorous** or **irreverent** tone.

In context of the unexpected assertion that the author makes in the next sentence (being a **vegetarian** is bad for animals and agriculture) the play on words also establishes a tone of light **mockery** and **sarcasm** toward the "critics:" people who believe that eating meat is bad for animals and the environment.

Because the author introduces his critique through a clever play on words rather than simply announcing that it is wrong to believe that vegetarianism helps the environment, his tone could also be called **ironic, facetious, wry, sardonic,** or **satirical.**

If you didn't immediately pick up on the sarcasm in those couple of sentences, though, don't be too hard on yourself. Recognizing sarcasm often requires that you *hear* the words, with their accompanying intonation and emphases, as they would sound when spoken aloud. If someone were to read the passage on the previous page out loud, they would probably draw out or put special emphasis on the word *grilled* in order to make it clear that it was being used in an unexpected way. In the absence of such auditory cues, you must do your best to "translate" the words on the page into everyday speech. As mentioned earlier, you should read the words (very, very) quietly to yourself, thinking about which words a speaker would naturally stress or pay particular attention to.

Sometimes, however, authors will "tell" you what to pay attention to by using punctuation such as italics, quotation marks, and exclamation points, or rhetorical techniques such as repetition, to indicate that you should give special emphasis to a given word or phrase. In such cases, you must pay close attention to those features of the text and consider how they would "translate" into a spoken phrase.

For example, consider the beginning of this passage (lines 1-11):

Some scientists, unsurprisingly, balk at *Jurassic Park*. After all, the science is so inaccurate! Velociraptor was smaller and had feathers. Dilophosaurus wasn't venomous. Tyrannosaurus rex could not run so fast.
5 That opening scene where the paleontologists just wipe sand off of an intact and perfectly preserved dino skeleton is hogwash. In any case, near-complete DNA molecules cannot survive in fossils for tens of thousands of years, much less tens of millions. Also:
10 did you know that most of the dinosaurs depicted in *Jurassic Park* actually lived in the Cretaceous period? This is the pedant's approach to science fiction, and it does have its uses. Among other things, how would scientists be able to maintain bonding rituals within
15 their tribe if they could not rally around movies that get their specialties wrong? Astronomers have *Armageddon* and *Contact*; volcanologists have *Volcano* and *Dante's Peak*; physicists have the *Stars Trek* and *Wars*; and paleontologists have *Jurassic Park*. (Artificial
20 intelligence researchers are another story — most of them would be out of a job if not for the movies.)

The phrase *Some scientists* in line 1 tells us immediately that the author is going to be discussing what "they say," and that his attitude toward the information that follows will be negative – an impression that is confirmed by the word *hogwash* (nonsense). The exclamation point in line 2 and the question mark in line 11 are both used for **rhetorical effect** (or as **rhetorical flourishes**) in order to poke fun at the unjustified outrage of "those scientists" at *Jurassic Park's* scientific inaccuracies.

Another characteristic of this type of humor appears later in the passage, in the rhetorical question in lines 13-16. There again, the author pokes fun at "those" scientists by using a type of language typically associated with anthropologists studying an exotic tribe (*maintain bonding rituals within their tribe*). The difference between who these scientists actually are (established professionals in a developed country) and what the author's language suggests they are (members of a primitive society) results in **dry** or **wry humor**.

Wistfulness and Nostalgia

A passage whose tone falls into this category will contain a clear indication that the author misses the way things were in the past and regrets that they are now different. For example:

No image **brings a tear to the eye of even the crustiest ink-on-paper romantic** like a **yellowing** photograph of the city room of a **deceased newspaper**. *The Journal-American* was once New York City's
5   most widely read afternoon newspaper—yes, afternoon paper, a **once-grand tradition** of American journalism that has gone the way of the Linotype machine, the gluepot and the spike onto which editors would stick stories they deemed unworthy of publication.

There are a number of words and phrases in this passage that indicate that the author regrets the demise of the *New York Journal-American*. The phrases *brings a tear to the eye* and *once-grand* clearly indicates how sorry he is that it has disappeared, and the personification in the phrase "*deceased* newspaper" (a newspaper is not a living creature and cannot actually be deceased) further conveys his attachment to it. His tone is decidedly **wistful** or **nostalgic**.

Defensiveness

A defensive tone indicates that an author feels that he or she is being unfairly criticized or accused, and feels the need to defend or justify a belief or action. For example, consider this passage from the opening of Kazuo Ishiguro's 2010 novel *Never Let Me Go*. It provides a stellar example of a defensive tone:

My name is Kathy H. I'm thirty-one years old, and I've been a carer now for over eleven years… Now I know my being a carer so long isn't necessarily because they think I'm fantastic at what I do…
5   So I'm not trying to boast. But then I do know for a fact they've been pleased with my work, and by and large, I have too. Anyway, I'm not making any big claims for myself. I know carers, working now, who are just as good and don't get half the credit. If you're one of
10 them, I can understand how you might get resentful. But I'm not the first to be allowed to pick and choose, and I doubt if I'll be the last. And anyway, I've done my share of looking after donors brought up in every kind of place. By the time I finish, remember, I'll have
15 done twelve years of this, and it's only for the last six they've let me choose.

Although we have no context for statements the narrator is making and have no information about what a "carer" is, we can discern that she feels she must protect herself against people who would think that she does not deserve her position.

How do we know this? Well, first of all, she spends quite a bit of time justifying herself: she tells us that *[she] hasn't necessarily lasted so long because she's fantastic at what [she] does*, then insists that she isn't bragging (*So I'm not trying to boast... Anyway, I'm not making any big claims for myself*) while simultaneously trying to prove her competence (*But then I do know for a fact they've been pleased with my work, and by and large, I have too.*)

Furthermore, she goes out of her way to remind the reader how much work she's put in to deserve her privileges. (*By the time I finish, remember, I'll have done twelve years of this, and it's only for the last six they've let me choose.*) Clearly, she's anticipating being criticized and demonstrates a need to defend herself against that criticism at every turn.

Thinking and Teaching

You may also encounter passages whose tone is **reflective** or **pensive**. These passages are also likely to make use of the first person and tend to include phrases such as *I think*, *I believe*, and *it seems to me*, although that will not always be the case.

For example:

The world is complex and interconnected, and the evolution of our communications system from a broadcast model to a networked one has added a new dimension to the mix. The Internet has made us all less
5 dependent on professional journalists and editors for information about the wider world, allowing us to seek out information directly via online search or to receive it from friends through social media. But this enhanced convenience comes with a considerable risk: that we
10 will be exposed to what we want to know at the expense of what we need to know. While we can find virtual communities that correspond to our every curiosity, there's little pushing us beyond our comfort zones to or into the unknown, even if the unknown may have
15 serious implications for our lives. There are things we should probably know more about—like political and religious conflicts in Russia or basic geography. But even if we knew more than we do, there's no guarantee that the knowledge gained would prompt us to act in a
20 particularly admirable fashion.

Although this passage is not written in the more common first person singular, *I*, it is written in the first person plural, *we* – a strategy intended to establish a connection between the author and the reader. The constant alternation between acknowledging the good points of the Internet (seeking out information directly, finding virtual communities) and the bad points (nothing to push people beyond their comfort zones, people won't necessarily use their knowledge for good) indicates that the author is thinking through some serious questions. His tone could therefore be characterized as **pensive** or **reflective**.

A **didactic** tone is associated with the **second person** point of view, in which the narrator addresses the reader or another character directly in order to instruct them. For example, consider this snippet from a Sherlock Holmes novel:

"Really Hopkins," said he, "I have high hopes for your career, but you must learn patience before rushing off to pursue the first conclusion which occurs to you. Examine every fact, test every link in your chain and only then take action.

The phrase *you must learn*, and the commands *examine*, *test*, and *take* indicate that Holmes is instructing Hopkins. His tone could therefore be called **didactic**.

Tone and Attitude Exercises

1.   The world is complex and interconnected, and the
evolution of our communications system from a
broadcast model to a networked one has added a new
dimension to the mix. The Internet has made us all less
5 dependent on professional journalists and editors for
information about the wider world, allowing us to seek
out information directly via online search or to receive
it from friends through social media. But this enhanced
convenience comes with a considerable risk: that we
10 will be exposed to what we want to know at the expense
of what we need to know. While we can find virtual
communities that correspond to our every curiosity,
there's little pushing us beyond our comfort zones
to or into the unknown, even if the unknown may have
15 serious implications for our lives. There are things we
should probably know more about—like political and
religious conflicts in Russia or basic geography. But even
if we knew more than we do, there's no guarantee that
the knowledge gained would prompt us to act in a
20 particularly admirable fashion

■ 1 ■

The author's attitude toward the Internet is best
described as one of

A) fearfulness.
B) enthusiasm.
C) ambivalence.
D) curiosity.

■ 2 ■

Which lines provide the best evidence for the
answer to the previous question?

A) Lines 1-3 ("The world...one")
B) Lines 4-6 ("The internet...world")
C) Lines 11-13 ("While...zones")
D) Lines 17-20 ("But...fashion")

2.   Chimps do it, birds do it, even you and I do it.
Once you see someone yawn, you are compelled to
do the same. Now it seems that wolves can be added
to the list of animals known to spread yawns like a
5 contagion.
   Among humans, even thinking about yawning can
trigger the reflex, leading some to suspect that catching
a yawn is linked to our ability to empathize with other
humans. For instance, contagious yawning activates the
10 same parts of the brain that govern empathy and social
know-how. And some studies have shown that humans
with more fine-tuned social skills are more likely to
catch a yawn.
   Similarly, chimpanzees, baboons and bonobos
15 often yawn when they see other members of their species
yawning. Chimps (Pan troglodytes) can catch yawns
from humans, even virtual ones. At least in primates,
contagious yawning seems to require an emotional
connection and may function as a demonstration of
20 empathy. Beyond primates, though, the trends are less
clear-cut. One study found evidence of contagious
yawning in birds but didn't connect it to empathy.
A 2008 study showed that dogs (Canis lupus familiaris)
could catch yawns from humans, and another showed
25 that dogs were more likely to catch the yawn of a familiar
human rather than a stranger. But efforts to see if dogs
catch yawns from each other and to replicate the results
with humans have so far had no luck.

■ 1 ■

The author's attitude toward the relationship
between yawning and empathy in non-primates is
best described as one of

A) dubiousness.
B) agreement.
C) nostalgia.
D) hostility.

■ 2 ■

Which lines provide the best evidence for the
answer to the previous question?

A) Lines 2-3 ("Once...same")
B) Lines 6-9 ("Among...humans")
C) Lines 14-16 ("Similarly...yawning")
D) Lines 26-28 ("But...luck")

3.   These are stimulating times for anyone interested
in questions of animal consciousness. On what seems
like a monthly basis, scientific teams announce the
results of new experiments, adding to a preponderance
5 of evidence that we've been underestimating animal
minds, even those of us who have rated them fairly
highly. New animal behaviors and capacities are
observed in the wild, often involving tool use—or at
least object manipulation—the very kinds of activity
10 that led the distinguished zoologist Donald R. Griffin to
found the field of cognitive ethology (animal thinking)
in 1978: octopuses piling stones in front of their
hideyholes, to name one recent example; or dolphins
fitting marine sponges to their beaks in order to dig for
15 food on the seabed; or wasps using small stones to
smooth the sand around their egg chambers, concealing
them from predators. At the same time neurobiologists
have been finding that the physical structures in our
own brains most commonly held responsible for
20 consciousness are not as rare in the animal kingdom as
had been assumed. Indeed they are common. All of this
work and discovery appeared to reach a kind of
crescendo last summer, when an international group of
prominent neuroscientists meeting at the University of
25 Cambridge issued "The Cambridge Declaration on
Consciousness in Non-Human Animals," a document
stating that "humans are not unique in possessing the
neurological substrates that generate consciousness."
It goes further to conclude that numerous documented
30 animal behaviors must be considered "consistent with
experienced feeling states."

1

The author's attitude toward Donald R. Griffin
(line 10) is best described as one of

A) resignation.
B) admiration.
C) defensiveness.
D) skepticism.

4.   Every time a car drives through a major intersection, it becomes a data point. Magnetic coils of wire lay just beneath the pavement, registering each passing car. This starts a cascade of information: Computers tally the
5 number and speed of cars, shoot the data through underground cables to a command center and finally translate it into the colors red, yellow and green. On the seventh floor of Boston City Hall, the three colors splash like paint across a wall-sized map.
10   To drivers, the color red means stop, but on the map it tells traffic engineers to leap into action. Traffic control centers like this one—a room cluttered with computer terminals and live video feeds of urban intersections— represent the brain of a traffic system. The city's network
15 of sensors, cables and signals are the nerves connected to the rest of the body. "Most people don't think there are eyes and ears keeping track of all this stuff," says John DeBenedictis, the center's engineering director. But in reality, engineers literally watch our every move,
20 making subtle changes that relieve and redirect traffic.
    The tactics and aims of traffic management are modest but powerful. Most intersections rely on a combination of pre-set timing and computer adaptation. For example, where a busy main road intersects with a quiet residential
25 street, the traffic signal might give 70 percent of "green time" to the main road, and 30 percent to the residential road. (Green lights last between a few seconds and a couple minutes, and tend to shorten at rush hour to help the traffic move continuously.) But when traffic
30 overwhelms the pre-set timing, engineers override the system and make changes.

1

What effect does the quotation by John DeBenedictis in lines 16-17 have on the tone of of the passage?

A) It creates a skeptical tone, implying that the power of computers to control traffic may be limited.
B) It creates an enthusiastic tone, emphasizing the power of technology to ensure safety.
C) It creates an ominous tone, suggesting the risks of unrestrained surveillance.
D) It creates an informal tone, pointing out a common misconception in everyday language.

5.   To understand what the new software—that is, analytics—can do that's different from more familiar software like spreadsheets, word processing, and graphics, consider the lowly photograph. Here the

5   relevant facts aren't how many bytes constitute a digital photograph, or a billion of them. That's about as instructive as counting the silver halide molecules used to form a single old-fashioned print photo. The important feature of a digital image's bytes is that, unlike

10 crystalline molecules, they are uniquely easy to store, transport, and manipulate with software. In the first era of digital images, people were fascinated by the convenience and malleability (think PhotoShop) of capturing, storing, and sharing pictures. Now, instead of

15 using software to manage photos, we can mine features of the bytes that make up the digital image. Facebook can, without privacy invasion, track where and when, for example, vacationing is trending, since digital images reveal at least that much. But more importantly, those

20 data can be cross-correlated, even in real time, with seemingly unrelated data such as local weather, interest rates, crime figures, and so on. Such correlations associated with just one photograph aren't revealing. But imagine looking at billions of photos over weeks,

25 months, years, then correlating them with dozens of directly related data sets (vacation bookings, air traffic), tangential information (weather, interest rates, unemployment), or orthogonal information (social or political trends). With essentially free super-computing,

30 we can mine and usefully associate massive, formerly unrelated data sets and unveil all manner of economic, cultural, and social realities.

   For science fiction aficionados, Isaac Asimov anticipated the idea of using massive data sets to predict

35 human behavior, coining it "psychohistory" in his 1951 Foundation trilogy. The bigger the data set, Asimov said then, the more predictable the future. With big-data analytics, one can finally see the forest, instead of just the capillaries in the tree leaves. Or to put it in more

40 accurate terms, one can see beyond the apparently random motion of a few thousand molecules of air inside a balloon; one can see the balloon itself, and beyond that, that it is inflating, that it is yellow, and that it is part of a bunch of balloons en route to a birthday party. The

45 data/software world has, until now, been largely about looking at the molecules inside one balloon.

1

What effect does the word "imagine" (line 24) have on the tone of the passage?

A) It creates a mysterious tone that suggests the unlimited potential of technology.

B) It creates a skeptical tone that suggests the necessity of resisting certain inventions.

C) It creates a speculative tone that encourages the reader to consider a scenario.

D) It creates a defiant tone that emphasizes the need to persevere in the face of adversity.

6. The following passage is adapted from Jane Austen, *Northanger Abbey*, originally published in 1817.

No one who had ever seen Catherine Morland in her infancy would have supposed her born to be an heroine. Her situation in life, the character of her father and mother, her own person and disposition, were all
5 equally against her.

Her father was a clergyman, without being neglected, or poor, and a very respectable man, though his name was Richard—and he had never been handsome. He had a considerable independence besides
10 two good livings—and he was not in the least addicted to locking up his daughters. Her mother was a woman of useful plain sense, with a good temper, and, what is more remarkable, with a good constitution. She had three sons before Catherine was born; and instead of
15 dying in bringing the latter into the world, as anybody might expect, she still lived on—lived to have six children more—to see them growing up around her, and to enjoy excellent health herself. A family of ten children will be always called a fine family, where there
20 are heads and arms and legs enough for the number; but the Morlands had little other right to the word, for they were in general very plain, and Catherine, for many years of her life, as plain as any. She had a thin awkward figure, a sallow skin without colour, dark lank
25 hair, and strong features—so much for her person; and not less unpropitious for heroism seemed her mind. She was fond of all boy's plays, and greatly preferred cricket not merely to dolls, but to the more heroic enjoyments of infancy, nursing a dormouse, feeding a
30 canary-bird, or watering a rose-bush. Indeed she had no taste for a garden; and if she gathered flowers at all, it was chiefly for the pleasure of mischief—at least so it was conjectured from her always preferring those which she was forbidden to take. Such were her
35 propensities—her abilities were quite as extraordinary She never could learn or understand anything before she was taught; and sometimes not even then, for she was often inattentive, and occasionally stupid. Her mother was three months in teaching her only
40 to repeat the "Beggar's Petition"; and after all, her next sister, Sally, could say it better than she did. Not that Catherine was always stupid—by no means; she learnt the fable of "The Hare and Many Friends" as quickly as any girl in England. Her mother wished her
45 to learn music; and Catherine was sure she should like it, for she was very fond of tinkling the keys of the old forlorn spinner; so, at eight years old she began. She learnt a year, and could not bear it; and Mrs. Morland, who did not insist on her daughters being accomplished
50 in spite of incapacity or distaste, allowed her to leave off. The day which dismissed the music-master was one of the happiest of Catherine's life. Her taste for drawing was not superior; though whenever she could obtain the outside of a letter from her mother or seize
55 upon any other odd piece of paper, she did what she could in that way, by drawing houses and trees, hens and chickens, all very much like one another. Writing and accounts she was taught by her father; French by her mother: her proficiency in either was not
60 remarkable, and she shirked her lessons in both whenever she could. What a strange, unaccountable character!—for with all these symptoms of profligacy at ten years old, she had neither a bad heart nor a bad temper, was seldom stubborn, scarcely ever
65 quarrelsome, and very kind to the little ones, with few interruptions of tyranny; she was moreover noisy and wild, hated confinement and cleanliness, and loved nothing so well in the world as rolling down the green slope at the back of the house.

1

What effect does the phrase "What a strange, unaccountable character!" (lines 61-62) have on the tone of the passage?

A) It creates a harsh tone that suggests Catherine's parents are responsible for her educational deficiencies.
B) It creates a gently ironic tone that implies Catherine's shortcomings are not unusual in a young girl.
C) It creates a puzzled tone that emphasizes the inexplicable nature of Catherine's difficulties.
D) It creates a resigned tone that suggests Catherine's difficulties are irreversible.

7. This passage is adapted from Barry Schwartz, "More Isn't Always Better," © 2006 by Harvard Business Review.

Marketers assume that the more choices they offer, the more likely customers will be able to find just the right thing. They assume, for instance, that offering 50 styles of jeans instead of two increases the chances that

5 shoppers will find a pair they really like. Nevertheless, research now shows that there can be too much choice; when there is, consumers are less likely to buy anything at all, and if they do buy, they are less satisfied with their selection.

10 It all began with jam. In 2000, psychologists Sheena Iyengar and Mark Lepper published a remarkable study. On one day, shoppers at an upscale food market saw a display table with 24 varieties of gourmet jam. Those who sampled the spreads received a coupon for $1 off

15 any jam. On another day, shoppers saw a similar table, except that only six varieties of the jam were on display. The large display attracted more interest than the small one. But when the time came to purchase, people who saw the large display were one-tenth as likely to buy as

20 people who saw the small display.

Other studies have confirmed this result that more choice is not always better. As the variety of snacks, soft drinks, and beers offered at convenience stores increases, for instance, sales volume and customer

25 satisfaction decrease. Moreover, as the number of retirement investment options available to employees increases, the chance that they will choose any decreases. These studies and others have shown not only that excessive choice can produce "choice

30 paralysis," but also that it can reduce people's satisfaction with their decisions, even if they made good ones. My colleagues and I have found that increased choice decreases satisfaction with matters as trivial as ice cream flavors and as significant as jobs.

35 These results challenge what we think we know about human nature and the determinants of well-being. Both psychology and business have operated on the assumption that the relationship between choice and well-being is straightforward: The more choices people

40 have, the better off they are. In psychology, the benefits of choice have been tied to autonomy and control. In business, the benefits of choice have been tied to the benefits of free markets more generally. Added options make no one worse off, and they are bound to make

45 someone better off.

Choice *is* good for us, but its relationship to satisfaction appears to be more complicated than we

had assumed. There is diminishing marginal utility in having alternatives; each new option subtracts a little

50 from the feeling of well-being, until the marginal benefits of added choice level off. What's more, psychologists and business academics alike have largely ignored another outcome of choice: More of it requires increased time and effort and can lead to

55 anxiety, regret, excessively high expectations, and self-blame if the choices don't work out. When the number of available options is small, these costs are negligible, but the costs grow with the number of options. Eventually, each new option makes us feel

60 worse off than we did before.

Without a doubt, having more options enables us, most of the time, to achieve better objective outcomes. Again, having 50 styles of jeans as opposed to two increases the likelihood that customers will find a pair

65 that fits. But the subjective outcome may be that shoppers will feel overwhelmed and dissatisfied. This dissociation between objective and subjective results creates a significant challenge for retailers and marketers that look to choice as a way to enhance the

70 perceived value of their goods and services.

Choice can no longer be used to justify a marketing strategy in and of itself. More isn't always better, either for the customer or for the retailer. Discovering how much assortment is warranted is a

75 considerable empirical challenge. But companies that get the balance right will be amply rewarded.

1

What effect does the author's reference to "My colleagues and I" (lines 31-32) have on the tone of the passage?

A) It creates a dubious tone that conveys the author's skepticism toward Iyengar and Lepper's research.

B) It creates a reassuring tone that conveys the power of individual experience.

C) It creates a conversational tone that conveys potentially dry information in a personal manner.

D) It creates a distraught tone that conveys the uncertainty accompanying excessive choice.

2

The author's attitude toward Iyengar and Lepper's research is best described as one of

A) skepticism.
B) approval.
C) defensiveness.
D) indifference.

3

Which lines provide the best evidence for the answer to the previous question?

A) Lines 17-18 ("The large...one")
B) Lines 31-34 ("My...jobs")
C) Lines 40-41 ("In...control")
D) Lines 48-49 ("There is...alternatives")

4

The author would most likely consider the viewpoint in lines 39-40 ("The more...are")

A) an example of a belief with which he does not agree.
B) a potentially valid assertion that has not yet been conclusively proven.
C) a straightforward statement of fact.
D) a belief that has long been considered controversial.

5

Which lines provide the best evidence for the answer to the previous question?

A) Line 15 ("On...table")
B) Lines 41-43 ("In...generally")
C) Lines 61-62 ("Without...outcomes")
D) Lines 72-73 ("More...retailer")

College Board/Khan Academy Tone and Attitude Questions

Test 1

6
15   Inference

Test 3

42

Test 4

1   No line reference
2   Evidence

19   Graphic
23

Explanations: Tone and Attitude Exercises

1.1-2 C, C

The author's mixed feelings about the Internet are indicated by the fact that he spends the first half of the passage discussing its advantages and the second half discussing its disadvantages. Lines 11-13 best indicate that ambivalence by mentioning both sides of the argument (the Internet allows people to seek out information directly vs. it doesn't encourage people to leave their comfort zones).

2.1-2 A, D

The fastest way to answer this question is to recall that yawning in primates is discussed in the first half of the passage, while yawning in non-primates is discussed at the end. If you do not remember, the phrase *Beyond primates* in line 20 is a big clue to the section of the passage you need to focus on. What does that line indicate? That the relationship between empathy and yawning in animals other than primates is *less clear-cut*. That's negative, but not overly so. The only answer that fits that criteria is *dubious* (doubtful); *hostility* is too strong. For the second question, lines 26-28 are the only lines cited after line 20, so you can start by assuming they are correct. Indeed, they support the idea that yawning may not be related to empathy in dogs (a non-primate) by indicating that dogs have not been shown to catch yawns from one another.

3. B

The fact that the author refers to Griffin as "distinguished" in line 10 indicates an extremely positive attitude. In addition, he indicates that Griffin founded the field of cognitive ethology, which the author clearly has a strong interest in. All of the other options are negative, making *admiration* the only possible answer.

4. D

Start by focusing on the language of the quote itself: *Most people don't think there are eyes and ears keeping track of all this stuff.* The most striking feature is the use of the word "stuff" – it's a very casual word, not one that normally appears in formal writing. In fact, that word creates an *informal* tone, making the answer D). You do not even need to consider any of the other information in the answer.

5. C

Despite the seeming complexity of the answer choices, this question can be answered without consideration of any information in the passage – the only relevant piece of information is the word *imagine* itself. Why would an author use that word? To encourage a reason to consider a possible situation or result, i.e. to *speculate*. That makes C) the answer.

6. B

Start by considering the context in which the phrase in question appears. The narrator has just finished describing Catherine's lack of perseverance in her music lessons and attempts to avoid studying accounting and French – all perfectly normal behaviors for a mischievous young girl. (How many children really *want* to practice piano, and study accounting and French?) The narrator, however, describes these behaviors as something astounding and perplexing. The key is to understand that the narrator's exaggerated description is deliberate; the narrator understands full well that Catherine's behavior is normal and is gently mocking the conventional expectation of how a heroine should behave. The discrepancy between the behaviors themselves and the narrator's exaggerated surprise creates an *ironic* tone, making B) the correct answer.

7.1 C

The key word is *I* – any time an author/narrator refers to her/himself in the first person, look for an answer that includes the idea of personal, informal, or conversation. Those ideas are present in C, making it the correct answer.

7.2-3 B, B

If you use the main point (too much choice = bad), 7.2 can be a very straightforward question, and you are most likely better off answering the questions in order. The discussion of Iyengar and Lepper indicates that they ran the pioneering experiment that demonstrated the negative effects of too much choice. Since the author agrees with Iyengar and Lepper, the correct answer must be positive; B) is therefore the only possible answer. Looking at the following question, you know that the correct lines must indicate that the author believes Iyengar and Lepper's research is accurate. You can also start by assuming that the correct lines are likely to be somewhere close to the spot where Iyengar and Lepper's names appear, making A) and B) top candidates for the correct answer. Careful with A) – although lines 17-18 do appear as part of the discussion of Iyengar and Lepper's research, they don't involve the results. In fact, they state what the conventional wisdom would predict: people spent more time looking at the table with more options. B) is correct because it indicates that the author's own research has confirmed Iyengar and Lepper's finding.

7.4-5 A, D

Again, using the main point is the fastest way to answer this pair of questions. Start by defining the viewpoint in lines 39-40: *The more choices people have, the better off they are*. If you know that the author's point is that too much choice *isn't* good, you can jump to A) as the correct answer. For 7.5, the main point is almost invariably reiterated at the end of a passage, and D) cites lines at the end. With that information, you can check D) first. Sure enough, it reiterates the point that *more isn't always better*.

11. Rhetorical Strategy and Organization

Rhetorical strategy questions come in a variety of forms. They may ask about how paragraphs/passages are organized, about the point of view from which the paragraph is written, and about how counterarguments are presented. They are typically phrased in the following ways:

- This passage is written from the perspective of someone who is…

- Which choice best describes the structure of the first paragraph/this passage?

- The statement in line x signals a shift from…

Point of View

There are several narrative points of view that you should be familiar with for the SAT. Some questions may ask you to identify them directly, but other questions may test them indirectly – in such cases, recognizing the point of view can provide an effective shortcut.

A **first person** narrative is written from the perspective of the narrator. Usually the word *I* will appear (first person singular), but occasionally *we* (first person plural) may also be used. All personal anecdotes are, by definition, written in the first person.

For example, let's return to this excerpt from Susan B. Anthony's speech:

    Mrs. President and Sisters, I might almost say daughters—**I** cannot tell you how much joy has filled my heart as **I** have sat here listening to these papers and noting those characteristics that made each in its
5 own way beautiful and masterful. **I** would in no ways lessen the importance of these expressions by your various representatives, but **I** want to say that the words that specially voiced what **I** may call the up-gush of my soul were to be found in the paper read by Mrs. Swalm
10 on "The Newspaper as a Factor of Civilization."

The repeated use of the word *I* indicates a first-person narration.

262

A **third person** narrative, on the other hand, is written from an objective or impersonal perspective and describes other people or things rather than the narrator him- or herself.

For example:

Every time a car drives through a major intersection, it becomes a data point. Magnetic coils of wire lay just beneath the pavement, registering each passing car. This starts a cascade of information: Computers tally the
5   number and speed of cars, shoot the data through underground cables to a command center and finally translate it into the colors red, yellow and green. On the seventh floor of Boston City Hall, the three colors splash like paint across a wall-sized map.

Although this passage is highly descriptive, it focuses on events, not on the narrator. Unlike the first passage, its tone is much more neutral and detached. **The majority of SAT passages are written from a third-person perspective.**

Second person narrations are less common than either first or third person narrations, but you may encounter them from time to time. They can address the reader directly by using the word *you*, or indirectly or by giving **commands**. For example, the following excerpt does both of these things:

10   … The idea is that once **you** have developed the ability to play an arpeggio on the piano, putt a golf ball or parallel park, attention to what you are doing leads to inaccuracies, blunders and sometimes even utter paralysis. As the great
15   choreographer George Balanchine would say to his dancers, "Don't think, dear; just do."
        Perhaps **you** have experienced this destructive force yourself. **Start thinking** about just how to carry a full glass of water without spilling, and **you'll** end up
20   drenched. How, exactly, do **you** initiate a telephone conversation? **Begin wondering**, and before long, the recipient of **your** call will notice the heavy breathing and hang up. Our actions, the French philosopher Maurice Merleau-Ponty tells us, exhibit a "magical"
25   efficacy, but when we focus on them, they degenerate into the absurd. A 13-time winner on the Professional Golfers Association Tour, Dave Hill, put it like this: "**You** can't be thinking about the mechanics of the sport while **you** are performing."

Noticing pronouns can also provide a very effective shortcut if you encounter questions asking you to identify where a change or **shift** occurs in the passage. In order to answer these questions, you must be able to recognize key places in the development of the argument: where new or contradictory information is introduced, where important ideas are emphasized, and where "they say" switches to "I say." You should also pay close attention to shifts in point of view.

For example, we going to take another look at this excerpt from Barbara Jordan's 1976 National Democratic Convention speech:

It was one hundred and forty-four years ago that members of the Democratic Party first met in convention to select a Presidential candidate. A lot of years passed since 1832, and during that time it would
5 have been most unusual for any national political party to ask a Barbara Jordan to deliver a keynote address. But tonight, here I am. And I feel that notwithstanding the past that my presence here is one additional bit of evidence that the American Dream need not forever be
10 deferred.
Now that **I** have this grand distinction, what in the world am **I** supposed to say? **I** could list the problems which cause people to feel cynical, angry, frustrated: problems which include lack of integrity in government;
15 the feeling that the individual no longer counts; feeling that the grand American experiment is failing or has failed. **I** could recite these problems, and then **I** could sit down and offer no solutions. But **I** don't choose to do that either. The citizens of America expect more.
20 **We** are a people in search of a national community. **We** are a people trying not only to solve the problems of the present, unemployment, inflation, but **we** are attempting on a larger scale to fulfill the promise of America. **We** are attempting to fulfill our national
25 purpose, to create and sustain a society in which all of us are equal.

1

Which choice best describes the shift that occurs in line 20?

A) A criticism of a situation to a acknowledgment of its significance
B) a discussion of a problem to a description of a solution
C) A personal reaction to a discussion of a general concern.
D) a presentation of a claim to a questioning of that claim

Like many questions, this one appears to be considerably more difficult than it actually is. The most important thing to understand is that the question is asking about the *shift* that occurs in line 20. By definition, a shift is a change from one thing to another, so to answer the question, we must look at the information before line 20 as well as line 20 itself.

If we just look at the previous paragraph as well as the paragraph that line 20 begins, we can notice that in the previous paragraph, the word *I* appears repeatedly, whereas the new paragraph refers to *we*. The shift is therefore from personal to general, making C) correct.

Some point of view questions may ask the author or narrator's **relationship** to the subject of the passage – that is, whether they are **personally involved**, or whether they are merely an **interested observer**. In such cases, it is important that you notice the pronoun (e.g. *I, we, it*) that the author uses throughout the passage. An author who is personally involved will use personal pronouns, and an author who is not directly involved will use impersonal pronouns.

Most authors of science and social science passages will be informed observers – people who are strongly interested in and highly knowledgeable about their subjects but who do not actually participate in the events/research they describe. As a result, they will often demonstrate a positive attitude toward their subjects. (Again: if they weren't interested, they wouldn't bother to write about them in the first place.)

In contrast, authors of fiction passages and historical documents may be either directly involved or knowledgeable observers.

For example, let's return to this social science passage:

Every time a car drives through a major intersection, it becomes a data point. Magnetic coils of wire lay just beneath the pavement, registering each passing car. This starts a cascade of information: Computers tally the
5 number and speed of cars, shoot the data through underground cables to a command center and finally translate it into the colors red, yellow and green. On the seventh floor of Boston City Hall, the three colors splash like paint across a wall-sized map.
10 To drivers, the color red means stop, but on the map it tells traffic engineers to leap into action. Traffic control centers like this one—a room cluttered with computer terminals and live video feeds of urban intersections— represent the brain of a traffic system. The city's network
15 of sensors, cables and signals are the nerves connected to the rest of the body. "Most people don't think there are eyes and ears keeping track of all this stuff," says John DeBenedictis, the center's engineering director. But in reality, engineers literally watch our every move,
20 making subtle changes that relieve and redirect traffic.
The tactics and aims of traffic management are modest but powerful. Most intersections rely on a combination of pre-set timing and computer adaptation. For example, where a busy main road intersects with a quiet residential
25 street, the traffic signal might give 70 percent of "green time" to the main road, and 30 percent to the residential road. (Green lights last between a few seconds and a couple minutes, and tend to shorten at rush hour to help the traffic move continuously.) But when traffic
30 overwhelms the pre-set timing, engineers override the system and make changes.

1

This passage is written from the perspective of someone who is

A) actively involved in promoting traffic safety throughout urban areas
B) familiar with the activities of traffic engineers
C) an employee of the traffic control center in Boston City Hall
D) opposed to the intrusion of traffic engineers into everyday life

This passage is essentially descriptive or informative: it provides information about what traffic engineers do and how a traffic control center functions, from an outsider's perspective. The tone is neutral/positive.

In addition to providing the most common description of a non-fiction writer, B) corresponds to this perspective: someone who knows about the subject but who is not directly involved in it.

Both A) and C) indicate personal involvement, eliminating them. Although D) does not indicate personal involvement, the word *opposed* is negative, and there is nothing in the passage to suggest that the author does not approve of traffic engineers' role in everyday life. While you personally may be somewhat put off by the fact that traffic engineers are *literally watch[ing] our every move*, there is absolutely no evidence that the author feels that way, and you cannot project your own impressions onto the author.

Other point of view questions could ask about the narrator's perspective in terms of **age** (child vs. adult) or **time**. These questions tend to occur when passages discuss events that took place at different times, often earlier, or when the narrator is looking back on an event. They are most likely to accompany fiction passages, although it is possible they could accompany other passage types as well.

Pay attention to the **tense** in which passages are written – that is, whether they are in the **present** (*is, are*) or **past** (*was, were*). The action of a passage written in the present is taking place as the author describes it, while the action of a passage written in the past has already taken place.

On the next page, we're going to look at an example. Pay attention to the passage's point of view and tense.

The following passage is adapted from a novel by Willa Cather, originally published in 1918. The narrator has been sent to live with his grandparents in Nebraska.

On the afternoon of that Sunday I took my first long ride on my pony, under Otto's direction. After that Dude and I went twice a week to the post-office, six miles east of us, and I saved the men a good
5 deal of time by riding on errands to our neighbors. When we had to borrow anything, I was always the messenger.

All the years that have passed have not dimmed my memory of that first glorious autumn. The new country
10 lay open before me: there were no fences in those days, and I could choose my own way over the grass uplands, trusting the pony to get me home again. Sometimes I followed the sunflower-bordered roads.

I used to love to drift along the pale-yellow cornfields,
15 looking for the damp spots one sometimes found at their edges, where the smartweed soon turned a rich copper color and the narrow brown leaves hung curled like cocoons about the swollen joints of the stem. Sometimes I went south to visit our German neighbors and to
20 admire their catalpa grove, or to see the big elm tree that grew up out of a deep crack in the earth and had a hawk's nest in its branches. Trees were so rare in that country, and they had to make such a hard fight to grow, that we used to feel anxious about them, and visit them
25 as if they were persons. It must have been the scarcity of detail in that tawny landscape that made detail so precious.

Sometimes I rode north to the big prairie-dog town to watch the brown earth-owls fly home in the late afternoon
30 and go down to their nests underground with the dogs. Antonia Shimerda liked to go with me, and we used to wonder a great deal about these birds of subterranean habit. We had to be on our guard there, for rattlesnakes were always lurking about. They came to pick up an easy
35 living among the dogs and owls, which were quite defenseless against them; took possession of their comfortable houses and ate the eggs and puppies. We felt sorry for the owls. It was always mournful to see them come flying home at sunset and disappear under
40 the earth.

But, after all, we felt, winged things who would live like that must be rather degraded creatures. The dog-town was a long way from any pond or creek. Otto Fuchs said he had seen populous dog-towns in the desert where
45 there was no surface water for fifty miles; he insisted that some of the holes must go down to water—nearly two hundred feet, hereabouts. Antonia said she didn't believe it; that the dogs probably lapped up the dew in the early morning, like the rabbits.

50 Antonia had opinions about everything, and she was soon able to make them known. Almost every day she came running across the prairie to have her reading lesson with me. Mrs. Shimerda grumbled, but realized it was important that one member of the family should
55 learn English. When the lesson was over, we used to go up to the watermelon patch behind the garden. I split the melons with an old corn-knife, and we lifted out the hearts and ate them with the juice trickling through our fingers. The white melons we did not touch, but we
60 watched them with curiosity. They were to be picked later, when the hard frosts had set in, and put away for winter use. After weeks on the ocean, the Shimerdas were famished for fruit. The two girls would wander for miles along the edge of the cornfields, hunting for
65 ground-cherries.

Antonia loved to help grandmother in the kitchen and to learn about cooking and housekeeping. She would stand beside her, watching her every movement. We were willing to believe that Mrs. Shimerda was a
70 good housewife in her own country, but she managed poorly under new conditions. I remember how horrified we were at the sour, ashy-grey bread she gave her family to eat. She mixed her dough, we discovered, in an old tin peck-measure that had been used about the
75 barn. When she took the paste out to bake it, she left smears of dough sticking to the sides of the measure, put the measure on the shelf behind the stove, and let this residue ferment. The next time she made bread, she scraped this sour stuff down into the fresh dough to
80 serve as yeast.

1

This passage is written from the perspective of

A) an adult recalling a memorable experience that occurred earlier in his adult life.
B) an adult recounting a significant childhood memory.
C) a child describing the development of a friendship.
D) a narrator analyzing a story told to him by an acquaintance.

The key to answering this question is the line *All the years that have passed have not dimmed my memory of that first glorious autumn.* The narrator is looking *looking back* on an event that occurred earlier in his life. Even though he's describing what happened when he was a boy, the phrase *All the years that have passed* indicates he's no longer a boy at the time he's telling the story. Which answer does that correspond to? B).

If you didn't notice that phrase and played process of elimination, you could eliminate D) immediately because the passage is written in the first person, as indicated by the repeated use of the word *I*.

Now we need to think carefully about the other answers. Let's start with A). Yes, the passage is told by an adult recounting a significant memory, but careful – it's not an *adult* memory. In addition to the key phrase *All the years that have passed* at the beginning of the passage, we can also infer that the narrator was young at the time of the passage from the fact that he and Antonia were having "reading lessons," and by the fact that the narrator refers to Antonia and her sister as girls.

To eliminate C), think about the **tense** in which the passage is written. All of the verbs are in the past (*went, rode, grumbled, touched*), indicating that the action took place in the past.

Paragraph and Passage Organization

Paragraph and passage organization questions test your understanding of rhetorical strategies on a large scale; occasionally, they may be paired with supporting evidence questions. To answer these questions correctly and quickly, you must be able to identify places where key ideas and arguments are introduced, as well transition words that indicate the relationships of those ideas to one another.

If a question asks about the **organization of a paragraph**, you should begin by skimming for important transitions within that paragraph; then consider how they relate to one another (comparison/contrast, sequence, etc.).

If a question asks about the **overall organization of a passage**, you should focus on the end of the introduction and the first sentence of each subsequent paragraph.

While you should be able to recognize how paragraphs and passages are organized, you should not take the time to label each section of a passage as you read it. If you are comfortable determining organization, you can most likely figure it out on the spot when necessary. As a preparation strategy, however, you may find it helpful to label the various parts of a passage (e.g. historical context, supporting example, counterargument, etc.).

You should also be on the lookout for changes in point of view, especially those involving first person narrations (*I*), because this information can provide an important shortcut for both identifying correct answers and eliminating incorrect ones.

In some cases, you may also be able to **simplify** some questions by **focusing on one part of an answer choice** and checking it against the corresponding part of the passage.

Let's look at some examples.

The sharing economy is a little like online shopping, which started in America 15 years ago. At first, people were worried about security. But having made a successful purchase from, say, Amazon, they
5 felt safe buying elsewhere. Similarly, using Airbnb or a car-hire service for the first time encourages people to try other offerings. Next, consider eBay. Having started out as a peer-to-peer marketplace, it is now dominated by professional "power sellers" (many of whom started
10 out as ordinary eBay users). The same may happen with the sharing economy, which also provides new opportunities for enterprise. Some people have bought cars solely to rent them out, for example. Incumbents are getting involved too. Avis, a car-hire firm, has a share
15 in a sharing rival. So do GM and Daimler, two carmakers. In the future, companies may develop hybrid models, listing excess capacity (whether vehicles, equipment or office space) on peer-to-peer rental sites. In the past, new ways of doing things online have not displaced the
20 old ways entirely. But they have often changed them. Just as internet shopping forced Walmart and Tesco to adapt, so online sharing will shake up transport, tourism, equipment-hire and more.
The main worry is regulatory uncertainty. Will
25 room-4-renters be subject to hotel taxes, for example? In Amsterdam officials are using Airbnb listings to track down unlicensed hotels. In some American cities, peer-to-peer taxi services have been banned after lobbying by traditional taxi firms. The danger is that
30 although some rules need to be updated to protect consumers from harm, incumbents will try to destroy competition. People who rent out rooms should pay tax, of course, but they should not be regulated like a Ritz-Carlton hotel. The lighter rules that typically govern
35 bed-and-breakfasts are more than adequate. The sharing economy is the latest example of the internet's value to consumers. This emerging model is now big and disruptive enough for regulators and companies to have woken up to it. That is a sign of its immense potential. It
40 is time to start caring about sharing.

1

Which choice best describes the structure of the first paragraph (lines 1-23)?

A) A comparison is presented and developed through supporting examples.
B) A principle is described, and an opposing principle is then introduced.
C) The strengths and weakness of several competing explanations are discussed.
D) A personal account of an experience is provided, followed by a reflection on that experience.

Before we start working through the answers carefully, we can eliminate D). A quick glance at the passage reveals that the word *I* does not appear anywhere, so it cannot be personal.

The next thing we want to do is simplify the question and the answers. The question asks about the entire first paragraph – that's 23 lines. **But a line reference that long is normally an indicator that it is not necessary to reread all the lines carefully.** So instead, we're going to just look at the beginning of the passage, say lines 1-7. The beginning of the correct answer must describe what's going on in those lines.

The sharing economy is a little like online shopping, which started in America 15 years ago. At first, people were worried about security. But having made a successful purchase from, say, Amazon, they
5 felt safe buying elsewhere. Similarly, using Airbnb or a car-hire service for the first time encourages people to try other offerings.

1

Which choice best describes the structure of the first paragraph (lines 1-23)?

A) A comparison is presented and developed through supporting examples.
B) A principle is described, and an opposing principle is then introduced.
C) The strengths and weakness of several competing explanations are discussed.
D) A personal account of an experience is offered, followed by a reflection on that experience.

What is happening at the beginning of the passage? Well, the first sentence presents a comparison, as indicated by the phrase *a little like*. If we just look at the beginning of each answer choice, we can see that A) is the only remaining answer that begins with the word *comparison*, suggesting that it is correct. When we read a little further, we see that the following lines do in fact develop that comparison, as indicated by the transition *similarly*. So A) is the correct answer.

The answer choices could, however, be written in a manner less conducive to this type of shortcut. What if they were presented like this?

The sharing economy is a little like online shopping, which started in America 15 years ago. **At first**, people were worried about security. **But** having made a successful purchase from, say, Amazon, they
5 felt safe buying elsewhere. **Similarly**, using Airbnb or a car-hire service for the first time encourages people to try other offerings. **Next**, consider eBay. Having started out as a peer-to-peer marketplace, it is now dominated by professional "power sellers" (many of whom started
10 out as ordinary eBay users). **The same** may happen with the sharing economy, which **also** provides new opportunities for enterprise.

1

Which choice best describes the structure of the first paragraph (lines 1-23)?

A) An assertion is presented, and supporting examples are provided.
B) A principle is described, and an opposing principle is then introduced.
C) The strengths and weakness of several competing explanations are discussed.
D) A personal account of an experience is presented followed by a reflection on that experience.

Now we can no longer use the word *comparison* as a shortcut. We can still eliminate D) right away, but we have to think about the other answers more carefully. That does not mean that we need to read the entire first paragraph, however – we can still get plenty of information from the beginning, even though we might want to read a little further. If an answer doesn't fit with the beginning of the passage, it won't be correct; reading further won't change that.

Looking at the first sentence, we can see that in addition to being a comparison, it is also an argument, i.e. an assertion, not a "principle" or "explanation." And when we look at the transitions, we can see that they are mostly continuers that support the claim. So A) is right.

Let's look at a full-length example.

The following passage is adapted from Michael Anft, "Solving the Mystery of Death Valley's Walking Rocks," © 2011 by Johns Hopkins Magazine.

For six decades, observers have been <u>confounded</u> by the movement of large rocks across a dry lake bed in California's Death Valley National Park. Leaving flat trails behind them, rocks that weigh up to 100
5 pounds seemingly do Michael Jackson's moonwalk across the valley's sere, cracked surface, sometimes traveling more than 100 yards. Without a body of water to pick them up and move them, the rocks at Racetrack Playa, a flat space between the valley's high cliffs,
10 have been the subject of much speculation, including whether they have been relocated by human pranksters or space aliens. The rocks have become the desert equivalent of Midwestern crop circles. "They really are a curiosity," says Ralph Lorenz, a planetary scientist at
15 the Applied Physics Laboratory. "Some [people] have mentioned UFOs. But I've always believed that this is something science could solve."

It has tried. **One theory** holds that the rocks are blown along by powerful winds. **Another** posits that
20 the wind pushes thin sheets of ice, created when the desert's temperatures dip low enough to freeze water from a rare rainstorm, and the rocks go along for the ride. But neither theory is rock solid. Winds at the playa aren't strong enough—some scientists believe that
25 they'd have to be 100 miles per hour or more—to blow the rocks across the valley. And rocks subject to the "ice sailing theory" wouldn't create trails as they moved.

Lorenz and a team of investigators believe that a
30 **combination of forces may work to rearrange Racetrack Playa's rocks.** "We saw that it would take a lot of wind to move these rocks, which are larger than you'd expect wind to move," Lorenz explains. "That led us to this idea that ice might be picking up the
35 rocks and floating them." As they explained in the January issue of *The American Journal of Physics*, instead of moving along with wind-driven sheets of ice, the rocks may instead be lifted by the ice, making them more subject to the wind's force. The key, Lorenz
40 says, is that the lifting by an "ice collar" reduces friction with the ground, to the point that the wind now has enough force to move the rock. The rock moves, the ice doesn't, and because part of the rock juts through the ice, it marks the territory it has covered.
45 Lorenz's team came to its conclusion through a combination of intuition, lab work, and observation— not that the last part was easy. Watching the rocks travel is a bit like witnessing the rusting of a hubcap. Instances of movement are rare and last for only a few
50 seconds. Lorenz's team placed low-resolution cameras on the cliffs (which are about 30 miles from the nearest paved road) to take pictures once per hour. For the past three winters, the researchers have weathered extreme temperatures and several flat tires to measure how
55 often the thermometer dips below freezing, how often the playa gets rain and floods, and the strength of the winds. "The measurements seem to back up our hypothesis," he says. "Any of the theories may be true at any one time, but ice rafting may be the best explan-
60 ation for the trails we've been seeing. We've seen trails like this documented in Arctic coastal areas, and the mechanism is somewhat similar. A belt of ice sur- rounds a boulder during high tide, picks it up, and then drops it elsewhere." His "ice raft theory" was also
65 borne out by an experiment that used the ingenuity of a high school science fair. Lorenz placed a basalt pebble in a Tupperware container with water so that the pebble projected just above the surface. He then turned the container upside down in a baking tray filled with a
70 layer of coarse sand at its base, and put the whole thing in his home freezer. The rock's "keel" (its protruding part) projected downward into the sand, which simu- lated the cracked surface of the playa (which scientists call "Special K" because of its resemblance to cereal
75 flakes). A gentle push or slight puff of air caused the Tupperware container to move, just as an ice raft would under the right conditions. The pebble made a trail in the soft sand. "It was primitive but effective," Lorenz says of the experiment. Lorenz has spent the
80 last 20 years studying Titan, a moon of Saturn. He says that Racetrack Playa's surface mirrors that of a dried lakebed on Titan. Observations and experiments on Earth may yield clues to that moon's geology. "We also may get some idea of how climate affects
85 geology—particularly as the climate changes here on Earth," Lorenz says. "When we study other planets and their moons, we're forced to use Occam's razor – sometimes the simplest answer is best, which means you look to Earth for some answers. Once you get out
90 there on Earth, you realize how strange so much of its surface is. So, you have to figure there's weird stuff to be found on Titan as well." Whether that's true or not will take much more investigation. He adds: "One day, we'll figure all this out. For the moment, the moving
95 rock present a wonderful problem to study in a beautiful place."

Which choice best describes the structure of this passage?

A) A theory is presented, and evidence to refute it is provided.
B) A mystery is described, explanations are considered, and a synthesis is proposed.
C) A hypothesis is introduced, and its strengths and weaknesses are analyzed.
D) A new technology is described, its application is discussed, and its implications are considered.

It's understandable that you might get a little nervous (or more than a little nervous) about having to boil 96 lines worth of information down into a single statement, but here again, you can actually answer the question using only the first sentence.

What do we learn from it? That observers have been *confounded* (utterly baffled) by the movement of the Racetrack Playa rocks – in other words, there's a mystery going on. Based on that piece of information alone, you can identify B) as the answer most likely to be correct.

If you want to check the answer out further, you can focus on the beginnings of subsequent paragraphs. The words *One theory* and *another [theory]* at the beginning of the second paragraph correspond to "explanations," and the phrase *a combination of forces* corresponds to "synthesis." So B) is correct.

Counterarguments

One important component of the "they say/I say" structure is the counterargument. Simply put, a counterargument is what "they say." "They" could be real people who have actually argued the opposite point of view, but the objections could also be **hypothetical** – that is, they represent what someone arguing the opposite point of view *might* say.

The following types of phrases are tipoffs that an author is introducing a counterargument:

• Some people/researchers have argued that…
• It might/could be argued that…
• A possible objection/concern is that…
• On the other hand, one could argue that…
• Of course, it is true that…

Although it may seem contradictory to you, authors use counterarguments in order to *strengthen* their own claims. By addressing – and refuting or **rebutting** – possible objections, they can explain why those objections do not outweigh their own argument and thus demonstrate that their own argument is stronger than the other side's.

Some counterarguments will appear near the beginning of a passage – authors often begin with what "they say" – but they can also show up closer to the end. Having finished explaining their argument, authors will sometimes then turn to potential objections.

It is important to understand that counterarguments will sometimes be presented in indirect ways. Instead of asserting that anyone who disagrees with them is wrong, authors may make **concessions**, acknowledging that some of the objections to their argument are valid. They may also agree with part of the objection while disagreeing with other parts. In such cases, you must read very carefully to determine which idea the author agrees/disagrees with. In the following passage, the counterargument is in bold, and the rebuttal is italicized.

The sharing economy is a little like online shopping, which started in America 15 years ago. At first, people were worried about security. But having made a successful purchase from, say, Amazon, they
5 felt safe buying elsewhere. Similarly, using Airbnb or a car-hire service for the first time encourages people to try other offerings. Next, consider eBay. Having started out as a peer-to-peer marketplace, it is now dominated by professional "power sellers" (many of whom started
10 out as ordinary eBay users). The same may happen with the sharing economy, which also provides new opportunities for enterprise. Some people have bought cars solely to rent them out, for example. Incumbents are getting involved too. Avis, a car-hire firm, has a share
15 in a sharing rival. So do GM and Daimler, two carmakers. In the future, companies may develop hybrid models, listing excess capacity (whether vehicles, equipment or office space) on peer-to-peer rental sites. In the past, new ways of doing things online have not displaced the
20 old ways entirely. But they have often changed them. Just as internet shopping forced Walmart and Tesco to adapt, so online sharing will shake up transport, tourism, equipment-hire and more.
The main worry is regulatory uncertainty. Will
25 **room-4-renters be subject to hotel taxes, for example? In Amsterdam officials are using Airbnb listings to track down unlicensed hotels. In some American cities, peer-to-peer taxi services have been banned after lobbying by traditional taxi firms.** *The danger is that*
30 *although some rules need to be updated to protect consumers from harm, incumbents will try to destroy competition. People who rent out rooms should pay tax, of course, but they should not be regulated like a Ritz-Carlton hotel. The lighter rules that typically govern*
35 *bed-and-breakfasts are more than adequate. The sharing economy is the latest example of the internet's value to consumers. This emerging model is now big and disruptive enough for regulators and companies to have woken up to it. That is a sign of its immense potential. It*
40 *is time to start caring about sharing.*

This passage contains an excellent example of a counterargument that is presented somewhat subtly. The author introduces a potential **drawback** (regulatory uncertainty, *the main worry*), poses a rhetorical question, and then provides examples of how different places (Amsterdam, some American cities) have responded in different ways. Finally, he makes his own: although some regulation is necessary to protect consumers, it must not stifle competition. The sharing economy is too big to go back now.

Notice that the parts of the counterargument are separated from one another. First, the author presents the counterargument, and only after he is done expanding on it does he respond with his own assertion. He does not flip between viewpoints; once he has discussed an idea, he leaves it and moves on.

Sometimes, however, authors may weave elements of the counterargument into their own arguments, flipping back and forth within the same section or even within the same sentence. The presence of contradictors such as *although*, *while*, and *whereas* often signals that this is the case. When this is the case, the information that follows the contradictor will correspond to what "I say."

In the passage below, for instance, the author repeatedly alternates between opposing viewpoints within sentences or pairs of sentences. Again, the counterarguments are in bold, whereas the author's arguments are italicized.

The world is complex and interconnected, and the evolution of our communications system from a broadcast model to a networked one has added a new dimension to the mix. **The Internet has made us all less**
5 **dependent on professional journalists and editors for information about the wider world, allowing us to seek out information directly via online search or to receive it from friends through social media.** <u>*But*</u> *this enhanced convenience comes with a considerable risk: that we*
10 *will be exposed to what we want to know at the expense of what we need to know.* **While we can find virtual communities that correspond to our every curiosity,** *there's little pushing us beyond our comfort zones to or into the unknown, even if the unknown may have*
15 *serious implications for our lives.* There are things we should probably know more about—like political and religious conflicts in Russia or basic geography. But even if we knew more than we do, there's no guarantee that the knowledge gained would prompt us to act in a
20 particularly admirable fashion.

Here, the author develops his counterargument primarily by considering the drawbacks of the Internet: that people will not pay attention to important information about the world because they are so focused on what they want to know, and that they have little reason to move beyond their comfort zones.

Effect of a Rhetorical Strategy

The final type of rhetorical strategy question asks you to identify the *effect* of a particular rhetorical strategy, such as repetition or word choice. Although these questions are phrased differently, they are more or less identical to certain function or main point questions – they are essentially asking you why information is presented in a particular way (i.e. its purpose) or what point it is used to support.

For example let's return to this excerpt from Barbara Jordan's 1976 speech:

...And now we must look to the future. Let us heed the
voice of the people and recognize their common sense.
If we do not, we not only blaspheme our political
heritage, we ignore the common ties that bind all
30 Americans. Many fear the future. Many are distrustful
of their leaders, and believe that their voices are never
heard. Many seek only to satisfy their private interests.
But this is the great danger America faces – that we will
cease to be one nation and become instead a collection
35 of interest groups: city against suburb, region against
region, individual against individual; each seeking to
satisfy private wants. If that happens, who then will speak
for America? Who then will speak for the common good?
　This is the question which must be answered in 1976:
40 Are we to be one people bound together by common
spirit, sharing in a common endeavor; or will we become
a divided nation? For all of its uncertainty, we cannot
flee the future. We must address and master the future
together. It can be done if we restore the belief that we
45 share a sense of national community, that we share a
common national endeavor.

1

What is the effect of the repetition of the word "we" in the fifth paragraph (lines 39-46)?

A) It evokes a sense of danger, calling attention to the dangers posed by political corruption.
B) It creates a sense of unity, emphasizing the connection between the author and the reader.
C) It reveals a need for sociability, pointing out the risks of excessive solitude.
D) It underscores the longstanding nature of a problem faced by citizens in the United States.

Although there is a considerable amount of information packed into the answer choices, the question is much simpler than it appears – it's almost unnecessary to even look at the passage. When authors write in the third person plural (*we*), there's really only one reason they do so: to create a sense of solidarity or **unity**, implying that a particular situation applies to everyone and that the author is as involved as the reader. With that information, you can immediately identify B) as the correct answer.

Rhetorical Strategy and Organization Exercises

1.   These are stimulating times for anyone interested in questions of animal consciousness. On what seems like a monthly basis, scientific teams announce the results of new experiments, adding to a preponderance
5 of evidence that we've been underestimating animal minds, even those of us who have rated them fairly highly. New animal behaviors and capacities are observed in the wild, often involving tool use—or at least object manipulation—the very kinds of activity
10 that led the distinguished zoologist Donald R. Griffin to found the field of cognitive ethology (animal thinking) in 1978: octopuses piling stones in front of their hideyholes, to name one recent example; or dolphins fitting marine sponges to their beaks in order to dig for
15 food on the seabed; or wasps using small stones to smooth the sand around their egg chambers, concealing them from predators. At the same time neurobiologists have been finding that the physical structures in our own brains most commonly held responsible for
20 consciousness are not as rare in the animal kingdom as had been assumed. Indeed they are common. All of this work and discovery appeared to reach a kind of crescendo last summer, when an international group of prominent neuroscientists meeting at the University of
25 Cambridge issued "The Cambridge Declaration on Consciousness in Non-Human Animals," a document stating that "humans are not unique in possessing the neurological substrates that generate consciousness." It goes further to conclude that numerous documented
30 animal behaviors must be considered "consistent with experienced feeling states."

1

Which choice best describes the organization of this passage?

A) A theory is offered, an experiment is presented, and a critique is offered.

B) An existing model is discussed, its flaws are examined, and a new model is proposed.

C) Several examples of animal behavior are presented, and their significance is analyzed.

D) An assertion is made, and specific examples are provided to support it.

2

In line 21, the author's focus shifts from

A) a series of examples to a description of an outcome.

B) focus on an individual to a consideration of a group.

C) an examination of a problem to a proposal of a solution.

D) a discussion of a claim to a questioning of that claim.

2. The following passage is adapted from Jane Austen, *Northanger Abbey*, originally published in 1817.

No one who had ever seen Catherine Morland in her infancy would have supposed her born to be an heroine. Her situation in life, the character of her father and mother, her own person and disposition, were all
5 equally against her.

Her father was a clergyman, without being neglected, or poor, and a very respectable man, though his name was Richard—and he had never been handsome. He had a considerable independence besides
10 two good livings—and he was not in the least addicted to locking up his daughters. Her mother was a woman of useful plain sense, with a good temper, and, what is more remarkable, with a good constitution. She had three sons before Catherine was born; and instead of
15 dying in bringing the latter into the world, as anybody might expect, she still lived on—lived to have six children more—to see them growing up around her, and to enjoy excellent health herself. A family of ten children will be always called a fine family, where there
20 are heads and arms and legs enough for the number; but the Morlands had little other right to the word, for they were in general very plain, and Catherine, for many years of her life, as plain as any. She had a thin awkward figure, a sallow skin without colour, dark lank
25 hair, and strong features—so much for her person; and not less unpropitious for heroism seemed her mind. She was fond of all boy's plays, and greatly preferred cricket not merely to dolls, but to the more heroic enjoyments of infancy, nursing a dormouse, feeding a
30 canary-bird, or watering a rose-bush. Indeed she had no taste for a garden; and if she gathered flowers at all, it was chiefly for the pleasure of mischief— at least so it was conjectured from her always preferring those which she was forbidden to take
35 Such were her propensities—her abilities were quite as extraordinary. She never could learn or understand anything before she was taught; and sometimes not even then, for she was often inattentive, and occasionally stupid. Her mother was three months in teaching her
40 only to repeat the "Beggar's Petition"; and after all, her next sister, Sally, could say it better than she did. Not that Catherine was always stupid—by no means; she learnt the fable of "The Hare and Many Friends" as quickly as any girl in England. Her mother wished her
45 to learn music; and Catherine was sure she should like it, for she was very fond of tinkling the keys of the old forlorn spinner; so, at eight years old she began. She learnt a year, and could not bear it; and Mrs. Morland, who did not insist on her daughters being accomplished in
50 spite of incapacity or distaste, allowed her to leave off. The day which dismissed the music-master was one of the happiest of Catherine's life. Her taste for drawing was not superior; though whenever she could obtain the outside of a letter from her mother or seize
55 upon any other odd piece of paper, she did what she could in that way, by drawing houses and trees, hens and chickens, all very much like one another. Writing and accounts she was taught by her father; French by her mother: her proficiency in either was not
60 remarkable, and she shirked her lessons in both whenever she could. What a strange, unaccountable character!—for with all these symptoms of profligacy at ten years old, she had neither a bad heart nor a bad temper, was seldom stubborn, scarcely ever
65 quarrelsome, and very kind to the little ones, with few interruptions of tyranny; she was moreover noisy and wild, hated confinement and cleanliness, and loved nothing so well in the world as rolling down the green slope at the back of the house.

1

This passage is written from the perspective of

A) a member of Catherine's family who is critical of Catherine's upbringing.
B) an observer familiar with Catherine and her family.
C) a character who finds herself at odds with her family.
D) a character who is puzzled by the constraints placed on her by society.

2

The words "never," "not even," and "inattentive" (lines 36-38) mainly have the effect of

A) rebuking Catherine's mother for her excessive demands on her daughter.
B) pointing out Catherine's contrary nature.
C) calling attention to Catherine's lack of precociousness.
D) provoking a sense of sympathy for Catherine's misbehavior.

3. This passage is adapted from Barry Schwartz, "More Isn't Always Better," © 2006 by Harvard Business Review.

Marketers assume that the more choices they offer, the more likely customers will be able to find just the right thing. They assume, for instance, that offering 50 styles of jeans instead of two increases the chances that
5 shoppers will find a pair they really like. Nevertheless, research now shows that there can be too much choice; when there is, consumers are less likely to buy anything at all, and if they do buy, they are less satisfied with their selection.
10 It all began with jam. In 2000, psychologists Sheena Iyengar and Mark Lepper published a remarkable study. On one day, shoppers at an upscale food market saw a display table with 24 varieties of gourmet jam. Those who sampled the spreads received a coupon for $1 off
15 any jam. On another day, shoppers saw a similar table, except that only six varieties of the jam were on display. The large display attracted more interest than the small one. But when the time came to purchase, people who saw the large display were one-tenth as likely to buy as
20 people who saw the small display.
   Other studies have confirmed this result that more choice is not always better. As the variety of snacks, soft drinks, and beers offered at convenience stores increases, for instance, sales volume and customer
25 satisfaction decrease. Moreover, as the number of retirement investment options available to employees increases, the chance that they will choose any decreases. These studies and others have shown not only that excessive choice can produce "choice
30 paralysis," but also that it can reduce people's satisfaction with their decisions, even if they made good ones. My colleagues and I have found that increased choice decreases satisfaction with matters as trivial as ice cream flavors and as significant as jobs.
35 These results challenge what we think we know about human nature and the determinants of well-being. Both psychology and business have operated on the assumption that the relationship between choice and well-being is straightforward: The more choices people
40 have, the better off they are. In psychology, the benefits of choice have been tied to autonomy and control. In business, the benefits of choice have been tied to the benefits of free markets more generally. Added options make no one worse off, and they are bound to make
45 someone better off.
   Choice *is* good for us, but its relationship to satisfaction appears to be more complicated than we had assumed. There is diminishing marginal utility in having alternatives; each new option subtracts a little
50 from the feeling of well-being, until the marginal benefits of added choice level off. What's more, psychologists and business academics alike have largely ignored another outcome of choice: More of it requires increased time and effort and can lead to
55 anxiety, regret, excessively high expectations, and self-blame if the choices don't work out. When the number of available options is small, these costs are negligible, but the costs grow with the number of options. Eventually, each new option makes us feel
60 worse off than we did before.
   Without a doubt, having more options enables us, most of the time, to achieve better objective outcomes. Again, having 50 styles of jeans as opposed to two increases the likelihood that customers will find a pair
65 that fits. But the subjective outcome may be that shoppers will feel overwhelmed and dissatisfied. This dissociation between objective and subjective results creates a significant challenge for retailers and marketers that look to choice as a way to enhance the
70 perceived value of their goods and services.
   Choice can no longer be used to justify a marketing strategy in and of itself. More isn't always better, either for the customer or for the retailer. Discovering how much assortment is warranted is a
75 considerable empirical challenge. But companies that get the balance right will be amply rewarded.

1

This passage is written from the perspective of

A) an individual interested who believes that customers should be offered as many choices as possible.

B) a person who is knowledgeable about economic theory but who lacks practical experience.

C) a researcher actively engaged in studying the effects of choice on consumer behavior.

D) a marketing expert who wants to advertise products more effectively.

Which of the following best describes the
organization of the first two paragraphs
(lines 1-20)?

A) A claim is presented, an opposing claim is
   offered, and evidence is provided.
B) An unexpected finding is described, and an
   attempt to dismiss the finding is made.
C) A hypothesis is proposed, an experiment is
   carried out, and the results are analyzed.
D) Competing explanations for a phenomenon
   are discussed, and the results of a study
   designed to test them are evaluated.

4. The following passaged is adapted from Olympe de Gouges, *Declaration of the Rights of Women*. It was initially published in 1791, during the French Revolution, and was written in response to the *Declaration of the Rights of Man* (1789).

Woman, wake up; the toxin of reason is being heard throughout the whole universe; discover your rights. The powerful empire of nature is no longer surrounded by prejudice, fanaticism, superstition, and
5 lies. The flame of truth has dispersed all the clouds of folly and usurpation. Enslaved man has multiplied his strength and needs recourse to yours to break his chains. Having become free, he has become unjust to his companion. Oh, women, women! When will you cease
10 to be blind? What advantage have you received from the Revolution? A more pronounced scorn, a more marked disdain. In the centuries of corruption you ruled only over the weakness of men. The reclamation of your patrimony, based on the wise decrees of nature –
15 what have you to dread from such a fine undertaking? Do you fear that our legislators, correctors of that morality, long ensnared by political practices now out of date, will only say again to you: women, what is there in common between you and us? Everything, you
20 will have to answer. If they persist in their weakness in putting this non sequitur* in contradiction to their principles, courageously oppose the force of reason to the empty pretensions of superiority; unite yourselves beneath the standards of philosophy; deploy all the
25 energy of your character. Regardless of what barriers confront you, it is in your power to free yourselves; you have only to want to. Let us pass not to the shocking tableau of what you have been in society; and since national education is in question at this moment, let us
30 see whether our wise legislators will think judiciously about the education of women.

Women have done more harm than good. Constraint and dissimulation have been their lot. What force has robbed them of, ruse returned to them; they had recourse
35 to all the resources of their charms, and the most irreproachable persons did not resist them. Poison and the sword were both subject to them; they commanded in crime as in fortune. The French government, especially,
depended throughout the centuries on the nocturnal
40 administrations of women; the cabinet could keep no secrets as a result of their indiscretions; all have been subject to the cupidity and ambition of this sex, formerly contemptible and respected, and since the revolution, respectable and scorned.

45   In this sort of contradictory situation, what remarks could I not make! I have but a moment to make them, but this moment will fix the attention of the remotest posterity. Under the Old Regime, all was vicious, all was guilty; but could not the amelioration of
50 conditions be perceived even in the substance of vices? A woman only had to be beautiful or amiable; when she possessed these two advantages, she saw a hundred fortunes at her feet. If she did not profit from them, she had a bizarre character or a rare philosophy
55 which made her scorn wealth; then she was deemed to be like a crazy woman. A young, inexperienced woman, seduced by a man whom she loves, will abandon her parents to follow him; the ingrate will leave her after a few years, and the older she has
60 become with him, the more inhuman is his inconstancy; if she has children, he will likewise abandon them. If he is rich, he will consider himself excused from sharing his fortune with his noble victims. If some involvement binds him to his duties, he will
65 deny them, trusting that the laws will support him. If he is married, any other obligation loses its rights. Then what laws remain to extirpate vice all the way to its root? The law of dividing wealth and public administration between men and women. It can easily
70 be seen that one who is born into a rich family gains very much from such equal sharing. But the one born into a poor family with merit and virtue – what is her lot? Poverty and opprobrium. If she does not precisely excel in music or painting, she cannot be admitted to
75 any public function when she has all the capacity for it.

1

Which of the following best characterizes the narrator's shift in focus in lines 45-46?

A) She shifts from criticizing a group of people to praising that group.
B) She shifts from discussing political affairs to discussing artistic affairs.
C) She shifts from discussing opposing views to attempting to reconcile those views.
D) She shifts from describing a problem to offering a personal opinion.

5. The following passage is adapted from "Scientists Discover Salty Aquifer, Previously Unknown Microbial Habitat Under Antarctica," © 2015 by Dartmouth College.

Using an airborne imaging system for the first time in Antarctica, scientists have discovered a vast network of unfrozen salty groundwater that may support previously unknown microbial life deep under the coldest, driest
5 desert on our planet. The findings shed new light on ancient climate change on Earth and provide strong evidence that a similar briny aquifer could support microscopic life on Mars. The scientists used SkyTEM, an airborne electromagnetic sensor, to detect and map
10 otherwise inaccessible subterranean features.

The system uses an antennae suspended beneath a helicopter to create a magnetic field that reveals the subsurface to a depth of about 1,000 feet. Because a helicopter was used, large areas of rugged terrain could
15 be surveyed. The SkyTEM team was funded by the National Science Foundation and led by researchers from the University of Tennessee, Knoxville (UTK), and Dartmouth College, which oversees the NSF's SkyTEM project.

20 "These unfrozen materials appear to be relics of past surface ecosystems and our findings provide compelling evidence that they now provide deep subsurface habitats for microbial life despite extreme environmental conditions," says lead author Jill Mikucki,
25 an assistant professor at UTK. "These new below-ground visualization technologies can also provide insight on glacial dynamics and how Antarctica responds to climate change."

Co-author Dartmouth Professor Ross Virginia is
30 SkyTEM's co-principal investigator and director of Dartmouth's Institute of Arctic Studies. "This project is studying the past and present climate to, in part, understand how climate change in the future will affect biodiversity and ecosystem processes," Virginia says.
35 "This fantastic new view beneath the surface will help us sort out competing ideas about how the McMurdo Dry Valleys have changed with time and how this history influences what we see today."

The researchers found that the unfrozen brines form
40 extensive, interconnected aquifers deep beneath glaciers and lakes and within permanently frozen soils. The brines extend from the coast to at least 7.5 miles inland in the McMurdo Dry Valleys, the largest ice-free region in Antarctica. The brines could be due to freezing and/or
45 deposits. The findings show for the first time that the Dry Valleys' lakes are interconnected rather than isolated; connectivity between lakes and aquifers is important in sustaining ecosystems through drastic climate change, such as lake dry-down events. The findings also challenge

50 the assumption that parts of the ice sheets below the pressure melting point are devoid of liquid water.

In addition to providing answers about the biological adaptations of previously unknown ecosystems that persist in the extreme cold and dark of the Antarctic
55 winter, the new study could help scientists to understand whether similar conditions might exist elsewhere in the solar system, specifically beneath the surface of Mars, which has many similarities to the Dry Valleys. Overall, the Dry Valleys ecosystem -- cold,
60 vegetation-free and home only to microscopic animal and plant life -- resembles, during the Antarctic summer, conditions on the surface on Mars.

SkyTEM produced images of Taylor Valley along the Ross Sea that suggest briny sediments exist at subsurface temperatures down to perhaps -68°F, which
65 is considered suitable for microbial life. One of the studied areas was lower Taylor Glacier, where the data suggest ancient brine still exists beneath the glacier. That conclusion is supported by the presence of Blood Falls, an iron-rich brine that seeps out of the glacier and
70 hosts an active microbial ecosystem.

Scientists' understanding of Antarctica's underground environment is changing dramatically as research reveals that subglacial lakes are widespread and that at least half of the areas covered by the ice
75 sheet are akin to wetlands on other continents. But groundwater in the ice-free regions and along the coastal margins remains poorly understood.

1

Which choice best describes the organization of this passage?

A) An experiment is discussed, and several interpretations of its results are analyzed.

B) A finding is described, and the implications of that finding are considered.

C) A hypothesis is presented, an attempt to validate it using new technology is described, and the resulting data are evaluated.

D) An ecosystem on Earth is compared to an an ecosystem on Mars, and the origin of each is discussed.

Official Guide/Khan Academy Rhetorical Strategy and Passage Organization Questions

Test 1

2   Passage structure
34   Function

Test 2

3   Point of view
12   Counterargument

Test 3

21   Passage organization

Test 4

43   Passage organization
44   Evidence

Explanations: Rhetorical Strategy and Passage Organization Exercises

1.1 D

Don't be distracted by the amount of information in the answer choices. Focus on the beginning of the passage, and work on matching it to the first part of one of the answers. In reality, all you need is the first sentence: *These are stimulating times for anyone interested in questions of animal consciousness.* That is a subjective statement, i.e. an *assertion*. That points right to D). The rest of the passage consists of details supporting the claim: first, the findings that animals exhibit sophisticated behaviors, and then the description of the "Cambridge Declaration."

1.2 A

What sort of information precedes line 21? A series of examples illustrating the idea that animals are likely capable of conscious thought. What happens in line 21? The author begins to describe the meeting of neuroscientists at Cambridge – the phrase *All of this work and discovery appeared to reach a kind of crescendo last summer* indicates that the meeting was the *result* of the discoveries described in the previous section of the passage. The shift from examples to result (=outcome) corresponds to A).

2.1 B

The key to this question is to recognize that the passage is written from an objective, third person point of view; Catherine and her family members are referred to as *she, he,* and *they*. Furthermore, the narration is purely descriptive. The narrator knows a lot about Catherine and her family but is not involved in the action. That eliminates C) and D). Choosing between A) and B), you might run into trouble if you don't realize that the description of Catherine's faults is ironic. The narrator is not actually criticizing Catherine but rather poking fun at the convention of a too-good-to-be-true heroine. That eliminates A). B) is correct because the narrator is simply an observer who is very familiar with the lives of Catherine and her family.

2.2 C

To simplify this question, rephrase it as, "what point are the words *never, not even,* and *inattentive* used to make?" Most simply, they are intended to emphasize the fact that Catherine's abilities aren't particularly extraordinary for a girl of her age, i.e. her "lack of precociousness" (*precocious* means "unusually mature"). That makes C) the answer.

3.1 C

This question throws an awful lot of information at you, but in fact it can be answered very quickly using only one tiny section of the passage – the use of the first person in the phrase *My colleagues and I* indicates that the writer is personally engaged in the type of research he describes. The answer is therefore C).

3.2 A

To simplify this question, match the beginning of the passage to the beginning of an answer choice. The repetition of the word *assume* (lines 1 and 3), followed by the phrase *Nevertheless, research now shows* indicates "they say/I say," i.e. claim and opposing claim. That corresponds directly to A).

4. D

The easiest way to answer this question is to recognize that the word *I* appears for the first time in line 46, indicating a shift to a first person (personal) point of view. That corresponds to D).

5. B

The easiest way to answer this question is to match the beginning of the passage to the beginning of an answer choice. The first sentence of the passage refers to a "discovery." The only answer that corresponds to that idea is B), which refers to a "finding" (discovery = finding). B) is thus correct.

12. Analogies

During the previous redesign of the SAT in 2005, one of the biggest alterations was the elimination of the analogy section. What most people don't realize, however, is that analogy questions were never eliminated entirely. While there are no longer vocabulary-based analogy questions, *passage-based* analogy questions do still appear.

I think it's pretty safe to say that analogy questions are among the most hated questions on the Reading section (if you don't think they're so bad, consider yourself lucky). They also tend to be among the most challenging: students already scoring around 700 often find that analogy questions are among those that regularly give them trouble.

The good news is that analogy questions appear relatively infrequently – and when they do show up, there's usually only one. The bad news, of course, is they do crop up sometimes, and you have to be prepared to handle them when that happens.

Analogy questions can be phrased in several ways: most frequently, you will be asked to identify the scenario from among the answer choices that is most *analogous* (similar) to the scenario described in several lines of the passage. You may also be asked to identify the answer choice that is *most like* or *most similar to* a scenario described in the passage. Either way, the answer choices will describe a series of situations and people completely unconnected to the passage itself. You are responsible for drawing the connection between the specific wording in the passage and the more general situation it describes, and for recognizing which of the answers describes the same essential situation.

Analogy questions do not typically have shortcuts but instead require multiple steps of logic. While there are tools you can use to recognize correct answers more confidently and efficiently, the answer will never be spelled out in any obvious way in the passage, and there are no general key words that regularly appear in answer choices to indicate either correct or incorrect responses. While the correct answer will typically contain a synonym or synonyms for words in the passage, you must identify those words on your own.
For that reason, the kind of systematic, step-by-step approach that is not always necessary for other kinds of questions is required here. Provided that you're willing to stick to it closely, however, analogy questions can be… well, I wouldn't go so far as to say pleasant, but definitely manageable enough to not make you want to rip your test in half whenever you see one.

1) Go back to the passage and read the exact lines provided in the question.

Analogy questions are not context-based questions. Provided you understand the general section of the passage well enough for those lines to make sense, you should be able to answer the question based only on the lines given. Reading more than a few words before/after for necessary context will most likely confuse you.

2) Quickly rephrase the scenario presented.

Take a moment and reiterate for yourself exactly what's going on in those lines. Who are the people in question, what are they doing, and what is the outcome?

3) Sum up the scenario <u>in general terms</u>. Write it down.

This is the crucial step – you have to understand what's going on in more abstract terms in order to draw the analogy. What you write can be very short and simple, but if you don't have something to look at to keep you focused, you'll usually have much more difficulty recognizing the correct answer.

4) Check the answers one by one, in order

As you read each answer, think about whether it matches the general "template" for the scenario you've established in step 3. If it clearly doesn't match, cross it out; if there's any chance it could work, leave it. If you're left with more than one answer, determine which one matches the template more closely – that will be the correct answer.

To reiterate: going through these steps need not be time-consuming. On the contrary, it is possible to complete them very, very quickly. But you should do your best to avoid skipping steps. If you don't define the relationships precisely upfront, it's very easy to get confused and to forget just what you're looking for.

Let's look at an example:

For science fiction aficionados, Isaac Asimov anticipated the idea of using massive data sets to predict
5 human behavior, coining it "psychohistory" in his 1951 Foundation trilogy. The bigger the data set, Asimov said then, the more predictable the future. With big-data analytics, one can finally see the forest, instead of just the capillaries in the tree leaves. Or to put it in more
10 accurate terms, one can see beyond the apparently random motion of a few thousand molecules of air inside a balloon; one can see the balloon itself, and beyond that, that it is inflating, that it is yellow, and that it is part of a bunch of balloons en route to a birthday party. The
15 data/software world has, until now, been largely about looking at the molecules inside one balloon.

1

Which of the following is most analogous to the situation described in lines 7-16 ("With...balloon")?

A) A scientist makes a groundbreaking discovery and receives an award.
B) A classical musician successfully releases an album of contemporary songs.
C) A tourist is able to observe an entire city and the surrounding region from a skyscraper.
D) A private company partners with a local government to build a new shopping district.

Now we're going to apply the process described above to figure out the solution:

1) Reread only the lines in question

Lines 7-14 state:

With big-data analytics, one can finally see the forest, instead of just the capillaries in the tree leaves. Or to put it in more accurate terms, one can see beyond the apparently random motion of a few thousand molecules of air inside a balloon; one can see the balloon itself, and beyond that, that it is inflating, that it is yellow, and that it is part of a bunch of balloons en route to a birthday party. The data/software world has, until now, been largely about looking at the molecules inside one balloon.

2) Reiterate lines in your own words

Before big data, could only see small picture; now can see big picture

If you feel that it helps to write this part down and you can do so quickly, write it down. If you think this step will take too much time or doesn't seem necessary skip it.

3) Rephrase #2 in a more general way

Small pic. → big pic.

Notice the shorthand here. This is similar to a "main point" exercise – the goal is to capture the general idea as simply and quickly as possible.

4) Find the answer that matches the summary in #3

One by one, we're going to check the answers in order.

A) A scientist makes a groundbreaking discovery and receives an award.

No. This has nothing to do with seeing the big picture. Don't get caught up in associative thinking here – the fact that the passage is talking about science does not mean that the *situation* in the passage is the same as the one in the answer choice.

B) A classical musician successfully releases an album of contemporary songs.

Successfully switching from one genre of music to another is not at all the same thing as moving from the small picture to the big one. So B) is out.

C) A tourist is able to observe an entire city and the surrounding region from a skyscraper.

Maybe. It doesn't explicitly discuss moving from the small picture to the big picture, but it does capture the idea of being able to see beyond one's immediate surroundings from a high-up vantage point. That is similar to *see[ing] beyond the apparently random motion of a few thousand molecules of air inside a balloon; one can see the balloon itself, and beyond that, that it is inflating.*

So we keep C).

**D) A private company partners with a local
      government to build a new shopping district.**

No, the collaboration between public and private has nothing to do with moving from the small picture to the big picture. This answer is completely off topic.

So the answer is C) It might not match exactly, but it comes closest of all the answers.

You could also be asked to identify an analogy within the passage itself.

For example:

Every time a car drives through a major intersection, it becomes a data point. Magnetic coils of wire lay just beneath the pavement, registering each passing car. This starts a cascade of information: Computers tally the
5 number and speed of cars, shoot the data through underground cables to a command center and finally translate it into the colors red, yellow and green. On the seventh floor of Boston City Hall, the three colors splash like paint across a wall-sized map.
10 To drivers, the color red means stop, but on the map it tells traffic engineers to leap into action. Traffic control centers like this one—a room cluttered with computer terminals and live video feeds of urban intersections— represent the brain of a traffic system. The city's network
15 of sensors, cables and signals are the nerves connected to the rest of the body. "Most people don't think there are eyes and ears keeping track of all this stuff," says John DeBenedictis, the center's engineering director. But in reality, engineers literally watch our every move,
20 making subtle changes that relieve and redirect traffic.
      The tactics and aims of traffic management are modest but powerful. Most intersections rely on a combination of pre-set timing and computer adaptation. For example, where a busy main road intersects with a quiet residential
25 street, the traffic signal might give 70 percent of "green time" to the main road, and 30 percent to the residential road. (Green lights last between a few seconds and a couple minutes, and tend to shorten at rush hour to help the traffic move continuously.) But when traffic
30 overwhelms the pre-set timing, engineers override the system and make changes.

1

Which of the following is most like the "sensors, cables, and signals?"

A) "Magnetic coils of wire" (line 2)
B) "the colors red, yellow, and green" (line 7)
C) "the brain of a traffic system" (line 14)
D) "a combination of pre-set timing and
      computer adaptation" (lines 22-23)

Sensors, cables, and signals refer to the specific instruments that traffic engineers use to channel information from the streets into traffic control centers, so we're essentially looking for an **example** of one of those things. There's no shortcut; we need to check the answers in order. That said, we'll find the answer pretty quickly. For A), the passage tells us that the magnetic coils of wire register the number/speed of cars and transmit that information through underground cables to traffic control centers, so this is exactly what we're looking for.

Otherwise, B) is wrong because the colors listed are a result of the information transmitted, not the tools for transmitting the information. C) is wrong because *the brain of a traffic system* is the actual traffic control center, and we're looking for the tools the control center uses. And D) is wrong because *a combination of pre-set timing and computer adaptations* is mentioned as an example of the tactics/aims of traffic management. It's a way of managing traffic at intersections, not a tool for relaying information back to traffic engineers.

Analogy Exercises

1. Around the middle of the 20th century, science
    dispensed with the fantasy that we could easily colonize
    the other planets in our solar system. Science fiction
    writers absorbed the new reality: soon, moon and
5   asteroid settings replaced Mars and Venus.

Which of the following is most analogous to the
situation described in the passage?

A) A writer realizes that he is unlikely to become
    a successful novelist and accepts a job at a
    magazine instead.
B) A musician continues to perform despite
    receiving unfavorable reviews from critics.
C) A pilot is forced to make an emergency
    landing after encountering bad weather during
    a flight.
D) A politician retires from office after becoming
    involved in a scandal.

2. Our psychological habitat is shaped by what you
    might call the magnetic property of home, the way it
    aligns everything around us. Perhaps you remember a
    moment, coming home from a trip, when the house you
5   call home looked, for a moment, like just another house
    on a street full of houses. But then the illusion faded
    and your house became home again. That, I think, is
    one of the most basic meanings of home—a place we
    can never see with a stranger's eyes for more than a
10 moment.

## 2

The situation described in lines 3-7 ("Perhaps…
again") is most analogous to which of the following?

A) a student's friends do not initially recognize
    him after he changes his appearance.
B) a mother briefly fails to recognize her son
    among a crowd of children.
C) a doctor greets a patient warmly because she is
    happy that he has been cured.
D) a teacher has difficulty distinguishing between
    a set of twins.

3. Why is the connection between smells and
    memories so strong? The reason for these associations
    is that the brain's olfactory bulb is connected to both
    the amygdala (an emotion center) and to the
5   hippocampus, which is involved in memory. And,
    because smells serve a survival function (odors can
    keep us from eating spoiled or poisonous foods), some
    of these associations are made very quickly, and may
    even involve a one-time association.

As described in the passage, the connection between
smells and memories is most similar to which of
the following?

A) a driver has an accident at an intersection and
    refuses to drive past it again.
B) a child insists of wearing clothes of a
    particular color every day.
C) a young woman inexplicably develops an
    allergy to a common household item.
D) a food manufacturer develops a technology to
    prevent its products from spoiling.

4. Experimental scientists occupy themselves with observing and measuring the cosmos, finding out what stuff exists, no matter how strange that stuff may be. Theoretical physicists, on the other hand, are not
5 satisfied with observing the universe. They want to know why. They want to explain all the properties of the universe in terms of a few fundamental principles and parameters. These fundamental principles, in turn, lead to the "laws of nature," which govern the
10 behavior of all matter and energy.

Theoretical physicists' goal, as indicated in the passage, is most similar to which of the following?

A) a biologist observing changes in a specimen over an extended period of time.
B) members of a community rebuilding a house destroyed in a storm.
C) an astronaut undergoes years of training to prepare for a journey into space.
D) a linguist seeking to discover the underlying features common to distantly related languages.

5. Yogi Berra, the former Major League baseball catcher and coach, once remarked that you can't hit and think at the same time. Of course, since he also reportedly said, "I really didn't say everything I said,"
5 it is not clear we should take his statements at face value. Nonetheless, a widespread view — in both academic journals and the popular press — is that thinking about what you are doing, as you are doing it, interferes with performance. The idea is that once you
10 have developed the ability to play an arpeggio on the piano, putt a golf ball or parallel park, attention to what you are doing leads to inaccuracies, blunders and sometimes even utter paralysis. As the great choreographer George Balanchine would say to his
15 dancers, "Don't think, dear; just do."
    Perhaps you have experienced this destructive force yourself. Start thinking about just how to carry a full glass of water without spilling, and you'll end up drenched. How, exactly, do you initiate a telephone
20 conversation? Begin wondering, and before long, the recipient of your call will notice the heavy breathing and hang up. Our actions, the French philosopher Maurice Merleau-Ponty tells us, exhibit a "magical" efficacy, but when we focus on them, they degenerate
25 into the absurd. A 13-time winner on the Professional Golfers Association Tour, Dave Hill, put it like this: "You can't be thinking about the mechanics of the sport while you are performing."

## 5

The situation described in lines 17-19 ("Start... drenched") is most similar to which of the following?

A) A magician refuses to reveal the secret to a popular trick.
B) A gymnast falls after worrying about the position of her legs during a routine move.
C) A student fails an exam after staying awake all night to study.
D) An executive loses an important deal because she was insufficiently prepared for a meeting.

Note: none of the tests in the Official Guide contains an analogy question; however, one does appear on the released PSAT (https://collegereadiness.collegeboard.org/psat-nmsqt-psat-10/practice/full-length-practice-test, Section 1, Question 9, p. 4), so it is reasonable to assume that some SATs will contain them as well.

Explanations: Analogy Exercises

1. A

What is the scenario described in the passage? Science fiction writers realized that it was not realistic for the Earth to easily colonize other planets, so they changed their works to incorporate that new reality by focusing on asteroids and the moon.

General scenario: realize x is unrealistic, adjust expectations to do y.

The key word in (A) is *instead*. The answer describes a person who realizes that a goal is unrealistic and changes plans accordingly (takes a job at a magazine).

B) describes the opposite of the original scenario because the musician *continues* to perform when faced with discouragement. In C), the pilot is *forced* to land, whereas the science fiction writers make a choice to focus on something new. And in D), the politician does not realize that something specific is unrealistic and replace his/her career with a new one but rather abandons the career altogether.

2. B

What's the situation described in lines 3-7? Not recognizing a very familiar place for a moment – a place that it is virtually impossible not to recognize.

General scenario: not recognize x, when x is something that you *always* recognize.

B) is the correct answer because a child is someone whose appearance a parent *cannot* forget (at least under normal circumstances), and the parent only fails to recognize the child *briefly* (=for a moment).

A) is not correct because the friend's appearance has changed – the passage says nothing about the house looking different; the scenario in C) is completely unrelated to that described in the passage; and in (D) the focus is on someone who cannot distinguish between two things that look the same, not on someone who does not recognize one familiar thing.

3. A

What characterizes the relationship between smells and memories? It's very strong because it serves a survival function: things that smell bad are more likely to be harmful, and thus people learn to avoid things associated with that smell.

General scenario: know that x is potentially harmful after a brief exposure, so avoid x.

A) is correct because it describes a situation in which a person was exposed to a bad situation once and as a result goes out of the way not to experience that situation again. B) is incorrect because the child's preference is clearly positive; there is no mention of a negative occurrence. Although the scenario in C) is negative, the word *inexplicably* indicates that there is no reason for the allergy, and we're looking for a specific negative experience. D) plays on associative interference by using the word *food*, which appears in the passage, but the situation described is both positive and unrelated to the scenario in the passage.

4. D

What is the theoretical physicists' goal? *They want to know why. They want to explain all the properties of the universe in terms of a few fundamental principles and parameters.* (lines 6-8)

General scenario: want to know the general rules governing a particular phenomenon.

D) is correct because the linguist wants to *uncover the underlying features* that distantly related languages have in common. The underlying assumption is that all languages must have similarities, or that there is a set of rules governing how language works. A) describes what biologist (an experimental scientist) does, *not* a theoretical physicist. B) and C) are entirely unrelated to the passage. The scenario in B) involves people collaborating to achieve a goal, and that in C) involves a person spending a lot of time to prepare for a difficult undertaking.

5. B

What is the situation described in lines 17-19? Someone thinks about how to carry a glass of water and end up spilling it.

General scenario: think too hard about a common/simple activity and mess up.

B) is correct because it describes a situation that should be very straightforward for the person involved (the gymnast's move is *routine*) but that is ruined because the person is thinking too hard about what they're doing. In A), don't get fooled by references to magic in the passage; this answer is designed to play on associative interference. C) and D) describe failures, but not ones that occur because a person has overthought an action.

13. Paired Passages

While Passage 1/Passage 2 relationship questions are often among the most difficult on the SAT, they are also the most direct embodiment of the "they say/I say" model and come closest to asking you to do the kind of reading you'll do in college. When you write research papers, you will be asked to consider multiple interpretations or points of view. The ability to understand differences between arguments, even subtle ones, is crucial to being able to analyze them and formulate a coherent argument in response.

That said, paired passages are many people's least favorite part of SAT Reading. They hit you just when you're most tired, and they demand a level of focus that goes even beyond that required for the rest of the section. Instead of asking you to deal with one or two viewpoints, they can sometimes ask you to deal with three or four: not only what the author of each passage thinks, but sometimes also what the author of each passage says that *other people* think (got that straight?). While there is no way to make these questions easy, breaking them down carefully can go a long way toward making them more manageable.

How to Read Paired Passages

As a general rule, **your goal should be to deal with the smallest amount of information possible at any given time**. The more work you do in terms of determining arguments upfront, the less work you'll have to do on the questions. When you break questions down and work through them methodically, you greatly reduce the chance of confusion.

So in a nutshell:

1. Clearly mark the questions that ask about Passage 1 only, the ones that ask about Passage 2 only, and the ones that ask about both passages.

2. Read Passage 1: write main point + tone

3. Answer Passage 1 questions

4. Read Passage 2: write main point + tone, AND relationship to Passage 1

5. Answer Passage 2 questions

6. Answer Passage 1/Passage 2 relationship questions

Common Passage 1/Passage 2 Relationships

Both passages will *always* revolve around the same basic idea or event, even if it isn't always immediately obvious how the two passages relate to one another. The most common P1/P2 relationship simply involves two authors with conflicting views on or interpretations of an idea or event; however, there are a handful of other relationships that can occur.

- Passage 1 and Passage 2 present opposing views of the same topic (P1 = positive, P2 = negative or vice-versa).

- Passage 1 and Passage 2 agree but have different focuses or stylistic differences (e.g. P1 is written in third person and P2 is written in first person).

- Passage 1 and Passage 2 discuss different aspects of the same event or idea (e.g. P1 focuses on how an event was perceived by the press, P2 focuses on how it affected women).

- Passage 2 provides an example of an idea described generally in Passage 1.

- Passage 2 provides an explanation for a phenomenon discussed in Passage 1.

Why is it so important to determine the relationship between the passages? First, because paired passages will almost always include a question that explicitly asks you to identify the relationship between the passages. If you've already defined the relationship, you've essentially answered the question before you've even looked at it.

It is also crucial to determine the relationship between the passages because you cannot infer what the author of one passage would likely think of an idea in the other passage without knowing whether the authors agree or disagree. When the authors of the two passages disagree, most of the answers to relationship questions will be negative, and you can often automatically eliminate any positive or neutral answer just by reading the first word or two. Likewise, when the authors agree, most correct answers will be positive.

You should, however, be aware that some questions will ask you to identify a statement with which both authors would clearly agree, even when the passages indicate that they hold conflicting opinions. (Conversely, you may also be asked to identify a point of disagreement for two authors who clearly agree.)

In such cases, you must proceed very carefully. Very often, the answers to such questions will often be based on an easily-overlooked detail in one or both of the passages. Sometimes that detail will in fact be located in a key place in one of the passages (introduction, last sentence, a topic sentence, close to a major transition or a dash/colon), but sometimes it will not. Because it is very unlikely that you will remember the information necessary to answer the question, you should always plan to return to the passages as necessary. You should also make sure that you do not eliminate any answer unless you have gone back to the passage and confirmed that it is incorrect.

I repeat: Do not even attempt to rely on your memory. Just read.

Relationship Questions are Inference Questions

Because there is absolutely no difference between questions that ask about only one passage in a P1/P2 set and any other question about a single passage elsewhere on the test, there is absolutely no difference in how you should approach questions asking about single passages.

For most people, the real challenge is the relationship questions, most of which ask you to infer what one author would think about a particular idea in the other passage. In such cases, you must break down the question, making sure to define each idea separately and clearly before you attempt to determine the relationship between them.

Note: If you find that paired passage "relationship" questions are consistently too confusing/time consuming for you, you should consider forgetting about them entirely (filling in your favorite letter) in order to spend more time on the questions that ask about only one passage. If you are not aiming for a perfect score and struggle excessively with these questions, you are probably better off using the time you would have spent on them to answer other questions you are more likely to answer correctly.

That said, "relationship" questions should be broken down in the following way:

1. Re-read the lines in question and sum up the idea in your own words.

2. Reiterate the main point of the other passage.

3. Determine whether the authors would agree or disagree.

4. Look at the answers: if the authors would agree, cross out all negative answers; if the authors would disagree, cross out all positive answers.

5. Check the remaining answers against the passage, focusing on the most specific part of each answer.

Important: as discussed earlier, answers that indicate a lack of interest on the part of one author (e.g. *apathetic, indifferent*) will almost always be incorrect. Passages are chosen precisely because there is a clear positive or negative relationship between their ideas, so by definition those words are unlikely to be right.

Also: if a question states that a particular feature of both passages is the same, (e.g. "The purposes of **both** passages is to…"), you can usually answer it by reading only one of the passages. The wording of the question indicates that if that feature is true for one passage, it must be true for the other.

On the next page, we're going to look at some examples.

Passage 1

Happiness – you know it when you see it, but it's hard to define. You might call it a sense of well-being, of optimism or of meaningfulness in life, although those could also be treated as separate entities. But
5 whatever happiness is, we know that we want it, and that it is just somehow *good*.

We also know that we don't always have control over our happiness. Research suggests that genetics may play a big role in our normal level of subjective well-
10 being, so some of us may start out at a disadvantage. On top of that, between unexpected tragedies and daily habitual stress, environmental factors can bring down mood and dry up our thirst for living.

Being able to manage the emotional ups and downs is
15 important for both body and mind, said Laura Kubzansky, professor of social and behavioral sciences at Harvard School of Public Health. "For physical health, it's not so much happiness per se, but this ability to regulate and have a sense of purpose and meaning," Kubzansky says.
20 Many scientific studies, including some by Kubzansky, have found a connection between psychological and physical well-being.

A 2012 review of more than 200 studies found a connection between positive psychological attributes,
25 such as happiness, optimism and life satisfaction, and a lowered risk of cardiovascular disease. Kubzansky and other Harvard School of Public Health researchers published these findings in the journal *Psychological Bulletin*.
30 It's not as simple as "you must be happy to prevent heart attacks," of course. If you have a good sense of well-being, it's easier to maintain good habits: Exercising, eating a balanced diet and getting enough sleep, researchers say. People who have an optimistic mindset
35 may be more likely to engage in healthy behaviors because they perceive them as helpful in achieving their goals, Kubzansky said.

For now these studies can only show associations; they do not provide hard evidence of cause and effect.
40 **But some researchers speculate that positive mental states do have a direct effect on the body, perhaps by reducing damaging physical processes.**

Passage 2

In reality, there is no clear-cut answer yet on whether being upbeat can keep you healthy or cure
45 **anything.** For some diseases, which may build over decades, the relationship between patients' attitudes and their prognosis is dubious at best. For other diseases, though, the scientific outlook is sunnier. There's evidence that mood can predict whether someone who
50 has had one heart attack will have another.

Little research has been done on the biological basis of positive thinking as a therapeutic treatment for illness, but scientists know the brain and the immune system communicate. Given that scientists also know
55 the immune system plays a role in inflammation of the arteries, which can play a role in heart attacks, it's reasonable to think that heart attacks could be tied back to things going on in the brain. However, when researchers tried to intercede and treat depression
60 among heart attack patients, they found the patient's moods improved, but the rates of second heart attack didn't. Ironically the most evidence for emotion affecting health actually favors negative emotions, not positive ones. For instance, we know anger and
65 depression are correlated with having a second heart attack; however, what's unproven is whether being positive can reduce the risk.

Another way emotion could affect health, even for complicated illnesses such as cancer, is by
70 affecting the patient's willingness to stick to the treatment plan. "It could be an indirect effect," said Anne Harrington, chair of Harvard University's history of science program and author of *The Cure Within: A History of Mind-Body Medicine*. If a person is
75 positive, he or she is more likely to show up for all the treatments, to have a better diet, to exercise. And if you're deeply depressed you sleep badly and that's bad for your health.

It's not an accident that the main point of each passage is located in a key place: focusing on the last sentence of the first passage and the first sentence of the second is often a quick way to identify the relationship between the passages, and you can sometimes save yourself a lot of time by paying extra attention to those places from the start.

So what do we have in terms of main point and tone?

Passage 1

Main point: happiness = probably good f/health
Tone: neutral
Attitude: positive, cautiously optimistic

Passage 2

Main point: Not sure if happiness = health
Tone: neutral
Attitude: skeptical, slightly negative

Relationship: Disagree

Notice that even though the authors disagree, the two passages contradict each other somewhat indirectly. Rather, the author of the first passage suggests that happiness *might* have a positive effect on people's health, while the author of the second passage admits that 1) we don't really know what effect happiness has on health, and 2) if emotions do have an effect on health, it's more likely the case for *negative* emotions.

Let's start by looking at a straightforward relationship question:

1

Which choice best states the relationship between the two passages?

A) Passage 2 proposes an alternate explanation for a phenomenon presented in Passage 1.
B) Passage 2 discredits the results of an experiment discussed in Passage 1.
C) Passage 2 considers the implications of a finding alluded to in Passage 1.
D) Passage 2 expresses skepticism about a theory that is described approvingly in Passage 1.

We know that the authors of the two passages disagree, so we're know the correct answer will probably be negative. If we start by looking at the beginning of each answer, we can see that only B) and D) are negative (*discredits, expresses skepticism*), suggesting that we should check them first. *Discredits* is almost certainly too strong – 40 lines isn't enough to discredit anything – but D) captures the fact that the author of Passage 1 is pretty positive toward the idea that happiness can improve health, while the author of Passage 2 isn't really buying it.

The relationship between the passages can also be tested on other ways. One possibility is to ask how the author of one passage would likely respond to the author of the other passage.

1

How would the author of Passage 2 most likely respond to the "researchers" referred to in line 40, Passage 1?

A) The immune system rather than the brain is primarily responsible for preventing illness.
B) Understanding the relationship between emotions and health could lead to new therapies.
C) There is insufficient evidence to establish a connection between health and happiness.
D) Studies about positive thinking are unreliable because they are typically biased.

The shortest way to answer this question is to use the main point of Passage 2, namely that it's unclear whether happiness affects health. That's pretty much what C) says. If an answer to a P1/P2 relationship question restates the main point of the appropriate passage, that answer will almost certainly be correct.

Otherwise, the fastest way to narrow down the choices and respond to the question is to ignore the choices provided and answer the question on your own. Although this may seem like a more time-consuming approach, it can actually save you a lot of time by allowing you to jump to the correct answer and bypass any potential confusion from the other answers.

1) Define the "researchers"

But some researchers speculate that positive mental states do have a direct effect on the body, perhaps by reducing damaging physical processes.

The "researchers" are people who believe that positive thinking might improve people's health – it's a cautious statement, but it's slightly positive. Note that the lines in question comprise the main point of Passage 1.

2) Look at the main point (1st sentence) of Passage 2

In reality, there is no clear-cut answer yet on whether being upbeat can keep you healthy or cure anything.

That's not an overwhelmingly negative statement, but still, it's mildly negative.

3) Consider the implications

P1 = Positive, P2 = Negative. The two passages clearly disagree, so we're looking for a negative answer. A) is neutral, and B) is positive, so both can be eliminated. The author of Passage 2 does not discuss bias in health/happiness studies, so that again leaves C).

This question could be rewritten from a slightly different angle, as an attitude question. In that case, it could also appear as part of a supporting evidence pair.

For example:

1

How would the author of Passage 2 most likely respond to the "researchers" referred to in line 40, Passage 1?

A) With dismissal, because the immune system is primarily responsible for preventing illness.
B) With approval, because understanding the relationship between emotions and health could lead to new therapies.
C) With skepticism, because there is insufficient evidence for a connection between health and positive thinking.
D) With indifference, because studies about positive thinking tend to be biased.

2

Which choice provides the best evidence for the answer to the previous question?

A) Lines 48-50 ("There's...another")
B) Lines 62-64 ("Ironically...ones")
C) Lines 66-67 ("however...risk")
D) Lines 68-71 ("Another...plan")

Let's start by just looking at the attitude word at the beginning of each answer.

    A) dismissal
    B) approval
    C) skepticism
    D) indifference

We know that the two passages disagree, so the correct answer will be negative. A) and C) fit, but B) is positive, and D) is pretty much always going to be wrong – *indifference* means that the author wouldn't care, and the question is being asked precisely because the author *would* have an opinion. So now we only have two answers to contend with.

What's the point of Passage 2? That we don't have enough evidence to judge whether positive thinking has any effect on health. Which is exactly what C) says.

To reiterate: the first question of the set is essentially the same question we just looked at. It's simply phrased a little differently. But with the supporting evidence question after it, there's a twist.

As we've seen, the most efficient ways to solve most supporting evidence pairs is to plug the answers to question #2 into question #1 and work from there. When supporting evidence questions are coupled with paired passage relationship questions, however, things get a bit more complicated. The reality is that there is no single most effective strategy for every question, and you must be flexible in order to consistently answer these questions correctly.

If you are able to answer question #1 quickly using the main point, you should answer the questions in order. Then, you can simply check each line reference in question #2 to see if it supports the correct idea.

If, on the other hand, the answer is based on a detail not directly related to the main point, you may be better served by plugging in the answers to question #2 into question #1.

For this pair, #1 is pretty straightforward if you know the point of the passage – the author is pretty clear that there isn't enough evidence to determine whether happiness can improve health, and that's what C) says.

For the supporting evidence question, you simply need to check each answer in turn to see if it reiterates the idea that the relationship between health and happiness is uncertain. Only C) discusses that idea (lines 62-64 state that *the most evidence for emotion affecting health actually favors negative emotions, not positive ones*), so it is the answer to the supporting evidence question as well.

Important: Remember that when it comes to Passage 1 vs. Passage 2 attitude questions, the moderate vs. extreme "rule" still applies. Extreme answers such as *anger, excitement,* and *incredulousness* (disbelief) are much less likely to be correct than answers such as *approval, concern,* and *skepticism*. If you are answering the questions in order, you may be able to make some educated guesses about answers likely to be right/wrong in question #1 of the pair.

Agreement Questions

As mentioned earlier, passages with conflicting viewpoints tend to include at least one question that asks you to identify a point that the authors would *agree* about. These questions are often targeted to test your understanding of the complexities of the relationship between the two passages – that is, the fact that an author can recognize the validity of part of an argument while disagreeing with another part.

Practically speaking, that means knowing the overall relationship between the passages is *not* sufficient to answer all of the questions. While the necessary information may be located in a key place (intro, conclusion, after a major transition) in one or both of the passages, it is also possible that the answer will hinge on information in the middle of a paragraph.

For example:

Which idea is supported by the authors of both passages?

A) Positive thinking is an essential component of a healthy lifestyle.
B) The relationship between the brain and the immune system is affected by a person's mental state.
C) A person's level of happiness is the most important factor in predicting illness.
D) Emotions may play a role in people's physical well-being.

If you're trying to answer the question using only the main points, you might eliminate D) immediately. After all, the author of Passage 2 focuses on the *lack* of evidence between happiness and health, and D) would seem to contradict that idea.

This, however, is where most people's memories fail them, and it illustrates perfectly why you shouldn't try to rely on your memory in the first place! The problem is that both authors present their arguments in nuanced ways – although Passage 1 is generally more open to the possibility that happiness might have a positive effect on health and Passage 2 is more negative toward that option, both state outright that there could be an indirect link between those things (Passage 1, lines 38-39; Passage 2, line 71). In addition the author of Passage 2 is pretty clear about the link between *negative* emotions and health, and D) only mentions *emotions* – it does not specify whether those emotions are positive or negative. So the answer is actually D).

Playing process of elimination, the extreme phrases *essential component* in A) and *most important factor* in C) suggest right away that both of those answers are incorrect. Indeed, when we look more closely at them, we can eliminate both because they directly contradict the main point of Passage 2. B) applies only to Passage 2 – the immune system is never even discussed in Passage 1. So that again leaves D) as the correct answer.

Similarities between two conflicting passages can also be tested indirectly, as one-question supporting evidence questions. For example, you could see a question that looks like this:

1

Which choice would best support the claim that the author of Passage 2 recognizes that an "optimistic mindset" (Passage 1, line 34) could have benefits for health?

A) Lines 45-48 ("For...sunnier")
B) Lines 51-54 ("Little...communicate")
C) Lines 64-66 ("For...attack")
D) Lines 74-76 ("If...exercise")

Although this question is phrased in an extremely roundabout manner, it is actually much simpler than it seems. The word *recognizes* is key – the question is essentially asking what part of Passage 2 supports the indicated claim in Passage 1.

To rephrase the question more simply, we could say something like, "What part of Passage 2 supports that there is a link between optimism and good health?" The correct answer must therefore be related to the idea that optimism can affect health. Now that we know what we're looking for, we can check the answers.

A) For some diseases, which may build over decades, the relationship between patients' attitudes and their prognosis is dubious at best. For other diseases, though, the scientific outlook is sunnier.

Don't get fooled by the word *sunnier*. The author is only saying that there *might* be a relationship between attitude and certain illnesses. This section does not mention the effects of optimism per se.

B) Little research has been done on the biological basis of positive thinking as a therapeutic treatment for illness, but scientists know the brain and the immune system communicate.

Careful. This section does *mention* the possibility of positive thinking as a treatment, but the author only says that little research has been done on it. Right words, wrong context.

C) For instance, we know anger and depression are correlated with having a second heart attack

No, this has nothing to do with the effects of optimism on health. It's completely off topic.

D) If a person is positive, he or she is more likely to show up for all the treatments, to have a better diet, to exercise.

Yes, this fits exactly. This sentence establishes a potential link between optimism and good health. Besides, it's the only answer we have left. So D) is correct.

Paired Passage Exercises

1. Passage 1 is adapted from the website locavores.com, © 2010. Passage 2 is adapted from Ronald Bailey, "The Food Miles Mistake," © 2008 *Reason* magazine.

Passage 1

Our food now travels an average of 1,500 miles before ending up on our plates. This globalization of the food supply has serious consequences for the environment, our health, our communities and our
5 tastebuds. Much of the food grown in the breadbasket surrounding us must be shipped across the country to distribution centers before it makes its way back to our supermarket shelves. Because uncounted costs of this long distance journey (air pollution and global
10 warming, the ecological costs of large scale monoculture, the loss of family farms and local community dollars) are not paid for at the checkout counter, many of us do not think about them at all.

What is eaten by the great majority of North
15 Americans comes from a global everywhere, yet from nowhere that we know in particular. How many of our children even know what a chicken eats or how an onion grows? The distance from which our food comes represents our separation from the
20 knowledge of how and by whom what we consume is produced, processed, and transported. And yet, the quality of a food is derived not merely from its genes and the greens that fed it, but from how it is prepared and cared for all the way until it reaches our mouths.
25 If the production, processing, and transport of what we eat is destructive of the land and of human community — as it very often is — how can we understand the implications of our own participation in the global food system when those processes are
30 located elsewhere and so are obscured from us? How can we act responsibly and effectively for change if we do not understand how the food system works and our own role within it.

Corporations, which are the principal beneficiaries
35 of a global food system, now dominate the production, processing, distribution, and consumption of food, but alternatives are emerging which together could together could form the basis for foodshed development. Just as many farmers are recognizing the social and
40 environmental advantages to sustainable agriculture, so are many consumers coming to appreciate the benefits of fresh and sustainably produced food. Such producers and consumers are being linked through such innovative arrangements as community supported
45 agriculture and farmers' markets. Alternative producers, alternative consumers, and alternative small entrepreneurs are rediscovering community and finding common ground.

Passage 2

In their recent policy primer for the Mercatus
50 Center at George Mason University, economic geographer Pierre Desrochers and economic consultant Hiroko Shimizu challenge the notion that food miles – the distance food travels from farm to plate – are a good sustainability indicator. As
55 Desrochers and Shimizu point out, the food trade has been historically driven by urbanization. As agriculture became more efficient, people were liberated from farms and able to develop other skills that helped raise general living standards. People
60 freed from having to scrabble for food, for instance, could work in factories, write software, or become physicians. Modernization is a process in which people get further and further away from the farm.

Modern technologies like canning and refrigeration
65 made it possible to extend the food trade from staple grains and spices to fruits, vegetables, and meats. As a result, world trade in fruits and vegetables—fresh and processed—doubled in the 1980s and increased by 30 percent between 1990 and 2001. Fruits and
70 vegetables accounted for 22 percent of the exports of developing economies in 2001. If farmers, processors, shippers, and retailers did not profit from providing distant consumers with these foods, the foods wouldn't be on store shelves. And consumers, of
75 course, benefit from being able to buy fresh foods year around.

So just how much carbon dioxide is emitted by transporting food from farm to fork? Desrochers and Shimizu cite a comprehensive study done by the
80 United Kingdom's Department of Environment, Food and Rural Affairs (DEFRA) which reported that 82 percent of food miles were generated within the U.K. Consumer shopping trips accounted for 48 percent and trucking for 31 percent of British
85 miles. Air freight amounted to less than 1 percent of food miles. In total, food transportation accounted for only 1.8 percent of Britain's carbon dioxide emissions.

Which choice best describes the relationship between the two passages?

A) Passage 2 offers an alternative explanation for a phenomenon that Passage 1 describes.
B) Passage 2 proposes a solution to a problem that Passage 1 presents.
C) Passage 2 expresses doubt about the benefits of a practice that Passage 1 advocates.
D) Passage 2 provides historical context for a tradition that Passage 1 discusses.

## 2

The authors of both passages would most likely agree with which of the following statements about food?

A) People must understand the food production system in order to make informed choices about their health.
B) A significant amount of the food consumed today is not produced locally.
C) Transporting food over long distances may reduce its quality.
D) The corporate model of food production is a necessary aspect of urbanization.

## 3

How would the author of Passage 2 most likely respond to the discussion in lines 8-14 of Passage 1 ("Because...all")?

A) He would claim that most pollution comes from sources other than food transportation.
B) He would assert that access to foods grown far away has led more people to adopt healthful diets.
C) He would argue that transporting food over long distances is the best way to feed an increasingly urban population.
D) He would point out that most family farms today exist by choice rather than necessity.

Which choice provides the best evidence for the answer to the previous question?

A) Lines 64-66 ("Modern...meats")
B) Lines 74-76 ("And...around")
C) Lines 82-83 ("82 percent...UK")
D) Lines 86-87 ("In...emissions")

How would the author of Passage 1 most likely respond to the authors of Passage 2's claim about "fresh foods" (line 75)?

A) With approval, because people should consume locally produced food whenever possible.
B) With skepticism, because the nutritional value of food transported over long distances may be compromised.
C) With apathy, because the corporate model of food production cannot be altered.
D) With interest, because new technologies may preserve foods for longer periods.

Which choice provides the best evidence for the answer to the previous question?

A) Lines 5-6 ("Much...country")
B) Lines 14-15 ("What...everywhere")
C) Lines 21-24 ("And...mouths")
D) Lines 37-38 ("alternatives...development")

2. Passage 1 is adapted from John Locke, *Two Treatises of Government*, originally published in 1690. Passage 2 is adapted from Alexander Hamilton, "A Full Vindication of the Measures of the Congress." Originally published in 1774, it was a key document in building support for the American Revolution.

Passage 1

To understand political power aright, and derive it from its original, we must consider what estate all men are naturally in, and that is, a state of perfect freedom to order their actions, and dispose of their
5 possessions and persons as they think fit, within the bounds of the law of Nature, without asking leave or depending upon the will of any other man.

A state also of equality, wherein all the power and jurisdiction is reciprocal, no one having more than
10 another, there being nothing more evident than that creatures of the same species and rank, promiscuously born to all the same advantages of Nature, and the use of the same faculties, should also be equal one amongst another, without subordination or subjection...
15 But though this be a state of liberty, yet it is not a state of license; though man in that state have an uncontrollable liberty to dispose of his person or possessions, yet he has not liberty to destroy himself, or so much as any creature in his possession, but where
20 some nobler use than its bare preservation calls for it. The state of Nature has a law of Nature to govern it, which obliges every one, and reason, which is that law, teaches all mankind who will but consult it, that being all equal and independent, no one ought to harm
25 another in his life, health, liberty or possessions... And, being furnished with like faculties, sharing all in one community of Nature, there cannot be supposed any such subordination among us that may authorize us to destroy one another, as if we were made for one
30 another's uses, as the inferior ranks of creatures are for ours.

Passage 2

That Americans are entitled to freedom, is incontrovertible upon every rational principle. All men have one common original: they participate in one
35 common nature, and consequently have one common right. No reason can be assigned why one man should exercise any power, or preeminence over his fellow creatures more than another; unless they have voluntarily veiled him with it. Since then, Americans
40 have not by any act of theirs empowered the British Parliament to make laws for them, it follows they can have no just authority to do it.

Besides the clear voice of natural justice in this respect, the fundamental principles of the English
45 constitution are in our favor. It has been repeatedly demonstrated, that the idea of legislation, or taxation, when the subject is not represented, is inconsistent with that. Nor is this all, our charters, the express conditions on which our progenitors relinquished
50 their native countries, and came to settle in this, preclude every claim of ruling and taxing us without our assent.

Every subterfuge that sophistry has been able to invent, to evade or obscure this truth, has been refuted
55 by the most conclusive reasonings; so that we may pronounce it a matter of undeniable certainty, that the pretensions of Parliament are contradictory to the law of nature, subversive of the British constitution, and destructive of the faith of the most solemn compacts.
60 What then is the subject of our controversy with the mother country? It is this, whether we shall preserve that security to our lives and properties, which the law of nature, the genius of the British constitution, and our charters afford us or whether we shall resign
65 them into the hands of the British House of Commons, which is no more privileged to dispose of them than the Grand Mogul? What can actuate those men, who labor to delude any of us into an opinion, that the object of contention between the parents and the
70 colonies is only three pence duty upon tea? or that the commotions in America originate in a plan, formed by some turbulent men to erect it into a republican government? The parliament claims a right to tax us in all cases whatsoever; its late laws are in virtue of
75 that claim. How ridiculous then is it to affirm, that we are quarrelling for the trifling Aim of three pence a pound on tea; when it is evidently the principle against which we contend.

1

Which choice best describes the relationship between the two passages?

A) Passage 2 presents a personal account of a conflict that Passage 1 describes in general terms.
B) Passage 2 presents the disadvantages of a perspective that Passage 1 celebrates.
C) Passage 2 takes a practical view of a reaction that Passage 1 approaches idealistically.
D) Passage 2 offers an example of a situation that Passage 1 discusses theoretically.

2

Both passages make the point that

A) individuals have the right to remain free from unjust domination.
B) the power of natural law outweighs the power of the laws developed by society.
C) societies must be governed by natural law as well as constitutional law.
D) societies must develop laws suited to the particular needs of their citizens.

3

The author of Passage 2 would most likely respond to the statement in lines 21-25 of Passage 1 ("The state...possessions") with

A) indifference, because people live in societies rather than in a state of nature.
B) agreement, because no individual has the inherent authority to rule over others.
C) doubt, because Locke does not directly address the question of leadership.
D) derision, because governments can ignore the dictates of natural law.

4

Which choice provides the best evidence for the answer to the previous question?

A) Lines 36-39 ("No...it")
B) Lines 45-48 ("It...that")
C) Lines 53-55 ("Every...reasonings")
D) Lines 61-64 ("It...us")

3. Passage 1 is adapted from Jonah Lehrer, "Under Pressure: the Search for a Stress Vaccine, © 2010 *Wired* magazine. Passage 2 is adapted from Kristin Sainani, "What, Me Worry?" © 2014, Stanford magazine.

Passage 1

Chronic stress, it turns out, is an extremely dangerous condition. While stress doesn't cause any single disease — in fact, the causal link between stress and ulcers has been largely disproved — it makes
5 most diseases significantly worse. The list of ailments connected to stress is staggeringly diverse and includes everything from the common cold and lower-back pain to Alzheimer's disease, major depressive disorder, and heart attack. Stress hollows out our bones
10 and atrophies our muscles. It triggers adult-onset diabetes and may also be connected to high blood pressure. In fact, numerous studies of human longevity in developed countries have found that psychosocial factors such as stress are the single most important
15 variable in determining the length of a life. It's not that genes and risk factors like smoking don't matter. It's that our levels of stress matter more.

Furthermore, the effects of chronic stress directly counteract improvements in medical care and public
20 health. Antibiotics, for instance, are far less effective when our immune system is suppressed by stress; that fancy heart surgery will work only if the patient can learn to shed stress. As pioneering stress researcher Robert Sapolsky notes, "You can give a guy a drug-
25 coated stent, but if you don't fix the stress problem, it won't really matter. For so many conditions, stress is the major long-term risk factor. Everything else is a short-term fix."

Passage 2

According to a 2013 national survey by the
30 American Psychological Association, the average stress level among adults is 5.1 on a scale of 10; that's one and a half points above what the respondents judged to be healthy. Two-thirds of people say managing stress is important, and nearly that
35 proportion had attempted to reduce their stress in the previous five years. Yet only a little over a third say they succeeded at doing so. More discouraging, teens and young adults are experiencing higher levels of stress, and also are struggling to manage it.
40 "Stress has a very bad reputation. It's in pretty bad shape, PR-wise," acknowledges Firdaus Dhabhar, an associate professor of psychiatry and behavioral science at Stanford. "And justifiably so," he adds.

Much of what we know about the physical and
45 mental toll of chronic stress stems from seminal work by Robert Sapolsky beginning in the late 1970s. Sapolsky, a neuroendocrinologist, was among the first to make the connection that the hormones released during the fight-or-flight response—the ones that
50 helped our ancestors avoid becoming dinner—have deleterious effects when the stress is severe and sustained. Especially insidious, chronic exposure to one of these hormones, cortisol, causes brain changes that make it increasingly difficult to shut the stress
55 response down.

But take heart: Recent research paints a different portrait of stress, one in which it indeed has a positive side. "There's good stress, there's tolerable stress, and there's toxic stress," says Bruce McEwen of
60 Rockefeller University, an expert on stress and the brain who trained both Sapolsky and Dhabhar.

Situations we typically perceive as stressful—a confrontation with a co-worker, the pressure to perform, a to-do list that's too long—are not the toxic
65 type of stress that's been linked to serious health issues such as cardiovascular disease, autoimmune disorders, severe depression and cognitive impairment. Short bouts of this sort of everyday stress can actually be a good thing: Just think of the exhilaration of
70 the deadline met or the presentation crushed, the triumph of holding it all together. And, perhaps not surprisingly, it turns out that beating yourself up about being stressed is counterproductive, as worrying about the negative consequences can in itself exacerbate any
75 ill effects.

1

Which of the following statements best describes the relationship between the passages?

A) Passage 2 considers some positive aspects of a phenomenon that Passage 1 presents in negative terms.
B) Passage 2 questions a finding that is praised in Passage 1.
C) Passage 2 provides an explanations for a longstanding problem that is discussed in Passage 1.
D) Passage 2 relates a personal experience that is described objectively in Passage 1.

2

The authors of both passages would most likely agree with which of the following statements?

A) Stress is directly responsible for causing many serious ailments.
B) Some types of stress can improve people's ability to cope with difficult situations.
C) Frequent exposure to stress can exacerbate existing conditions.
D) Stress levels in are genetically determined in some groups of people.

3

Which choice provides the best evidence that the author of Passage 2 would agree with the claim made in lines 1-2 of passage 1?

A) Lines 33-36 ("Two-thirds…years")
B) Lines 48-52 ("the hormones…sustained")
C) Lines 62-66 ("Situations…issues")
D) Lines 71-73 ("And…counterproductive")

4

The author of Passage 2 would most likely attribute the effects of chronic stress described in lines 18-20 of Passage 1 to

A) familial obligations.
B) Increased academic demands.
C) professional conflicts.
D) body chemicals.

5

Which choice provides the best evidence for the answer to the previous question?

A) Lines 29-31 ("According…10")
B) Lines 37-39 ("More…stress")
C) Lines 52-55 ("Especially…down")
D) Lines 56-58 ("But…side")

Official Guide/Khan Academy Paired Passage Questions

Test 1

49
50

51
52   **Evidence**

Test 2

30
31
32

Test 3

38   Function
39
40   Agree
41

Test 4

36
37   **Evidence**

38
39   **Evidence**

40

Explanations: Paired Passage Exercises

1.1 C

The easiest way to answer this question is to use the main points. Main point P1: industrial food = bad, buy local (=a practice). Main point P2: Buying local doesn't help the environment (=expresses doubt). Relationship: negative. The only answer with negative wording is C), making it the answer.

1.2 B

Lines 5-8 of P1 state that *Much of the food grown in the breadbasket surrounding us must be shipped across the country to distribution centers before it makes its way back to our supermarket shelves.* The author of Passage 2 does not make the point nearly as explicitly, but he does state in lines 67-69 that *world trade in fruits, vegetables – fresh and processed – doubled in the 1980s and increased by 30 percent between 1990 and 2001*, directly suggesting that people consume an enormous amount of food produced far away. The author of P1 only would agree with A) and C), and the author of P2 only would agree with D).

1.3-4 C, D

Start by defining "the discussion" in lines 8-14 of P1: transporting food is bad for the environment. What would the author of P2 think of that? If you pay close attention to the conclusion, the answer is fairly straightforward and gives you the answer to both this question and the following question. Even if you don't remember the conclusion, the fact that 1.4 provides a line reference at the end of passage – where the main point is usually located – indicates you should check that section first. In the conclusion, the author of P2 is pretty clear that "food miles" account for only a small portion (1.8 percent) of Britain's carbon dioxide emission. Therefore, most carbon dioxide emissions (98.2 percent, to be exact) must come from "other sources." That corresponds most directly to C).

1.5-6 B, C

The biggest danger with this question is that you will take it at face value – you might reason that because the authors of P1 are in favor of fresh food, they would obviously have a positive attitude toward it. The problem, however, is that the author of P2 is talking about "fresh" food that has been transported long distances – exactly what the author of P1 is against. So the answer must indicate opposition, making B) the only option. The correct lines in 1.6 must therefore convey the idea that food transported over long distances isn't quite so healthy. C) is correct because in context of the author of P1's argument, the statement that *the quality of a food is derived…from how it is prepared and cared for all the way until it reaches our mouths* implies that food transported halfway around the world might not be so fresh and high-quality after all.

2.1 D

The key to answering this question correctly is simply to understand the most basic relationship between the passages – P1 discusses a situation in general (=theoretically), as indicated by the repeated references to "Nature," "a state," "creatures," and "man," whereas P2 is specific, alluding to particular individuals and institutions (Parliament, the British constitution, the tea tax). That corresponds to D). Careful with A), though. It's almost right, but not quite. Hamilton does not provide a *personal account* – the word *I* never appears.

2.2 A

The author of P1 states that men can naturally *order their actions…without asking leave or depending upon the will of another man.* The author of P2 states that *No reason can be assigned why one man should exercise any power, or preeminence over his fellow creatures more than another; unless they have <u>voluntarily</u> veiled him with it.* In other words, both authors believe that people are naturally free and should remain so.

2.3-4 B, A

If you understand the point of both passages and know that the authors of the passages generally agree, then you can make an assumption upfront that B) is likely to be correct. You just need to find the lines that support that answer. Since the latter part of the passage is devoted to discussing the specific conflict between the British and the colonists, you can assume the answer to 2.4 will be at the beginning of the passage, narrowing your choices to A) and B). Sure enough, Hamilton essentially echoes Locke in lines 36-39, repeating the idea that everyone is equal in a state of nature. Hamilton simply adds one extra condition, namely that no one can legitimately hold authority unless it is explicitly granted. That is simply another way of saying that no one has "inherent authority" to rule.

3.1 A

The easiest way to answer this question is to use the main points. P1: stress = bad. P2 = stress = bad + good. That is essentially what A) says. B) is incorrect because although there is some disagreement between the passages, P2 does not question a specific finding; it simply provides a more nuanced look at stress. C) is incorrect because P1 does not discuss a "longstanding problem" – it simply describes the dangerous effects of stress. D) is incorrect because the author of P2 does not provide a "personal" account; the word *I* never appears.

3.2 C

The statement *While stress doesn't cause any single disease…it makes most diseases significantly worse* in P1 directly supports C); and the statement *hormones released during the fight-or-flight response…have deleterious effects when the stress is severe and sustained* in P2 suggests that the author of P2 would be likely to agree with C) as well. A) is directly contradicted by P1; the author of P2 only would agree with B); and neither passage provides support for D).

3.3 B

This is essentially the same question as 3.2, just worded slightly differently. Because the question is phrased in such a complex manner, you need to break it down. Start by defining the claim in lines 1-2 of P1: stress is very dangerous. Next, what lines in P2 support that idea? P2 is arranged in classic "they say/I say" format, and the discussion of the dangerous effects of stress is what "they say." The correct lines are thus most likely to be located at the beginning of the passage, narrowing the choices to A) and B). A) does not work because lines 33-36 simply discuss people's attempts to reduce stress; they do not directly state that stress is dangerous. B) is correct because lines 48-52 explicitly state that stress has "deleterious" (harmful) effects.

3.4-5 D, C

What does the author of P1 says about the effects of chronic stress? Basically, they're very dangerous. Unless you happen to remember the answer from Passage 2, the easiest way to approach this question is to plug in line references from 3.5 in order. The negative effects of stress are discussed at the beginning of the passage, but unfortunately, all of the line references provided are fairly close to the beginning. A) is incorrect because lines 29-31 only provide statistics about stress levels; they say nothing about why stress is dangerous. B) is incorrect for the same reason as A); careful not to extrapolate that academic demands are the cause of stress, just because the passage mentions teens and young adults. There is absolutely no mention of academics whatsoever. C) provides the answer to 3.4 and 3.5 because lines 52-55 provide a clear-cut explanation for why stress is so harmful: cortisol (= a hormone) prevents the brain from shutting the stress response down.

14. Infographics

If you're not accustomed to working with graphs and tables, infographic questions can be intimidating. Without a doubt, shifting from dealing sentences to lines and numbers can be jarring. You're solidly in reading mode, then wham! You have to answer a question about a…graph? This shift can easily leave you feeling overwhelmed and anxious.

The good news, however, is that graphic questions are rarely as complicated as they appear. No matter how unfamiliar the terminology may be, all the information you need to answer graph-related questions will be right in front of you. These questions are set up precisely so that you *can* figure them without outside knowledge; if you stay calm and consider things carefully, there's a good chance you'll be fine.

In fact, questions that involve graphics are often simpler than they initially appear. While graphs/charts are always related in some way to the passages they accompany, **many infographic questions can be answered on the basis of the graph or chart alone; you do not need to take the passage into account at all**.

Infographic questions can be divided into three main types:

1) Questions that require that graph only.

2) Questions that refer to both the graph and the passage but that can be answered using only one or the other.

3) Questions that require both the graph and the passage.

While the first and third types are fairly straightforward in terms of what information you need to consider, the second type can be somewhat trickier. Because these questions refer to both the graph and the passage, is very easy to think that you **must** look at both; however, doing so can be unnecessarily time consuming and confusing. In this chapter, we're going to break down examples of all three types so that you can understand what you need to do when.

Reading Graphs: Finding the Point and Skimming

Although graphs and passages might strike you as two completely different entities, reading a text and interpreting a graph have more in common than you might suspect. One simply conveys information in words while the other conveys it in bars and numbers.

Like passages, most graphs have a "point" to convey, and they are often much more efficient about conveying it than written words. In fact, that's precisely why authors use them. (Ever heard the expression "a picture is worth a thousand words?") Representing data visually can allow readers to quickly grasp what a writer might otherwise use up a lot of space explaining, saving both readers and writers considerable mental exertion.

Just as you can skim passages to get a general idea of what they are saying, you can also "skim" graphs visually to get a general sense of the information they convey. And again, your goal is to avoid getting caught in the details for as long as possible.

Here are some things to notice:

- What is the shape of the graph? Does it go up, down, or both?

- Are changes steady, or is there a big jump somewhere? If so, where?

- Is there an "outlier" point with a value very different from that of the other points?

- Are there items whose values don't change at all?

If you approach graphic questions with a general understanding of what the graph conveys, you can often identify the incorrect answer or eliminate multiple incorrect answers quickly.

For example, consider the following graph.

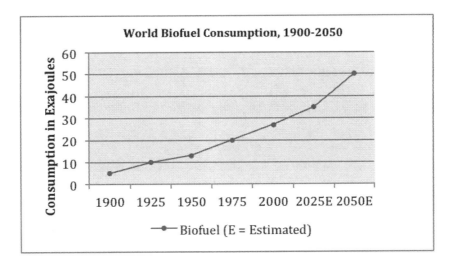

The first thing to notice is that this graph uses a unit of measurement – the exajoule (y-axis title) – that very few high school students will be familiar with. That's the type of wording that makes these questions *seem* so difficult. In reality, the terminology is **completely irrelevant**. If you understand that an exajoule is a unit of measurement, you can ignore it.

So what you're looking at is this:

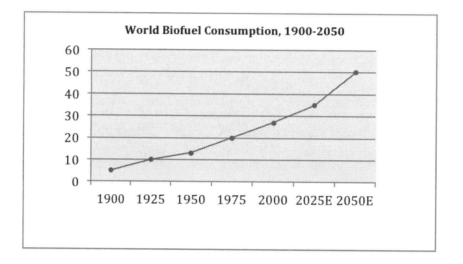

With the terminology taken away, you can focus on the essential: the graph represents a steady increase over time. In addition, values increase by about the same amount (5-10 points) during most of the intervals, except for the period from 2025 to 2050, which is larger (about 15 points). At no point do values fall, and no two values are ever the same.

Now, let's consider the title of the graph: World Biofuel Consumption, 1900-2050. The point of a title is to tell you what something is about, and graphs are no different. In this case, the title combined with what we've already determined tells us that biofuel use rose steadily throughout the 20th century and will continue to rise steadily into the 21st.

The "main point" could thus be something along the lines of "biofuel use UP 20-21C." Using that information, we can infer that the correct answer to any accompanying question must be consistent with that idea.

We can also infer that answer choices indicating any of the following would be **incorrect**:

- Biofuel consumption peaked in a year prior to 2050.

- Biofuel consumption decreased at any point.

- Biofuel consumption in the 20th century was greater than it will be in the 21st.

- The largest rise in biofuel consumption occurred at a point other than 2025-2050.

To be clear, you do not need to figure all of this out before looking at the answers. Your goal is simply to get the gist so that you can eliminate any answer that is inconsistent with it.

Reading Between the Lines

One thing to be aware of is that some questions may ask you to read between the lines of the graph – literally. That is, they will ask you to determine information about points that are not directly represented on the graph but can be determined from the information provided.

For example, take a look at this graph:

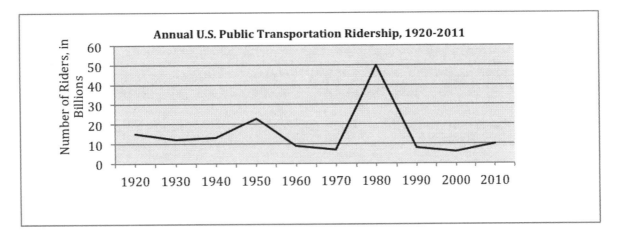

All of the years listed along the x-axis are in multiples of 10 (1920, 1930, etc.); however, there are also tick marks halfway *between* each set of years. You could therefore encounter a question that looks like this:

1

According to the graph, which statement is true about the number of riders who used public transportation in 1945?

A) It was substantially higher than the number of riders who used public transportation in 1950.
B) It was wildly out of proportion to the number of riders who used transportation during the previous two decades.
C) It was similar to the number of riders who used public transportation a decade later.
D) It was lower than the number of riders who used public transportation in 2010.

When you look at the graph, you will of course notice that 1945 does not appear. Both 1940 and 1950 do appear, however, so logically the tick mark between them represents 1945.

What does the graph tell us about the number of public transportation riders in 1945? Drawing a line from the tick mark, we can see that it was a little under 20 billion. (Remember that the numbers represent billions; the zeroes are omitted for the sake of clarity). It's a little lower than in 1950 but otherwise around the same as it was during the surrounding decades. Now that we've figured out some basics, we're going to look at the answers.

A) No. Remember we just said that the number in 1945 was *lower* than it was in 1950.

B) The extreme phrase *wildly out of proportion* immediately suggests that this answer is wrong. Besides, the only part of the graph that's really out of proportion to the rest is the part representing 1980. So we're going to assume this is wrong.

C) A decade later was 1955. If we look at the tick mark between 1950 and 1960 and trace a line up (or just compare visually), we end up with a point in roughly the same range as that for 1945. So C) works. Just to be safe, though, we're going to check D).

D) No, this is backwards. Ridership in 2010 was lower. That means ridership in 1945 was *higher*.

So the answer is C).

Multiple Variables

The graphs we've looked at so far have only contained one variable – that is, they have only charted the rise and/or fall of a single factor. Unfortunately, many of the graphs you are asked to work with on the SAT will contain more than one variable. When this is the case, you should **always start by noting the key difference between the lines** (or sectors, in the case of a bar graph).

The biggest difference (or similarity) between the lines is the "point" of the graph.

Here are some questions to consider

- Do the lines move in a similar way, or do they move in different ways? (e.g. do both lines rise or fall, or does one line rise while the other falls?)

- Is one line consistently high and the other consistently low?

- Do both lines ever pass through the same point?

- If a large increase/decline occurs, does it occur in the same place for both lines, or does it occur in different places?

I cannot stress how important this step is. While it may seem as if these questions are asking you to process an enormous amount of information, the reality is that only a small portion of what you see will actually be relevant. Furthermore, the questions will almost invariably target the most significant differences between the lines or sectors. If you've already established those differences upfront, you're already most of the way to the answer.

316

Let's consider this somewhat altered version of a graph we examined a little while ago:

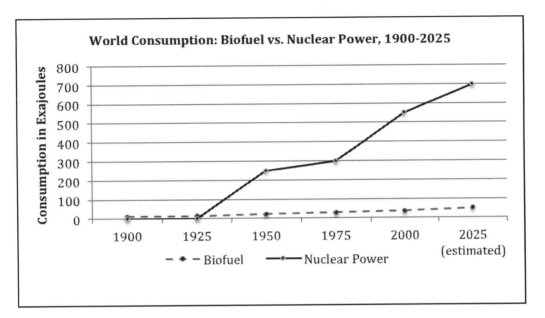

When we look at the graph, we can immediately perceive the difference between the two energy sources: biofuel use rose slowly throughout the 20th century and will continue to rise slowly throughout the 21st century. In contrast, nuclear power use rose very quickly in the mid-20th century and is continuing to rise quickly into the 21st century.

Our "main point" could therefore be something like "NP way up, BF up slowly" (nuclear power use is going way up, while biofuel use is rising slowly).

We could even be asked to deal with three variables:

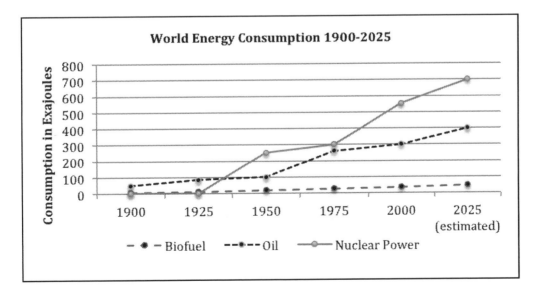

In this case, the main thing to notice is that biofuel use rose slowly, nuclear power use rose quickly, and oil use was somewhere in the middle.

Now let's look at a couple more graph-only questions. The most straightforward of these will simply ask you to identify the answer best supported by the graph. In other words, what is the point of the graph?

Let's consider the second version of the graph on the previous page, the one with the three variables. (Note that on the SAT, graphic questions will often appear on a different page from the graphs themselves, so you will need to be comfortable flipping back and forth.)

Remember the big picture: nuclear energy – high; oil – medium; biofuel – low. In addition, the lines for oil and nuclear power are about equal at 1975.

1

Which choice is supported by data in the graph?

A) The amount of oil and the amount of nuclear power used in 1950 were roughly the same.
B) By 2025, more energy will be obtained from nuclear energy than from oil or biofuel.
C) The use of biofuels is predicted to decline between 2000 and 2025.
D) Oil use rose at a dramatically higher rate than did biofuel use between 1975 and 2000.

We could work through these answers one-by-one (and in fact we're going to do so in a moment), but first let's consider the **shortcut**. The overall "point" of the graph is that nuclear energy has been way outstripping biofuel and oil for more than a century and will continue to do so in the immediate future.

Which answer comes closest to saying that? B). It simply states what the graph shows most obviously – by 2025, nuclear energy will be far ahead.

Playing process of elimination:

A) is incorrect because the oil and biofuel use were about the same in 1975, not 1950.

C) is incorrect because the use of biofuel is expected to increase slightly, not decrease.

D) is incorrect because although oil use did rise at a higher rate than biofuel use between 1975 and 2000, it did so at a *slightly* higher rate, not a *dramatically* higher rate. Don't forget that it only takes one wrong word to make an answer wrong.

Now we're going to try something a little bit more challenging.

"Backwards" Graphs and "Trick" Answers

In all of the graphs we've looked at so far, one thing was pretty straightforward: a line going up indicated that values were rising, and a line going down indicated that values were falling. Simple...right? Well, maybe not always.

We're going to try an experiment. Look at the graph below, and do your best to answer the question that follows.

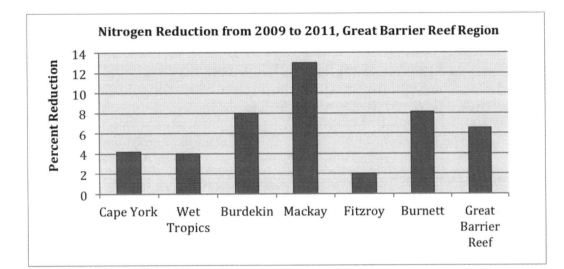

1

Which choice about nitrogen levels in 2011 is supported by data in the graph?

A) The amount of nitrogen in the water was highest at Mackay.
B) Nitrogen levels at Fitzroy were lower than than those at Cape York.
C) The amount of nitrogen in the water at Mackay declined by the largest percentage.
D) The amount of nitrogen in the water was generally comparable at Cape York and Wet Tropics.

If you picked A) or thought that there was more than one correct answer, congratulations – you've just fallen into the trap designed to ensnare all but the savviest graph readers.

The key to this question is to pay very close attention to its title. The title tells us that the bars indicate nitrogen *reduction*. The higher the bar, the larger the reduction, i.e. the amount by which nitrogen decreased. So higher bars = *lower* levels of nitrogen. If you miss that very important fact, you risk misinterpreting the graph entirely.

Let's work through the answer choices to see how that misunderstanding can play out.

A) is a classic "trick" answer, placed first to sidetrack you. It plays on the assumption that you'll see the highest bar in A) and leap to assume that indicates that nitrogen *levels* were highest there. But of course it's not nitrogen levels that increased, but rather nitrogen reduction. Moral of the story: if you see an answer that looks too easy when you haven't actually thought about the question, there's a good chance it's wrong.

B) has a similar problem. It assumes that you'll see that the bar for Fitzroy is lower than that for Cape York and leap to what seems to be a logical conclusion. The problem is that the graph actually tells us that nitrogen levels decreased less at Fitzroy than they did at Cape York. Furthermore, we know nothing about the original amount of nitrogen at either place – it's entirely possible that nitrogen levels at Fitzroy were higher than those at Cape York.

C) is correct because it states the "point" of the graph: nitrogen levels declined by a greater percentage at Mackay than they did at any of the other regions shown. Remember: in this case, a high bar = a large *decrease*.

D) is incorrect for the same reason as B) – we know nothing about the nitrogen amounts themselves. The graph only tells us that nitrogen levels at Cape York and Wet Tropics declined by similar percentages.

Another potential "trick" the SAT could throw at you involves not graphs but the wording of the questions. It is important to understand that although infographic questions may look very different from other questions, **they are still reading questions**; you must pay careful attention to how they are phrased. **An answer may accurately convey the information represented in the graph but not answer the particular question asked.**

One factor that you must consider is **scope** – that is, whether the question asks about a **specific feature** or piece of data in the graph, or whether it asks you to **provide an overview** or understand a **general trend**. If, for example, a question asks you which answer best summarizes the information in the graph, you could see an option that correctly describes a specific aspect of that graph. Although that answer may be factually correct, it will still be wrong because it does not answer the question at hand.

For example, consider this graph:

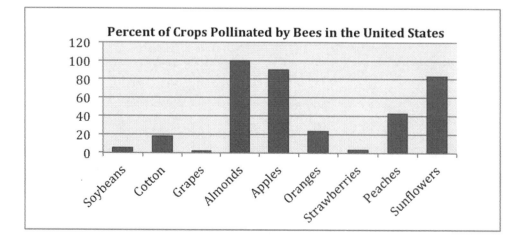

Which information best summarizes the information presented in the graph?

A) Every crop grown in the United States relies on bees for at least 20 percent of its pollination.
B) Bees are responsible for pollinating 100 percent of almonds around the world.
C) The percent of peaches pollinated by bees is more than double the percent of cotton.
D) The percent of United States crops pollinated by bees varies dramatically.

The question tells us that are looking for an answer that provides an **overview** of the information represented in the graph. **Answers that contain specific facts and/or figures are therefore likely to be wrong.**

Let's start by considering the big picture of the graph. One striking feature is how **varied** the bars are. A few of the bars are clustered near the top, a few are near the bottom, and only one is right in the middle. If we wanted to write a "main point," we could say something like "percent/bee poll. varies, but mostly very high/low."

While we could check out the answers one by one, we're actually going to apply that information to create a **shortcut**.

Three of the answers contain specific amounts – A) contains 20 percent, B) contains 100 percent, and C) contains *double*. Only D) does not contain a specific amount, and sure enough, it is consistent with our summary: the percent of US crops pollinated by bees ranges from just above zero all the way up to 100. So D) is the correct answer.

If you had checked the answers out one at a time, you could have gotten into some trouble.

A) is pretty obviously wrong. Some of the bars are much lower than 20 percent.

B) is a little trickier – it's half-right, half wrong. The title of the graph tells us that we're only dealing with crops in the United States, but this answer refers to the *world*. So even though the graph does in fact indicate that bees pollinate 100% of almonds in the U.S., this answer is beyond the scope of the passage. It could be true, but we don't know.

C) is the answer you really need to be careful with. The bar for peaches is indeed a little more than twice as high as it is for cotton, but this answer choice only deals with **two specific crops**, whereas the question asks us to **summarize**. So even though this answer is true, it's still wrong. If you checked the answers in order, though, there's a reasonable chance you'd get fooled and never even look at D).

Tables

Some infographic questions will not use graphs at all but rather tables. For example, in a science passage discussing the antibiotic-resistant bacteria, you could see something like the table below. MRSA is a type of bacteria that is especially resistant to common antibiotics.

Antibiotic	General Effectiveness %	General Resistance %	MRSA Effectiveness %	MRSA Resistance %
Erithromycin	31.94	68.06	26.92	73.08
Vancomycin	100	0	100	0
Mupirocin	90.28	9.72	73.08	26.92
Penicillin	5	95	0	100
Clindamicin	83.33	16.67	69.23	30.77
Rifampicin	86.11	13.89	61.54	38.46

Don't let the complicated names distract you. Focus on the numbers, and compare the similar columns: effective vs. effective, resistant vs. resistant.

The major thing to notice is that the "effective" numbers are always higher than the "MRSA effective" numbers. So basically, the chart is telling us that antibiotics that are generally effective are a lot less effective against MRSA. That makes sense: as stated above, MRSA is a particularly antibiotic-resistant type of bacteria.

1

Based on the table, which antibiotic showed the greatest discrepancy between its general effectiveness and its effectiveness against MRSA?

A) Erithryomycin
B) Vancomycin
C) Penicillin
D) Rifampicin

This question isn't necessarily hard – remember, all the information you need is right in front of you – but it does have the potential to be confusing.

The first thing to do is to make sure you're clear on what the question is asking and do some basic work upfront to determine what sort of information the correct answer must contain.

In this case, the key word is *discrepancy* – the question is asking which antibiotic shows the greatest **difference** between its general effectiveness and its effectiveness against MRSA.

The correct answer will therefore have a much higher number in the "general effectiveness" column than in the "MRSA effectiveness" column. One by one, we're going to check each answer. We're going to round the numbers to make things easy.

A) 32 vs. 27. That's pretty close. We'll leave it but assume it's wrong.

B) 100 vs. 100. There's no difference. Eliminate it.

C) 5 vs. 0. Pretty much the same as A). That leaves…

D) 86 vs. 62. That's a significant difference. So D) is correct.

Paired Graphics

Another potential twist the SAT could throw at you is to pair two graphics and ask about the relationship between them.

Once again, while these questions may look enormously complicated, the reality is that they will almost certainly focus on the graphs' most striking features. Only a couple of pieces of information will actually be relevant to you.

For example, consider the graphics below:

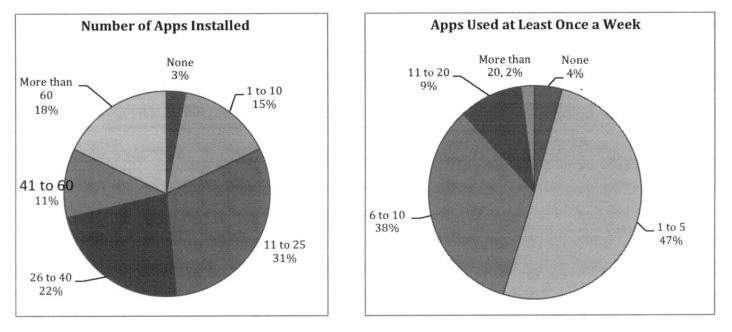

Adapted from "People Love Their Smartphones, but…" Scientific American.

Taken together, the graphs most directly support the idea that

A) the number of apps people install has risen significantly.
B) The majority of people use more than 10 different apps at least once per week.
C) people download many more apps than they actually use.
D) people's social networks strongly influence their choice of apps.

When you look at a pair of graphs like this, the first thing you want to notice is whether any of the sectors are particularly large or small. The second graph should grab your attention because one of its sectors is so large – almost 50% of the total. In contrast, the first graph is distributed somewhat more evenly. You can assume that difference will be significant.

Now consider what information the graphs depict.

The first graph shows the number of apps people download, indicating that the majority of people (53%) have between 11 and 40 apps, and 51% have more than 25 apps. So basically, most people have a lot of apps.

The second graph shows how many apps people actually use on a regular basis. This is where that huge sector becomes important. It indicates that a significant number (47%) of people only use between one and five apps. Furthermore, the next-largest sector indicates that an additional 38% only use between 6 and 10 apps. We know from the first graph, however, that most people have over 11 apps installed, with significant numbers having more than 25.

The difference between the number of apps people have and the number of apps they use therefore suggests that people are installing an awful lot of apps that they don't really use. And that's what C) says.

A) is off topic. The graphs show nothing about how the number of apps installed has changed over time. They only show how many apps people install vs. how many they use.

B) is incorrect because information from the second graph shows that the majority of people (51%) either use no apps weekly (4%) or between 1 and 5 apps (47%).

D) is off topic as well. There's no information about social networks in either of the graphs. So that again leaves C).

To Synthesize...Or Not

Now that we've looked at bunch of graph-only questions, we're going to add in a passage.

As discussed earlier in this chapter, questions that refer to both the graphic and the passage come in two varieties: one type requires you to take both sources into account. These questions tend to be the most difficult, but there is also no "trick" to them. They simply tell you what information to obtain to answer the question.

The other type refers to both sources but can actually be answered using only one source. You can check the other source for confirmation, but you don't necessarily need it. Let's start with a relatively straightforward question of this type.

We're going to come back to this graph:

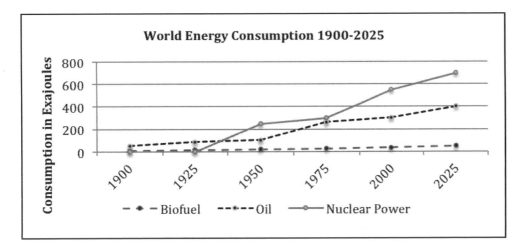

1

The passage and the graph are in agreement that in the twenty-first century, nuclear power will

A) constitute a significant source of energy.
B) lag behind other major energy sources.
C) eliminate the reliance on biofuel and oil.
D) allow for the creation of new technologies.

There's a reason we're looking at this question without a passage – we don't actually need one. The question *tells* us that the passage and the question are in agreement, so if it's true for one, it must be true for the other. The question is so specific and the graph so basic that it would be virtually impossible to create answers true for the graph but not the passage.

So once again, what's the "point" of this graph? The use of nuclear power has been rising, and nuclear power will provide a lot of energy in the 21st century. That's what A) says.

Now let's look at a graph paired with a passage.

This passage is adapted from Sharon Tregaskis, "What Bees Tell Us About Global Climate Change," © 2010 by *Johns Hopkins Magazine*.

Standing in the apiary on the grounds of the U.S. Department of Agriculture's Bee Research Laboratory in Beltsville, Maryland, Wayne Esaias digs through the canvas shoulder bag leaning against his leg in search of
5 the cable he uses to download data. It's dusk as he runs the cord from his laptop—precariously perched on the beam of a cast-iron platform scale—to a small, battery-operated data logger attached to the spring inside the scale's steel column. In the 1800s, a scale like this
10 would have weighed sacks of grain or crates of apples, peaches, and melons. Since arriving at the USDA's bee lab in January 2007, this scale has been loaded with a single item: a colony of *Apis mellifera*, the fuzzy, black-and-yellow honey bee. An attached, 12-bit
15 recorder captures the hive's weight to within a 10th of a pound, along with a daily register of relative ambient humidity and temperature.

On this late January afternoon, during a comparatively balmy respite between the blizzards that
20 dumped several feet of snow on the Middle Atlantic states, the bees, their honey, and the wooden boxes in which they live weigh 94.5 pounds. In mid-July, as last year's unusually long nectar flow finally ebbed, the whole contraption topped out at 275 pounds, including
25 nearly 150 pounds of honey. "Right now, the colony is in a cluster about the size of a soccer ball," says Esaias, who's kept bees for nearly two decades and knows without lifting the lid what's going on inside this hive. "The center of the cluster is where the queen is, and
30 they're keeping her at 93 degrees—the rest are just hanging there, tensing their flight muscles to generate heat." Provided that they have enough calories to fuel their winter workout, a healthy colony can survive as far north as Anchorage, Alaska. "They slowly eat their
35 way up through the winter," he says. "It's a race: Will they eat all their honey before the nectar flows, or not?" To make sure their charges win that race, apiarists have long relied on scale hives for vital management clues. By tracking daily weight variations, a beekeeper can
40 discern when the colony needs a nutritional boost to carry it through lean times, whether to add extra combs for honey storage and even detect incursions by marauding robber bees—all without disturbing the colony. A graph of the hive's weight—which can

45 increase by as much as 35 pounds a day in some parts of the United States during peak nectar flow — reveals the date on which the bees' foraging was was most productive and provides a direct record of successful pollination. "Around here, the bees make
50 their living in the month of May," says Esaias, noting that his bees often achieve daily spikes of 25 pounds, the maximum in Maryland. "There's almost no nectar coming in for the rest of the year." A scientist by training and career oceanographer at NASA, Esaias
55 established the Mink Hollow Apiary in his Highland, Maryland, backyard in 1992 with a trio of hand-me-down hives and an antique platform scale much like the one at the Beltsville bee lab. Ever since, he's maintained a meticulous record of the bees' daily
60 weight, as well as weather patterns and such details as his efforts to keep them healthy. In late 2006, honey bees nationwide began disappearing in an ongoing syndrome dubbed colony collapse disorder (CCD). Entire hives went empty as bees inexplicably
65 abandoned their young and their honey. Commercial beekeepers reported losses up to 90 percent, and the large-scale farmers who rely on honey bees to ensure rich harvests of almonds, apples, and sunflowers became very, very nervous. Looking for clues, Esaias
70 turned to his own records. While the resulting graphs threw no light on the cause of CCD, a staggering trend emerged: In the span of just 15 seasons, the date on which his Mink Hollow bees brought home the most nectar had shifted by two weeks—from late May
75 to the middle of the month. "I was shocked when I plotted this up," he says. "It was right under my nose, going on the whole time." The epiphany would lead Esaias to launch a series of research collaborations, featuring honey bees and other pollinators, to investigate
80 the relationships among plants, pollinators, and weather patterns. Already, the work has begun to reveal insights into the often unintended consequences of human interventions in natural and agricultural ecosystems, and exposed significant gaps in how we understand the
85 effect climate change will have on everything from food production to terrestrial ecology.

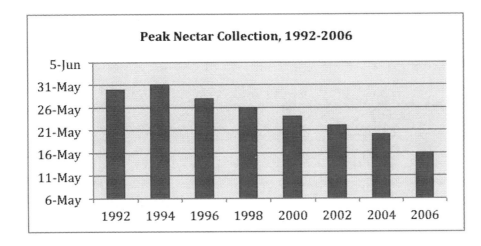

Peak Nectar Collection, 1992-2006

1

Data in the graph provide the most direct support for which idea in the passage?

OR:

Which concept is supported by the passage and by the information in the graph?

A) Human intervention in agriculture can have unintended consequences.
B) Peak nectar collection now occurs earlier than it did in recent years.
C) Bees that consume sufficient nutrients during the winter can survive in northern regions.
D) Bees collect the largest amount of honey during the month of May.

Let's consider how the question is constructed. **All of the answers restate points that are mentioned in the passage, so you don't need to look at the passage to check whether a given answer is there.** The question itself gives you all the necessary information from the passage. Your only job is to figure out which one of the points the graph supports. The simplest way to do that is figure out the "point" of the graph – by definition, it must be the same point as that presented in the passage.

How do you figure out the point of the graph? Start by looking at the title and the data in each of the axes. The title indicates the graph represents when peak nectar collection occurred (when the highest amount of nectar was collected). The x-axis shows years, and the y-axis shows dates in May, with high bars representing dates late in May and low bars representing dates early in May.

The fact that the bars get progressively shorter indicates that the peak nectar collection occurred steadily earlier in May between 1992 and 2006. That's exactly what B) says.

The question could also be asked this way:

Do the data in the graph provide support for Wayne Esaias's claim that the time when his bees were collecting the most nectar had shifted by two weeks?

A) Yes, because the data provide evidence that peak collection moved from late May to mid-May.
B) Yes, because in each year, peak collection occurred during the month of May.
C) No, because the graph indicates that peak collection shifted from the beginning of June to the beginning of May.
D) No, because peak collection time did not move earlier in every two-year period.

Once again, the question itself provides all the information from the passage you need to know, namely that Esaias claimed that his bees were collecting the most honey two weeks earlier than they used to. You do not need to consult the passage at all.

And once again, the easiest way to approach this question is to answer it for real upfront so that you do not become confused by the answer choices.

As discussed before, the graph shows that peak nectar production declined from late May to mid-May between 1992 and 2006. That's two weeks, so yes, the graph does support Esaias's claim. That makes A) the correct answer.

Note: Answer choices will sometimes use slightly different terminology from the passage or the question, requiring you to connect the original idea and the rephrased version. Here, for example, the question refers to the bees "collecting the most nectar" while the graph refers to "peak nectar production." It's the same concept, just expressed two different ways.

Now we're going to look at a question that actually requires you to work with both a graph and a passage. We're going to keep the same passage but use this graph instead:

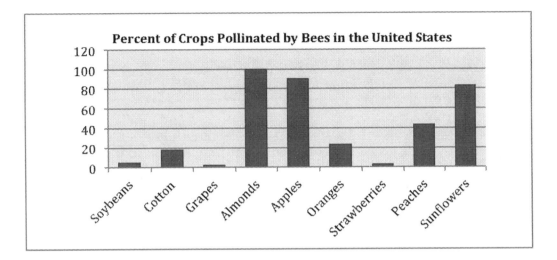

Percent of Crops Pollinated by Bees in the United States

1

The information in the graph best supports which idea in the passage?

A) Lines 9-11 ("In the 1800s...melon")
B) Lines 44-49 ("A graph...pollination")
C) Lines 65-69 ("Commercial...nervous")
D) Lines 72-75 ("In...month")

In this case, the line-reference construction of the answer choices leaves you no choice but to go back to the passage. That does not, however, mean that you are exempt from figuring some basic things out beforehand.

First, we're going to take a moment and summarize the information presented in the graph. Let's reiterate the main point: "percent/bee poll. varies, but mostly very high/low."

How does the graph relate to the passage? The passage discusses the decline in the bee population, and the graph shows the percentage of pollination from bees that each crop receives.

The graph therefore allows us to make some reasonable assumptions about how different crops would be affected by the bees' disappearance. Crops that receive most of the pollination from bees (high bars) would be strongly affected, while crops that receive less pollination from bees (low bars) would be less affected.

Now that we've figure out the basics, we're going to look at the answer choices.

A) **In the 1800s, a scale like this would have weighed sacks of grain or crates of apples, peaches, and melons.**

Apples and peaches are *included* in the graph, but this answer is otherwise off-topic. The graph shows the percent of each crop pollinated by bees; weight has nothing to do with that.

B) **A graph of the hive's weight—which can increase by as much as 35 pounds a day in some parts of the United States during peak nectar flow – reveals the date on which the bees' foraging was most productive and provides a direct record of successful pollination.**

Don't be fooled by the word *graph*. This answer has the same problem as A): the lines are about the relationship between weight and foraging, and the graph is about pollination.

C) **Commercial beekeepers reported losses up to 90 percent, and the large-scale farmers who rely on honey bees to ensure rich harvests of almonds, apples, and sunflowers became very, very nervous.**

The graph doesn't depict losses, but it does depict almonds, apples, and sunflowers. In fact, those are the crops that get the highest percentage of the pollination from bees (highest bars). It follows logically that the bees' disappearance would affect those crops the most severely, making beekeepers nervous. So C) works.

D) **In the span of just 15 seasons, the date on which his Mink Hollow bees brought home the most nectar had shifted by two weeks—from late May to the middle of the month.**

Once again, completely off-topic. The graph tells us absolutely nothing about dates, or when the change in nectar production occurred.

So the answer is C).

You could also encounter a question asking you to infer the author's attitude toward the information in the graphic:

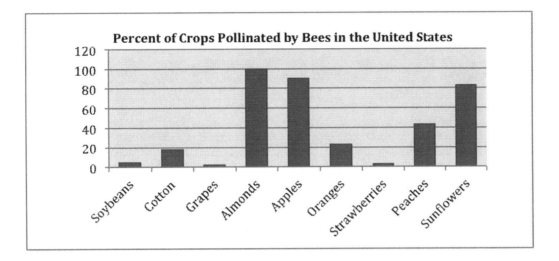

1

The author of the passage would most likely consider the information in the graph to be

A) questionable data that the author would dispute.
B) intriguing but unsupported by personal observations.
C) an accurate illustration of why some farmers are concerned.
D) more accurate for some regions than for others.

At first glance, it might look as if the answer could be anywhere. The question is very general, and there are no line references. If you stop and think about what's actually in the graph, however, you can narrow things down a bit.

The title of the graph provides some very important information. It tells you that the graph is about *crops*. Logically, then, the necessary section of the passage must relate to crops in some way. Based on that information, the words *farmers* in C) and *some regions* in D) seem to suggest that the answer is likely to be one of the places, with C) the more likely option. You don't know for sure, of course, but they're worth checking *first*.

If you scan for the word *farmers*, you'll discover it appears in one place: line 67. And if you read the entire sentence in which it appears, you'll see that large scale farmers are particularly concerned because they rely on almonds, apples, and sunflowers – exactly the crops that are most dependent on bee pollination and therefore most likely to be affected by the bees' disappearance. So the answer is in fact C).

In another twist, this question could be paired with a supporting evidence question:

1

Which lines from the passage provide the best
evidence for the previous question?

A) Lines 49-50 ("Around…May")
B) Lines 65-69 ("Commercial…nervous)
C) Lines 72-75 ("In…month")
D) Lines 81-83 ("Already…ecosystems")

In this case, the process for answering the previous question is similar. Although the paired
structure looks more complicated, it actually gives you some help by providing specific
possibilities for where the answer is located.

You still need to start by reiterating the big picture of the graph for yourself, though. If you
know that it focuses on specific crops, you can check each set of lines for references to
crops. Then, simply plug the line references into the previous question as you would for any
other supporting evidence question:

1

The author of the passage would most likely
consider the information in the graph to be

A) Lines 49-50 ("Around…May")
B) Lines 65-69 ("Commercial…nervous)
C) Lines 72-75 ("In…month")
D) Lines 81-83 ("Already…ecosystems")

When you get to B), the content overlap with the graph should be clear. Even if you don't
immediately make the connection between the bars of the graph and the relative
vulnerability of various crops, the fact that both the graph and this section of the passage
have the same focus provides an important clue that B) is the correct answer.

Infographic Exercises

Note: Some graphs in this exercise refer to a passage when none is provided. This is a deliberate strategy to reinforce the point that many questions can be answered using the graph alone, even when the passage is mentioned in the question.

1.

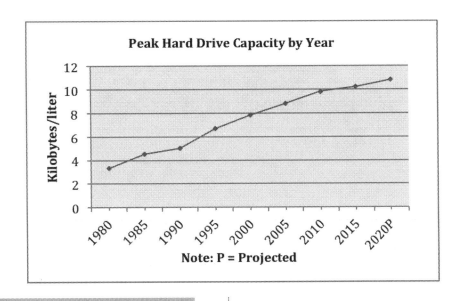

1

According to the graph, which statement is true about peak hard drive capacity in 2005?

A) It was double the peak hard drive capacity of a decade earlier.
B) It was around one kilobyte/liter higher than it had been five years earlier.
C) It was higher than peak hard drive capacity in 2010.
D) It was nine kilobytes/liter lower than it was in 2010.

2

Which choice best summarizes the information presented in the graph?

A) Hard drive capacity is expected to peak sometime before 2020.
B) Peak hard drive capacity was slightly higher in 2000 than in 1995.
C) Expanding peak hard drive capacity has led to a large increase in computer sales.
D) Peak hard drive capacity has increased dramatically since 1980.

2.

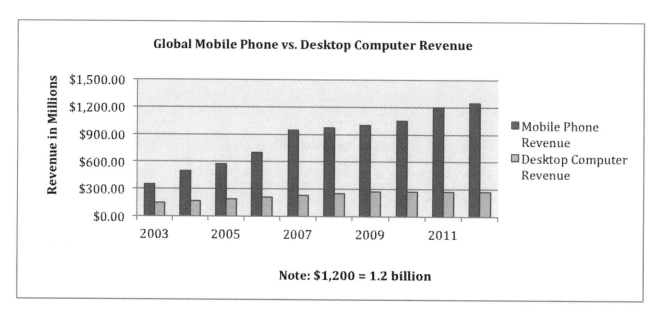

1.

According to the graph, which statement is true about the amount of revenue from mobile phone sales in 2008?

A) It was slightly higher than the amount of revenue from PC sales in 2008.
B) It was similar to the amount of revenue from PC sales in 2009.
C) it was similar to the amount of revenue from mobile phone sales in 2009.
D) It was wildly out of proportion to the amount of revenue from mobiles phone sales the previous year.

2.

Which information best summarizes the information presented in the graph?

A) The gap between revenue from mobile phone sales and PC sales has increased significantly.
B) Revenue from PC sales increased more rapidly than did revenue from mobile phone sales.
C) Revenue from tablet sales may soon overtake revenue from mobile phone sales.
D) Revenue from mobile phone sales has risen steadily, while revenue from PC sales has declined.

3.

Data in the graph provide most direct support for which idea in the passage?

A) People increasingly prefer mobile devices for numerous common tasks.
B) Consumers prefer to buy from companies whose products are familiar to them.
C) Mobile sales in new markets are substantially higher than are mobile sales in established markets.
D) Tablets can now perform many of the same functions as mobile phones.

3.

Figure 1

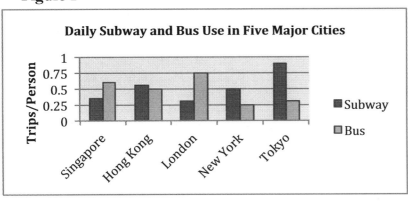

Daily Subway and Bus Use in Five Major Cities

Figure 2

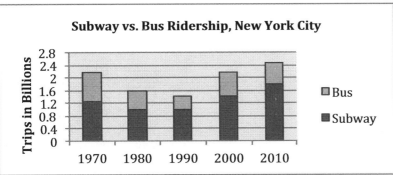

Subway vs. Bus Ridership, New York City

1

Information in figure 1 suggests that public transportation users in London

A) take subways and buses at similar rates.
B) are unusually reliant on buses.
C) take at least one subway trip daily.
D) take subways at about the same rate as people in New York.

2

Which of the following statements about bus use in New York City is best supported by information in figure 2?

A) It reached its highest point in 2010.
B) It was lower in 1980 than it was in 1990.
C) It began to rebound after 1990.
D) It declined in every decade.

3

Information in figure 1 supports the author's point that buses are growing in popularity as a means of urban transport by indicating that

A) many people around the world take at least one bus trip every day.
B) bus ridership surpasses subway ridership in some major cities.
C) people in Tokyo make far more trips by bus daily than they do trips by subway.
D) the number of bus trips taken by people in major cities has substantially increased.

4

Taken together, the graphs suggest that public transit users in New York City

A) use buses more often today than they did in previous decades.
B) use buses about as often as they use the subway.
C) rely more heavily on buses than do public transit users in other cities.
D) increasingly prefer to travel by subway.

4. The following passage is adapted from Michael Anft, "Solving the Mystery of Death Valley's Walking Rocks," © 2011 by Johns Hopkins Magazine.

For six decades, observers have been confounded by the movement of large rocks across a dry lake bed in California's Death Valley National Park. Leaving flat trails behind them, rocks that weigh up to 100
5 pounds seemingly do Michael Jackson's moonwalk across the valley's sere, cracked surface, sometimes traveling more than 100 yards. Without a body of water to pick them up and move them, the rocks at Racetrack Playa, a flat space between the valley's high cliffs,
10 have been the subject of much speculation, including whether they have been relocated by human pranksters or space aliens. The rocks have become the desert equivalent of Midwestern crop circles. "They really are a curiosity," says Ralph Lorenz, a planetary scientist at
15 the Applied Physics Laboratory. "Some [people] have mentioned UFOs. But I've always believed that this is something science could solve."

It has tried. One theory holds that the rocks are blown along by powerful winds. Another posits that
20 the wind pushes thin sheets of ice, created when the desert's temperatures dip low enough to freeze water from a rare rainstorm, and the rocks go along for the ride. But neither theory is rock solid. Winds at the playa aren't strong enough—some scientists believe that
25 they'd have to be 100 miles per hour or more—to blow the rocks across the valley. And rocks subject to the "ice sailing theory" wouldn't create trails as they moved.

Lorenz and a team of investigators believe that a
30 combination of forces may work to rearrange Racetrack Playa's rocks. "We saw that it would take a lot of wind to move these rocks, which are larger than you'd expect wind to move," Lorenz explains. "That led us to this idea that ice might be picking up the
35 rocks and floating them." As they explained in the January issue of *The American Journal of Physics*, instead of moving along with wind- driven sheets of ice, the rocks may instead be lifted by the ice, making them more subject to the wind's force. The key, Lorenz
40 says, is that the lifting by an "ice collar" reduces friction with the ground, to the point that the wind now has enough force to move the rock. The rock moves, the ice doesn't, and because part of the rock juts through the ice, it marks the territory it has covered.
45 Lorenz's team came to its conclusion through a combination of intuition, lab work, and observation— not that the last part was easy. Watching the rocks travel is a bit like witnessing the rusting of a hubcap. Instances of movement are rare and last for only a few

50 seconds. Lorenz's team placed low-resolution cameras on the cliffs (which are about 30 miles from the nearest paved road) to take pictures once per hour. For the past three winters, the researchers have weathered extreme temperatures and several flat tires to measure how
55 often the thermometer dips below freezing, how often the playa gets rain and floods, and the strength of the winds. "The measurements seem to back up our hypothesis," he says. "Any of the theories may be true at any one time, but ice rafting may be the best explan-
60 ation for the trails we've been seeing. We've seen trails like this documented in Arctic coastal areas, and the mechanism is somewhat similar. A belt of ice sur- rounds a boulder during high tide, picks it up, and then drops it elsewhere." His "ice raft theory" was also
65 borne out by an experiment that used the ingenuity of a high school science fair. Lorenz placed a basalt pebble in a Tupperware container with water so that the pebble projected just above the surface. He then turned the container upside down in a baking tray filled with a
70 layer of coarse sand at its base, and put the whole thing in his home freezer. The rock's "keel" (its protruding part) projected downward into the sand, which simu- lated the cracked surface of the playa (which scientists call "Special K" because of its resemblance to cereal
75 flakes). A gentle push or slight puff of air caused the Tupperware container to move, just as an ice raft would under the right conditions. The pebble made a trail in the soft sand. "It was primitive but effective," Lorenz says of the experiment. Lorenz has spent the
80 last 20 years studying Titan, a moon of Saturn. He says that Racetrack Playa's surface mirrors that of a dried lakebed on Titan. Observations and experiments on Earth may yield clues to that moon's geology. "We also may get some idea of how climate affects
85 geology—particularly as the climate changes here on Earth," Lorenz says. "When we study other planets and their moons, we're forced to use Occam's razor – sometimes the simplest answer is best, which means you look to Earth for some answers. Once you get out
90 there on Earth, you realize how strange so much of its surface is. So, you have to figure there's weird stuff to be found on Titan as well." Whether that's true or not will take much more investigation. He adds: "One day, we'll figure all this out. For the moment, the moving
95 rock present a wonderful problem to study in a beautiful place."

Racetrack Playa Average vs. Maximum Wind Speed

	Average Wind Speed (miles/hour)	Peak Wind Speed (miles/hour)
2008		
November	20	67
December	19	72
January	21	78
February	23	92
March	25	87
2009		
November	19	69
December	21	71
January	20	76
February	22	90
March	24	89

1

According to the graph, which statement is true about wind speeds at Racketrack Playa in 2009?

A) Peak wind speeds increased during every month between November and March.
B) Average wind speeds increased during every month between November and March.
C) Average wind speed in February was substantially higher than it was in December.
D) The lowest peak wind speed occurred in November.

2

Which choice is best supported by the information in the chart?

A) Peak wind speeds in 2009 were higher in every month than they were in 2008.
B) Average wind speeds in some months exceeded peak wind speeds in others.
C) The windiest months at Racetrack Playa were February and March.
D) Peak wind speed in February 2009 was higher than peak wind speed in February 2008.

3

Which of the following statements from the passage is represented by the chart?

A) Lines 16-17 ("But...solve")
B) Lines 23-26 ("Winds...valley")
C) Lines 39-42 ("The key...rock")
D) Lines 58-60 ("Any...seeing")

337

5. The following passage is adapted from "Makerspaces, Hackerspaces, and Community Scale Production in Detroit and Beyond," © 2013 by Sean Ansanelli.

During the mid-1980s, spaces began to emerge across Europe where computer hackers could convene for mutual support and camaraderie. In the past few years, the idea of fostering such shared, physical spaces
5 has been rapidly adapted by the diverse and growing community of "makers", who seek to apply the idea of "hacking" to physical objects, processes, or anything else that can be deciphered and improved upon.

A hackerspace is described by hackerspaces.org as
10 a "community-operated physical space where people with common interests, often in computers, technology, science, digital art or electronic art, can meet, socialize, and/or collaborate." Such spaces can vary in size, available technology, and membership structure (some
15 being completely open), but generally share community-oriented characteristics. Indeed, while the term "hacker" can sometimes have negative connotations, modern hackerspaces thrive off of community, openness, and assimilating diverse viewpoints – these often being the
20 only guiding principles in otherwise informal organizational structures.

In recent years, the city of Detroit has emerged as a hotbed for hackerspaces and other DIY ("Do-It-Yourself") experiments. Several hackerspaces
25 can already be found throughout the city and several more are currently in formation. Of course, Detroit's attractiveness for such projects can be partially attributed to cheap real estate, which allows aspiring hackers to acquire ample space for experimentation. Some observers
30 have also described this kind of making and tinkering as embedded in the DNA of Detroit's residents, who are able to harness substantial intergenerational knowledge and attract like-minded individuals.

Hackerspaces (or "makerspaces") can be found in
35 more commercial forms, but the vast majority of spaces are self-organized and not-for-profit. For example, the OmniCorp hackerspace operates off member fees to cover rent and new equipment, from laser cutters to welding tools. OmniCorp also hosts an "open hack night"
40 every Thursday in which the space is open to the general public. Potential members are required to attend at least one open hack night prior to a consensus vote by the existing members for admittance; no prospective members have yet been denied.

45 A visit to one of OmniCorp's open hack nights reveals the vast variety of activity and energy existing in the space. In the main common room alone, activities range from experimenting with sound installations and learning to program Arduino boards to building speculative "oloid"

50 shapes – all just for the sake of it. With a general atmosphere of mutual support, participants in the space are continually encouraged to help others.

One of the most active community-focused initiatives in the city is the Mt. Elliot Makerspace. Jeff Sturges,
55 former MIT Media Lab Fellow and Co-Founder of OmniCorp, started the Mt. Elliot project with the aim of replicating MIT's Fab Lab model on a smaller, cheaper scale in Detroit. "Fab Labs" are production facilities that consist of a small collection of flexible computer
60 controlled tools that cover several different scales and various materials, with the aim to make "almost anything" (including other machines). The Mt. Elliot Makerspace now offers youth-based skill development programs in eight areas: Transportation, Electronics,
65 Digital Tools, Wearables, Design and Fabrication, Food, Music, and Arts. The range of activities is meant to provide not only something for everyone, but a well-rounded base knowledge of making to all participants.

While the center receives some foundational support,
70 the space also derives significant support from the local community. Makerspaces throughout the city connect the space's youth-based programming directly to school curriculums.

The growing interest in and development of
75 hacker/makerspaces has been explained, in part, as a result of the growing maker movement. Through the combination of cultural norms and communication channels from open source production as well as increasingly available technologies for physical
80 production, amateur maker communities have developed in virtual and physical spaces.

Publications such as *Wired* are noticing the transformative potential of this emerging movement and have sought to devote significant attention to its
85 development. Chief editor Chris Anderson recently published a book entitled *Makers*, in which he proclaims that the movement will become the next Industrial Revolution. Anderson argues such developments will allow for a new wave of business opportunities by
90 providing mass-customization rather than mass-production.

The transformative potential of these trends goes beyond new business opportunities or competitive advantages for economic growth. Rather, these trends
95 demonstrate the potential to actually transform economic development models entirely.

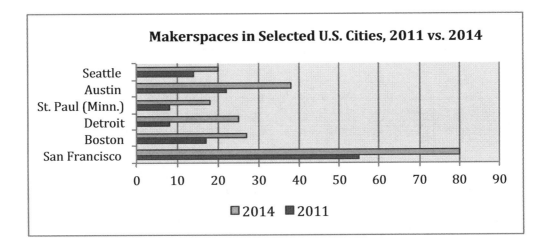

Makerspaces in Selected U.S. Cities, 2011 vs. 2014

■ 2014 ■ 2011

1

According to the graph, which statement is true about the number of makerspaces in Austin in 2014?

A) It was smaller than the number of makerspaces in Detroit in 2014.
B) It was almost half the number of makerspaces in San Francisco the same year.
C) It was the same as the number of makerspaces in Austin in 2011.
D) It lagged behind the number of makerspaces in Boston in 2014.

2

The author of the passage would most likely regard the graph with

A) enthusiasm, because it demonstrates that makerspaces can revolutionize the United States economy.
B) skepticism, because it show a relatively small number of makerspaces in Detroit.
C) approval, because it indicates that the makerspace movement has grown across the United States.
D) indifference, because it reveals that San Francisco has the greatest number of makerspaces.

3

Which of the following statements from the passage is supported by information in the graph?

A) Lines 3-6 ("In...makers")
B) Lines 26-29 ("Of...experimentation")
C) Lines 69-71 ("While...community")
D) Lines 92-94 ("The transformative...growth")

6. The following passage is adapted from Julian Jackson, "New Research Suggests Dinosaurs Were Warm-Blooded and Active" © 2011 by Julian Jackson.

New research from the University of Adelaide has added to the debate about whether dinosaurs were cold-blooded and sluggish or warm-blooded and active. Professor Roger Seymour from the University's School
5 of Earth & Environmental Sciences has applied the latest theories of human and animal anatomy and physiology to provide insight into the lives of dinosaurs.

Human thigh bones have tiny holes – known as the
10 "nutrient foramen" – on the shaft that supply blood to living bone cells inside. New research has shown that the size of those holes is related to the maximum rate that a person can be active during aerobic exercise. Professor Seymour has used this principle to evaluate
15 the activity levels of dinosaurs.

"Far from being lifeless, bone cells have a relatively high metabolic rate and they therefore require a large blood supply to deliver oxygen. On the inside of the bone, the blood supply comes usually from a single
20 artery and vein that pass through a hole on the shaft – the nutrient foramen," he says.

Professor Seymour wondered whether the size of the nutrient foramen might indicate how much blood was necessary to keep the bones in good repair. For
25 example, highly active animals might cause more bone 'microfractures,' requiring more frequent repairs by the bone cells and therefore a greater blood supply. "My aim was to see whether we could use fossil bones of dinosaurs to indicate the level of bone metabolic rate
30 and possibly extend it to the whole body's metabolic rate," he says. "One of the big controversies among paleobiologists is whether dinosaurs were cold-blooded and sluggish or warm-blooded and active. Could the size of the foramen be a possible gauge for dinosaur
35 metabolic rate?"

Comparisons were made with the sizes of the holes in living mammals and reptiles, and their metabolic rates. Measuring mammals ranging from mice to elephants, and reptiles from lizards to crocodiles, one
40 of Professor Seymour's Honors students, Sarah Smith, combed the collections of Australian museums, photographing and measuring hundreds of tiny holes in thigh bones.

"The results were unequivocal. The sizes of the holes
45 were related closely to the maximum metabolic rates during peak movement in mammals and reptiles," Professor Seymour says. "The holes found in mammals were about 10 times larger than those in reptiles."

These holes were compared to those of fossil
50 dinosaurs. Dr. Don Henderson, Curator of Dinosaurs from the Royal Tyrrell Museum in Alberta, Canada, and Daniela Schwarz-Wings from the Museum für Naturkunde Humboldt University Berliny, German measured the holes in 10 species of
55 dinosaurs from five different groups, including bipedal and quadrupedal carnivores and herbivores, weighing 50kg to 20,000kg.

"On a relative comparison to eliminate the differences in body size, all of the dinosaurs had
60 holes in their thigh bones larger than those of mammals," Professor Seymour says.

"The dinosaurs appeared to be even more active than the mammals. We certainly didn't expect to see that. These results provide additional weight to
65 theories that dinosaurs were warm-blooded and highly active creatures, rather than cold-blooded and sluggish."

Professor Seymour says following the results of this study, it's likely that a simple measurement of
70 foramen size could be used to evaluate maximum activity levels in other vertebrate animals.

Blood Flow Index Q$_1$ (mm^3)

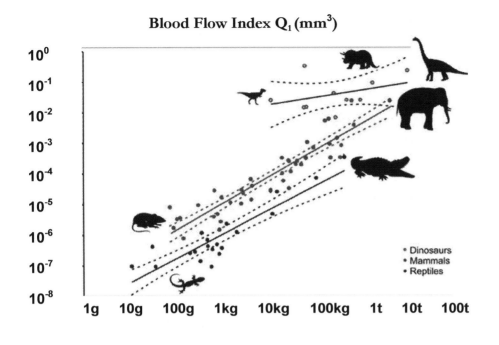

Seymour et al 2011

1

Which statement is best supported by data in the graph?

A) Light reptiles have higher blood flow than heavier reptiles.
B) Heavy mammals have lower blood flow than heavy reptiles.
C) Blood flow in the heaviest mammals is slightly higher than in light dinosaurs.
D) Blood flow is fairly uniform in dinosaurs at a wide range of weights.

2

The author of the passage would most likely consider the information in the graph to be

A) a compelling piece of evidence in support of Professor Seymour's theory.
B) a potentially interesting but premature finding.
C) conclusive proof that dinosaurs were active and warm-blooded.
D) suggestive of a point of view towards which the author is skeptical.

3

Do the data in the table provide support for Professor Seymour's claim that dinosaurs were warm-blooded and highly active?

A) Yes, because they indicate that dinosaurs' foramen size was larger than that of the largest mammals.
B) Yes, because they suggest that dinosaurs had even higher metabolic rates than animals known to be warm-blooded.
C) No, because they show that dinosaurs had lower blood flow than reptiles.
D) No, because they reveal only minimal changes in metabolic rate between small and large dinosaurs.

Official Guide/Khan Academy Infographic Questions

Test 1

28	Graphic only
29	Graphic + passage
30	Graphic only
31	Graphic + passage

Test 2

50	Graphic only
51	Graphic + passage
52	Graphic only

Test 3

50	Graphic only
51	Graphic only
52	Graphic only

Test 4

50	Graphic only
51	Graphic + passage
52	Graphic only

Explanations: Infographic Exercises

1.1 B

B) is correct because the point for 2005 indicates that peak hard drive capacity was around 9 kilobytes/liter. Even though the number nine does not appear on the graph, you can infer that this is the case because 8 and 10 do appear, and the point for 2005 is situated between them. If you look back to 2000 (five years earlier), you can see that the graph indicates a peak capacity of 8 kilobytes/liter, or one less than in 2005. Note that this question can be tricky if you forget that each line on the graph represents *two* kilobytes/liter. A point halfway between two lines therefore equals one kilobyte/liter.

A) is incorrect because peak hard drive capacity in 1995 (a decade earlier) was 7 – only 2 kilobytes less, not half (that would be 4). C) is incorrect because peak hard drive capacity in 2010 was higher than in 2005; you can tell just by looking at the graph. And D) is incorrect for the same reason as C) – don't get thrown off by the mention of the number 9. In this case, it indicates the peak hard drive capacity was 9 kilobytes/liter, not that it was 9 kilobytes/liter *less*.

1.2 D

Remember that this question is asking you to *summarize* the graph, not just to identify which statement it supports. The "main point" of the graph is that peak hard drive capacity has increased enormously since 1980 and is predicted to continue expanding. Based on that information alone, you should be able to identify D) as the answer.

Playing process of elimination, A) is incorrect because the graph indicates that peak hard drive capacity will keep expanding through 2020; it will not peak before then. For B), it is true that the peak hard drive capacity was slightly higher in 2000 than in 1995, but that statement only describes a small portion of the graph, and the question asks for a summary. C) is incorrect because the graph provides no information at all about computer sales; it is beyond the bounds of what can be inferred.

2.1 C

If you look at the graph as a whole, you should notice that mobile phone revenue has gone up very substantially, while PC revenue has been much lower and grown much more slowly. Furthermore, mobile phone revenue has been consistently much higher than PC revenue. Using that information, you can assume both A) and B) are wrong – at no point was mobile phone revenue only *slightly* higher than PC revenue, nor was it ever similar to PC revenue. In D), the phrase *wildly out of proportion* should also give you pause. Indeed the graph indicates that mobile phone revenue leveled off beginning in 2007; 2008 (the tick mark between 2007 and 2009) was only marginally higher than 2007. That leaves C), which is correct: the mobile phone bars for 2008 and 2009 are almost the same.

2.2. A

Again, take a moment to reiterate the point of the graph: mobile phone revenue has gone way up, while PC revenue has increased much more slowly and stayed far below mobile phone revenue. By the most recent year indicated in the graph, the PC bars are only about a quarter as high as the mobile phone bars, whereas they are half as high at the beginning. That indicates a larger gap between mobile phone and PC sales, making A) correct. B) is incorrect because the graph indicates the opposite: revenue from PC sales increased more slowly than revenue from mobile phone sales; C) is incorrect because the graph shows nothing about tablets; and D) is incorrect because PC revenue did not decline – it simply increased less than mobile phone revenue.

2.3 A

Forget about the reference to the passage that isn't there – the question is really asking what the graph shows, i.e. its "point." What is that point? That mobile phone revenue is increasingly outstripping desktop computer revenue. What does that suggest?

That mobile phones have become much, much more popular than desktop computers. Which answer is most consistent with that idea? A). Even though that answer does not mention anything about desktop computers, it is still generally consistent with the graph – if people increasingly prefer mobile "devices" (note the slight change of terminology from the graph) for "numerous common tasks," then logically revenue from sales of mobile devices would increase as well (and implicitly, sales of desktop computers, which were previously used for those tasks, would go down). B) is incorrect because the graph provides no information about companies, familiar to consumers or otherwise; C) is incorrect because the graph likewise provides no information about established vs. un-established markets; and D) is incorrect because the graph provides information about mobile *phones* only, not mobile devices in general. Note how this is different from A): a correct answer choice may phrase information from the graph in a more general way ("mobile *phones*" in the graph vs. "mobile *devices*" in the correct answer), but a correct answer cannot replace specific information in a graph with something equally specific (e.g. tablets).

3.1 B

When you look at the bar for London on the graph, there are two things to notice: one is that the bar for buses is much higher than the bar for subways, and the other is that the bar for buses is higher than it is in any other city. That indicates that people in London take buses at a higher rate than people in other cities, i.e. that they are *unusually reliant on buses.* The answer is therefore B). A) is incorrect because, as stated, the bar for buses is much higher than that for subways; C) is incorrect because the graph indicates just over .25 trips/person daily (remember that the bars represent increments of .25, not 1); and D) is incorrect because the bar for subway use in New York is much higher than the bar for subway use in London.

3.2 C

Start by making sure that you're looking at the bar for buses (top bar, light gray). If you consider the

graph as a whole, you can notice that the "bus" bars get smaller and then larger again; you can assume that the correct answer will be related to that fact. C) correctly states that bus use began to rebound (become larger) after 1990, which is precisely what the graph shows – there is a big leap from 1990 to 2000. A) is incorrect because the graph indicates that bus use was higher in 1970 than in 2010; B) is incorrect because the bar for bus use in 1990 is clearly *smaller* than that for 1980; D) is incorrect because bus use only declined until 1990, after which it began to increase.

3.3 B

This question is phrased in a fairly complicated way, so start by simplifying it. First, don't be too distracted by the reference to the (non-existent) passage. The question is only telling you that the graph supports a point in the passage, and that point will by necessity be the point of the graph. So the question is really only asking you to determine the point of the graph. What is the "point" of the graph? Bus use is more common in some cities, and subway use is more common in others. That is consistent with B), which is the answer. If you think about the question some more, that makes sense: the fact that people in some cities use buses more heavily than subways would indeed support the idea that buses are growing in popularity. A) is incorrect because the graph does not indicate that people take more than one bus trip/day in any city – remember that each bar represents .25 trips, not one. C) is incorrect because it states the opposite of what the graph shows – people in Tokyo take far more *subway* trips than bus trips. D) is incorrect because the graph indicates nothing about whether bus trips have increased or not – it only gives us a snapshot of how many trips people take on average at one point in time.

3.4 D

The question is essentially telling you that both graphs indicate similar phenomena, so start by figuring out what one graph reveals, then use the other graph to confirm that idea. If you look at figure 1, you can see that subway ridership is a lot higher than bus ridership, so the correct answer must be related to that idea. That is essentially what D) says, so you can assume that it is right. If you look at figure 2, you'll see that subway use has risen significantly since 1990, indicating that people in New York *increasingly* prefer the subway. A) is incorrect because the graph shows the opposite – bus use has declined, suggesting that preference for it has *declined*; B) is incorrect because the graphs show that subway use is much higher than bus use; and C) is incorrect because Figure 1 shows that bus use is higher in London and Singapore than in New York. Figure 2 also shows nothing about bus use in cities other than New York.

4.1 D

A) is incorrect because peak wind speed was lower in March than in February (89 vs. 90); B) is incorrect because average wind speed was higher in December than in January (21 vs. 20); C) is incorrect because average wind speed in February was only 1 mph higher than in December (22 vs. 21), not *substantially* higher; and D) is correct because 69 mph is the lowest peak wind speed provided for any month in 2009.

4.2 C

Unlike a graph, from which you can get a very quick overview of a situation, a chart isn't nearly as easy to get the big picture from. For that reason, you are better off working through the answers one-by-one rather than trying to get an overview of the chart as a whole. A) can be eliminated easily if you start from November and compare peak wind speeds in 2008 to those in 2009: peak speed in December 2008 was higher than in December 2009. B) is phrased in a general way, but that answer can be eliminated easily as well: all of the values for average speed are clearly far below all those for peak speed. C) is correct because the values for both average and peak wind speeds are higher than they are in any other month; and D) is incorrect because peak wind speed in February 2009 was lower (90) than peak wind speed in February 2008 (92).

4.3 B

Before you start hunting through the passage, figure out what sort of statement you're looking for. The chart indicates various wind speeds, so the correct section of the passage must focus on wind speeds as well. A) is off topic – those lines have nothing to do with wind speeds. B) is correct because those lines indicate that the winds at Racetrack Playa would have needed to blow more than 100 mph to move the rocks, and the chart indicates that their highest speed was 92 mph. Be careful with C) – lines 39-40 do refer to the wind, but the chart shows nothing about "ice collars" or rock movement. D) is likewise incorrect because the chart reveals nothing directly about ice rafting, only wind speed.

5.1 B

This is a straightforward "detail" question, so you don't need to worry about the "point" of the graph. A) is incorrect because there were more makerspaces in Austin in 2014 than in Detroit the same year; careful not to get confused by the fact that there were fewer makerspaces in Austin in *2011* than in Detroit in 2014. B) is correct because the number of makerspaces is Austin in 2014 is just under 40, while the number in San Francisco is 80 – that's almost half. C) is incorrect because the number of makerspaces in Austin grew from 2011 to 2014. D) is incorrect because the bar for 2014 Austin makerspaces is longer than that for Boston that year.

5.2 C

This question requires you to do some work upfront before looking at the answers. First, what is the "point" of the graph? Basically, there were far more makerspaces in various U.S. cities in 2014 than in 2011. What is the point of the passage? That makerspaces are a major, growing phenomenon that could transform the economy. Would the author's attitude toward the graph be positive or negative? Positive. Eliminate B) and D). Now look at A) and C). Be very, very careful with A). It is true that the author *states* makerspaces will revolutionize the economy, but the graph provides no information whatsoever about the economy, and there's also nothing that would allow us to infer the effects of the makerspace movement on economy. A) can thus be eliminated, leaving C). The author would indeed be likely to approve of the fact that makerspaces are proliferating so rapidly across the U.S.

5.3 A

If you've written – or better – underlined the point of the passage, this question should be fairly straightforward. You're looking for the lines that indicate that makerspaces are sprouting up all over the place. That's "big picture" information, so logically, the answer is most likely to be located at the beginning or the end of the passage. A) or D) are your top candidates for an answer. If you work in order, you'll hit the answer quickly: lines 3-6 state that *the idea of fostering such shared, physical spaces has been rapidly adapted by the diverse and <u>growing</u> community of "makers"* – that corresponds to the growth of makerspaces depicted in the graph.

6.1 D

Since the question is phrased so generally, you can assume that the answer will be related to the "point" or big picture of the graph. There's more information in this one than in the others, but if you had to sum up the most important information, it would probably have something to do with the fact that dinosaurs are way up at the top (indicating very high blood flow), above both mammals and reptiles. Keeping that information in mind, you can check the answers. A) is incorrect because the relationship between weight and blood flow is linear – heavy reptiles have higher blood flow than light reptiles. B) is incorrect because the line for heavy mammals is clearly well above that for heavy reptiles. You can use the "point" to eliminate C) – all of the dinosaurs are heavier than even the heaviest mammals. D) is correct because the graph indicates that blood flow is similarly high (=relatively uniform) in dinosaurs at weights ranging from 1 kilogram to 10 tons.

6.2 A

Start by breaking the question down. What does the author think? He has a pretty positive attitude toward Professor Seymour's theory; the passage indicates that there's a fair amount of evidence to suggest it's accurate. What is that theory? That dinosaurs were warm-blooded and active, as indicated by their high maximum blood flow (i.e. their metabolic rate). What does the graph show? That dinosaurs had extremely high blood flow, indicating extremely high metabolism. So logically, the author would have a positive attitude toward the graph. That eliminates B) and D). Now consider A) and C). The wording of C) should make you immediately suspicious; a single graph isn't enough to "conclusively prove" anything. The graph does, however, provide excellent *support* for Seymour's theory, making A) correct.

6.3 B

Although the question alludes to the passage, you don't actually need it. The question itself tells you the relevant piece of information, namely that Professor Seymour claims that dinosaurs are warm-blooded and active. Your only job is to determine whether the graph supports that claim. What does the graph show? That dinosaurs had extremely high blood flow, which is consistent with Professor Seymour's theory (high maximum blood flow = high metabolic rate = warm-bloodedness). That eliminates C) and D). A) can be eliminated because the graph provides no information about foramen size, leaving B). That answer is correct because the graph indicates that blood flow is higher in all dinosaurs than in even the heaviest mammals, which are known to be warm-blooded.

Appendix: Official Guide/Khan Academy Questions by Test

Test 1

#	Category	Sub-Category
1	Big Picture	Summary
2	Rhetorical Strategy	Passage Structure
3	Vocabulary	
4	**Literal Comp.**	**No line reference**
5	**Evidence**	
6	Attitude	
7	Function	Paragraph
8	Vocabulary	
9	Literal Comp.	Line reference
10	Supp. Evidence	
11	Main Point	Examples
12	Vocabulary	
13	**Literal Comp.**	**No line reference**
14	**Evidence**	
15	Attitude	Inference
16	**Literal Comp.**	**Line reference**
17	**Evidence**	
18	Vocabulary	
19	Function	
20	Graphic	
21	Inference	Main point
22	Function	Word
23	Support/Undermine	Undermine
24	Literal Comp.	Line reference
25	Function	
26	Inference	
27	Function	
28	Graphic	Graphic only
29	Graphic	Graphic + passage
30	Evidence	Graphic only
31	Graphic	Graphic + passage
32	Big Picture	Purpose of a passage
33	Big Picture	Main point
34	Function	Rhetorical strategy
35	Literal Comp.	
36	**Literal Comp.**	**No line reference**
37	**Evidence**	
38	**Literal Comp.**	**Line reference**
39	**Evidence**	
40	Vocabulary	
41	Function	Main point
42	Function	
43	**Literal Comp.**	**No line reference**
44	**Evidence**	
45	Vocabulary	
46	Function	
47	Literal Comp.	No line reference
48	Vocabulary	
49	P1/P2 Relationship	
50	**P1/P2 Relationship**	**Line reference**
51	**Evidence**	
52	P1/P2 Relationship	

Test 2

#	Category	Sub-Category
1	Big Picture	Summary
2	Function	
3	Rhetorical Strategy	Point of view
4	Function	
5	Literal Comp.	No line reference
6	**Literal Comp.**	**No line reference**
7	**Evidence**	
8	Function	
9	**Literal Comp.**	**No line reference**
10	**Evidence**	
11	Big Picture	Purpose of a passage
12	**Rhetorical Strategy**	**Counterargument**
13	**Evidence**	
14	Vocabulary	
15	Function	
16	Vocabulary	
17	Support/Undermine	Support
18	Main Point	
19	Graphic	Graphic only
20	Graphic	Graphic only
21	Graphic	Graphic + passage
22	**Literal Comp.**	**No line reference**
23	**Evidence**	
24	Literal Comp.	
25	Vocabulary	
26	Inference	
27	Literal Comp.	
28	Function	
29	Big Picture	Purpose of a passage
30	P1/P2 Relationship	

#	Type	Detail
31	P1/P2 Relationship	Agree
32	P1/P2 Relationship	
33	Big Picture	Main point
34	Function	
35	**Literal Comp.**	**No line reference**
36	**Evidence**	
37	Vocabulary	
38	Inference	
39	Vocabulary	
40	Literal Comp.	No line reference
41	Literal Comp.	Line reference
42	Function	Purpose of a paragraph
43	Vocabulary	
45	**Literal Comp.**	**No line reference**
46	**Evidence**	
47	Vocabulary	
48	**Inference**	**No line reference**
49	**Evidence**	
50	Graphic	Graphic only
51	Graphic	Graphic + passage
52	Graphic	Graphic only

Test 3

#	Type	Detail
1	Big Picture	Summary
2	Vocabulary	
3	**Inference**	**No line reference**
4	**Evidence**	
5	Function	
6	Vocabulary	
7	Literal Comp.	No line reference
8	Inference	
9	**Literal Comp.**	**No line reference**
10	**Evidence**	
11	Function	
12	**Literal Comp.**	**No line reference**
13	**Evidence**	
14	**Big Picture**	**Point of a paragraph**
15	**Evidence**	
16	Vocabulary	
17	Vocabulary	
18	Support/Undermine	Support
19	Graphic	Graphic only
20	Graphic	Graphic only
21	Rhetorical Strategy	Passage organization
22	Vocabulary	
23	**Inference**	**Assumption**
24	**Evidence**	

#	Type	Detail
25	Function	
26	Literal Comp.	Line reference
27	Literal Comp.	No line reference
28	Vocabulary	
29	**Inference**	**No line reference**
30	**Evidence**	
31	Vocabulary	
32	**Inference**	**No line reference**
33	**Evidence**	
34	Literal Comp.	No line reference
35	Vocabulary	
36	**Literal Comp.**	**No line reference**
37	**Evidence**	
38	P1/P2 Relationship	Function
39	P1/P2 Relationship	
40	P1/P2 Relationship	Agree
41	P1/P2 Relationship	
42	Tone	
43	**Inference**	**Line reference**
44	**Evidence**	
45	**Inference**	**No line reference**
46	**Evidence**	
47	Vocabulary	
48	Big Picture	Purpose of a paragraph
49	Inference	Assumption
50	Graphic	Graphic only
51	Graphic	Graphic only
52	Graphic	Graphic only

Test 4

#	Type	Detail
1	**Attitude**	**No line reference**
2	**Evidence**	
3	Vocabulary	
4	Function	
5	Literal Comp.	No line reference
6	Evidence	
7	Literal Comp.	No line reference
8	Inference	
9	Vocabulary	
10	Vocabulary	
11	Big Picture	Paragraph summary
12	Literal Comp.	No line reference
13	Vocabulary	
14	**Literal Comp.**	**No line reference**
15	**Evidence**	
16	**Inference**	**No line reference**
17	**Evidence**	

18	Vocabulary	
19	Attitude	Graphic
20	Graphic	Graphic only
21	Graphic	Graphic only
22	Big Picture	Purpose of a passage
23	Attitude	
24	Vocabulary	
25	**Inference**	**No line reference**
26	**Evidence**	
27	**Literal Comp.**	**No line reference**
28	**Evidence**	
29	Inference	
30	Function	Punctuation
31	Inference	
32	Literal Comp.	No line reference
33	Vocabulary	
34	Vocabulary	
35	Inference	
36	**P1/P2 Relationship**	**Line Reference**
37	**Evidence**	
38	**P1/P2 Relationship**	**Line Reference**
39	**Evidence**	
40	P1/P2 Relationship	
41	Big Picture	Purpose of a passage
42	Big Picture	Purpose of a passage
43	**Rhetorical Strategy**	**Passage organization**
44	**Evidence**	
45	Function	
46	**Literal Comp.**	**No line reference**
47	**Evidence**	
48	Inference	
49	Support/Undermine	Support
50	Graphic	Graphic only
51	Graphic	Graphic + passage
52	Graphic	Graphic only

Reprints and Permissions

Acheson, Dean. From "Speech at Berkeley, California, March 16, 1950. http://teachingamericanhistory.org/library/document/speech-at-berkeley-california/

Adee, Sally. From "Roughnecks in Space: Moon Mining in Science Fiction," *New Scientist*, 27 April 2012, 3:39 PM
http://www .newscientist.com/gallery/moon-mining

Anft, Michael. "Solving the Mystery of Death Valley's Walking Rocks," *Johns Hopkins Magazine*, 6/1/11. Reprinted by permission of *Johns Hopkins Magazine*. http://archive.magazine.jhu.edu/2011/06/solving-the-mystery-of-death-valley's-walking-rocks/

Ansanelli, Sean. "Makerspaces, Hackerspaces and Community-Scale Production in Detroit and Beyond," *Urban Magazine*, Spring 2013, p. 31. Reprinted by permission of the author. http://blogs.cuit.columbia.edu/urbanmagazine/files/2015/02/URBAN_Spring2013_WEB.pdf

Anthony, Susan B. From "Remarks to the Woman's Auxiliary Congress of the Public Press Congress," May 23, 1893. http://ecssba.rutgers.edu/docs/sbaexpo.html

Archer, Mike. From "Ordering the vegetarian meal? There's more animal blood on your hands," *The Conversation*, 16 December 2011, 6.34am http://theconversation.edu.au/ordering-the-vegetarian-meal-theres-more-animal-blood-on-your-hands-4659

Austen, Jane. *Northanger Abbey*. Originally published 1803. Excepted from Chapter 1 through Project Gutenberg, http://www.gutenberg.org/files/121/121-h/121-h.htm

Bailey, Ronald. Adapted from "The Food Miles Mistake," Reason.com, 4 November 2008. http://reason.com/archives/2008/11/04/the-food-miles-mistake

Ball, Philip. From "The Trouble With Scientists," *Nautilus*, 5/14/15. http://nautil.us/issue/24/error/the-trouble-with-scientists

Brauer, Wiebke. Adapted from "The Miracle of Space," *Smart Magazine*, 10/31/14. Reprinted by permission of *Smart Magazine*. http://smart-magazine.com/space/the-miracle-of-space/

Conniff, Richard. From "What the Luddites Really Fought Against," Smithsonian.com, March 2011. Reprinted by permission of the author.

de Gouges, Olympe. Adapted from *The Declaration of the Rights of Woman*, 1791. https://chnm.gmu.edu/revolution/d/293/

Gompers, Samuel. From "What Does the Working Man Want?" Address to Workers in Louisville, Kentucky, 1890. http://jackiewhiting.net/HonorsUS/Labor/gompers.pdf

Gross, Daniel. From "Will We Ever Be Able to Make Traffic Disappear?" Smithsonian.com, 5/7/2015. http://www.smithsonianmag.com/innovation/will-we-ever-be-able-to-make-traffic-disappear-180955164/

Ishiguro, Kazuo. From *Never Let Me Go*. Toronto: Vintage Canada (Random House), 2005, pp. 3-4.

Jackson, Julian. "New Research Suggests that Dinosaurs Were Active and Warm-Blooded." *Earth Times*, 7/12/11. http://www.earthtimes.org/nature/new-research-suggests-dinosaurs-warm-blooded-active/1138/. Reprinted by permission of the author.

Jordan, Barbara. Adapted from the Keynote Speech, Democratic National Convention, delivered July 12, 1976. http://www.americanrhetoric.com/speeches/barbarajordan1976dnc.html

Kelemen, Peter B. From "The Origin of the Ocean Floor," *Scientific American*, February 2009. **Reproduced with permission, © 2009, Scientific American, Inc. All rights reserved.** http://www.scientificamerican.com/article/the-origin-of-the-ocean-floor/

Kincaid, Jamaica. Excerpt from "Gwen" from ANNIE JOHN by Jamaica Kincaid. Copyright © 1985 by Jamaica Kincaid. Reprinted by permission of Farrar, Straus and Giroux, LLC.

Klinkenborg, Verlyn. Adapted from "Our Vanishing Night," *National Geographic*, November 2008. Reprinted by permission of the author.

Koerth-Baker, Maggie: From "The Power of Positive Thinking," Truth or Myth? *Live Science*, 29 August 2008, 5:20 AM, 05:20 http://www.livescience.com/2814-power-positive-thinking-truth-myth.html

Leech, Kirk: From "Why Moralism Spoils the Appetite," *Spiked Review of Books*. No. 53, February 2012. http://www.spiked-online.com/review_of_books/article/12154#.VaV2PFoT-fQ

Lehrer, Jonah. Adapted from "Under Pressure: The Search for Stress Vaccine," *Wired*, 7/28/10, 2:00 p.m. http://www.wired.com/2010/07/ff_stress_cure/

Locke, John. From *Two Treatises of Government*, 1691. http://socserv2.socsci.mcmaster.ca/econ/ugcm/3ll3/locke/government.pdf

McConnell, David. From "Playing with Infinity on Riker's Island," *Prospect*, February 2012. http://www.prospectmagazine.co.uk/science-and-technology/playing-with-infinity-on-rikers-island

Miller, Greg. From "How Our Brains Make Memories," Smithsonian.com, May 2010. http://www.smithsonianmag.com/science-nature/how-our-brains-make-memories-14466850/

Mills, Mark. From "Every Breath You Take," *City Journal*, 7/2/13. http://www.city-journal.org/2013/bc0702mm.html

Montero, Barbara Gail. From "The Myth of 'Just Do It,'" *The New York Times*, 6/9/13. http://opinionator.blogs.nytimes.com/author/barbara-gail-montero/

Nuwer, Rachel. "What is a Species?" Smithsonian.com, 11/6/13. http://www.smithsonianmag.com/science-nature/what-is-a-species-insight-from-dolphins-and-humans-180947580/?no-ist

Orwell, George. Adapted from "Keep the Apidastra Flying," originally published 1936. Accessed from Project Gutenberg, http://gutenberg.net.au/ebooks02/0200021.txt

"The Rise of the Sharing Economy," *The Economist*, 3/9/2013. http://www.economist.com/news/leaders/21573104-internet-everything-hire-rise-sharing-economy

Rousseau, Jean-Jacques. From *The Social Contract*, 1762, trans. GDH Cole. http://www.gutenberg.org/files/46333/46333-h/46333-h.htm

Rupp, Rebecca. From "Surviving the Sneaky Psychology of Supermarkets," *National Geographic*, 6/15/15. http://theplate.nationalgeographic.com/2015/06/15/surviving-the-sneaky-psychology-of-supermarkets/

Riggio, Ronald. Excerpted from "Why Certain Smells Trigger Positive Memories," *Psychology Today*, May 1, 2012. Reprinted by permission of the author.

Sainani, Kristin. Adapted from "What, Me Worry?" *Stanford Magazine*, May/June 2014. https://alumni.stanford.edu/get/page/magazine/article/?article_id=70134

Schulman, Ari N. From "*Jurassic* Generation," *The New Atlantis*, Winter/Spring 2013. http://www.thenewatlantis.com/publications/jurassic-generation

Schwartz, Barry. "More Isn't Always Better," *Harvard Business Review*, June 2006. Reprinted by permission of Harvard Business Publishing. https://hbr.org/2006/06/more-isnt-always-better

"Scientists Discover Salty Aquifer, Previously Unknown Microbial Habitat Under Antarctica," © 2015, Dartmouth College. http://www.sciencenewsline.com/articles/2015042815560014.html

Sullivan, John Jeremiah. "One of Us," *Lapham's Quarterly*, Spring 2013. http://www.laphamsquarterly.org/animals/one-us

Taylor, Astra. "A Small World After All," *Bookforum*, June/July/August 2013. http://www.bookforum.com/inprint/020_02/11685

Thompson, Helen. "Yawning Spreads Like a Plague in Wolves," Smithsonian.com, 8/27/14, http://www.smithsonianmag.com/science-nature/yawning-spread-plague-wolves-180952484/

Tregaskis, Sharon. "The Buzz: What Bees Tell Us About Global Climate Change, *Johns Hopkins Magazine*. 6/2/2010. Reprinted with permission by *Johns Hopkins Magazine*. http://archive.magazine.jhu.edu/2010/06/the-buzz-what-bees-tell-us-about-global- climate-change/

Wharton, Edith. *Summer*, originally published 1917. Excerpted from Chapter 1 through Project Gutenberg, http://www.gutenberg.org/files/166/166-h/166-h.htm

Webster, Daniel. Adapted from the "Seventh of March Speech to the Senate," 1850. https://www.dartmouth.edu/~dwebster/speeches/seventh-march.html

"Why Eat Locally?" *The Regal Vegan*, http://www.regalvegan.com/site/local-yokels/

About the Author

Since 2007, Erica Meltzer has worked as a tutor and test-prep writer, helping numerous students raise their SAT, ACT, GRE, and GMAT Verbal scores and gain acceptance to their top-choice schools. In addition to *The Critical Reader*, she is also the author of *The Ultimate Guide to SAT Grammar* (2011) and *The Complete Guide to ACT English* (2014). Her books have been widely praised as the most effective resources available for the verbal portions of the SAT and ACT, and are used by tutors and test-prep companies across the United States. A graduate of Wellesley College, she is based in New York City. You can visit her online at http://www.thecriticalreader.com.

Access™ 2007 For Dummies®

Cheat Sheet

Navigating the Ribbon with Key Tips

1. **Press the Alt key.**

   Key Tips appear on the Ribbon, the Microsoft Office Button, and the Quick Access Toolbar.

2. **Press a Key Tip to set the focus to that item (like C in this case for the Create tab).**

   Key Tips appear for the item.

3. **Press a Key Tip (like T to create a new table).**

   The command assigned to the Key Tip runs.

Basic Comparison Operators

Name	Symbol	What It Means	Example
Equals	=	Displays all records that exactly match whatever you type.	To find all items from customer 37, type **37** into the Criteria row.
Less Than	<	Lists all values that are less than your criterion.	Typing **<50000** in the Salary field finds all employees who earn less than $50K.
Greater Than	>	Lists all values in the field that are greater than the criterion.	Typing **>50000** in the Salary field finds all employees who I'll be hitting up for a loan because they earn more than $50K.
Greater Than or Equal To	>=	Works just like Greater Than, except it also includes all entries that exactly match the criterion.	**>=50,000** finds all values from 50,000 to infinity.
Less Than or Equal To	<=	If you add = to Less Than, your query includes all records that have values below or equal to the criterion value.	**<=50000** includes not only those records with values less than 50,000, but also those with a value of 50,000.
Not Equal To	<>	Finds all entries that don't match the criteria.	If you want a list of all records except those with a value of 50,000, enter **<>50000**.

Access™ 2007 For Dummies®

Cheat Sheet

Keyboard Shortcuts

Keystroke	Function
Ctrl+n	Create a new blank database
Ctrl+o	Open an existing database
F11	Show/hide Navigation Pane
Alt+f	Opens the Microsoft Office Button menu
Alt+h	Displays Home tab on the Ribbon
Alt+c	Displays the Create tab on the Ribbon
Alt+x	Displays the External Data tab on the Ribbon
Alt+a	Displays the Database Tools tab on the Ribbon
Ctrl+c	Copies selection to the clipboard
Ctrl+v	Pastes selection to the clipboard
Ctrl+z	Undoes last operation
Ctrl+;	Inserts the current date
Ctrl+:	Inserts the current time
Ctrl+'	Copies same field data from previous record
F2	Selects all data in the field or places cursor in edit mode
F9	Recalculates fields on a form or refreshes a lookup combo or list box list
Ctrl+Enter	Inserts a line break in datasheet and form view
Ctrl+Shift++	Inserts a new record
Ctrl+Shift+-	Deletes current record
Ctrl+Enter	Opens selected object from Navigation Pane in design view
F4	Toggles property sheet in design or layout view
Ctrl+Right Arrow	Moves selected control to the right in design or layout view
Ctrl+ Left Arrow	Moves selected control to the left in design or layout view
Ctrl+ Down Arrow	Moves selected control down in design or layout view
Ctrl+ Up Arrow	Moves selected control up in design or layout view
Shift+Right Arrow	Increases selected control width in design or layout view
Shift+ Left Arrow	Decreases selected control width in design or layout view
Shift+ Down Arrow	Increases selected control height in design or layout view
Shift+ Up Arrow	Decreases selected control height in design or layout view
F4	Toggles property sheet in design view
Shift+F2	Zooms in on current field in datasheet and form view

For Dummies: Bestselling Book Series for Beginners